Teach...
Inspire...
Lead...

With REA's FTCE General Knowledge test prep, you'll be in a class all your own.

We'd like to hear from you!

Visit **www.rea.com/teacher** *to send us your comments or e-mail us at* **info@rea.com**.

D0932576

Research & Education Association

The Best Teachers' Test Preparation for the

FTCE

General
Knowledge

Edited by

Leasha M. Barry, Ph.D.
Associate Professor
University of West Florida

Alicia Mendoza, Ed.D.
Associate Professor
Florida International University

And the Staff of
Research & Education Association

Visit our Educator Support Center at:
www.REA.com/teacher

The competencies presented in this book were created and implemented by the Florida Department of Education. For further information visit the FTCE website at *www.fl.nesinc.com.*

Research & Education Association
61 Ethel Road West
Piscataway, New Jersey 08854
E-mail: info@rea.com

The Best Teachers' Test Preparation for the Florida FTCE General Knowledge Test

Published 2009

Printed in the United States of America

Library of Congress Control Number 2006923803

ISBN-13: 978-0-7386-0169-4
ISBN-10: 0-7386-0169-1

REA® is a registered trademark of Research & Education Association, Inc.

About the Editors

Leasha M. Barry, Ph.D., received her graduate training in Special Education, disability, and at-risk populations at the University of California at Santa Barbara. She is an Associate Professor in the Division of Teacher Education within the College of Professional Studies at the University of West Florida. Her work focuses on early intervention with at-risk populations, including individuals with disabilities and those who experience traumatic stress at home and in educational and healthcare settings. Dr. Barry is interested in identifying and documenting developmentally appropriate supports and interventions that set the stage for independence and self-determination for individuals who are identified as at-risk.

Alicia Mendoza, Ed.D., formerly chair of the Elementary Education Department at Florida International University, has held the position of Associate Professor at the same academic institution for more than 31 years. Before coming to FIU, she was an Associate Professor at Clarion State College in Clarion, Pennsylvania and served as a consultant to Head Start classes in Western Pennsylvania. She also taught in the public schools of New York City. She earned her Ed.D. and M.Ed. at the University of Miami, and her B.A. at Queens College in New York City. Dr. Mendoza has been the recipient of the Distinguished Member Award of the Association of Teacher Educators in 2005, a Teaching Incentive award, and an Excellence in Advising award during her time at Florida International University. She is the author of numerous published articles, book chapters, and curriculum materials. Dr. Mendoza also recently authored a book, titled *The Essentials of Elementary Education and Current Controversies.*

About Research & Education Association

Founded in 1959, Research & Education Association is dedicated to publishing the finest and most effective educational materials—including software, study guides, and test preps—for students in middle school, high school, college, graduate school, and beyond.

REA's Test Preparation series includes books and software for all academic levels in almost all disciplines. Research & Education Association publishes test preps for students who have not yet entered high school, as well as for high school students preparing to enter college. Students from countries around the world seeking to attend college in the United States will find the assistance they need in REA's publications. For college students seeking advanced degrees, REA publishes test preps for many major graduate school admission examinations in a wide variety of disciplines, including engineering, law, and medicine. Students at every level, in every field, with every ambition can find what they are looking for among REA's publications.

REA's practice tests are always based upon the most recently administered exams and include every type of question that you can expect on the actual exams.

REA's publications and educational materials are highly regarded and continually receive an unprecedented amount of praise from professionals, instructors, librarians, parents, and students. Our authors are as diverse as the fields represented in the books we publish. They are well-known in their respective disciplines and serve on the faculties of prestigious high schools, colleges, and universities throughout the United States and Canada.

Today, REA's wide-ranging catalog is a leading resource for teachers, students, and professionals.

We invite you to visit us at *www.rea.com* to find out how "REA is making the world smarter."

Acknowledgments

We would like to thank REA's Larry B. Kling, Vice President, Editorial, for supervising development; Pam Weston, Vice President, Publishing, for setting the quality standards for production integrity and managing the publication to completion; Christine Reilley, Senior Editor, for project management and preflight editorial review; Diane Goldschmidt, Senior Editor, for post-production quality assurance; Anne Winthrop Esposito, Senior Editor, Hadassa Goldsmith, Ellen Gong, and Sandra Rush for their editorial contributions; Christine Saul, Senior Graphic Artist, for cover design; Jeff LoBalbo, Senior Graphic Artist, for post-production file mapping; Alice Leonard, Senior Editor, for coordinating revisions; and Rachel DiMatteo, Graphic Artist, for typesetting revisions.

We also gratefully acknowledge the team at Aquent Publishing Services for typesetting and indexing the manuscript.

CONTENTS

FTCE

Florida Teacher Certification Examinations
General Knowledge Test

Review

Passing the FTCE General Knowledge Test

About This Book

You are preparing to take the Florida Teacher Certification Exam General Knowledge Test (FTCE-GKT). Perhaps you are taking it for the first time. Perhaps you are retaking the exam. Whatever the case, this book will help you pass.

While working through this book, you will acquire a thorough and accurate understanding of what it takes to master the FTCE-GKT. The comprehensive review material in this book covers all subject areas known to appear on the FTCE-GKT, providing you with all the information you need to take this challenging certification exam.

Test-takers should note that every time the FTCE-GKT is administered, multiple versions of the exam are created and distributed to each testing center. These versions may contain a mix of different questions with different answers. This test versioning can add a greater level of uncertainty for the test-taker. Are you sure you are studying every topic enough? Are you adequately prepared for every test subject you may encounter on the FTCE-GKT? You can rest assured. One important purpose of this book is to prepare you for every possible version of the FTCE-GKT. We at REA believe you cannot prepare enough for this career-building exam.

About Our Practice Exams

You will be allotted three and one half hours to take the actual exam. This same amount of time is allotted to take each of our practice tests. REA's tests are carefully based on the current FTCE-GKT exams, and thus contain every type of question that you can expect to see on test day. Each practice test question is thoroughly explained in easy-to-follow detail. Sample responses are also provided for the essays to help you better understand and master the test material.

The FTCE is scored on a pass/fail basis. The following are the maximum percentages of questions in each subtest you need to answer correctly in order to pass:

- 65% Reading
- 73% English Language
- 58% Mathematics

In order to pass the Essay subtest, you need a score of at least 6 out of 12. Two raters will grade your exam independently and their grades will be combined to arrive at your final score.

About the Test

Who Takes the Test, and What Is It Used For?

The FTCE-GKT is used by the State of Florida to assess knowledge of teacher certification candidates. If you do not achieve a passing score on the FTCE-GKT, don't panic. You can take the test again, so you can work on improving your score in preparation for your next administration.

When Should the FTCE-GKT Be Taken?

The FTCE-GKT is usually taken immediately before the completion of a teacher certification program at a college or university. This gives candidates enough time to retake the test if they are not pleased with their score. Our practice tests will familiarize you with the format of the exam so that you do not have to go through the anxiety of learning about the FTCE-GKT during the actual exam.

When and Where Is the Test Given?

The FTCE-GKT is administered five times a year at testing centers across Florida. Tests are usually administered on a Saturday; however, the test may be taken on an alternate day if a conflict, such as a religious obligation, exists.

The registration bulletin for the FTCE-GKT contains test dates and administration sites. You may obtain a registration bulletin by contacting:

FTCE/FELE Program
Evaluation Systems Group of Pearson
PO Box 226   Phone: (413) 256-2893
Amherst, MA 01004   Website: *www.fl.nesinc.com*

Is There a Registration Fee?

Yes, you must pay a fee to take the FTCE-GKT. Fee waivers are available for candidates who are unable to afford registration. You must be enrolled in a college undergraduate program and must prove that you are required by a registered score recipient to take the exam. Details regarding income eligibility levels are contained in the registration bulletin.

How to Use This Book

What should I Study First?

Read over our review material, and then take the first practice test. This will help you pinpoint your areas of weakness. Study those sections in which you had the most difficulty first, and then move on to those areas that presented less of a challenge to you.

When should I Start Studying?

It is never too early to begin studying for the FTCE-GKT. The earlier you begin, the more time you will have to sharpen your skills. Do not procrastinate! Cramming is not an effective way to study. Give yourself enough time to become familiar with the format of the test and the material it covers. The sooner you learn the format of the exam, the more comfortable and confident you will be on the day of the test.

Format of the FTCE-GKT

The FTCE-GKT is divided into four sections:

The Reading Test

The Reading Test measures your ability to understand and analyze written information. The test consists of several written passages and about 40 multiple-choice questions to test your understanding of those passages. You have 40 minutes to complete this section of the exam.

The Mathematics Test

The Mathematics Test measures competency in mathematical skills that an educated adult will require. It focuses on the ability to solve problems in a quantitative context. Several problems involve the integration of several skills into one problem-solving situation. The test consists of about 45 multiple-choice questions, which you have 100 minutes to complete.

The English Language Skills Test

The English Language Skills Test assesses your facility with the use of standard English, and you have 40 minutes to complete 40 multiple-choice questions.

The Essay Test

The Essay Test assesses the ability to communicate in written form using appropriate language and grammar. For your essay, you will choose between two topics. The 50 minutes allotted for this section of the exam includes time to prepare, write, and edit your essay.

About the Review Sections

The Reading Comprehension Review

The Reading Comprehension Review is designed to enhance the reading comprehension skills necessary to achieve a high score on the FTCE-GKT. Strategies for attacking reading comprehension questions are thoroughly explained, and a four-step approach to answering the test questions is completely outlined. In addition, a vocabulary enhancer is included to help you better understand the passages on the test.

The Basic Math Skills Review

The Mathematics Review will help you reinforce the arithmetic, algebraic, and geometric concepts that will be tested on the FTCE-GKT. Drill questions are included that will help you sharpen your mathematical skills. A valuable reference table offers quick access to important formulae and an index of mathematical symbols. Careful review of this section should give you all the information you need to pass this section of the FTCE-GKT.

The English Language Skills Review

The English Language Skills Review will help you prepare for the test by offering instruction and drills to enhance your conceptual and organizational skills; word choice skills; sentence structure skills; and grammar, spelling, capitalization, and punctuation skills.

The Writing Skills Review

The Writing Skills Review contains a wealth of information concerning the structure, content, and form of the FTCE-GKT essay. Regardless of the topic you are assigned on the exam, a concise, well-constructed essay is essential to achieve a passing score. Careful study of the Essay Writing Review will hone your essay writing abilities, so that you will be able to write your essay with confidence.

Studying for the FTCE-GKT

Everyone has a different learning environment that works best for them, and it is very important that you find the one that works best for you. Some students prefer to set aside a few hours every morning to study, while others prefer to study at night before going to sleep. Some students are capable of studying while waiting on line at the supermarket, or even while eating lunch. Other students require absolute silence in a well-lit room to study. Only you can determine what works best for you, but be consistent and use your time wisely. Develop a routine that works for you and stick to it.

When you are taking the practice tests, you should try to duplicate the testing conditions as closely as possible. Turn off the television and radio, and sit down in a quiet area as free from distraction as possible.

Make sure to time yourself, and allow yourself no more time for the practice tests than you would have on the actual exam. Start off by setting a timer for the time that is allotted to each section of the exam, and be sure to reset it for the appropriate amount of time whenever you start a new section.

As you complete each practice test, score your exam and thoroughly review the detailed explanations to all the questions you answered incorrectly. Concentrate on one question at a time by reviewing the question and the explanation, and by studying the appropriate review material until you are confident that you completely understand the material.

Keep track of your scores on the individual practice tests. Doing this will enable you to gauge your progress and discover general weaknesses in particular sections. You should carefully study the review sections that cover your areas of difficulty to help reinforce your skills in those areas.

Test-Taking Tips

Even though you have probably taken standardized tests like the FTCE-GKT before, you may still be experiencing some anxiety about the exam. This is perfectly normal and there are several ways to help alleviate it listed below.

- **Become comfortable with the format of the FTCE-GKT.** When you are taking the practice tests, simulate the testing conditions as closely as possible. Stay calm and pace yourself. After simulating the test a few times, you will boost your chances of doing well. The test-taking experience will not be unfamiliar to you, and this will allow you to take the FTCE-GKT with much more confidence.

- **Read all of the possible answers.** Just because you think you have found the correct response, do not automatically assume that it is the best answer. Read all the answer choices so that you do not make a mistake by jumping to conclusions.

- **Use the process of elimination.** Go through all the answer choices and eliminate obviously incorrect answers immediately. If you are able to eliminate one or two answer choices, you will be able to make an educated guess.

- **Work quickly and steadily.** You only have one hour for each section, so pace yourself carefully. Do not spend too much time on any one question. By taking the practice tests included in this book, you will become better able to manage your time.

- **Learn the directions for each test section.** Familiarizing yourself with the directions for each section will not only save time, but also help you avoid anxiety and the mistakes that anxiety breeds.

- **Be sure that the answer oval you are marking corresponds to the number of the question in the test booklet.** Since the multiple-choice sections of the FTCE-GKT are graded by a machine, mismarking one response can throw off your entire score. Periodically check to be sure that you have not unintentionally left a space blank, or filled in two answer choices for a single question.

- **Guess, guess, guess.** You are not penalized for incorrect responses on the FTCE-GKT. Your score is based on the number of questions you have answered correctly. Therefore, even if you have absolutely no idea what the answer to a given question might be, you still have a 20 percent chance of being right. If you are able to eliminate even one or two of the answer choices, your chances of guessing correctly are greatly increased.

The Day of the Test

Before the Test

On the day of the test, you should wake up early after a good night's rest. You should have a good breakfast and dress in layers that can be removed or added as the conditions in the testing center require. Arrive at the testing center early. This will allow you to relax and collect your thoughts before the test, and will also spare you the anguish that comes with being late. As an added incentive to make sure that you arrive early, keep in mind that *no one will be admitted into the testing center after the test has begun.*

Before you leave for the testing center, make sure that you have your admission ticket and two unexpired forms of identification, written in English. The first must be government-issued, and must contain a recent photograph and your signature (i.e., your driver's license, passport, or alien registration card). The second identification must have either a photo or signature (i.e., a Social Security card or student I.D.). You will not be admitted to the testing center if you do not have proper identification.

You must also bring a blue or black ball-point pen and *several sharpened No. 2 pencils*, as none will be provided at the testing center!

You may wear a watch to the testing center; however, try to avoid wearing a watch with an audible alarm or signal. Dictionaries, notebooks, briefcases, cell phones, electronic devices, scratch paper, correction fluid, calculators, and packages are not permitted in the testing center. Drinking, smoking, and eating are also prohibited.

During the Test

Once you enter the test center, follow all the rules and instructions given by your test supervisor. Failure to do so runs you the risk of being dismissed from the testing center. You may also have your scores canceled.

After all testing materials have been distributed, the test supervisor will give you directions for filling out your answer sheet. Fill out this sheet carefully since the information you enter will be printed on your score report. Remember to fill in your name exactly as it appears on the admission ticket to avoid confusion later on.

Scrap paper is not provided, but you are permitted write in your test booklet. Mark your answers in the appropriate spaces on the answer sheet. Each numbered row will contain four ovals corresponding to each answer choice for that question. Fill in the oval that corresponds to your answer darkly, completely, and neatly. Should you change your answer, remember to erase the old answer entirely from the page. Only one answer should be marked for each question. This is very important, because answer sheets are machine scored, and stray marks can cause the machine to score your answers incorrectly.

After the Test

Once your test materials have been collected, you will be dismissed. Proceed to the exit.

Congratulations! You are well on your way to certification.

Talking to Your Fellow Test-Takers After the Test. Keep in mind that several versions of the FTCE-GKT are administered during each testing period. The test-takers around you were very likely working on tests with completely different questions and answers than yours. So, do not be alarmed when talking to friends and acquaintances about their FTCE-GKT test-taking experiences and you do not "remember" the questions they are discussing.

Reading Comprehension Review

Overview

This review was developed to prepare you for the Reading Section of the FTCE-GKT. You will be guided through a step-by-step approach to attacking reading passages and questions. Also included are tips to help you quickly and accurately answer the questions that will appear in this section. By studying our review, you will greatly increase your chances of achieving a passing score on the Reading Section of the FTCE-GKT.

Remember, the more you know about the skills tested, the better you will perform on the test. In this section, the skills you will be tested on are

1. Knowledge of literal comprehension

2. Knowledge of inferential comprehension

To help you master these skills, we present examples of the types of questions you will encounter and explanations of how to answer them. A drill section is also provided for further practice. Even if you are sure you will perform well on this section, make sure to complete the drills, as they will help sharpen your skills.

The Passages

The four reading passages in the Reading Section are specially designed to be on the level of the types of material that you will encounter in college textbooks. They will present you with very diverse subjects. The passages will be both expository and narrative. Although you will not be expected to have prior knowledge of the information presented in the passages, you will be expected to know the fundamental reading comprehension techniques presented in this chapter. Only your ability to read and comprehend material will be tested.

The Questions

Each passage will be followed by a number of questions, with the total number appearing in the section being 40 questions. The questions will ask you to make determinations based on what you have read. You will encounter 11 main types of questions in this test. These questions will ask you to

- recognize main ideas.

- identify supporting details.

- determine meaning of words or phrases in context.

- determine purpose.

- identify overall organizational pattern.

- distinguish between fact and opinion.

- recognize bias.

- recognize tone.

- determine relationships between sentences.

- analyze the validity of arguments.

- draw logical inferences and conclusions.

General Strategies

- Look over all the passages first and then attack the passages that seem easiest and most interesting.

- Identify and underline what sentences are the main ideas of each paragraph.

- When a question asks you to draw inferences, your answer should reflect what is implied in the passage, rather than what is directly stated.

- Use the context of the sentence to find the meaning of an unfamiliar word.

- Identify what sentences are example sentences and label them with an "E." Determine whether or not the writer is using facts or opinions.

- Circle key transitions and identify dominant patterns of organization.

- Make your final response and move on. Don't dawdle or get frustrated by the really troubling passages. If you haven't gotten answers after two attempts, answer as best you can and move on.

- If you have time at the end, go back to the passages that were difficult and review them again.

Strategies for Reading Passages

When reading the passage, this is your plan of attack:

Step 1: Read quickly while keeping in mind that questions will follow.

Step 2: Uncover the main idea or theme of the passage. Many times it is contained within the first few lines of the passage.

Step 3: Uncover the main idea of each paragraph. Usually it is contained in either the first or last sentence of the paragraph.

Step 4: Skim over the detailed points of the passage while circling key words or phrases. These are words or phrases such as *but, on the other hand, although, however, yet,* and *except.*

When you take the Reading Section of the FTCE-GKT, you will have two tasks:

1. to read the passage and

2. to answer the questions.

Of the two, carefully reading the passage is the most important; answering the questions is based on an understanding of the passage. Here is a four-step approach to reading:

Step 1: preview,

Step 2: read actively,

Step 3: review the passage, and

Step 4: answer the questions.

You should study the following exercises and use these four steps when you complete the Reading Section of the FTCE-GKT.

STEP 1: Preview

A preview of the reading passage will give you a purpose and a reason for reading; previewing is a good strategy to use in test-taking. Before beginning to read the passage (usually a four-minute activity if you preview and review), you should take about 30 seconds to look over the passage and questions. An effective way to preview the passage is to read quickly the first sentence of each paragraph, the concluding sentence of the passage, and the questions—not all the answers—following the passage. A passage is given below. Practice previewing the passage by reading the first sentence of each paragraph and the last line of the passage.

PASSAGE

1   That the area of obscenity and pornography is a difficult one for the Supreme Court is well documented. The Court's numerous attempts to define obscenity have proven unworkable and left the decision to the subjective preferences of the justices. Perhaps Justice Stewart put it

5 best when, after refusing to define obscenity, he declared, "But I know it when I see it." Does the Court literally have to see it to know it? Specifically, what role does the fact-pattern, including the materials' medium, play in the Court's decision?

    Several recent studies employ fact-pattern analysis in modeling the

10 Court's decision making. These studies examine the fact-pattern or case characteristics, often with ideological and attitudinal factors, as a determinant of the decision reached by the Court. In broad terms, these studies owe their theoretical underpinnings to attitude theory. As the name suggests, attitude theory views the Court's attitudes as an explanation

15 of its decisions.

    These attitudes, however, do not operate in a vacuum. As Spaeth explains, "the activation of an attitude involves both an object and the situation in which that object is encountered." The objects to which the court directs its attitudes are litigants. The situation—the subject matter

20 of the case—can be defined in broad or narrow terms. One may define the situation as an entire area of the law (e.g., civil liberties issues). On an even broader scale the situation may be defined as the decision to grant certiorari or whether to defect from a minimum-winning coalition.

    Defining the situation with such broad strokes, however, does not

25 allow one to control for case content. In many specific issue areas, the cases present strikingly similar patterns. In examining the Court's search and seizure decisions, Segal found a relatively small number of situational and case characteristic variables explain a high proportion of the Court's decisions.

30   Despite Segal's success, efforts to verify the applicability of fact-pattern analysis in other issue areas and using broad-based factors have been slow in forthcoming. Renewed interest in obscenity and pornography by federal and state governments, the academic community, and numerous antipornography interest groups indicates the Court's

35 decisions in this area deserve closer examination.

The Court's obscenity and pornography decisions also present an opportunity to study the Court's behavior in an area where the Court has granted significant decision-making authority to the states. In *Miller vs. California* (1973) the Court announced the importance of local community standards in obscenity determinations. The Court's subsequent behavior may suggest how the Court will react in other areas where it has chosen to defer to the states (e.g., abortion).

40

QUESTIONS

1. The main idea of the passage is best stated in which of the following?

    (A) The Supreme Court has difficulty convicting those who violate obscenity laws.

    (B) The current definitions for obscenity and pornography provided by the Supreme Court are unworkable.

    (C) Fact-pattern analysis is insufficient for determining the attitude of the Court toward the issues of obscenity and pornography.

    (D) Despite the difficulties presented by fact-pattern analysis, Justice Segal found the solution in the patterns of search and seizure decisions.

2. The main purpose of the writer in this passage is to

    (A) convince the reader that the Supreme Court is making decisions about obscenity based on their subjective views only.

    (B) explain to the reader how fact-pattern analysis works with respect to cases of obscenity and pornography.

    (C) define obscenity and pornography for the layperson.

    (D) demonstrate the role fact-pattern analysis plays in determining the Supreme Court's attitude about cases in obscenity and pornography.

3. Of the following, which fact best supports the writer's contention that the Court's decisions in the areas of obscenity and pornography deserve closer scrutiny?

    (A) The fact that a Supreme Court Justice said, "I know it when I see it."

    (B) Recent studies that employ fact-pattern analysis in modeling the Court's decision-making process.

    (C) The fact that attitudes do not operate in a vacuum.

    (D) The fact that federal and state governments, interest groups, and the academic community show renewed interest in the obscenity and pornography decisions by the Supreme Court.

4. Among the following statements, which states an opinion expressed by the writer rather than a fact?

    (A) That the area of obscenity and pornography is a difficult one for the Supreme Court is well documented.

(B)   The objects to which a court directs its attitudes are the litigants.

(C)   In many specific issue areas, the cases present strikingly similar patterns.

(D)   The Court's subsequent behavior may suggest how the Court will react in other legal areas.

5.   The list of topics below that best reflects the organization of the topics of the passage is

(A)   I.   The difficulties of the Supreme Court

  II.   Several recent studies

  III.   Spaeth's definition of "attitude"

  IV.   The similar patterns of cases

  V.   Other issue areas

  VI.   The case of *Miller vs. California*

(B)   I.   The Supreme Court, obscenity, and fact-pattern analysis

  II.   Fact-pattern analyses and attitude theory

  III.   The definition of "attitude" for the Court

  IV.   The definition of "situation"

  V.   The breakdown in fact-pattern analysis

  VI.   Studying Court behavior

(C)   I.   Justice Stewart's view of pornography

  II.   Theoretical underpinnings

  III.   A minimum-winning coalition

  IV.   Search and seizure decisions

  V.   Renewed interest in obscenity and pornography

  VI.   The importance of local community standards

(D)   I.   The Court's numerous attempts to define obscenity

  II.   Case characteristics

  III.   The subject matter of cases

  IV.   The Court's proportion of decisions

  V.   Broad-based factors

  VI.   Obscenity determination

6.   Which paragraph below is the best summary of the passage?

(A)   The Supreme Court's decision-making process with respect to obscenity and pornography has become too subjective. Fact-pattern analyses, used to determine the overall attitude of the Court, reveal only broad-based attitudes on the part of the Court toward the situations of obscenity cases. But these patterns cannot fully account for the Court's attitudes toward case content. Research is not conclusive that fact-pattern analyses work when applied to legal areas. Renewed public and local interest suggests continued study and close examination of how the Court makes decisions. Delegating authority to the states may reflect patterns for Court decisions in other socially sensitive areas.

(B)   Though subjective, the Supreme Court decisions are well documented. Fact-pattern analyses reveal the attitude of the Supreme Court toward its decisions in cases. Spaeth explains that an attitude involves both an object and a situation. For the Court, the situation may be defined as the decision to grant certiorari. Cases present strikingly similar patterns, and a small number of variables explain a high proportion of the Court's decisions. Segal has made an effort to verify the applicability of fact-pattern analysis with some success. The Court's decisions on obscenity and pornography suggest weak Court behavior, such as in *Miller vs. California.*

(C)   To determine what obscenity and pornography mean to the Supreme Court, we must use fact-pattern analysis. Fact-pattern analysis reveals the ideas that the Court uses to operate in a vacuum. The litigants and the subject matter of cases is defined in broad terms (such as an entire area of law) to reveal the Court's decision-making process. Search and seizure cases reveal strikingly similar patterns, leaving the Court open to grant certiorari effectively. Renewed public interest in the Court's decisions proves how the Court will react in the future.

(D)   Supreme Court decisions about pornography and obscenity are under examination and are out of control. The Court has to see the case to know it. Fact-pattern analyses reveal that the Court can only define cases in narrow terms, thus revealing individual egotism on the part of the Justices. As a result of strikingly similar patterns in search and seizure cases, the Court should be studied further for its weakness in delegating authority to state courts, as in the case of *Miller vs. California.*

7.   Based on the passage, the rationale for fact-pattern analyses arises out of what theoretical groundwork?

(A)   Subjectivity theory

(B)   The study of cultural norms

(C)   Attitude theory

(D)   Cybernetics

8.   Based on data in the passage, what would most likely be the major cause for the difficulty in pinning down the Supreme Court's attitude toward cases of obscenity and pornography?

(A)   The personal opinions of the Court Justices

(B)   The broad nature of the situations of the cases

(C)   The ineffective logistics of certiorari

(D)   The inability of the Court to resolve the variables presented by individual case content

9.   In the context of the passage, *subjective* might be most nearly defined as

   (A)   personal.

   (B)   wrong.

   (C)   focused.

   (D)   objective.

By previewing the passage, you should have learned the following:

- The fact that the area of obscenity and pornography is a difficult one for the Supreme Court is well documented.

- Several recent studies employ fact-pattern analysis in modeling the Court's decision making.

- These attitudes are not formed and expressed in a vacuum.

- Defining the situation with such broad strokes does not allow one to control for case content.

- Despite Segal's success, efforts to verify the applicability of fact-pattern analysis in other issue areas and using broad-based factors have been slow in coming.

- The Court's obscenity and pornography decisions also present an opportunity to study the Court's behavior in an area where the Court has granted significant decision-making authority to the states.

- The Court's subsequent behavior may suggest how the Court will react in other areas where it has chosen to defer to the states (e.g., abortion).

These few sentences tell you much about the entire passage.

As you begin to examine the passage, you should first determine the main idea of the passage and underline it, so that you can easily refer back to it if a question requires you to do so (see question 1). The main idea should be found in the first paragraph of the passage, and may even be the first sentence. From what you have read thus far, you now know that the main idea of this passage is that: the Supreme Court has difficulty in making obscenity and pornography decisions.

In addition, you also know that recent studies have used fact-pattern analysis in modeling the Court's decision. You have learned also that attitudes do not operate independently and that case content is important. The feasibility of using fact-pattern analysis in other areas and broad-based factors have not been quickly verified. To study the behavior of the Court in an area in which they have granted significant decision-making authority to the states, one has only to consider the obscenity and pornography decisions. In summary, the author suggests that the Court's subsequent behavior may suggest how the Court will react in those other areas in which decision-making authority has previously been granted to the states. As you can see, having this information will make the reading of the passage much easier.

You should have also looked at the stem of the question in your preview. You do not necessarily need to spend time reading the answers to each question in your preview. The stem alone can help to guide you as you read.

The stems in this case are:

1. The main idea of the passage is best stated in which of the following?

2. The main purpose of the writer in this passage is to

3. Of the following, which fact best supports the writer's contention that the Court's decisions in the areas of obscenity and pornography deserve closer scrutiny?

4. Among the following statements, which states an opinion expressed by the writer rather than a fact?

5. The list of topics below that best reflects the organization of the topics of the passage is

6. Which paragraph below is the best summary of the passage?

7. Based on the passage, the rationale for fact-pattern analyses arises out of what theoretical groundwork?

8. Based on data in the passage, what would most likely be the major cause for the difficulty in pinning down the Supreme Court's attitude toward cases of obscenity and pornography?

9. In the context of the passage, *subjective* might be most nearly defined as

STEP 2: Read Actively

After your preview, you are now ready to read actively. This means that as you read, you will be engaged in such things as underlining important words, topic sentences, main ideas, and words denoting the tone of the passage. If you think underlining can help you save time and help you remember the main ideas, feel free to use your pencil.

Read carefully the first sentence of each paragraph since this often contains the topic of the paragraph. You may wish to underline each topic sentence.

During this stage, you should also determine the writer's purpose in writing the passage (see question 2), as this will help you focus on the main points and the writer's key points in the organization of a passage. You can determine the author's purpose by asking yourself, Does *the relationship* between the writer's main idea plus evidence the writer uses answer one of four questions?

- What is the writer's overall primary goal or objective?

- Is the writer trying primarily to persuade you by proving or using facts to make a case for an idea? (P)

- Is the writer trying only primarily to inform and enlighten you about an idea, object, or event? (I)

- Is the writer attempting primarily to amuse you? To keep you fascinated? To keep you laughing? (A)

Read these examples and see if you can decide what the primary purpose of the following statements might be.

(A) Jogging too late in life can cause more health problems than it solves. I will allow that the benefits of jogging are many: lowered blood pressure, increased vitality, better cardiovascular health, and better muscle tone. However, an older person may have a history of injury or chronic ailments that makes jogging counterproductive. For example, the elderly jogger may have hardening of the arteries, emphysema, or undiscovered aneurysms just waiting to burst and cause stroke or death. Chronic arthritis in the joints will only be aggravated by persistent irritation and use. Moreover, for those of us with injuries sustained in our youth—such as torn Achilles' tendons or torn knee cartilage—jogging might just make a painful life more painful, cancelling out the benefits the exercise is intended to produce.

(B) Jogging is a sporting activity that exercises all the main muscle groups of the body. That the arms, legs, buttock, and torso voluntary muscles are engaged goes without question. Running down a path makes you move your upper body as well as your lower body muscles. People do not often take into account, however, how the involuntary muscle system is also put through its paces. The heart, diaphragm, even the eye and face muscles, take part as we hurl our bodies through space at speeds up to five miles per hour over distances as long as 26 miles.

(C) It seems to me that jogging styles are as identifying as fingerprints! People seem to be as individual in the way they run as they are in personality. Here comes the Duck, waddling down the track, little wings going twice as fast as the feet in an effort to stay upright. At about the quarter mile mark, I see the Penguin, quite natty in the latest jogging suit, body stiff as a board from neck to ankles and the ankles flexing a mile a minute to cover the yards. And down there at the half-mile post—there comes the Giraffe—a tall fellow in a spotted electric yellow outfit, whose long strides cover about a dozen yards each, and whose neck waves around under some old army camouflage hat that probably served its time in a surplus store in the Bronx rather than in Desert Storm. Once you see the animals in the jogger woods once, you can identify them from miles away just by seeing their gait. And by the way, be careful whose hoof you're stepping on, it may be mine!

In (A) the writer makes a statement that a number of people would debate and which isn't clearly demonstrated in science or common knowledge. In fact, common wisdom usually maintains the opposite thesis. Many would say that jogging improves the health of the aging—even slows down the aging process. As soon as you see a writer point to or identify *an issue open to debate* and standing in need of proof, s/he is setting out to persuade you of one side or the other. You'll notice, too, that the writer in this case takes a stand, here. It's almost as if s/he is saying, "I have concluded that . . ." But a thesis or arguable idea is only a *hypothesis* until evidence is summoned by the writer to prove it. Effective arguments are based on serious, factual, or demonstrable evidence, not opinion.

In (B) the writer is just stating a fact. This is not a matter for debate. From here, the writer's evidence is to *explain* and *describe* what is meant by the fact. S/he proceeds to *analyze* (break down into its elements) the way the different muscle groups come into play or do work when jogging, thus explaining the fact stated as a main point in the opening sentence. That jogging exercises all the muscle groups is not in question or a matter of debate. Besides taking the form of explaining how something works, what parts it is made of (for example, the basic parts of a bicycle are . . .), writers may show how the idea, object, or event functions. A writer may use this information to prove something. But if s/he doesn't argue to prove a debatable point, then the purpose must be either to inform (as here) or to entertain.

In (C) the writer is taking a stand, but s/he is not attempting to prove anything, merely pointing to a light-hearted observation. Moreover, all of the examples s/he uses to support the statement are either fanciful, funny, odd, or peculiar to the writer's particular vision. Joggers aren't really animals, after all.

Make sure to examine all of the facts that the author uses to support his/her main idea. This will allow you to decide whether or not the writer has made a case, and what sort of purpose s/he supports. Look for supporting details—facts, examples, illustrations, the testimony or research of experts, that are about the topic in question and *show* what the writer *says* is so. In fact, paragraphs and theses consist of *show* and *tell*. The writer *tells* you something is so or not so and then *shows* you facts, illustrations, expert testimony, or experience to back up what s/he says is or is not so. As you determine where the author's supporting details are, you may want to label them with an "S" so that you can refer back to them easily when answering questions (see question 3).

It is also important for you to be able to recognize the difference between the statements of fact presented and statements of the author's opinion. You will be tested on this skill in this section of the test (see question 4). Let's look at the following examples. In each case ask yourself if you are reading a fact or an opinion.

1. Some roses are red.

2. Roses are the most beautiful flower on earth.

3. After humans smell roses, they fall in love.

4. Roses are the worst plants to grow in your backyard.

Number 1 is a fact. All you have to do is go look at the evidence. Go to a florist. You will see that number 1 is true. A fact is anything that can be demonstrated to be true in reality or that has been demonstrated to be true in reality and is documented by others. For example, the moon is in orbit about 250,000 miles from the earth.

Number 2 is an opinion. The writer claims this as truth, but since it is an abstract quality (beauty), it remains to be seen. Others will hold different opinions. This is a matter of taste, not fact.

Number 3 is an opinion. There is probably some time-related coincidence between these two, but there is no verifiable or repeatable and observable evidence that this is always true—at least not the way it is true that if you throw a ball into the air, it will always come back down to earth if left on its own without interference. Opinions have a way of sounding absolute, are held by the writer with confidence, but are not backed up by factual evidence.

Number 4, though perhaps sometimes true, is a matter of opinion. Many variables contribute to the health of a plant in a garden: soil, temperature range, amount of moisture, number, and kinds of bugs. This is a debatable point that the writer would have to prove.

As you read, you should note the structure of the passage. There are several common structures for the passages. Some of these structures are described below.

Main Types of Paragraph Structures

1. The structure is a main idea plus supporting arguments.

2. The structure is a main idea plus examples.

3. The structure includes comparisons or contrasts.

4. There is a pro and a con structure.

5. The structure is chronological.

6. The structure has several different aspects of one idea. For example, a passage on education in the United States in the 1600s and 1700s might first define education, then describe colonial education, then give information about separation of church and state, and then outline the tax opposition and supportive arguments. Being able to recognize these structures will help you recognize how the author has organized the passage.

Examining the structure of the passage will help you answer questions that ask you to organize (see question 5) the information in the passage, or to summarize (see question 6) the information presented in that passage.

For example, if you see a writer using a transitional pattern that reflects a sequence moving forward in time, such as "In 1982 . . . Then, in the next five years . . . A decade later, in 1997, the xxxx will . . ." chances are the writer is telling a story, history, or the like. Writers often use transitions of classification to analyze an idea, object, or event. They may say something like, "The first part . . . Secondly . . . Thirdly . . . Finally." You may then ask yourself what is this analysis for? To explain or to persuade me of something? These transitional patterns may also help reveal the relationship of one part of a passage to another. For example, a writer may be writing "on the one hand, . . . on the other hand . . ." This should alert you to the fact that the writer is comparing two things or contrasting them. What for? Is one better than the other? Worse?

By understanding the *relationship* among the main point, transitions, and supporting information, you may more readily determine the pattern of organization as well as the writer's purpose in a given piece of writing.

As with the paragraph examples above showing the difference among possible purposes, you must look at the relationship between the facts or information presented (that's the show part) and what the writer is trying to point out to you (that's the tell part) with that data. For example, in the data given in number 6 above, the discussion presented about education in the 1600s might be used

- to prove that it was a failure (a form of argument),

- to show that it consisted of these elements (an analysis of the status of education during that time), or

- to show that education during that time was silly.

To understand the author's purpose, the main point and the evidence that supports it must be considered together to be understood. In number 6, no statement appears that controls these disparate areas of information. To be meaningful, a controlling main point is needed. You need to know that that main point is missing. You need to be able to distinguish between the writer showing data and the writer telling or making a point.

In the two paragraphs below, consider the different relationship between the same data above and the controlling statement, and how that controlling statement changes the discussion from explanation to argument:

(A) Colonial education was different than today's and consisted of several elements. Education in those days meant primarily studying the three "r's" (reading, writing, and arithmetic) and the Bible. The church and state were more closely aligned with one another—education was, after all, for the purpose of serving God better, not to make more money.

(B) Colonial "education" was really just a way to create a captive audience for the Church. Education in those days meant studying the three "r's" in order to learn God's word—the Bible—not commerce. The Church and state were closely aligned with one another, and what was good for the Church was good for the state—or else you were excommunicated, which kept you out of Heaven for sure.

The same information areas are brought up in both cases, but in (A) the writer treats it analytically (". . . consisted of several elements . . ."), not taking any real debatable stand on the issue. What is, is. However, the controlling statement in (B) puts forth a volatile hypothesis, and then uses the same information to support that hypothesis.

STEP 3: Review the Passage

After you finish reading actively, take 10 or 20 seconds to look over the main idea and the topic sentences that you have underlined, and the key words and phrases you have marked. Now you are ready to enter Step 4 and answer the questions.

STEP 4: Answer the Questions

In Step 2, Read Actively, you gathered enough information from the passage to answer questions dealing with the main idea, support, meaning, purpose, organization, fact vs. opinion, bias, tone, relationships between sentences, validity, and logic. Let's look again at these questions.

Strategies for Answering Questions

Competency 1: Knowledge of Literal Comprehension

When answering the questions, this is your plan of attack:

Step 1: Attack each question one at a time. Read it carefully.

Step 2: If the question is asking for a general answer, such as the main idea or the purpose of the passage, answer it immediately.

Step 3: If the question is asking for an answer that can only be found in a specific place in the passage, save it for last since this type of question requires you to go back to the passage and therefore takes more of your time.

Step 4: For the detail-oriented questions, try to eliminate or narrow down your choices before looking for the answer in the passage.

Step 5: Go back into the passage, utilizing the key words you circled, to find the answer.

Step 6: Any time you cannot find the answer, use the process of elimination to the greatest extent and then guess.

Skill 1: Recognize the Main Idea

Looking back at the questions that follow the passage, you see that question 1 is a "main idea" question:

1.   The main idea of the passage is best stated in which of the following?

(A)   The Supreme Court has difficulty convicting those who violate obscenity laws.

(B)   The current definitions for obscenity and pornography provided by the Supreme Court are unworkable.

(C)   Fact-pattern analysis is insufficient for determining the attitude of the Court toward the issues of obscenity and pornography.

(D)   Despite the difficulties presented by fact-pattern analysis, Justice Segal found the solution in the patterns of search and seizure decisions.

In answering the question, you see that answer choice (C) is correct. The writer uses the second, third, fourth, and fifth paragraphs to show how fact-pattern analysis is an ineffective determinant of Court attitude toward obscenity and pornography.

Answer (A) is incorrect. Nothing is ever said directly about "convicting" persons accused of obscenity, only that the Court has difficulty defining it.

Choice (B) is also incorrect. Though it is stated as a fact by the writer, it is only used as an effect that leads the writer to examine how fact-pattern analysis does or does not work to reveal the "cause" or attitude of the Court toward obscenity and pornography.

Finally, answer choice (D) is incorrect. The statement is contrary to what Segal found when he examined search and seizure cases.

Skill 2: Identify Supporting Details

Question 3 requires you to analyze the author's supporting details:

3.   Of the following, which fact best supports the writer's contention that the Court's decisions in the areas of obscenity and pornography deserve closer scrutiny?

(A)   The fact that a Supreme Court Justice said, "I know it when I see it."

(B) Recent studies that employ fact-pattern analysis in modeling the Court's decision-making process.

(C) The fact that attitudes do not operate in a vacuum.

(D) The fact that federal and state governments, interest groups, and the academic community show renewed interest in the obscenity and pornography decisions by the Supreme Court.

To answer this question, let's look at the answer choices. Choice (D) must be correct. In the fifth paragraph, the writer states that the "renewed interest"—a real and observable fact—from these groups "indicates the Court's decisions . . . deserve closer examination," another way of saying scrutiny.

Answer (A) is incorrect. The writer uses this remark to show how the Court cannot effectively define obscenity and pornography, relying on "subjective preferences" to resolve issues.

In addition, choice (B) is incorrect because the writer points to the data in (D), not fact-pattern analyses, to prove this.

(C), too, is incorrect. Although it is true, the writer makes this point to show how fact-pattern analysis doesn't help clear up the real-world "situation" in which the Court must make its decisions.

Skill 3: Determine the Meaning of Words or Phrases in Context

Returning to question 9, we can now determine an answer:

9.   In the context of the passage, *subjective* might be most nearly defined as

    (A) personal.

    (B) wrong.

    (C) focused.

    (D) objective.

Choice (A) is best. By taking note of the example of Justice Stewart provided by the writer, we can see that Justice Stewart's comment is an example not of right or wrong. (He doesn't talk about right or wrong. He uses the verb "know"—whose root points primarily to *know*ledge, understanding, and insight, *not* ethical considerations.) He probably doesn't mean "focused by" since the focus is provided by the appearance or instance of the case itself. By noting the same word ending and the appearance of the root "object"—meaning an observable thing existing outside of ourselves in time and space, and comparing it with the root of subjective, "subject"—often pointing to something personally studied, we can begin to rule out "objective" as the opposite of "subjective." Usually when we talk about people's "preferences," we are referring to matters of taste or quality; preferences don't usually result from scientific study or reasoning but instead arise out of a combination of personal taste and idiosyncratic intuitions. Thus, (A) becomes the most likely choice.

(C) is incorrect because the Court's focus is already in place—obscenity and pornography.

Answer (B) is incorrect. Nothing is implied or stated about the rightness or wrongness of the decisions themselves. Rather, it is the definition of obscenity that seems "unworkable."

(D) is also incorrect. "Objective" is the direct opposite of "subjective." To reason based on the object of study is the opposite of reasoning based upon the beliefs, opinions, or ideas of the one viewing the object, rather than consideration of the evidence presented by the object itself *independent* of the observer.

You may not have been familiar with the word "subjective," but from your understanding of the writer's intent, you should have been able to figure out what s/he was after. Surrounding words and phrases almost always provide clues in determining a word's meaning. In addition, any examples that appear in the text may also provide some hints.

Competency 2: Knowledge of Inferential Comprehension

Skill 1: Determine the Purpose

In examining question 2, you see that you must determine the author's purpose in writing the passage:

2.   The main purpose of the writer in this passage is to

   (A)   convince the reader that the Supreme Court is making decisions about obscenity based on their subjective views only.

   (B)   explain to the reader how fact-pattern analysis works with respect to cases of obscenity and pornography.

   (C)   define obscenity and pornography for the layperson.

   (D)   demonstrate the role fact-pattern analysis plays in determining the Supreme Court's attitude about cases in obscenity and pornography.

Looking at the answer choices, you see that choice (D) is correct. Though the writer never states it directly, s/he summons data consistently to show that fact-pattern analysis only gives us part of the picture, or "broad strokes" about the Court's attitude, but cannot account for the attitude toward individual cases.

Choice (A) is incorrect. The writer doesn't try to convince us of this fact, but merely states it as an opinion resulting from the evidence derived from the "well-documented" background to the problem.

(B) is also incorrect. The writer does more than just explain the role of fact-pattern analysis, but rather shows how it cannot fully apply.

The passage is about the Court's difficulty in defining these terms, not the man or woman in the street. Nowhere do definitions for these terms appear. Therefore, choice (C) is incorrect.

Skill 2: Identify Overall Organizational Pattern

Question 5 asks you to organize given topics to reflect the organization of the passage:

5.   The list of topics below that best reflects the organization of the topics of the passage is

   (A)   I.   The difficulties of the Supreme Court

              II.   Several recent studies

            III.   Spaeth's definition of "attitude"

            IV.   The similar patterns of cases

              V.   Other issue areas

            VI.   The case of *Miller vs. California*

   (B)   I.   The Supreme Court, obscenity, and fact-pattern analysis

              II.   Fact-pattern analyses and attitude theory

            III.   The definition of "attitude" for the Court

            IV.   The definition of "situation"

              V.   The breakdown in fact-pattern analysis

            VI.   Studying Court behavior

   (C)   I.   Justice Stewart's view of pornography

              II.   Theoretical underpinnings

            III.   A minimum-winning coalition

            IV.   Search and seizure decisions

              V.   Renewed interest in obscenity and pornography

            VI.   The importance of local community standards

   (D)   I.   The Court's numerous attempts to define obscenity

              II.   Case characteristics

            III.   The subject matter of cases

            IV.   The Court's proportion of decisions

              V.   Broad-based factors

            VI.   Obscenity determination

After examining all of the choices, you will determine that choice (B) is the correct response. These topical areas lead directly to the implied thesis that the "role" of fact-pattern analysis is insufficient for determining the attitude of the Supreme Court in the areas of obscenity and pornography. (See question 1.)

Answer (A) is incorrect because the first topic stated in the list is not the topic of the first paragraph. It is too global. The first paragraph is about the difficulties the Court has with defining obscenity and how fact-pattern analysis might be used to determine the Court's attitude and clear up the problem.

(C) is incorrect because each of the items listed in this topic list are supporting evidence or data for the real topic of each paragraph. (See the list in (B) for correct topics.) For example, Justice Stewart's statement about pornography is only cited to indicate the nature of the problem with obscenity for the Court. It is not the focus of the paragraph itself.

Finally, (D) is incorrect. As with choice (C) these are all incidental pieces of information or data used to make broader points.

Skill 3: Distinguish Between Fact and Opinion

By examining question 4, you can see that you are required to know the difference between fact and opinion:

4.   Among the following statements, which states an opinion expressed by the writer rather than a fact?

   (A)   That the area of obscenity and pornography is a difficult one for the Supreme Court is well documented.

   (B)   The objects to which a court directs its attitudes are the litigants.

   (C)   In many specific issue areas, the cases present strikingly similar patterns.

   (D)   The Court's subsequent behavior may suggest how the Court will react in other legal areas.

Keeping in mind that an opinion is something that cannot be proven to hold true in all circumstances, you can determine that choice (D) is correct. It is the only statement among the four for which the evidence is yet to be gathered. It is the writer's opinion that this may be a way to predict the Court's attitudes.

(A), (B), and (C) are all taken from data or documentation in existence already in the world, and are, therefore, incorrect.

Skill 4: Recognize Bias

While reading, make a distinction between key ideas author bias, and the evidence for those ideas. *Evidence* is anything used to prove that an idea is true, real, correct, or probable. Bias is the author's personal feelings on the topic and what they believe which may not be based in fact.

Types of Evidence

Only a few forms of evidence are available to the writer. The kinds of evidence that a writer can summon to support his or her position or point are as follows: (1) facts and statistics, (2) the testimony of an authority, (3) personal anecdote, (4) hypothetical illustrations, and (5) analogy. Strictly speaking, the last two in this list are not true evidence but only offer commonsense probability to the support of an argument. In fact, there is a hierarchy for evidence similar to that of purpose. The most powerful evidence is fact, supported by statistics; the least powerful is analogy. The following table suggests the relationship:

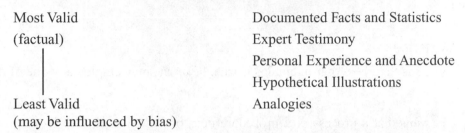

Hierarchy of Validity of Evidence

Most Valid	Documented Facts and Statistics
(factual)	Expert Testimony
	Personal Experience and Anecdote
	Hypothetical Illustrations
Least Valid	Analogies
(may be influenced by bias)	

Documented facts and statistics are the most powerful evidence a writer can bring to bear on proving an idea or supporting a main thesis. Documented facts and statistics must be used fairly and come from reliable sources. For example, *Funk and Wagnall's Encyclopedia* is a reliable source but Joe the plumber's *Guide to Waterfowl in Hoboken* is not. This is true because, first of all, Joe is a plumber, not an ornithologist (a bird scientist), and second, no one has ever heard of Joe the plumber as an expert. Reliable sources for facts and statistics are the best information that can be offered.

Expert testimony is the reported positions, theses, or studies of people who are recognized experts in the field under discussion in the literature. A writer may use books, articles, essays, interviews, and so on by trained scientists and other professionals to support a thesis or position. Most often, this testimony takes the form of quotations from the expert or a paraphrasing of his or her important ideas or findings.

Personal experience and anecdote is the evidence of a writer's own personal experience, or a "little story" about an event, person, or idea that exemplifies the point he or she is trying to make. It holds weight if the reader trusts the writer, and it is valuable; it is not as powerful or as conclusive as documented facts or the testimony of experts (unless the writer is a recognized authority in the field about which he or she has written).

Hypothetical illustrations are examples that suggest probable circumstances in which something would be true. Strictly speaking, a hypothetical illustration is not "hard" evidence, but rather evidence of probability. For example, to demonstrate that "people will do whatever they can get away with," a writer might bring up the hypothetical illustration of someone at a ticket counter who gets back more change than he or she paid for the ticket. The chances are, the writer might point out, that the person would pocket the extra money rather than be honest and return it. In this case, the writer is not naming anybody in particular or citing statistics to make the point, but rather is pointing to *a situation that is likely but is not an actual documented case.* This situation has either the weight of common sense for the reader or none at all.

Analogies are the last and weakest form of evidence. It is not actually evidence at all. An analogy is simply a comparison between items that are different but that also have some striking similarities. Analogies often use the term "like" to show the relationship of ideas. For example, the writer might say,

"Life is like a tree: we start out struggling in the dirt, grow into the full bloom of youth, and become deeply rooted in our ways, until, in the autumn of our years, we lose our hair like leaves, and succumb ultimately to the bare winter of death."

While reading, determine what sort of evidence the writer is using and how effective it is in proving his or her point.

Reasons for Evidence

To prove any thesis that the writer maintains is true, he or she may employ any one of the following seven strategies:

1. *show* that a process or a procedure does or should work step by step in time;

2. *compare or contrast* two or more things or ideas to show important differences or similarities;

3. *identify* a problem and then explain how to solve it;

4. *analyze* into its components, or *classify* by its types or categories, an idea or thing to show how it is put together, how it works, or how it is designed;

5. *explain* why something happens to produce a particular result or set of results;

6. *describe* the particular individual characteristics of a place, person, time, or idea;

7. *define* what a thing is or what an idea means.

Bias can be identified in passages in which the author is comparing and contrasting two arguments.

To analyze the relationship between ideas in opposition (pro and con), first identify the claim each side is making. (Of course, in many situations there are more than two sides.) Pay attention to the intricacies of the position; many arguments are not simply for or against something, but instead are qualified positions with exceptions. For example, the claim that Medicare should pay for standard prescriptions is different from the claim that Medicare should pay for prescriptions. The word 'standard' qualifies the argument; perhaps experimental drugs or preventative treatments are excluded from the proposal. In analyzing an argument, be sure to find the edges of the argument, where the arguer would not want to press the argument further and where there may be bias.

After analyzing the argument, locate and evaluate the reasons that the author uses to support the claim. Ask yourself, "Why is the author's claim important?" Then examine the reasons the author gives: are they good reasons and are they connected to the claim? Finally, examine the evidence the author uses to support the reasons. The evidence should come from reliable sources and be pertinent to the reasons and claim. In examining two or more opposing arguments, you will judge which best supports its claim. However, the best argument may fail to convince its reader, especially on politically volatile topics such as abortion rights.

Skill 5: Recognize Tone

The general tone of the passage can indicate something about the unfamiliar word. For instance, whether the word is positive or negative can often be deduced by tone clues.

His speech ostracized his audience, who found his sarcastic, mordant, and rude comments disturbing. (definition: to exclude willingly. The reader cannot miss the heavy negative tone of the words in the passage.)

Drill 1: Vocabulary

DIRECTIONS: Determine a working meaning for the underlined word in each of the following passages.

1. Romeyn de Hooghe, the first <u>limner</u> to limit his work to narrative strips, used his talent to create pictorial criticism of the persecution of the Huguenots under Louis XIV.

2. The somber clouds and the dreary rain caused the child to <u>mope</u> about the house.

3. The <u>veracity</u> of the witness's testimony, revealed through his eye-to-eye contact with the jury and lack of stumbling over words, was not doubted.

4. Why isn't the evening sun described as <u>moribund</u>, not setting; after all, it is coming to the day's end?

5. As president, state warden, and security chief, the leader described in Gilbert and Sullivan's "The Mikado" is a <u>poohbah</u>.

6. Robin Hood's <u>audacious</u> actions included conducting dangerous rescues of Maid Marian and visiting enemy territory disguised as a local.

7. Among common household health products are <u>St. John's Wort</u> and <u>Echinacea</u>, herbs from the garden.

8. My father is a <u>numismatist</u>; he spends several hours each week studying his coins from other countries and time periods.

Drill 1: Answers

1. artist; line drawer

2. unhappily move about

3. truthfulness

4. dying or dead

5. leader who holds several offices

6. daring

7. herbs used for good health

8. coin collector

Skill 6: Recognize Relationships Between Sentences

If the literature is a textbook, read the *introduction*, scan the *chapter titles*, and quickly review any *subheadings, charts, pictures, appendices,* and *indexes* that the book includes. If it is an article, read the first and last paragraphs. These are the most likely places to find the writer's *main point* or *thesis*.

Note that there is a significant difference between a thesis and a main point. Here is an example of a *main point*:

> The Rocky Mountains have three important geological features: abundant water, gold- and silver-bearing ore, and oil-bearing shale.

Notice that this statement is not a matter of the writer's opinion. It is a fact. Now, notice the following *thesis*:

> The Rocky Mountains are the most important source of geological wealth in the United States.

What is the difference? The second statement offers an arguable conclusion or informed opinion. It may be an informed opinion on the part of the writer, but it is still an opinion. A thesis, then, is a statement offered by a writer as true or correct, although it is actually a matter of opinion.

In the first statement, whether the author has an opinion about it or not, these features are an important part of the makeup of the Rocky Mountains. In the second statement, the author may have contrary evidence to offer about Alaska or the Everglades. The second statement bears proving; the first is self-evident. The writer would go on to show the existence of these features, not—as in the second case—the quality or value of those features. The writer of a main point paper is reporting to or informing his or her audience; the writer of a thesis is attempting to sway the audience to his or her point of view.

Key Sections to Recognize

In reading a particular passage, you want to identify what portions or sections of a whole essay you confront. Depending upon which section of an essay is offered, you may decide whether you are reading the writer's main point, thesis, purpose, or evidence.

Introduction: The introductory paragraph usually shows the writer's point of view, or thesis, and introduces that position with some lead-in or general data to support it. The thesis of an essay is the writer's stated or implied position on a particular issue or idea. Identify the writer's purpose and point of view.

Development: This part consists of three or more middle paragraphs that prove the writer's position from different angles, using evidence from real-life experience and knowledge. Evidence may take the form of facts, examples, statistics, illustrations, opinions, or analogies.

In addition, each paragraph within the development section will have a stated or implied main point used to support the thesis of the whole passage. For example, a thesis might be "Dogs are better than cats." Having said that, a whole paragraph might be written with supporting examples to show a main point in support of that idea. The main point of the paragraph that needs support, then, might be as follows:

First of all, dogs are more loyal than cats.

The evidence that is summoned to support that point which, in turn, supports the overall thesis would therefore have to be facts, statistics, expert testimony, or anecdotal knowledge that shows that dogs are indeed more loyal than cats. For example: "The A.S.P.C.A. reports that 99 out of 100 dogs cannot adjust to new owners after the death of their original masters, while only 2 out of 100 cats cannot adjust in the same situation."

Conclusion: The last paragraph usually (but not always) sums up the writer's position and may add some final reminder of what the issue is, some speculation, or some call to action that the writer suggests.

Skill 7: Analyze the Validity of Arguments

Induction, Deduction, and Fallacies

In formulating critical evaluations of a piece of writing, it is important to understand the problems, if any, with the logic of the piece that has been read. Does it make sense? If not, why doesn't it? It is up to the reader to find the errors in any piece of writing he or she reads. Of course, if the writer is effective, the reader won't find these fallacies. Be on the lookout for them because it is often a good way to refute, criticize, or counterargue if called upon to respond critically to any author's central idea, thesis, or main point. Make sure the evidence proves the writer's point and not something else.

Pay special attention to conclusions. The writer may not have proved the point. An essay is essentially a *syllogism* that proves something by *induction* or *deduction*. The *syllogism* is that *basic form of deductive reasoning* that is the cornerstone of most logic. It consists of a *major premise*, a *minor premise*, and a *conclusion*. Note how they are used in the discussion below. *Induction* is the sort of reasoning that arrives at a general conclusion based on the relationship among the contributing elements of an idea.

For example, a writer may observe under experimental conditions that whenever a spider begins to spin a web, it first rubs its back legs over its silk gland. The author may have observed 100,000 different species of spiders display this behavior. He or she may have also observed that they never rub their hind legs over the gland at any other time, only when they are about to put out silk to start a web. He or she may then *induce* from these observations that spiders must rub their hind legs over their silk glands in order to begin the production of silk to spin a web. Another individual may prove this theory wrong later because new evidence shows up to invalidate the induction. Until that happens, this will be the conclusion drawn from observations of the behavior of spiders.

Deduction, by way of contrast, reasons from the general to the particular. For example, an author may assert that all trees grow upward from the earth, not downward from the sky. Until someone finds a tree that grows from the sky to the earth, an individual will assume that every tree started growing out of the earth and base all other conclusions about the growth and flowering of trees upon this *deduction* as well.

Occasionally, however, the *premises* of a deductive argument are false or unprovable. The *premises* of an argument are those *definitions* or *assumptions* that are givens (concepts that do not stand in need of proof but are either self-evident, common knowledge, or agreed upon as terms between the writer and the reader). For example,

> Major Premise: All goats have beards.
>
> Minor Premise: Harry Jones has a beard.
>
> Conclusion: Therefore, Harry is a goat.

The conclusion is incorrect. It could be true if only goats have beards, but this is not the case; male human beings may have beards as well. Therefore, the conclusion is insupportable. In this example, we lack sufficient information to draw a conclusion about who or what Harry is.

Typical Logical Fallacies

Below is a list of typical logical errors that weak writers commit. The list is not exhaustive. Know how they occur and practice finding them in others' arguments, either in conversation or in essays they may have written.

1. *Either/or:* The writer assumes only two opposing possibilities: "Either we abolish cars, or the environment is doomed." This argument is weak because other factors may contribute to the destruction of the environment as well.

2. *Oversimplification:* Here the author might first state, "Only motivated athletes become champions." Perhaps not; though unfortunate, unmotivated athletes who use enhancing steroids occasionally become champions, too.

3. *Begging the question:* The writer assumes he or she has proved something that has not been proven. "He is unintelligent because he is stupid." A lack of intelligence is almost synonymous with being stupid. It cannot be proven that he is stupid by saying he is unintelligent; that "he" is either or both of these is exactly what needs to be proved.

4. *Ignoring the issue:* An argument against the truth of a person's testimony in court shifts from what the witness observed to how the witness's

testimony is inadmissible. "The witness is obviously unkempt and home-less." One has nothing to do with the other.

5. *Arguing against a person, not an idea:* The writer argues that somebody's idea has no merit because he or she is immoral or unintelligent: "John can't prove anything about dogs being faithful; he can't even understand basic mathematics."

6. *"It does not follow…"* or *non sequitur:* The writer leaps to a wrong conclusion: "John is tall; he must know a lot about mountains."

7. *Drawing the wrong conclusion from a sequence:* "He trained, read, then trained some more and, therefore, won the match." It is quite possible that other factors led to his winning the match.

Drill 2: Inferential Comprehension

DIRECTIONS: Read the passages and answer the questions that follow.

Passage 1

The Mitsushita Electric Industrial Company of Japan has developed a computer program that can use photographs of faces to predict the aging process and, also, how an unborn child may look. The system can show how a couple may look after 40 years of marriage and how newlyweds' future children may look. The computer analyzes facial characteristics from a photograph, based on shading and coloring differences, and then creates a three-dimensional model in its memory. The system consists of a personal computer with a program and circuit board. It will be marketed soon by the Mitsushita Company.

1. This passage is written in the point of view called

    (A) first person.

    (B) second person.

    (C) third person.

    (D) a combination of first and third person.

2. The intended purpose of this passage is to

    (A) persuade a couple to send in their photographs to use to predict their children's appearance.

    (B) explain how the aging process of adults and the appearance of their children can be predicted by a computer.

    (C) express an opinion about the technology of the future in Japan.

    (D) describe one way a computer uses photographs.

Passage 2

As a farmer from Conrad, Montana, I might be the last person expected to invent and patent a motorcycle helmet. (No, I don't wear a helmet while I am driving my tractor.) The law in the United States requires that all cars sold must carry a third, high-mounted brake light on the rear of the vehicle. If cars need this light, I thought, how much safer life would be for motorcyclists if they, too, had such a light. The problem, however, was to install it "high-mounted." I have designed a helmet with a brake light in the rear. Thus, motorcyclists wearing a helmet like mine are much safer on the road.

3.   The intended purpose of the passage is to

    (A)   tell about a farmer in Montana.

    (B)   explain a safety requirement for cars in the United States.

    (C)   describe a man's motorcycle helmet invention that makes riding motorcycles safer.

    (D)   show the versatility of some people.

4.   The point of view of this passage is

    (A)   first person.   (C)   third person.

    (B)   second person.   (D)   first and third person.

Drill 2: Detailed Explanations of Answers

1.   **(C)**

Choice (C) is the correct answer because the passage employs the point of view of an outsider through the use of pronouns such as *he, she,* and *it*.

2.   **(B)**

The intended purpose is to explain. Although couples might be interested in sending in their photographs to see what their children may look like, choice (A), the passage is not encouraging this reaction from those who read it. Choice (C) is much too broad a response; also, the passage is not expressing an opinion. Choice (D) is too vague, although what it says is incomplete truth.

3.   **(C)**

The focus of the passage is the motorcycle helmet, and the intended purpose is to explain why and how the helmet was invented. Choice (A) is a fact about the inventor—he is a farmer. Choice (B) is a true statement as well, but it is what prompted the writer's idea for a helmet. (D) is a general statement that is unrelated to this passage.

4.   **(A)**

The personality of the speaker is revealed along with his ideas and actions. Notice also the use of the pronoun *I*. Choice (D) will attract some test-takers, but the first person point of view often uses third person pronouns along with first person pronouns.

Skill 8: Draw Logical Inferences and Conclusions

Returning to question 6 in the practice passage, you must be able to summarize the passage and draw logical inferences and conclusions.

6. Which paragraph below is the best summary of the passage?

(A) The Supreme Court's decision-making process with respect to obscenity and pornography has become too subjective. Fact-pattern analyses, used to determine the overall attitude of the Court, reveal only broad-based attitudes on the part of the Court toward the situations of obscenity cases. But these patterns cannot fully account for the Court's attitudes toward case content. Research is not conclusive that fact-pattern analyses work when applied to legal areas. Renewed public and local interest suggests continued study and close examination of how the Court makes decisions. Delegating authority to the states may reflect patterns for Court decisions in other socially sensitive areas.

(B) Though subjective, the Supreme Court decisions are well documented. Fact-pattern analyses reveal the attitude of the Supreme Court toward its decisions in cases. Spaeth explains that an attitude involves both an object and a situation. For the Court, the situation may be defined as the decision to grant certiorari. Cases present strikingly similar patterns, and a small number of variables explain a high proportion of the Court's decisions. Segal has made an effort to verify the applicability of fact-pattern analysis with some success. The Court's decisions on obscenity and pornography suggest weak Court behavior, such as in *Miller vs. California.*

(C) To determine what obscenity and pornography mean to the Supreme Court, we must use fact-pattern analysis. Fact-pattern analysis reveals the ideas that the Court uses to operate in a vacuum. The litigants and the subject matter of cases is defined in broad terms (such as an entire area of law) to reveal the Court's decision-making process. Search and seizure cases reveal strikingly similar patterns, leaving the Court open to grant certiorari effectively. Renewed public interest in the Court's decisions proves how the Court will react in the future.

(D) Supreme Court decisions about pornography and obscenity are under examination and are out of control. The Court has to see the case to know it. Fact-pattern analyses reveal that the Court can only define cases in narrow terms, thus revealing individual egotism on the part of the Justices. As a result of strikingly similar patterns in search and seizure cases, the Court should be studied further for its weakness in delegating authority to state courts, as in the case of *Miller vs. California.*

The paragraph that best and most accurately reports what the writer demonstrated based on the implied thesis (see question 1) is answer choice (C) which is correct.

Choice (A) is incorrect. While it reflects some of the evidence presented in the passage, the passage does not imply that all Court decisions are subjective, just the ones about pornography and obscenity. Similarly, the writer does not suggest that delegating authority to the states as in *Miller vs. California* is a sign of some weakness, but merely that it is worthy of study as a tool for predicting or identifying the Court attitude.

Response (B) is also incorrect. The writer summons information over and over to show how fact-pattern analysis cannot pin down the Court's attitude toward case content.

(D) is incorrect. Nowhere does the writer say or suggest that the justice system is "out of control" or that the justices are "egotists," only that they are liable to be reduced to being "subjective" rather than based on an identifiable shared standard.

Drill 3: Reading Comprehension

> **DIRECTIONS:** Read the passage and answer the questions that follow.

WATER

1   The most important source of sediment is earth and rock material carried to the sea by rivers and streams; the same materials may also have been transported by glaciers and winds. Other sources are volcanic ash and lava, shells and skeletons of organisms, chemical precipitates
5   formed in seawater, and particles from outer space.

      Water is a most unusual substance because it exists on the surface of the earth in its three physical states: ice, water, and water vapor. There are other substances that might exist in a solid and liquid or gaseous state at temperatures normally found at the earth's surface,
10   but there are fewer substances which occur in all three states.

      Water is odorless, tasteless, and colorless. It is the only substance known to exist in a natural state as a solid, liquid, or gas on the surface of the earth. It is a universal solvent. Water does not corrode, rust, burn, or separate into its components easily. It is chemically inde-
15   structible. It can corrode almost any metal and erode the most solid rock. A unique property of water is that it expands and floats on water when frozen or in the solid state. Water has a freezing point of 0°C and a boiling point of 100°C. Water has the capacity for absorbing great quantities of heat with relatively little increase in temperature.
20   When *distilled*, water is a poor conductor of electricity but when salt is added, it is a good conductor of electricity.

      Sunlight is the source of energy for temperature change, evaporation, and currents for water movement through the atmosphere. Sunlight controls the rate of photosynthesis for all marine plants,
25   which are directly or indirectly the source of food for all marine animals. Migration, breeding, and other behaviors of marine animals are affected by light.

      Water, as the ocean or sea, is blue because of the molecular scattering of the sunlight. Blue light, being of short wavelength, is scat-
30   tered more effectively than light of longer wavelengths. Variations in color may be caused by particles suspended in the water, water depth, cloud cover, temperature, and other variable factors. Heavy concentrations of dissolved materials cause a yellowish hue, while algae will cause the water to look green. Heavy populations of plant and animal
35   materials will cause the water to look brown.

1. Which of the following lists of topics best organizes the information in the selection?

    (A) I.   Water as vapor

        II. Water as ice

        III. Water as solid

    (B) I.   Properties of seawater

        II. Freezing and boiling points of water

        III. Photosynthesis

        IV. Oceans and seas

    (C) I.   Water as substance

        II. Water's corrosion

        III. Water and plants

        IV. Water and algae coloration

    (D) I.   Water's physical states

        II. Properties of water

        III. Effects of the sun on water

        IV. Reasons for color variation in water

2. According to the passage, what is the most unique property of water?

    (A) Water is odorless, tasteless, and colorless.

    (B) Water exists on the surface of the earth in three physical states.

    (C) Water is chemically indestructible.

    (D) Water is a poor conductor of electricity.

3. Which of the following best defines the word *distilled* as it is used in the last sentence of the third paragraph?

    (A) Free of salt content   (C) Dehydrated

    (B) Free of electrical energy   (D) Containing wine

4. The writer's main purpose in this selection is to

    (A) explain the colors of water.

    (B) examine the effects of the sun on water.

    (C) define the properties of water.

    (D) describe the three physical states of all liquids.

5. The writer of this selection would most likely agree with which of the following statements?

    (A) The properties of water are found in most other liquids on this planet.

(B) Water should not be consumed in its most natural state.

(C) Water might be used to serve many different functions.

(D) Water is too unpredictable for most scientists.

> **DIRECTIONS: Read the passage and answer the questions that follow.**

THE BEGINNINGS OF THE SUBMARINE

1   A submarine was first used as an offensive weapon during the American Revolutionary War. The Turtle, a one-man submersible designed by an American inventor named David Bushnell and hand-operated by a screw propeller, attempted to sink a British man-of-war

5   in New York Harbor. The plan was to attach a charge of gunpowder to the ship's bottom with screws and explode it with a time fuse. After repeated failures to force the screws through the copper sheathing of the hull of H.M.S. *Eagle*, the submarine gave up and withdrew, exploding its powder a short distance from the *Eagle*. Although the attack

10   was unsuccessful, it caused the British to move their blockading ships from the harbor to the outer bay.

     On 17 February 1864, a Confederate craft, a hand-propelled submersible, carrying a crew of eight men, sank a Federal corvette that was blockading Charleston Harbor. The hit was accomplished by a

15   torpedo suspended ahead of the Confederate *Hunley* as she rammed the Union frigate *Housatonic*, and is the first recorded instance of a submarine sinking a warship.

     The submarine first became a major component in naval warfare during World War I, when Germany demonstrated its full potential.

20   Wholesale sinking of Allied shipping by the German U-boats almost swung the war in favor of the Central Powers. Then, as now, the submarine's greatest advantage was that it could operate beneath the ocean surface where detection was difficult. Sinking a submarine was comparatively easy, once it was found—but finding it before it could

25   attack was another matter.

     During the closing months of World War I, the Allied Submarine Devices Investigation Committee was formed to obtain from science and technology more effective underwater detection equipment. The committee developed a reasonably accurate device for locating a sub-

30   merged submarine. This device was a trainable hydrophone, which was attached to the bottom of the ASW ship, and used to detect screw noises and other sounds that came from a submarine. Although the committee disbanded after World War I, the British made improvements on the locating device during the interval between then and

35   World War II, and named it ASDIC after the committee.

American scientists further improved on the device, calling it SONAR, a name derived from the underlined initials of the words <u>so</u>und <u>na</u>vigation and <u>r</u>anging.

40   At the end of World War II, the United States improved the snorkel (a device for bringing air to the crew and engines when operating submerged on diesels) and developed the Guppy (short for greater underwater propulsion power), a conversion of the fleet-type submarine of World War II fame. The superstructure was changed by reducing the surface area, streamlining every protruding object, and

45   enclosing the periscope shears in a streamlined metal fairing. Performance increased greatly with improved electronic equipment, additional battery capacity, and the addition of the snorkel.

6. The passage implies that one of the most pressing modifications needed for the submarine was to

    (A) streamline its shape.

    (B) enlarge the submarine for accommodating more torpedoes and men.

    (C) reduce the noise caused by the submarine.

    (D) add a snorkel.

7. It is inferred that

    (A) ASDIC was formed to obtain technology for underwater detection.

    (B) ASDIC developed an accurate device for locating submarines.

    (C) the hydrophone was attached to the bottom of the ship.

    (D) ASDIC was formed to develop technology to defend U.S. shipping.

8. SONAR not only picked up the sound of submarines moving through the water but also

    (A) indicated the speed at which the sub was moving.

    (B) gave the location of the submarine.

    (C) indicated the speed of the torpedo.

    (D) placed the submarine within a specified range.

9. According to the passage, the submarine's success was due in part to its ability to

    (A) strike and escape undetected.

    (B) move swifter than other vessels.

    (C) submerge to great depths while being hunted.

    (D) run silently.

10. From the passage, one can infer

    (A) David Bushnell was indirectly responsible for the sinking of the Federal corvette in Charlestown Harbor.

    (B)   David Bushnell invented the Turtle.

    (C)   the Turtle was a one-man submarine.

    (D)   the Turtle sank the *Eagle* on February 17, 1864.

Drill 3: Detailed Explanations of Answers

1.   **(D)**

The correct response is (D) because its precepts are summations of each of the composition's main paragraphs. (A) only mentions points made in the second paragraph. (B) and (C) only mention scattered points made throughout the passage, each of which does not represent a larger body of information within the passage.

2.   **(B)**

The second paragraph states that this is the reason that water is a most unusual substance. (A) and (C) list unusual properties of water, but are not developed in the same manner as the property stated in (B). (D) is not even correct under all circumstances.

3.   **(A)**

The sentence contrasts distilled water to that which contains salt, so (A) is correct. (B), (C), and (D) are not implied by the passage.

4.   **(C)**

The writer's didactic summary of water's properties is the only perspective found in the passage. (A) and (B) are the subjects of individual paragraphs within the passage, but hardly represent the entire passage itself. An in-depth discussion of the physical states of liquids (D) is not offered within the passage.

5.   **(C)**

The correct choice is (C) because of the many properties of water ascribed to it in the passage, each of which might serve one practical purpose or another. (A) and (D) are contradicted within the passage, while (B) is not implied at all by the passage.

6.   **(A)**

Answer (A) is correct because of the importance of streamlining mentioned in the final paragraph. (B) and (C) are not suggested in the paragraph, and (D) is secondary in importance to (A).

7.   **(D)**

Since it may be inferred from the general purpose of underwater detection equipment, (D) is correct. While (A) and (B) are true statements, they are not inferences. (C) is not implied in the passage.

8. **(D)**

Answer (D) is correct because the "R" in SONAR stands for "Ranging." (A), (B), and (C) are neither mentioned nor implied by the passage.

9. **(A)**

As was mentioned in the third sentence of the third paragraph, (A) is correct. (B), (C), and (D) are not mentioned in the passage.

10. **(A)**

It may be inferred that Bushnell's invention led to the success of the later version of the submarine. (B) and (C) are true, but are not inferences because they are directly stated in the first paragraph. (D) is not a true statement; the Turtle had no direct link to the 1864 incident.

Mathematics Review

Are you ready to tackle the math section of the FTCE-GKT? Well, the chances are that you will be, but only after some reviewing of basic concepts. The more familiar you are with these fundamental principles, the better you will do on the math section. Our math review represents the various mathematical topics that will appear on the FTCE-GKT.

Competency 1: Knowledge of Number Sense, Concepts, and Operations

Compare the Relative Value of Real Numbers

Integers and Real Numbers

Most of the numbers used in algebra belong to a set called the **real numbers** or **reals**. This set can be represented graphically by the real number line, and includes whole numbers and all the numbers between them, such as 2.7, 3/4, and $\sqrt{2}$.

Given the number line below, we arbitrarily fix a point and label it with the number 0. In a similar manner, we can label any point on the line with one of the real numbers, depending on its position relative to 0. Numbers to the right of 0 are positive, while those to the left are negative. Value increases from left to right, so that if a is to the right of b, it is said to be greater than b.

If we now divide the number line into equal segments, we can label the points on this line with real numbers. For example, the point 2 lengths to the left of 0 is −2, and the point 3 lengths to the right of 0 is +3 (the + sign is usually assumed, so +3 is written simply as 3). The number line now looks like this:

These points represent the subset of the reals known as the **integers**. The set of integers is made up of both the positive and negative whole numbers and zero:

$$\{\ldots, -4, -3, -2, -1, 0, 1, 2, 3, 4, \ldots\}.$$

Some subsets of integers are:

Natural Numbers or Positive Numbers—the set of integers starting with 1 and increasing:

$$N = \{1, 2, 3, 4, \ldots\}.$$

Whole Numbers—the set of integers starting with 0 and increasing:

$$W = \{0, 1, 2, 3, \ldots\}.$$

Negative Numbers—the set of integers starting with −1 and decreasing:

$$Z = \{-1, -2, -3, \ldots\}.$$

Prime Numbers—the set of positive integers greater than 1 that are divisible only by 1 and themselves:

$$\{2, 3, 5, 7, 11, \ldots\}.$$

Even Integers—the set of integers divisible by 2:

$$\{\ldots, -4, -2, 0, 2, 4, 6, \ldots\}.$$

Odd Integers—the set of integers not divisible by 2:

$$\{\ldots, -3, -1, 1, 3, 5, 7, \ldots\}.$$

Consecutive Integers—the set of integers that differ by 1:

$$\{n, n + 1, n + 2, \ldots\} \ (n = \text{an integer}).$$

PROBLEM

Classify each of the following numbers into as many different sets as possible. Example: real, integer ...

(1) 0

(2) 9

(3) $\sqrt{6}$

(4) $\dfrac{1}{2}$

(5) $\dfrac{2}{3}$

(6) 1.5

SOLUTION

(1) 0 is a real number, an integer, and a whole number.

(2) 9 is a real number, an odd integer, and a natural number.

(3) $\sqrt{6}$ is a real number (and a radical).

(4) $\dfrac{1}{2}$ is a real number (and a fraction).

(5) $\dfrac{2}{3}$ is a real number (and a fraction).

(6) 1.5 is a real number (and a decimal).

Absolute Value

The **absolute value** of a number is represented by a vertical line on each side of the number, and is equal to the given number, regardless of sign.

The absolute value of a real number A is defined as follows:

$$|A| = \begin{cases} A \text{ if } A \geq 0 \\ -A \text{ if } A < 0 \end{cases}$$

- **EXAMPLES**

$$|5| = 5, |-8| = -(-8) = 8$$

Absolute values follow the given rules:

(A) $|-A| = |A|$

(B) $|A| \geq 0$ equality holding only if $A = 0$

(C) $\left|\dfrac{A}{B}\right| = \dfrac{|A|}{|B|}, \ B \neq 0$

(D) $|AB| = |A| \times |B|$

(E) $|A|^2 = A^2$

Absolute value can also be expressed on the real number line as the distance of the point represented by the real number from the point labeled 0.

So $|-3| = 3$ because -3 is 3 units to the left of 0.

PROBLEM

Classify each of the following statements as true or false. If it is false, explain why.

(1) $|-120| > 1$ (2) $|4-12| = |4| - |12|$ (3) $|4-9| = 9-4$

(4) $|12-3| = 12-3$ (5) $|-12a| = 12|a|$

SOLUTION

(1) True

(2) False,

$$|4-12| = |4| - |12|$$
$$|-8| = 4-12$$
$$8 \neq -8$$

(3) True

(4) True

(5) True

Order of Operations

When a series of operations involving addition, subtraction, multiplication, or division is indicated, first resolve any operations in parentheses, then resolve exponents, then resolve multiplication and/or division, and finally perform addition and/or subtraction. One way to remember this is to recite "Please excuse my dear Aunt Sally." The *P* stands for parentheses, the *E* for exponents, the *M* for multiplication, the *D* for division, the *A* for addition and the *S* for subtraction. Now let's try using the order of operations.

Consider

$$60 - 25 \div 5 + 15 - 100 + 4 \times 10$$
$$= 60 - 25 \div 5 + 15 - 100 + 40$$
$$= 60 - 5 + 15 - 100 + 40$$
$$= 115 - 105$$
$$= 10$$

Notice that $25 \div 5$ could be evaluated at the same time that 4×10 is evaluated, since they are both part of the multiplication/division step.

PROBLEM

Calculate the value of each of the following expressions:

(1) $||4-10|+12-20|$ (2) $|-5|\times|4|+\dfrac{|-12|}{4}$

SOLUTION

Before solving this problem, one must remember the order of operations: parentheses (or absolute value), multiplication and division, addition and subtraction.

(1) $||-6|+12-20|=|6+12-20|=|18-20|=|-2|=2$

(2) $(5\times4)+{}^{12}\!/_4=20+3=23$

PROBLEM

Find the absolute value for each of the following:

(1)   0   (2)   4

(3) $-\pi$ (4) a, where a is a real number

SOLUTION

(1) $|0|=0$

(2) $|4|=4$

(3) $|-\pi|=\pi$

(4)   for $a>0$, $|a|=a$

for $a=0$, $|a|=0$

for $a<0$, $|a|=a$

or $|a|=\begin{cases} a & \text{if } a>0 \\ 0 & \text{if } a=0 \\ -a & \text{if } a<0 \end{cases}$

Positive and Negative Numbers

A)   **To add two numbers with like signs,** add their absolute values and write the sum with the common sign. So,

$$6+2=8, (-6)+(-2)=-8$$

B) **To add two numbers with unlike signs,** find the difference between their absolute values, and write the result with the sign of the number with the greater absolute value. So,

$$(-4) + 6 = 2, \ 15 + (-19) = -4$$

C) **To subtract a number *b* from another number *a*,** change the sign of *b* and add to *a*. Examples:

$$10 - (3) = 10 + (-3) = 7 \tag{1}$$
$$2 - (-6) = 2 + 6 = 8 \tag{2}$$
$$(-5) - (-2) = -5 + 2 = -3 \tag{3}$$

D) **To multiply (or divide) two numbers having like signs,** multiply (or divide) their absolute values and write the result with a positive sign. Examples:

$$(5)(3) = 15 \tag{1}$$
$$(-6) \div (-3) = 2 \tag{2}$$

E) **To multiply (or divide) two numbers having unlike signs,** multiply (or divide) their absolute values and write the result with a negative sign. Examples:

$$(-2)(8) = -16 \tag{1}$$
$$9 \div (-3) = -3 \tag{2}$$

According to the law of signs for real numbers, the square of a positive or negative number is always positive. This means that it is impossible to take the square root of a negative number in the real number system.

PROBLEM

Calculate the value of each of the following expressions:

$$(1) \quad ||2 - 5| + 6 - 14| \qquad\qquad (2) \quad |-8| \times 2 + \frac{|-12|}{4}$$

SOLUTION

Before solving this problem, one must use the rules for the **order of operations**. Always work within the parentheses or within absolute values first while keeping in mind that multiplication and division are carried out before addition and subtraction, working from left to right.

$$
\begin{aligned}
(1) \quad ||-3| + 6 - 14| &= |3 + 6 - 14| \\
&= |9 - 14| \\
&= |-5| \\
&= 5
\end{aligned}
$$

(2) $(8 \times 2) + \dfrac{12}{4} = 16 + 3$
$= 19$

Odd and Even Numbers

When dealing with odd and even numbers, keep in mind the following:

Adding:

even + even = even

odd + odd = even

even + odd = odd

Multiplying:

even × even = even

even × odd = even

odd × odd = odd

Drill: Integers and Real Numbers

Addition

1.   Simplify $4 + (-7) + 2 + (-5)$.

(A) −6   (B) −4   (C) 0   (D) 6   (E) 18

2.   Simplify $144 + (-317) + 213$.

(A) −357   (B) −40   (C) 40   (D) 257   (E) 674

3.   Simplify $|4 + (-3)| + |-2|$.

(A) −2   (B) −1   (C) 1   (D) 3   (E) 9

4.   What integer makes the equation $-13 + 12 + 7 + ? = 10$ a true statement?

(A) −22   (B) −10   (C) 4   (D) 6   (E) 10

5.   Simplify $4 + 17 + (-29) + 13 + (-22) + (-3)$.

(A) −44   (B) 20   (C) 23   (D) 34   (E) 78

Subtraction

6.   Simplify $319 - 428$.

(A) −111   (B) −109   (C) −99   (D) 109   (E) 747

7. Simplify $91,203 - 37,904 + 1,073$.

     (A) 54,372   (B) 64,701   (C) 128,034   (D) 129,107   (E) 130,180

8. Simplify $|43 - 62| - |-17 - 3|$.

     (A) −39   (B) −19   (C) −1   (D) 1   (E) 39

9. Simplify $-(-4 - 7) + (-2)$.

     (A) −22   (B) −13   (C) −9   (D) 7   (E) 9

10. In the St. Elias Mountains, Mt. Logan rises from 1,292 meters above sea level to 7,243 meters above sea level. How tall is Mt. Logan?

     (A) 4,009 m   (B) 5,951 m   (C) 5,699 m   (D) 6,464 m   (E) 7,885 m

Multiplication

11. Simplify $(-3) \times (-18) \times (-1)$.

     (A) −108   (B) −54   (C) −48   (D) 48   (E) 54

12. Simplify $|-42| \times |7|$.

     (A) −294   (B) −49   (C) −35   (D) 284   (E) 294

13. Simplify $(-6) \times 5 \times (-10) \times (-4) \times 0 \times 2$.

     (A) −2,400   (B) −240   (C) 0   (D) 280   (E) 2,700

14. Simplify $-|-6 \times 8|$.

     (A) −48   (B) −42   (C) 2   (D) 42   (E) 48

15. A city in Georgia had a record low temperature of −3°F one winter. During the same year, a city in Michigan experienced a record low that was nine times the record low set in Georgia. What was the record low in Michigan that year?

     (A) −31°F   (B) −27°F   (C) −21°F   (D) −12°F   (E) −6°F

Division

16. Simplify $(-24) \div 8$.

     (A) −4   (B) −3   (C) −2   (D) 3   (E) 4

17. Simplify $(-180) \div (-12)$.

    (A) -30 (B) -15 (C) 1.5 (D) 15 (E) 216

18. Simplify $|-76| \div |-4|$.

    (A) -21 (B) -19 (C) 13 (D) 19 (E) 21.5

19. Simplify $|216 \div (-6)|$

    (A) -36 (B) -12 (C) 36 (D) 38 (E) 43

20. At the end of the year, a small firm has \$2,996 in its account for bonuses. If the entire amount is equally divided among the 14 employees, how much does each one receive?

    (A) \$107   (B) \$114   (C) \$170   (D) \$210   (E) \$214

Order of Operations

21. Simplify $\dfrac{4+8\times2}{5-1}$.

    (A) 4 (B) 5 (C) 6 (D) 8 (E) 12

22. $96 \div 3 \div 4 \div 2 =$

    (A) 65 (B) 64 (C) 16 (D) 8 (E) 4

23. $3 + 4 \times 2 - 6 \div 3 =$

    (A) -1 (B) $\dfrac{5}{3}$ (C) $\dfrac{8}{3}$ (D) 9 (E) 12

24. $[(4 + 8) \times 3] \div 9 =$

    (A) 4 (B) 8 (C) 12 (D) 24 (E) 36

25. $18 + 3 \times 4 \div 3 =$

    (A) 3 (B) 5 (C) 10 (D) 22 (E) 28

26. $(29 - 17 + 4) \div 4 + |-2| =$

    (A) $2\dfrac{2}{3}$ (B) 4 (C) $4\dfrac{2}{3}$ (D) 6 (E) 15

27. $(-3) \times 5 - 20 \div 4 =$

   (A) -75 (B) -20 (C) -10 (D) $-8\frac{3}{4}$ (E) 20

28. $\dfrac{11 \times 2 + 2}{16 - 2 \times 2} =$

   (A) $\dfrac{11}{16}$ (B) 1 (C) 2 (D) $3\frac{2}{3}$ (E) 4

29. $|-8 - 4| \div 3 \times 6 + (-4) =$

   (A) 20 (B) 26 (C) 32 (D) 62 (E) 212

30. $32 \div 2 + 4 - 15 \div 3 =$

   (A) 0 (B) 7 (C) 15 (D) 23 (E) 63

Fractions

The fraction, $\dfrac{a}{b}$, where the **numerator** is a and the **denominator** is b, implies that a is being divided by b. The denominator of a fraction can never be zero since a number divided by zero is not defined. If the numerator is greater than the denominator, the fraction is called an **improper fraction. A mixed number** is the sum of a whole number and a fraction, or

$$4\frac{3}{8} = 4 + \frac{3}{8}.$$

Operations with Fractions

A) **To change a mixed number to an improper fraction**, simply multiply the whole number by the denominator of the fraction and add the numerator. This product becomes the numerator of the result and the denominator remains the same; for example,

$$5\frac{2}{3} = \frac{(5 \times 3) + 2}{3} = \frac{15 + 2}{3} = \frac{17}{3}$$

To change an improper fraction to a mixed number, simply divide the numerator by the denominator. The remainder becomes the numerator of the fractional part of the mixed number, and the denominator remains the same; for example,

$$\frac{35}{4} = 35 \div 4 = 8\frac{3}{4}$$

To check your work, change your result back to an improper fraction to see if it matches the original fraction.

B) **To find the sum of fractions having a common denominator**, simply add together the numerators of the given fractions and put this sum over the common denominator.

$$\frac{11}{3}+\frac{5}{3}=\frac{11+5}{3}=\frac{16}{3}, \text{ or } 5\frac{1}{3}$$

Similarly for subtraction,

$$\frac{11}{3}-\frac{5}{3}=\frac{11-5}{3}=\frac{6}{3}=2$$

C) **To find the sum of two fractions having different denominators**, it is necessary to find the **lowest common denominator (LCD)** of the different denominators using a process called **factoring**.

To **factor** a number means to find two or more numbers that when multiplied together have a product equal to the original number. These numbers are then said to be **factors** of the original number; for example, the factors of 6 are

(1)   1 and 6 since $1 \times 6 = 6$.

(2)   2 and 3 since $2 \times 3 = 6$.

Every number is the product of itself and 1. A **prime factor** is a number that does not have any factors besides itself and 1. This is important when finding the LCD of two fractions having different denominators because the LCD is the product of the prime factors (eliminating any duplicates).

To find the LCD of $\frac{11}{6}$ and $\frac{5}{16}$, we must first find the prime factors of each of the two denominators.

$$6 = 2 \times 3$$
$$16 = 2 \times 2 \times 2 \times 2$$
$$\text{LCD} = 2 \times 2 \times 2 \times 2 \times 3 = 48$$

Note that we do not need to repeat the duplicate 2 that appears in both the factors of 6 and 16.

Once we have determined the LCD of the denominators, each of the fractions must be converted into equivalent fractions having the LCD as a denominator.

Rewrite $\frac{11}{6}$ and $\frac{5}{16}$ to have 48 as their denominators.

$$6 \times ? = 48$$
$$6 \times 8 = 48$$
$$16 \times ? = 48$$
$$16 \times 3 = 48$$

If the numerator and denominator of each fraction are each multiplied (or divided) by the same number, the value of the fraction will not change. This is because a fraction b/b, where b is any number, is equal to the multiplicative identity, 1.

Therefore (see the product rule (E) below):

$$\frac{11}{6}\times\frac{8}{8}=\frac{88}{48} \qquad \frac{5}{16}\times\frac{3}{3}=\frac{15}{48}$$

We may now find

$$\frac{11}{6} + \frac{5}{16} = \frac{88}{48} + \frac{15}{48} = \frac{103}{48}$$

Similarly, for subtraction,

$$\frac{11}{6} - \frac{5}{16} = \frac{88}{48} - \frac{15}{48} = \frac{73}{48}$$

D) **To add mixed fractions** (those made up of a whole number and a fraction), add the fractions first, then—separately—the whole numbers. If the fractions add up to more than 1, add 1 to the whole number sum. For example, if after adding we have 3 and $1\frac{3}{4}$, the final sum is $4\frac{3}{4}$.

The algorithm for subtracting fractions is generally the same as that for adding: Common denominators are required. A problem, however, may be encountered when attempting to subtract mixed fractions such as $3\frac{2}{5}$ and $1\frac{4}{5}$. Note that $\frac{4}{5}$ can't be subtracted from $\frac{2}{5}$ (without involving negative numbers.) The solution is to rename $3\frac{2}{5}$ as $2\frac{7}{5}$. (This is accomplished by "borrowing" 1, or $\frac{5}{5}$, from the 3.) The new problem—still equivalent to the original—is $2\frac{7}{5}$ minus $1\frac{4}{5}$, or $1\frac{3}{5}$.

E) **To find the product of two or more fractions**, simply multiply the numerators of the given fractions to find the numerator of the product and multiply the denominators of the given fractions to find the denominator of the product; for example,

$$\frac{2}{3} \times \frac{1}{5} \times \frac{4}{7} = \frac{2 \times 1 \times 4}{3 \times 5 \times 7} = \frac{8}{105}$$

If the numbers to be multiplied are mixed fractions, first rewrite them as "improper" fractions, such as $\frac{14}{3}$.

F) **To find the quotient of two fractions,** simply invert (or flip-over) the divisor and multiply; for example,

$$\frac{8}{9} \div \frac{1}{3} = \frac{8}{9} \times \frac{3}{1} = \frac{24}{9}$$

G) **To simplify a fraction** is to convert it into a form in which the numerator and denominator have no common factor other than 1; for example,

$$\frac{12}{18} = \frac{12 \div 6}{18 \div 6} = \frac{2}{3}, \text{ or the answer to the example in (F) would be } \frac{24}{9} = \frac{8 \div 3}{3 \div 3} = \frac{8}{3}.$$

H) A **complex fraction** is a fraction whose numerator and/or denominator is made up of fractions. To simplify the fraction, find the LCD of all the fractions. Multiply both the numerator and denominator by this number and simplify.

PROBLEM

If $a = 4$ and $b = 7$, find the value of $\dfrac{a + \frac{a}{b}}{a - \frac{a}{b}}$.

SOLUTION

By substitution,

$$\frac{a + \frac{a}{b}}{a - \frac{a}{b}} = \frac{4 + \frac{4}{7}}{4 - \frac{4}{7}}$$

In order to combine the terms, we must find the LCD of 1 and 7. Since both are prime factors, the LCD = $1 \times 7 = 7$.

$$\frac{4 + \frac{4}{7}}{4 - \frac{4}{7}} = \frac{\frac{32}{7}}{\frac{24}{7}}$$

$$\frac{32}{7} \div \frac{24}{7} = \frac{32}{7} \times \frac{7}{24} = \frac{32}{24}$$

By dividing both the numerator and denominator by 8, $^{32}\!/_{24}$ can be reduced to $^{4}\!/_{3}$.

Drill: Fractions

Changing an Improper Fraction to a Mixed Number

DIRECTIONS: Write each improper fraction as a mixed number in simplest form.

1. $\dfrac{50}{4}$

     (A) $10\dfrac{1}{4}$ (B) $11\dfrac{1}{2}$ (C) $12\dfrac{1}{4}$ (D) $12\dfrac{1}{2}$ (E)   25

2. $\dfrac{17}{5}$

   (A) $3\dfrac{2}{5}$ (B) $3\dfrac{3}{5}$ (C) $3\dfrac{4}{5}$ (D) $4\dfrac{1}{5}$ (E) $4\dfrac{2}{5}$

3. $\dfrac{42}{3}$

   (A) $10\dfrac{2}{3}$ (B) 12 (C) $13\dfrac{1}{3}$ (D) 14 (E) $21\dfrac{1}{3}$

4. $\dfrac{85}{6}$

   (A) $9\dfrac{1}{6}$ (B) $10\dfrac{5}{6}$ (C) $11\dfrac{1}{2}$ (D) 12 (E) $14\dfrac{1}{6}$

5. $\dfrac{151}{7}$

   (A) $19\dfrac{6}{7}$ (B) $20\dfrac{1}{7}$ (C) $21\dfrac{4}{7}$ (D) $31\dfrac{2}{7}$ (E) $31\dfrac{4}{7}$

Changing a Mixed Number to an Improper Fraction

> **DIRECTIONS**: Change each mixed number to an improper fraction in simplest form.

6. $2\dfrac{3}{5}$

   (A) $\dfrac{4}{5}$ (B) $\dfrac{6}{5}$ (C) $\dfrac{11}{5}$ (D) $\dfrac{13}{5}$ (E) $\dfrac{17}{5}$

7. $4\dfrac{3}{4}$

   (A) $\dfrac{7}{4}$ (B) $\dfrac{13}{4}$ (C) $\dfrac{16}{3}$ (D) $\dfrac{19}{4}$ (E) $\dfrac{21}{4}$

8. $6\dfrac{7}{6}$

   (A) $\dfrac{13}{6}$ (B) $\dfrac{43}{6}$ (C) $\dfrac{19}{36}$ (D) $\dfrac{42}{36}$ (E) $\dfrac{48}{6}$

9. $12\dfrac{3}{7}$

    (A) $\dfrac{87}{7}$ (B) $\dfrac{164}{14}$ (C) $\dfrac{34}{3}$ (D) $\dfrac{187}{21}$ (E) $\dfrac{252}{7}$

10. $21\dfrac{1}{2}$

    (A) $\dfrac{11}{2}$ (B) $\dfrac{22}{2}$ (C) $\dfrac{24}{2}$ (D) $\dfrac{42}{2}$ (E) $\dfrac{43}{2}$

Adding Fractions with the Same Denominator

DIRECTIONS: Add and write the answer in simplest form or as a mixed number.

11. $\dfrac{5}{12} + \dfrac{3}{12} =$

    (A) $\dfrac{5}{24}$ (B) $\dfrac{1}{3}$ (C) $\dfrac{8}{12}$ (D) $\dfrac{2}{3}$ (E) $1\dfrac{1}{3}$

12. $\dfrac{5}{8} + \dfrac{7}{8} + \dfrac{3}{8} =$

    (A) $\dfrac{15}{24}$ (B) $\dfrac{3}{4}$ (C) $\dfrac{5}{6}$ (D) $\dfrac{7}{8}$ (E) $1\dfrac{7}{8}$

13. $131\dfrac{2}{15} + 28\dfrac{3}{15} =$

    (A) $159\dfrac{1}{6}$ (B) $159\dfrac{1}{5}$ (C) $159\dfrac{1}{3}$ (D) $159\dfrac{1}{2}$ (E) $159\dfrac{3}{5}$

14. $3\dfrac{5}{18} + 2\dfrac{1}{18} + 8\dfrac{7}{18} =$

    (A) $13\dfrac{13}{18}$ (B) $13\dfrac{3}{4}$ (C) $13\dfrac{7}{9}$ (D) $14\dfrac{1}{6}$ (E) $14\dfrac{2}{9}$

15. $17\dfrac{9}{20} + 4\dfrac{3}{20} + 8\dfrac{11}{20} =$

    (A) $29\dfrac{23}{60}$ (B) $29\dfrac{23}{20}$ (C) $30\dfrac{3}{20}$ (D) $30\dfrac{1}{5}$ (E) $30\dfrac{3}{5}$

Subtracting Fractions with the Same Denominator

DIRECTIONS: Subtract and write the answer in simplest form or as a mixed number.

16. $4\frac{7}{8} - 3\frac{1}{8} =$

    (A) $1\frac{1}{4}$ (B) $1\frac{3}{4}$ (C) $1\frac{12}{16}$ (D) $1\frac{7}{8}$ (E) 2

17. $132\frac{5}{12} - 37\frac{3}{12} =$

    (A) $94\frac{1}{6}$ (B) $95\frac{1}{12}$ (C) $95\frac{1}{6}$ (D) $105\frac{1}{6}$ (E) $169\frac{2}{3}$

18. $19\frac{1}{3} - 2\frac{2}{3} =$

    (A) $16\frac{2}{3}$ (B) $16\frac{5}{6}$ (C) $17\frac{1}{3}$ (D) $17\frac{2}{3}$ (E) $17\frac{5}{6}$

19. $\frac{8}{21} - \frac{5}{21} =$

    (A) $\frac{1}{21}$ (B) $\frac{1}{7}$ (C) $\frac{3}{21}$ (D) $\frac{2}{7}$ (E) $\frac{3}{7}$

20. $82\frac{7}{10} - 38\frac{9}{10} =$

    (A) $43\frac{4}{5}$ (B) $44\frac{1}{5}$ (C) $44\frac{2}{5}$ (D) $45\frac{1}{5}$ (E) $45\frac{2}{10}$

Finding the LCD

DIRECTIONS: Find the lowest common denominator of each group of fractions.

21. $\frac{2}{3}, \frac{5}{9},$ and $\frac{1}{6}$

    (A) 9 (B) 18 (C) 27 (D) 54 (E) 162

22. $\dfrac{1}{2}, \dfrac{5}{6}$, and $\dfrac{3}{4}$

  (A) 2   (B) 4   (C) 6   (D) 12   (E) 48

23. $\dfrac{7}{16}, \dfrac{5}{6}$, and $\dfrac{2}{3}$

  (A) 3   (B) 6   (C) 12   (D) 24   (E) 48

24. $\dfrac{8}{15}, \dfrac{2}{5}$, and $\dfrac{12}{25}$

  (A) 5   (B) 15   (C) 25   (D) 75   (E) 375

25. $\dfrac{2}{3}, \dfrac{1}{5}$, and $\dfrac{5}{6}$

  (A) 15   (B) 30   (C) 48   (D) 90   (E) 120

26. $\dfrac{1}{3}, \dfrac{9}{42}$, and $\dfrac{4}{21}$

  (A) 21   (B) 42   (C) 126   (D) 378   (E) 4,000

27. $\dfrac{4}{9}, \dfrac{2}{5}$, and $\dfrac{1}{3}$

  (A) 15   (B) 17   (C) 27   (D) 45   (E) 135

28. $\dfrac{7}{12}, \dfrac{11}{36}$, and $\dfrac{1}{9}$

  (A) 12   (B) 36   (C) 108   (D) 324   (E) 432

29. $\dfrac{3}{7}, \dfrac{5}{21}$, and $\dfrac{2}{3}$

  (A) 21   (B) 42   (C) 31   (D) 63   (E) 441

30. $\dfrac{13}{16}, \dfrac{5}{8}$, and $\dfrac{1}{4}$

  (A) 4   (B) 8   (C) 16   (D) 32   (E) 64

Adding Fractions with Different Denominators

> **DIRECTIONS**: Add and write the answer in simplest form.

31. $\dfrac{1}{3}+\dfrac{5}{12}=$

    (A) $\dfrac{2}{5}$　　(B) $\dfrac{1}{2}$　　(C) $\dfrac{9}{12}$　　(D) $\dfrac{3}{4}$　　(E) $1\dfrac{1}{3}$

32. $3\dfrac{5}{9}+2\dfrac{1}{3}=$

    (A) $5\dfrac{1}{2}$　　(B) $5\dfrac{2}{3}$　　(C) $5\dfrac{8}{9}$　　(D) $6\dfrac{1}{9}$　　(E) $6\dfrac{2}{3}$

33. $12\dfrac{9}{16}+17\dfrac{3}{4}+8\dfrac{1}{8}=$

    (A) $37\dfrac{7}{16}$　　(B) $38\dfrac{7}{16}$　　(C) $38\dfrac{1}{2}$　　(D) $38\dfrac{2}{3}$　　(E) $39\dfrac{3}{16}$

34. $28\dfrac{4}{5}+11\dfrac{16}{25}=$

    (A) $39\dfrac{2}{3}$　　(B) $39\dfrac{4}{5}$　　(C) $40\dfrac{9}{25}$　　(D) $40\dfrac{2}{5}$　　(E) $40\dfrac{11}{25}$

35. $2\dfrac{1}{8}+1\dfrac{3}{16}+\dfrac{5}{12}=$

    (A) $3\dfrac{35}{48}$　　(B) $3\dfrac{3}{4}$　　(C) $3\dfrac{19}{24}$　　(D) $3\dfrac{13}{16}$　　(E) $4\dfrac{1}{12}$

Subtracting Fractions with Different Denominators

> **DIRECTIONS**: Subtract and write the answer in simplest form.

36. $8\dfrac{9}{12}-2\dfrac{2}{3}=$

    (A) $6\dfrac{1}{12}$　　(B) $6\dfrac{1}{6}$　　(C) $6\dfrac{1}{3}$　　(D) $6\dfrac{7}{12}$　　(E) $6\dfrac{2}{3}$

37. $185\frac{11}{15} - 107\frac{2}{5} =$

    (A) $77\frac{2}{15}$ (B) $78\frac{1}{5}$ (C) $78\frac{3}{10}$ (D) $78\frac{1}{3}$ (E) $78\frac{9}{15}$

38. $34\frac{2}{3} - 16\frac{5}{6} =$

    (A) 16 (B) $16\frac{1}{3}$ (C) 17 (D) 17 (E) $17\frac{5}{6}$

39. $3\frac{11}{48} - 2\frac{3}{16} =$

    (A) $\frac{47}{48}$ (B) $1\frac{1}{48}$ (C) $1\frac{1}{24}$ (D) $1\frac{8}{48}$ (E) $1\frac{7}{24}$

40. $81\frac{4}{21} - 31\frac{1}{3} =$

    (A) $47\frac{3}{7}$ (B) $49\frac{6}{7}$ (C) $49\frac{1}{6}$ (D) $49\frac{5}{7}$ (E) $49\frac{13}{21}$

Multiplying Fractions

DIRECTIONS: Multiply and reduce the answer.

41. $\frac{2}{3} \times \frac{4}{5} =$

    (A) $\frac{6}{8}$ (B) $\frac{3}{4}$ (C) $\frac{8}{15}$ (D) $\frac{10}{12}$ (E) $\frac{6}{5}$

42. $\frac{7}{10} \times \frac{4}{21} =$

    (A) $\frac{2}{15}$ (B) $\frac{11}{31}$ (C) $\frac{28}{210}$ (D) $\frac{1}{6}$ (E) $\frac{4}{15}$

43. $5\dfrac{1}{3} \times \dfrac{3}{8} =$

    (A) $\dfrac{4}{11}$ (B) 2 (C) $\dfrac{8}{5}$ (D) $5\dfrac{1}{8}$ (E) $5\dfrac{17}{24}$

44. $6\dfrac{1}{2} \times 3 =$

    (A) $9\dfrac{1}{2}$ (B) $18\dfrac{1}{2}$ (C) $19\dfrac{1}{2}$ (D) 20 (E) $12\dfrac{1}{2}$

45. $3\dfrac{1}{4} \times 2\dfrac{1}{3} =$

    (A) $5\dfrac{7}{12}$ (B) $6\dfrac{2}{7}$ (C) $6\dfrac{5}{7}$ (D) $7\dfrac{7}{12}$ (E) $7\dfrac{11}{12}$

Dividing Fractions

DIRECTIONS: Divide and reduce the answer.

46. $\dfrac{3}{16} \div \dfrac{3}{4} =$

    (A) $\dfrac{9}{64}$ (B) $\dfrac{1}{4}$ (C) $\dfrac{6}{16}$ (D) $\dfrac{9}{16}$ (E) $\dfrac{3}{4}$

47. $\dfrac{4}{9} \div \dfrac{2}{3} =$

    (A) $\dfrac{1}{3}$ (B) $\dfrac{1}{2}$ (C) $\dfrac{2}{3}$ (D) $\dfrac{7}{11}$ (E) $\dfrac{8}{9}$

48. $5\dfrac{1}{4} \div \dfrac{7}{10} =$

    (A) $2\dfrac{4}{7}$ (B) $3\dfrac{27}{40}$ (C) $5\dfrac{19}{20}$ (D) $7\dfrac{1}{2}$ (E) $8\dfrac{1}{4}$

49. $4\dfrac{2}{3} \div \dfrac{7}{9} =$

    (A) $2\dfrac{24}{27}$ (B) $3\dfrac{2}{9}$ (C) $4\dfrac{14}{27}$ (D) $5\dfrac{12}{27}$ (E) 6

50. $3\dfrac{2}{5} \div 1\dfrac{7}{10} =$

    (A) 2 (B) $3\dfrac{4}{7}$ (C) $4\dfrac{7}{25}$ (D) $5\dfrac{1}{10}$ (E) $5\dfrac{2}{7}$

Decimals

When we divide the denominator of a fraction into its numerator, the result is a **decimal**. The decimal is based upon a fraction with a denominator of 10, 100, 1,000, . . . and is written with a **decimal point**. Whole numbers are placed to the left of the decimal point where the first place to the left is the units place; the second to the left is the tens; the third to the left is the hundreds, etc. The fractions are placed on the right where the first place to the right is the tenths; the second to the right is the hundredths, etc.

- **EXAMPLES**

$$12\frac{3}{10} = 12.3 \qquad 4\frac{17}{100} = 4.17 \qquad \frac{3}{100} = .03$$

Since a **rational number** is of the form a/b, $b \neq 0$, then all rational numbers can be expressed as decimals by dividing b into a. The result is either a **terminating decimal**, meaning that b divides into a with a remainder of 0 after a certain point; or a **repeating decimal**, meaning that b continues to divide into a so that the decimal has a repeating pattern of integers.

- **EXAMPLES**

    (A) $\dfrac{1}{2} = 0.5$

    (B) $\dfrac{1}{3} = .333...$

    (C) $\dfrac{11}{16} = .6875$

    (D) $\dfrac{4}{7} = .571428571428...$

(A) and (C) are terminating decimals; (B) and (D) are repeating decimals. This explanation allows us to define **irrational numbers** as numbers whose decimal form is non-terminating and non-repeating; for example

$$\sqrt{2} = 1.4142...$$
$$\sqrt{3} = 1.7320...$$

PROBLEM

Express $-\dfrac{10}{20}$ as a decimal.

SOLUTION

$$-\frac{10}{20} = -\frac{50}{100} = -.5$$

PROBLEM

Write $\dfrac{2}{7}$ as a repeating decimal.

SOLUTION

To write a fraction as a repeating decimal, divide the numerator by the denominator until a pattern of repeated digits appears.

$$2 \div 7 = .285714285714...$$

Identify the entire portion of the decimal that is repeated. The repeating decimal can then be written in the shortened form:

$$\frac{2}{7} = .\overline{285714}$$

Operations with Decimals

A) **To add numbers containing decimals,** write the numbers in a column making sure the decimal points are lined up, one beneath the other. Add the numbers as usual, placing the decimal point in the sum so that it is still in line with the others. It is important not to mix the digits in the tenths place with the digits in the hundredths place, and so on. Note that if two numbers differ according to the number of digits to the right of the decimal point, zeros must be added.

- **EXAMPLES**

$$2.558 + 6.391 \qquad\qquad 57.51 + 6.2$$

$$
\begin{array}{r}
2.558 \\
+\,6.391 \\
\hline
8.949
\end{array}
\qquad\qquad
\begin{array}{r}
57.51 \\
+\;\,6.20 \\
\hline
63.71
\end{array}
$$

Similarly with subtraction,

78.54 − 21.33	7.11 − 4.2

$$\begin{array}{r} 78.54 \\ -\,21.33 \\ \hline 57.21 \end{array} \qquad \begin{array}{r} 7.11 \\ -\,4.20 \\ \hline 2.91 \end{array}$$

.63 − .214	15.224 − 3.6891

$$\begin{array}{r} .630 \\ -\,.214 \\ \hline .416 \end{array} \qquad \begin{array}{r} 15.2240 \\ -\,3.6891 \\ \hline 11.5349 \end{array}$$

B) **To multiply numbers with decimals,** simply multiply as usual. Then, to figure out the number of decimal places that belong in the product, find the total number of decimal places in the numbers being multiplied and place the decimal point that many places in from the right.

• **EXAMPLES**

$$\begin{array}{r} 6.555 \text{ (3 decimal places)} \\ \times \quad 4.5 \text{ (1 decimal place)} \\ \hline 32775 \\ 26220 \\ \hline 294975 \\ 29.4975 \text{ (4 decimal places)} \end{array} \qquad \begin{array}{r} 5.32 \text{ (2 decimal places)} \\ \times \quad .04 \text{ (2 decimal places)} \\ \hline 2128 \\ 000 \\ \hline 2128 \\ .2128 \text{ (4 decimal places)} \end{array}$$

C) **To divide numbers with decimals,** you must first make the divisor a whole number by moving the decimal point the appropriate number of places to the right. The decimal point of the dividend should also be moved that same number of places. Place a decimal point in the quotient, directly in line with the new decimal point in the dividend.

• **EXAMPLES**

12.92 ÷ 3.4	40.376 ÷ 7.21

$$\begin{array}{r} 3.8 \\ 3.4.\overline{)12.9.2} \\ -102 \\ \hline 272 \\ -272 \\ \hline 0 \end{array} \qquad \begin{array}{r} 5.6 \\ 7.21.\overline{)40.37.6} \\ -3605 \\ \hline 4326 \\ -4326 \\ \hline 0 \end{array}$$

If you are asked to find the correct answer to two decimal places, simply divide until you have three decimal places and then round off. If the third decimal place is a 5 or larger, the number in the second decimal place is increased by 1. If the third decimal place is less than 5, that number is simply dropped.

PROBLEM

> Find the answers to the following to two decimal places:
>
> (1) $44.3 \div 3$ (2) $56.99 \div 6$

SOLUTION

(1)
```
       14.766
   3 ) 44.300
      -3
      ──
       14
      -12
      ───
        23
       -21
       ───
         20
        -18
        ───
          20
         -18
         ───
           2
```

(2)
```
      9.498
  6 ) 56.990
     -54
     ───
      29
     -24
     ───
      59
     -54
     ───
      50
     -48
     ───
       2
```

14.766 can be rounded off to 14.77

9.498 can be rounded off to 9.50. Note that the zero remains after the 5 because the answer is supposed to be to two decimal places.

D)   **To compare two decimals to see which is the larger,** first look at the tenths place. The larger digit in this place represents the larger number. If the two digits are the same, however, look at the digits in the hundredths place, and so on.

- **EXAMPLES**

  .518 and .216   .723 and .726

  5 is larger than 2; therefore,   The first two digits, 72 are the same, but 6 is larger than 3; therefore,

  .518 is larger than .216   .726 is larger than .723

Drill: Decimals

Addition

> **DIRECTIONS: Perform the following additions.**

1. $1.032 + 0.987 + 3.07 =$

(A) 4.089   (B) 5.089   (C) 5.189   (D) 6.189   (E) 13.972

2. $132.03 + 97.1483 =$

    (A) 98.4686   (B) 110.3513   (C) 209.1783   (D) 229.1486 (E) 229.1783

3. $7.1 + 0.62 + 4.03827 + 5.183 =$

    (A) 0.2315127 (B) 16.45433   (C) 16.94127   (D) 18.561   (E) 40.4543

4. $8 + 17.43 + 9.2 =$

    (A) 34.63   (B) 34.86   (C) 35.63   (D) 176.63 (E) 189.43

5. $1{,}036.173 + 289.04 =$

    (A) 382.6573   (B) 392.6573   (C) 1,065.077   (D) 1,325.213 (E) 3,926.573

Subtraction

DIRECTIONS: Perform the following subtractions.

---

6. $3.972 - 2.04 =$

    (A) 1.932   (B) 1.942   (C) 1.976   (D) 2.013   (E) 2.113

7. $16.047 - 13.06 =$

    (A) 2.887   (B) 2.987   (C) 3.041   (D) 3.141   (E) 4.741

8. $87.4 - 56.27 =$

    (A) 30.27   (B) 30.67   (C) 31.1   (D) 31.13   (E) 31.27

9. $1{,}046.8 - 639.14 =$

    (A) 303.84   (B) 313.74   (C) 407.66   (D) 489.74   (E) 535.54

10. $10{,}000 - 842.91 =$

    (A) 157.09   (B) 942.91   (C) 5,236.09   (D) 9,057.91 (E) 9,157.09

Multiplication

DIRECTIONS: Perform the following multiplications.

---

11. $1.03 \times 2.6 =$

    (A) 2.18   (B) 2.678   (C) 2.78   (D) 3.38   (E) 3.63

12. 93 × 4.2 =

(A) 39.06   (B) 97.2   (C) 223.2   (D) 390.6   (E) 3,906

13. 0.04 × 0.23 =

(A) 0.0092   (B) 0.092   (C) 0.27   (D) 0.87   (E) 0.920

14. 0.0186 × 0.03 =

(A) 0.000348   (B) 0.000558   (C) 0.0548   (D) 0.0848   (E) 0.558

15. 51.2 × 0.17 =

(A) 5.29   (B) 8.534   (C) 8.704   (D) 36.352   (E) 36.991

Division

> **DIRECTIONS**: Perform the following divisions.

16. 123.39 ÷ 3 =

(A) 31.12   (B) 41.13   (C) 401.13   (D) 411.3   (E) 4,113

17. 1,428.6 ÷ 6

(A) 0.2381   (B) 2.381   (C) 23.81   (D) 238.1   (E) 2,381

18. 25.2 ÷ 0.3 =

(A) 0.84   (B) 8.04   (C) 8.4   (D) 84   (E) 840

19. 14.95 ÷ 6.5 =

(A) 2.3   (B) 20.3   (C) 23   (D) 230   (E) 2,300

20. 46.33 ÷ 1.13 =

(A) 0.41   (B) 4.1   (C) 41   (D) 410   (E) 4,100

Comparing

> **DIRECTIONS**: Answer the following questions.

21. Which is the **largest** number in this set—{0.8, 0.823, 0.089, 0.807, 0.852}?

(A) 0.8   (B) 0.823   (C) 0.089   (D) 0.807   (E) 0.852

22. Which is the **smallest** number in this set—{32.98, 32.099, 32.047, 32.5, 32.304}?

    (A) 32.98   (B) 32.099   (C) 32.047   (D) 32.5   (E) 32.304

23. In which set below are the numbers arranged correctly from smallest to largest?

    (A) {0.98, 0.9, 0.993}   (B) {0.113, 0.3, 0.31}

    (C) {7.04, 7.26, 7.2}   (D) {0.006, 0.061, 0.06}

    (E) {12.84, 12.801, 12.6}

24. In which set below are the numbers arranged correctly from largest to smallest?

    (A) {1.018, 1.63, 1.368}   (B) {4.219, 4.29, 4.9}

    (C) {0.62, 0.6043, 0.643}   (D) {16.34, 16.304, 16.3}

    (E) {12.98, 12.601, 12.86}

25. Which is the **largest** number in this set—{0.87, 0.89, 0.889, 0.8, 0.987}?

    (A) 0.87   (B) 0.89   (C) 0.889   (D) 0.8   (E) 0.987

Changing a Fraction to a Decimal

DIRECTIONS: Answer the following questions.

26. What is $\frac{1}{4}$ written as a decimal?

    (A) 1.4   (B) 0.14   (C) 0.2   (D) 0.25   (E) 0.3

27. What is $\frac{3}{5}$ written as a decimal?

    (A) 0.3   (B) 0.35   (C) 0.6   (D) 0.65   (E) 0.8

28. What is $\frac{7}{20}$ written as a decimal?

    (A) 0.35   (B) 0.4   (C) 0.72   (D) 0.75   (E) 0.9

29. What is $\frac{2}{3}$ written as a decimal?

    (A) 0.23   (B) 0.33   (C) 0.5   (D) 0.6   (E) $0.\overline{6}$

30. What is $\dfrac{11}{25}$ written as a decimal?

    (A)   0.1125   (B)   0.25   (C)   0.4   (D)   0.44   (E)   0.5

Percent

A **percent** is a way of expressing the relationship between a part and the whole, where the whole is defined as 100%. A percent can be defined by a fraction with a denominator of 100. Decimals can also represent a percent. For instance,

$$56\% = 0.56 = \frac{56}{100}$$

PROBLEM

Compute the values of

     (1)   90% of 400   (2)   180% of 400

     (3)   50% of 500   (4)   200% of 4

SOLUTION

The symbol % means per hundred, therefore $5\% = \frac{5}{100} = .05$.

(1)   90% of 400 = .90 × 400 = 360

(2)   180% of 400 = 1.80 × 400 = 720

(3)   50% of 500 = .50 × 500 = 250

(4)   200% of 4 = 2.00 × 4 = 8

Equivalent Forms of a Number

Some problems may call for converting numbers into an equivalent or simplified form in order to make the solution more convenient.

A)   **Converting a fraction to a decimal:**

$$\frac{1}{2} = 0.50$$

Divide the numerator by the denominator:

```
        .50
    2⟌1.00
     −10
       00
```

B) **Converting a number to a percent:**

$$0.50 = 50\%$$

Multiply by 100:

$$0.50 = (0.50 \times 100)\% = 50\%$$

C) **Converting a percent to a number (decimal):**

$$30\% = 0.30$$

Divide by 100:

$$30\% = 30 \div 100 = 0.30$$

D) **Converting a decimal to a fraction:**

$$0.500 = \frac{1}{2}$$

Convert .500 to $^{500}\!/_{1000}$ and then simplify the fraction by dividing the numerator and denominator by common factors:

$$\frac{5 \times 100}{10 \times 100} = \frac{5}{10} = \frac{1 \times 5}{2 \times 5} = \frac{1}{2}$$

PROBLEM

Express

(1) 1.65 as a percent (2) 0.7 as a fraction

(3) $-\dfrac{10}{20}$ as a decimal (4) $\dfrac{4}{2}$ as an integer

SOLUTION

(1) $1.65 \times 100 = 165\%$

(2) $0.7 = \dfrac{7}{10}$

(3) $-\dfrac{10}{20} = -0.5$

(4) $\dfrac{4}{2} = 2$

PROBLEM

> What percent of
>
> (1)   100 is 99.5?   (2)   200 is 4?

SOLUTION

(1) $\dfrac{99.5}{100} = .995 = 99.5\%$

(2) $\dfrac{4}{200} = .02 = 2\%$

Drill: Percent

Finding Percents

> **DIRECTIONS:** Solve to find the correct percentages.

1.   Find 3% of 80.

(A) 0.24   (B) 2.4   (C) 24   (D) 240   (E) 2,400

2.   Find 50% of 182.

(A) 9   (B) 90   (C) 91   (D) 910   (E) 9,100

3.   Find 83% of 166.

(A) 0.137   (B) 1.377   (C) 13.778   (D) 137   (E) 137.78

4.   Find 125% of 400.

(A) 425   (B) 500   (C) 525   (D) 600   (E) 825

5.   Find 300% of 4.

(A) 12   (B) 120   (C) 1,200   (D) 12,000   (E) 120,000

6.   Forty-eight percent of the 1,200 students at Central High are males. How many male students are there at Central High?

(A) 57   (B) 576   (C) 580   (D) 600   (E) 648

7. For 35% of the last 40 days, there has been measurable rainfall. How many days out of the last 40 days have had measurable rainfall?

    (A) 14   (B) 20   (C) 25   (D) 35   (E) 40

8. Of every 1,000 people who take a certain medicine, 0.2% develop severe side effects. How many people out of every 1,000 who take the medicine develop the side effects?

    (A) 0.2   (B) 2   (C) 20   (D) 22   (E) 200

9. Of 220 applicants for a job, 75% were offered an initial interview. How many people were offered an initial interview?

    (A) 75   (B) 110   (C) 120   (D) 155   (E) 165

10. Find 0.05% of 4,000.

    (A) 0.05   (B) 0.5   (C) 2   (D) 20   (E) 400

Changing Percents to Fractions

DIRECTIONS: Solve to find the correct fractions.

11. What is 25% written as a fraction?

    (A) $\dfrac{1}{25}$ (B) $\dfrac{1}{5}$ (C) $\dfrac{1}{4}$ (D) $\dfrac{1}{3}$ (E) $\dfrac{1}{2}$

12. What is $33\dfrac{1}{3}\%$ written as a fraction?

    (A) $\dfrac{1}{4}$ (B) $\dfrac{1}{3}$ (C) $\dfrac{1}{2}$ (D) $\dfrac{2}{3}$ (E) $\dfrac{5}{9}$

13. What is 200% written as a fraction?

    (A) $\dfrac{1}{2}$ (B) $\dfrac{2}{1}$ (C) $\dfrac{20}{1}$ (D) $\dfrac{200}{1}$ (E) $\dfrac{2,000}{1}$

14. What is 84% written as a fraction?

    (A) $\dfrac{1}{84}$ (B) $\dfrac{4}{8}$ (C) $\dfrac{17}{25}$ (D) $\dfrac{21}{25}$ (E) $\dfrac{44}{50}$

15. What is 2% written as a fraction?

    (A) $\dfrac{1}{50}$ (B) $\dfrac{1}{25}$ (C) $\dfrac{1}{10}$ (D) $\dfrac{1}{4}$ (E) $\dfrac{1}{2}$

Changing Fractions to Percents

> **DIRECTIONS**: Solve to find the following percentages.

16. What is $\dfrac{2}{3}$ written as a percent?

    (A) 23%   (B) 32%   (C) $33\dfrac{1}{3}\%$ (D) $57\dfrac{1}{3}\%$ (E) $66\dfrac{2}{3}\%$

17. What is $\dfrac{3}{5}$ written as a percent?

    (A) 30%   (B) 35%   (C) 53%   (D) 60%   (E) 65%

18. What is $\dfrac{17}{20}$ written as a percent?

    (A) 17%   (B) 70%   (C) 75%   (D) 80%   (E) 85%

19. What is $\dfrac{45}{50}$ written as a percent?

    (A) 45%   (B) 50%   (C) 90%   (D) 95%   (E) 97%

20. What is $1\dfrac{1}{4}$ written as a percent?

    (A) 114%   (B) 120%   (C) 125%   (D) 127%   (E) 133%

Changing Percents to Decimals

> **DIRECTIONS**: Convert the percentages to decimals.

21. What is 42% written as a decimal?

    (A) 0.42   (B) 4.2   (C) 42   (D) 420   (E) 422

22. What is 0.3% written as a decimal?

    (A) 0.0003   (B) 0.003   (C) 0.03   (D) 0.3   (E) 3

23. What is 8% written as a decimal?

    (A) 0.0008   (B) 0.008   (C) 0.08   (D) 0.80   (E) 8

24. What is 175% written as a decimal?

    (A) 0.175   (B) 1.75   (C) 17.5   (D) 175   (E) 17,500

25. What is 34% written as a decimal?

    (A) 0.00034   (B) 0.0034   (C) 0.034   (D) 0.34   (E) 3.4

Changing Decimals to Percents

DIRECTIONS: Convert the following decimals to percents.

26. What is 0.43 written as a percent?

    (A) 0.0043%   (B) 0.043%   (C) 4.3%   (D) 43%   (E) 430%

27. What is 1 written as a percent?

    (A) 1%   (B) 10%   (C) 100%   (D) 111%   (E) 150%

28. What is 0.08 written as a percent?

    (A) 0.08%   (B) 8%   (C) 8.8%   (D) 80%   (E) 800%

29. What is 3.4 written as a percent?

    (A) 0.0034%   (B) 3.4%   (C) 34%   (D) 304%   (E) 340%

30. What is 0.645 written as a percent?

    (A) 64.5%   (B) 65%   (C) 69%   (D) 70%   (E) 645%

Rational and Irrational Numbers

A rational number is any number that can be written in the simple fraction form $\frac{a}{b}$ where a is any integer and b is any integer except zero. An irrational number is a number that cannot be written as a simple fraction. It is an infinite and non-repeating decimal.

The tree diagram below shows you the relationships between the different types of numbers.

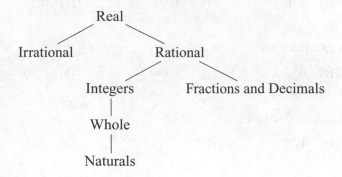

- **EXAMPLE**

Here are some examples of rational numbers.

2	3	5	10	32	−2	−4	−18	−25
$\frac{1}{4}$	$\frac{1}{2}$	$\frac{2}{3}$	$-\frac{1}{4}$	$-\frac{4}{7}$	$-\frac{10}{55}$	$\frac{21}{9}$	$\frac{101}{635}$	

- **EXAMPLE**

Here are some examples of irrational numbers.

π — approximately equal to 3.14159

e — approximately equal to 2.71828

$\sqrt{2}$ — approximately equal to 1.41421

$\sqrt{3}$ — approximately equal to 1.73205

$\sqrt{5}$ — approximately equal to 2.23607

PROBLEM

List the numbers shown below from least to greatest.

$$\frac{1}{3}, \qquad \sqrt{3}, \qquad 3, \qquad 0.3$$

SOLUTION

$\frac{1}{3} \approx 0.33333$

$\sqrt{3} \approx 1.73205$

Therefore, the numbers from least to greatest are: $0.3, \frac{1}{3}, \sqrt{3}, 3$

PROBLEM

List the numbers shown below from greatest to least.

2^2, $\sqrt{9}$, e, π

SOLUTION

$2^2 = 4$; $\sqrt{9} = 3$; $e \approx 2.71828$; $\pi \approx 3.14159$

Therefore, the numbers from greatest to least are: $2^2, \pi, \sqrt{9}, e$

PROBLEM

List the numbers shown below from least to greatest.

-5, $\sqrt{5}$, -8, $\frac{16}{7}$

SOLUTION

$\sqrt{5} \approx 2.23607$

$\frac{16}{7} \approx 2.28571$

Therefore, the numbers from least to greatest are: $-8, -5, \sqrt{5}, \frac{16}{7}$

PROBLEM

Classify each of the following numbers into as many different sets as possible. Example: real, integer …

(1)   0   (2)   9   (3) $\sqrt{6}$

(4)   1/2   (5)   2/3   (6)   1.5

SOLUTION

(1)   Zero is a real number and an integer.

(2)   9 is a real, natural number, and an integer.

(3) $\sqrt{6}$ is a real, irrational number.

(4)   1/2 is a real, rational number, and a fraction.

(5)   2/3 is a real, rational number, and a fraction.

(6)   1.5 is a real, rational and a decimal number.

PROBLEM

Write each integer below as a product of its primes.

2   12   5   22   18   36

SOLUTION

A prime number is a number that has no factors other than itself and 1. For example, the numbers 1, 3, 5, and 7 are prime numbers. Write each integer as a product of its primes.

$$2 = 2 \times 1$$
$$12 = 4 \times 3 = 2 \times 2 \times 3$$
$$5 = 5 \times 1$$
$$22 = 11 \times 2$$
$$18 = 6 \times 3 = 2 \times 3 \times 3$$
$$36 = 6 \times 6 = 3 \times 2 \times 3 \times 2$$
$$\text{or } 18 \times 2 = 9 \times 2 \times 2 = 3 \times 3 \times 2 \times 2$$

PROBLEM

Find the greatest common divisor (GCD) for the following numbers: 12 and 24.

SOLUTION

Step 1 is to write out each number as a product of its primes.

$$12 = 6 \times 2 \qquad 24 = 12 \times 2$$
$$= 3 \times 2 \times 2 \qquad = 6 \times 2 \times 2$$
$$= 3 \times 2 \times 2 \times 2$$

$3 \times 2 \times 2$ is the common factor in both sets of prime factors.

Step 2 is to multiply the common factors together to get the GCD.

$$3 \times 2 \times 2 = 12$$

Therefore, 12 is the GCD.

Radicals

The **square root** of a number is a number that when multiplied by itself results in the original number. Thus, the square root of 81 is 9 since $9 \times 9 = 81$. However, -9 is also a root of 81 since $(-9)(-9) = 81$. Every positive number will have two roots. The principal root is the positive one. Zero has only one square root, and negative numbers do not have real numbers as their roots.

A **radical sign** indicates that the root of a number or expression will be taken. The **radicand** is the number whose root will be taken. The **index** tells how many times the root needs to be multiplied by itself to equal the radicand,

(1) $\sqrt[3]{64}$;

3 is the index and 64 is the radicand. Since $4 \times 4 \times 4 = 64$, then $\sqrt[3]{64} = 4$.

(2) $\sqrt[5]{32}$;

5 is the index and 32 is the radicand. Since $2 \times 2 \times 2 \times 2 \times 2 = 32$, then $\sqrt[5]{32} = 2$.

Operations with Radicals

A) **To multiply two or more radicals**, we utilize the law that states,

$$\sqrt{a} \times \sqrt{b} = \sqrt{ab}.$$

Simply multiply the radicands, put the product under the radical sign, and simplify; for example,

(1) $\sqrt{12} \times \sqrt{5} = \sqrt{60} = \sqrt{4 \times 15} = \sqrt{4} \times \sqrt{15} = 2 \times \sqrt{15}$

(2) $3\sqrt{2} \times 4\sqrt{8} = 3 \times 4 \times \sqrt{2 \times 8} = 12 \times \sqrt{16} = 12 \times 4 = 48$

(3) $2\sqrt{10} \times 6\sqrt{5} = 2 \times 6 \times \sqrt{50} = 12 \times \sqrt{25 \times 2} = 12 \times 5 \times \sqrt{2} = 60\sqrt{2}$

B) **To divide radicals,** factor both the numerator and the denominator. By multiplying the radical in the denominator by itself, you can make the denominator a rational number. The numerator, however, must also be multiplied by this radical so that the value of the original expression does not change.

Then simplify the fraction; for example,

(1) $\dfrac{\sqrt{128}}{\sqrt{2}} = \dfrac{\sqrt{64} \times \sqrt{2}}{\sqrt{2}} = \dfrac{8\sqrt{2}}{\sqrt{2}} = 8$

(2) $\dfrac{\sqrt{10}}{\sqrt{3}} = \dfrac{\sqrt{10} \times \sqrt{3}}{\sqrt{3} \times \sqrt{3}} = \dfrac{\sqrt{30}}{3}$

(3) $\dfrac{\sqrt{8}}{2\sqrt{3}} = \dfrac{\sqrt{8} \times \sqrt{3}}{2\sqrt{3} \times \sqrt{3}} = \dfrac{\sqrt{24}}{2 \times 3} = \dfrac{2\sqrt{6}}{6} = \dfrac{\sqrt{6}}{3}$

C)   **To add two or more radicals**, the radicals must have the same index and the same radicand. These similarities be determined. only in simplified radicals.

- **EXAMPLES**

    (1) $6\sqrt{2} + 2\sqrt{2} = (6+2)\sqrt{2} = 8\sqrt{2}$

    (2) $\sqrt{27} + 5\sqrt{3} = \sqrt{9}\sqrt{3} + 5\sqrt{3} = 3\sqrt{3} + 5\sqrt{3} = 8\sqrt{3}$

    (3) $7\sqrt{3} + 8\sqrt{2} + 5\sqrt{3} = 12\sqrt{3} + 8\sqrt{2}$

    Similarly, for subtraction,

    (1) $12\sqrt{3} - 7\sqrt{3} = (12-7)\sqrt{3} = 5\sqrt{3}$

    (2) $\sqrt{80} - \sqrt{20} = \sqrt{16}\sqrt{5} - \sqrt{4}\sqrt{5} = 4\sqrt{5} - 2\sqrt{5} = 2\sqrt{5}$

    (3) $\sqrt{50} - \sqrt{3} = 5\sqrt{2} - \sqrt{3}$

Drill: Radicals

Multiplication

DIRECTIONS: Multiply and simplify each answer.

1. $\sqrt{6} \times \sqrt{5} =$

    (A) $\sqrt{11}$ (B) $\sqrt{30}$ (C) $2\sqrt{5}$ (D) $3\sqrt{10}$ (E) $2\sqrt{3}$

2. $\sqrt{3} \times \sqrt{12} =$

   (A) 3   (B) $\sqrt{15}$ (C) $\sqrt{36}$ (D) 6   (E) 8

3. $\sqrt{7} \times \sqrt{7} =$

   (A) 7   (B) 49   (C) $\sqrt{14}$ (D) $2\sqrt{7}$ (E) $2\sqrt{14}$

4. $3\sqrt{5} \times 2\sqrt{5} =$

   (A) $5\sqrt{5}$ (B) 25   (C) 30   (D) $5\sqrt{25}$ (E) $6\sqrt{5}$

5. $4\sqrt{6} \times \sqrt{12} =$

   (A) $4\sqrt{8}$ (B) $8\sqrt{2}$ (C) $5\sqrt{8}$ (D) $4\sqrt{12}$ (E) $24\sqrt{2}$

Division

DIRECTIONS: Divide and simplify the answer.

6. $\sqrt{10} \div \sqrt{2} =$

   (A) $\sqrt{8}$ (B) $2\sqrt{2}$ (C) $\sqrt{5}$ (D) $2\sqrt{5}$ (E) $2\sqrt{3}$

7. $\sqrt{30} \div \sqrt{15} =$

   (A) $\sqrt{2}$ (B) $\sqrt{45}$ (C) $3\sqrt{5}$ (D) $\sqrt{15}$ (E) $5\sqrt{3}$

8. $\sqrt{100} \div \sqrt{25} =$

   (A) $\sqrt{4}$ (B) $5\sqrt{5}$ (C) $5\sqrt{3}$ (D) 2   (E) 4

9. $\sqrt{48} \div \sqrt{8} =$

   (A) $4\sqrt{3}$ (B) $3\sqrt{2}$ (C) $\sqrt{6}$ (D) 6   (E) 12

10. $3\sqrt{12} \div \sqrt{3} =$

    (A) $3\sqrt{15}$ (B) 6   (C) 9   (D) 12   (E) $3\sqrt{36}$

Addition

DIRECTIONS: Simplify each radical and add.

---

11. $\sqrt{7} + 3\sqrt{7} =$

    (A) $3\sqrt{7}$ (B) $4\sqrt{7}$ (C) $3\sqrt{14}$ (D) $4\sqrt{14}$ (E) $3\sqrt{21}$

12. $\sqrt{5} + 6\sqrt{5} + 3\sqrt{5} =$

    (A) $9\sqrt{5}$ (B) $9\sqrt{15}$ (C) $5\sqrt{10}$ (D) $10\sqrt{5}$ (E) $18\sqrt{15}$

13. $3\sqrt{32} + 2\sqrt{2} =$

    (A) $5\sqrt{2}$ (B) $\sqrt{34}$ (C) $14\sqrt{2}$ (D) $5\sqrt{34}$ (E) $6\sqrt{64}$

14. $6\sqrt{15} + 8\sqrt{15} + 16\sqrt{15} =$

    (A) $15\sqrt{30}$ (B) $30\sqrt{45}$ (C) $30\sqrt{30}$ (D) $15\sqrt{45}$ (E) $30\sqrt{15}$

15. $6\sqrt{5} + 2\sqrt{45}$

    (A) $12\sqrt{5}$ (B) $8\sqrt{50}$ (C) $40\sqrt{2}$ (D) $12\sqrt{50}$ (E) $8\sqrt{5}$

Subtraction

DIRECTIONS: Simplify each radical and subtract.

---

16. $8\sqrt{5} - 6\sqrt{5} =$

    (A) $2\sqrt{5}$ (B) $3\sqrt{5}$ (C) $4\sqrt{5}$ (D) $14\sqrt{5}$ (E) $48\sqrt{5}$

17. $16\sqrt{33} - 5\sqrt{33} =$

    (A) $3\sqrt{33}$ (B) $33\sqrt{11}$ (C) $11\sqrt{33}$ (D) $11\sqrt{0}$ (E) $\sqrt{33}$

18. $14\sqrt{2} - 19\sqrt{2} =$

    (A) $5\sqrt{2}$ (B) $-5\sqrt{2}$ (C) $-33\sqrt{2}$ (D) $33\sqrt{2}$ (E) $-4\sqrt{2}$

19. $10\sqrt{2} - 3\sqrt{8} =$

    (A) $6\sqrt{6}$ (B) $-2\sqrt{2}$ (C) $7\sqrt{6}$ (D) $4\sqrt{2}$ (E) $-6\sqrt{6}$

20. $4\sqrt{3} - 2\sqrt{12} =$

    (A) $-2\sqrt{9}$ (B) $-6\sqrt{15}$ (C) 0   (D) $6\sqrt{15}$ (E) $2\sqrt{12}$

Exponents

When a number is multiplied by itself a specific number of times, it is said to be **raised to a power**. The way this is written is $a^n = b$ where a is the number or **base**, n is the **exponent** or **power** that indicates the number of times the base is to be multiplied by itself, and b is the product of this multiplication.

In the expression 3^2, 3 is the base and 2 is the exponent. This means that 3 is multiplied by itself 2 times and the product is 9.

An exponent can be either positive or negative. A negative exponent implies a fraction such that if n is a negative integer

$$a^{-n} = \frac{1}{a^n}, \ a \neq 0. \text{ So, } 2^{-4} = \frac{1}{2^4} = \frac{1}{16}.$$

An exponent that is 0 gives a result of 1, assuming that the base is not equal to 0.

$$a^0 = 1, a \neq 0.$$

An exponent can also be a fraction in which the numerator remains the exponent of a, but the denominator tells what root to take. Thus, if m and n are positive integers,

$$a^{\frac{m}{n}} = \sqrt[n]{a^m}$$

For example,

(1) $4^{\frac{3}{2}} = \sqrt[2]{4^3} = \sqrt{64} = 8$ (2) $3^{\frac{4}{2}} = \sqrt[2]{3^4} = \sqrt{81} = 9$

For a negative fractional exponent, the same operation would take place, but the result would be a fraction. For example,

(1) $27^{-\frac{2}{3}} = \frac{1}{27^{2/3}} = \frac{1}{\sqrt[3]{27^2}} = \frac{1}{\sqrt[3]{729}} = \frac{1}{9}$

PROBLEM

Simplify the following expressions:

(1) -3^{-2} (2) $(-3)^{-2}$ (3) $\dfrac{-3}{4^{-1}}$

SOLUTION

(1) Here the exponent applies only to 3. Thus,

$$-3^{-2} = -(3)^{-2} = -\left(\frac{1}{3^2}\right) = -\frac{1}{9}$$

(2) In this case the exponent applies to the negative base as well due to the parentheses. Thus,

$$(-3)^{-2} = \frac{1}{(-3)^2} = \frac{1}{(-3)(-3)} = \frac{1}{9}$$

(3) $$\frac{-3}{4^{-1}} = \frac{-3}{\left(\frac{1}{4}\right)^1} = \frac{-3}{\frac{1}{4^1}} = \frac{-3}{\frac{1}{4}} = -3 \times \frac{4}{1} = -12$$

remembering that division by a fraction is equivalent to multiplication by that fraction's reciprocal.

General Laws of Exponents

A) $a^p a^q = a^{p+q}$

$4^2 4^3 = 4^{2+3} = 1{,}024$

B) $(a^p)^q = a^{pq}$

$(2^3)^2 = 2^6 = 64$

C) $\dfrac{a^p}{a^q} = a^{p-q}$

$\left(\dfrac{a}{b}\right)^p = \dfrac{a^p}{b^p},\ b \neq 0$

D) $(ab)^p = a^p b^p$

$(3 \times 2)^2 = 3^2 \times 2^2 = (9)(4) = 36$

E) $\left(\dfrac{a}{b}\right)^p = \dfrac{a^p}{b^p},\ b \neq 0$

$\left(\dfrac{4}{5}\right)^2 = \dfrac{4^2}{5^2} = \dfrac{16}{25}$

Drill: Exponents

Multiplication

DIRECTIONS: Simplify.

1. $4^6 \times 4^2 =$

    (A) 4^4 (B) 4^8 (C) 4^{12} (D) 16^8 (E) 16^{12}

2. $2^2 \times 2^5 \times 2^3 =$

    (A) 2^{10} (B) 4^{10} (C) 8^{10} (D) 2^{30} (E) 8^{30}

3. $6^6 \times 6^2 \times 6^4 =$

    (A) 18^8 (B) 18^{12} (C) 6^{12} (D) 6^{48} (E) 18^{48}

4. $a^4b^2 \times a^3b =$

    (A) ab (B) $2a^7b^2$ (C) $2a^{12}b$ (D) a^7b^3 (E) a^7b^2

5. $m^8n^3 \times m^2n \times m^4n^2 =$

    (A) $3m^{16}n^6$ (B) $m^{14}n^6$ (C) $3m^{14}n^5$ (D) $3m^{14}n^5$ (E) m^2

Division

DIRECTIONS: Simplify.

6. $6^5 \div 6^3 =$

    (A) 0 (B) 1 (C) 6 (D) 12 (E) 36

7. $11^8 \div 11^5 =$

    (A) 1^3 (B) 11^3 (C) 11^{13} (D) 11^{40} (E) 88^5

8. $x^{10}y^8 \div x^7y^3 =$

    (A) x^2y^5 (B) x^3y^4 (C) x^3y^5 (D) x^2y^4 (E) x^5y^3

9. $a^{14} \div a^9 =$

   (A) 1^5 (B) a^5 (C) $2a^5$ (D) a^{23} (E) $2a^{23}$

10. $c^{17}d^{12}e^4 \div c^{12}d^8e =$

   (A) $c^4d^5e^3$ (B) $c^4d^4e^3$ (C) $c^5d^8e^4$ (D) $c^5d^4e^3$ (E) $c^5d^4e^4$

Power to a Power

DIRECTIONS: Simplify.

---

11. $(3^6)^2 =$

   (A) 3^4 (B) 3^8 (C) 3^{12} (D) 9^6 (E) 9^8

12. $(4^3)^5 =$

   (A) 4^2 (B) 2^{15} (C) 4^8 (D) 20^3 (E) 4^{15}

13. $(a^4b^3)^2 =$

   (A) $(ab)^9$ (B) a^8b^6 (C) $(ab)^{24}$ (D) a^6b^5 (E) $2a^4b^3$

14. $(r^3p^6)^3 =$

   (A) r^9p^{18} (B) $(rp)^{12}$ (C) r^6p^9 (D) $3r^3p^6$ (E) $3r^9p^{18}$

15. $(m^6n^5q^3)^2 =$

   (A) $2m^6n^5q^3$ (B) m^4n^3q (C) $m^8n^7q^5$ (D) $m^{12}n^{10}q^6$ (E) $2m^{12}n^{10}q^6$

Scientific Notation

Technicians, engineers, and others engaged in scientific work are often required to solve problems involving very large and very small numbers. Problems such as

$$\frac{22{,}684 \times 0.00189}{0.0713 \times 83 \times 7}$$

are not uncommon. Solving such problems by the rules of ordinary arithmetic is laborious and time consuming. Moreover, the tedious arithmetic process lends itself to operational errors. Also, it isn't easy to locate the decimal point in the result. These difficulties can be greatly reduced by a knowledge of the powers of 10 and their use.

The laws of exponents form the basis for calculation using powers of 10. The following list includes several decimals and whole numbers expressed as powers of 10:

$$10,000 = 10^4 \qquad\qquad 0.1 \quad\; = 10^{-1}$$
$$1,000 = 10^3 \qquad\qquad 0.01 \quad = 10^{-2}$$
$$100 = 10^2 \qquad\qquad 0.001 \; = 10^{-3}$$
$$10 = 10^1 \qquad\qquad 0.0001 = 10^{-4}$$
$$1 = 10^0$$

The concept of scientific notation may be demonstrated as follows:

$$60,000 = 6.0000 \times 10,000$$
$$= 6 \times 10^4$$
$$538 = 5.38 \times 100$$
$$= 5.38 \times 10^2$$

Notice that the final expression in each of the foregoing examples involves a number between 1 and 10, multiplied by a power of 10. Furthermore, in each case the exponent of the power of 10 is a number equal to the number of digits between the new position of the decimal point and the original position (understood) of the decimal point.

We apply this reasoning to write any number in scientific notation; that is, as a number between 1 and 10 multiplied by the appropriate power of 10. The appropriate power of 10 is found by the following mechanical steps:

1. Shift the decimal point to standard position, which is the position immediately to the right of the first nonzero digit.

2. Count the number of digits between the new position of the decimal point and its original position. This number indicates the value of the exponent for the power of 10.

3. If the decimal point is shifted to the left, the sign of the exponent of 10 is positive; if the decimal point is shifted to the right, the sign of the exponent is negative.

The validity of this rule, for those cases in which the exponent of 10 is negative, is demonstrated as follows:

$$0.00657 = 6.57 \times 0.001$$
$$= 6.57 \times 10^{-3}$$
$$0.348 = 3.48 \times 0.1$$
$$= 3.48 \times 10^{-1}$$

Further examples of the use of scientific notation are given as follows:

$$543,000,000 = 5.43 \times 10^8$$
$$186 = 1.86 \times 10^2$$
$$243.01 = 2.4301 \times 10^2$$
$$0.0000007 = 7 \times 10^{-7}$$
$$0.00023 = 2.3 \times 10^{-4}$$

Applying Number Theory Concepts

To factor a polynomial completely is to find the prime factors of the polynomial.

The following concepts are important while factoring or simplifying expressions.

A)   The factors of a given algebraic expression consist of two or more algebraic expressions which, when multiplied together, produce the given algebraic expression. A **prime factor** is a polynomial with no factors other than itself and 1.

B)   The **least common multiple (LCM)** for a polynomial is the smallest quantity divisible by every term of the polynomia. For algebraic expressions the least common numerical coefficients for each of the given expressions will be a factor of the LCM.

C)   The **greatest common factor (GCF)** for a polynomial is the largest factor that is common to all terms of the polynomial.

ARITHMETIC DRILLS

ANSWER KEY

Drill: Integers and Real Numbers

1. (A)	6. (B)	11. (B)	16. (B)	21. (B)	26. (D)
2. (C)	7. (A)	12. (E)	17. (D)	22. (E)	27. (B)
3. (D)	8. (C)	13. (C)	18. (D)	23. (D)	28. (C)
4. (C)	9. (E)	14. (A)	19. (C)	24. (A)	29. (A)
5. (B)	10. (B)	15. (B)	20. (E)	25. (D)	30. (C)

Drill: Fractions

1. (D)	10. (E)	19. (B)	28. (B)	37. (D)	46. (B)
2. (A)	11. (D)	20. (A)	29. (A)	38. (E)	47. (C)
3. (D)	12. (E)	21. (B)	30. (C)	39. (C)	48. (D)
4. (E)	13. (C)	22. (D)	31. (D)	40. (B)	49. (E)
5. (C)	14. (A)	23. (E)	32. (C)	41. (C)	50. (A)
6. (D)	15. (C)	24. (D)	33. (B)	42. (A)	
7. (D)	16. (B)	25. (B)	34. (E)	43. (B)	
8. (B)	17. (C)	26. (B)	35. (A)	44. (C)	
9. (A)	18. (A)	27. (D)	36. (A)	45. (D)	

Drill: Decimals Pg 68

1. (B)	6. (A)	11. (B)	16. (B)	21. (E)	26. (D)
2. (E)	7. (B)	12. (D)	17. (D)	22. (C)	27. (C)
3. (C)	8. (D)	13. (A)	18. (D)	23. (B)	28. (A)
4. (A)	9. (C)	14. (B)	19. (A)	24. (D)	29. (E)
5. (D)	10. (E)	15. (C)	20. (C)	25. (E)	30. (D)

Drill: Percent Pg 74

1. (B)	6. (B)	11. (C)	16. (E)	21. (A)	26. (D)
2. (C)	7. (A)	12. (B)	17. (D)	22. (B)	27. (C)
3. (E)	8. (B)	13. (B)	18. (E)	23. (C)	28. (B)
4. (B)	9. (E)	14. (D)	19. (C)	24. (B)	29. (E)
5. (A)	10. (C)	15. (A)	20. (C)	25. (D)	30. (A)

Drill: Radicals Pg 82

1. (B)	5. (E)	9. (C)	13. (C)	17. (C)
2. (D)	6. (C)	10. (B)	14. (E)	18. (B)
3. (A)	7. (A)	11. (B)	15. (A)	19. (D)
4. (C)	8. (D)	12. (D)	16. (A)	20. (C)

Drill: Exponents

1. (B)	4. (D)	7. (B)	10. (D)	13. (B)
2. (A)	5. (B)	8. (C)	11. (C)	14. (A)
3. (C)	6. (E)	9. (B)	12. (E)	15. (D)

Competency 2: Knowledge of Measurement

Measurement

Measurements are numbers that describe the amount or quantity of some attribute. These attributes can be time, distance, speed, weight, area, volume, or temperature. Further, these attributes can be measured in different units. Distance can be expressed in various units of measurement including inches, feet, yards, and miles. Distance is a one-dimensional measurement. Weight is a common measurement that can be expressed in grams, ounces, pounds, and tons. Area is an important measurement that can be expressed in terms of square inches, square feet, and square yards. In addition, area can be measured in square miles and acres. Area is a two-dimensional measurement. Volume is a three-dimensional measurement. For solids, volume can be measured in terms of cubic inches, cubic feet, or cubic yards. For liquids, volume can be measured in ounces, cups, pints, quarts, and gallons. Temperature can be measured in degrees Fahrenheit or degrees Centigrade.

Here are some key measurement terms and ideas:

Customary units are generally the same as *U.S. units* and are also called English units. Customary units of length include inches, feet, yards, and miles. Customary units of weight include ounces, pounds, and tons. Customary units of capacity (or volume) include teaspoons, tablespoons, cups, pints, quarts, and gallons.

1 yard = 3 feet = 36 inches	1 cup = 8 fluid ounces
1 mile = 1,760 yards = 5,280 feet	1 pint = 2 cups
1 acre = 43,560 square feet	1 quart = 2 pints
1 hour = 60 minutes	1 gallon = 4 quarts
1 minute = 60 seconds	1 pound = 16 ounces
	1 ton = 2,000 pounds

Metric units of length include millimeters, centimeters, meters, and kilometers. The centimeter is the basic metric unit of length, at least for short distances. There are about 2.5 centimeters to 1 inch. The kilometer is a metric unit of length used for longer distances. It takes more than 1.5 kilometers to make a mile. A very fast adult runner could run a kilometer in about three minutes.

Metric units of weight include grams and kilograms. The gram is the basic metric unit of mass (which for many purposes is the same as *weight*). A large paper clip weighs about 1 gram. It takes about 28 grams to make 1 ounce. Metric units of capacity include milliliters and liters. The liter is the basic metric unit of volume (or capacity). A liter is slightly smaller than a quart, so it takes more than four liters to make a gallon.

1 liter = 1000 milliliters = 1000 cubic centimeters

1 meter = 100 centimeters = 1000 millimeters

1 kilometer = 1000 meters

1 gram = 1000 milligrams

1 kilogram = 1000 grams

Prefixes in the metric system indicate the number of multiples of the base units, so it is simple to determine the conversion factors between units.

Prefix	Multiplication Factor	Unit Symbols
kilo	× 1000	km, kg, kl
no prefix (base unit)	× 1	m, g, l
deci	× 0.1	dm, dg, dl
centi	× 0.01	cm, cg, cl
milli	× 0.001	mm, mg, ml

Here are some frequently used customary-to-metric ratios. Values are approximate.

1 inch = 2.54 centimeters

1 yard = 0.91 meters

1 mile = 1.61 kilometers

1 ounce = 28.35 grams

1 pound = 2.2 kilograms

1 quart = 0.94 liters

Metric-to-customary conversions can be found by taking the reciprocals of each of the factors noted above. For instance, 1 kilometer = 0.62 mile (computed by dividing 1 by 1.61).

An important step in solving problems involving measurement is figuring out its category. Generally, such problems will fall under one of these categories: length, area, angles, volume, mass, time, money, and temperature. Solving measurement problems will likely have you calling on your knowledge in several other areas of mathematics, especially algebra. The following is an example measurement problem that requires knowledge of several math topics:

Sophie's Carpet Store charges $19.40 per square yard for the type of carpeting you'd like (padding and labor included). How much will you pay to carpet your 9 foot by 12 foot room?

One way to find the solution is to convert the room dimensions to yards (3 yards by 4 yards), then multiply to get 12 square yards. Finally, multiply 12 by the price of $19.40 per square yard, for a total price of $232.80.

• **EXAMPLE**

If there are 5,280 feet in one mile, how many yards are there in 4 miles?

First, divide the number of feet in a mile by 3 in order to find the number of yards in a mile: $5,280 \div 3 = 1,760$ yards. Second, multiply 1,760 by 4 in order to find the number of yards in 4 miles: $1,760 \times 4 = 7,040$ yards.

• **EXAMPLE**

How many pounds are there in 25 tons?

There are 2,000 pounds in one ton, so we multiply 2,000 by 25 to find the number of pounds in 25 tons: $2,000 \times 25 = 50,000$ pounds.

• **EXAMPLE**

Candle-Wick is a company that manufactures candles. Their standard candle weighs 5 ounces. In order to calculate shipping charges for a case of candles, a worker needs to know the weight of 24 candles.

$$
\begin{array}{ll}
\quad 24 \quad \text{candles} \\
\underline{\times\ 5} \quad \text{ounces per candle} \\
\quad 120 \quad \text{ounces}
\end{array}
$$

120 ounces ÷ 16 ounces per pound = 7.5 pounds, which equals 7 pounds and 8 ounces

• **EXAMPLE**

Calculate the number of square yards in an area that measures 162 square feet.

162 square feet ÷ 9 square feet per square yard = 18 square yards

• **EXAMPLE**

How many ounces are there in 2¾ cups?

Express 2¾ in decimal form: 2.75. Because there are 8 ounces in a cup, multiply 2.75 cups by 8: $2.75 \times 8 = 22$ ounces.

• **EXAMPLE**

How many gallons are there in 246 quarts?

There are 4 quarts in one gallon, so divide 246 quarts by 4: $246 \div 4 = 61.5$ gallons.

Change in Units

When measurement problems are presented that involve conversion to either metric or English units, the appropriate data will be given in the problem.

PROBLEM

The Eiffel Tower is 984 feet high. Express this height in meters, in kilometers, in centimeters, and in millimeters.

SOLUTION

A meter is equivalent to 39.370 inches. In this problem, the height of the tower in feet must be converted to inches and then the inches can be converted to meters. There are 12 inches in 1 foot. Therefore, feet can be converted to inches by using the factor 12 inches/1 foot.

984 feet × 12 inches/1 foot = 11,808 inches

Once the height is found in inches, this can be converted to meters by the factor 1 meter/39.370 inches.

11808 inches × 1 meter/39.370 inches = 300 m.

Therefore, the height in meters is 300 m.

There are 1,000 meters in one kilometer. Meters can be converted to kilometers by using the factor 1 km/1000 m.

300 m × 1 km/1000 m = .300 km.

As such, there are .300 kilometers in 300 m.

There are 100 centimeters in 1 meter, thus meters can be converted to centimeters by multiplying by the factor 100 cm/1 m.

300 m × 100 cm/1 m = 30,000 cm.

There are 30,000 centimeters in 300 m.

There are 1,000 millimeters in 1 meter; therefore, meters can be converted to millimeters by the factor 1000 mm/1 m.

300 m × 1,000 mm/1 m = 300,000 mm.

There are 300,000 millimeters in 300 meters.

PROBLEM

The unaided eye can perceive objects that have a diameter of 0.1 mm. What is the diameter in inches?

SOLUTION

From a standard table of conversion factors, one can find that 1 inch = 2.54 cm. Thus, cm can be converted to inches by multiplying by 1 inch/2.54 cm. Here, the diameter is given as 0.1 mm. Millimeters are converted to cm by multiplying the number of mm by .1 cm/1 mm. Solving for cm, you obtain:

$$0.1 \text{ mm} \times .1 \text{ cm/1 mm} = .01 \text{ cm}.$$

Solving for inches:

$$0.01 \text{ cm} \times 1 \text{ inch/2.54 cm} = 0.00394 \text{ inches} = 3.94 \times 10^{-3} \text{ inches}.$$

- **EXAMPLE**

One inch is approximately equal to 2.54 centimeters. Calculate the approximate number of centimeters in 5 inches.

$$2.54 \text{ centimeters} \times 5 = 12.7 \text{ centimeters}$$

- **EXAMPLE**

One cubic inch is approximately equal to 16.38 cubic centimeters. Calculate the approximate number of cubic centimeters in 5 cubic inches.

$$16.38 \text{ cubic centimeters} \times 5 = 81.9 \text{ cubic centimeters}$$

PROBLEM

How many ounces are there in 4¾ pounds?

SOLUTION

Convert 4¾ into its decimal form: 4.75. Because there are 16 ounces in a pound, we can find the number of ounces in 4.75 pounds by multiplying: 4.75 × 16 = 76 ounces.

PROBLEM

A parent is planning a birthday party for a child. The parent has 3¼ gallons of fruit punch. How many cups is this?

SOLUTION

There are 4 quarts in a gallon and 4 cups in a quart. Therefore, there are 16 cups in a gallon. $3.25 \times 16 = 52$ cups.

Temperature

There are two commonly used temperature scales. The Fahrenheit temperature scale is widely used in the United States, but the Celsius temperature scale (also called the Centigrade scale) is equally useful in other countries and frequently in scientific work.

Water boils at 212 degrees Fahrenheit and 100 degrees Celsius, and freezes at 32 degrees Fahrenheit and 0 degrees Celsius.

At −40 degrees, the Fahrenheit and Celsius temperature scales meet.

Celsius temperature (C) can be converted into Fahrenheit temperature (F) by using the following formula:

$$F = \frac{9}{5}C + 32$$

Conversely, Fahrenheit temperature can be converted to Celsius temperature by using the formula:

$$C = \frac{5}{9}(F - 32)$$

A third measurement system, the International System of Units, or Système International D'Unités (SI), is based on the metric system. SI differs from the metric system by using the Kelvin temperature scale. The size of a degree in the Celsius and Kelvin scales are the same, but "0°" is different. 0 Kelvin = −273°Celsius. 0 Kelvin, also known as absolute zero, is the temperature at which, theoretically, all molecular movement ceases.

• **EXAMPLE**

A traveler from the United States is visiting a country that uses the Celsius temperature scale. The temperature on the thermometer reads 25 degrees Celsius. Calculate the temperature in degrees Fahrenheit.

$$F = \frac{9}{5}(25) + 32$$

$$F = \frac{225}{5} + 32$$

$$= 45 + 32 = 77 \text{ degrees Fahrenheit}$$

- **EXAMPLE**

    A traveler visiting the United States comes from a foreign country that uses the Celsius temperature scale. The temperature on the thermometer reads 86 degrees Fahrenheit. Calculate the temperature in degrees Celsius.

$$C = \frac{5}{9}(86 - 32)$$

$$C = \frac{5}{9}(54)$$

$$= \frac{270}{9} = 30 \text{ degrees Celsius}$$

PROBLEM

A thermometer reads 20 degrees Celsius. How many degrees Fahrenheit is this?

SOLUTION

Use the following formula to solve this problem:

$$F = \frac{9}{5}C + 32$$

$$F = \frac{9}{5}(20) + 32$$

$$F = \frac{180}{5} + 32$$

$$= 36 + 32 = 68 \text{ degrees Fahrenheit}$$

PROBLEM

The temperature on a Fahrenheit thermometer reads 59 degrees. How many degrees Celsius is this?

SOLUTION

Use the following formula to solve this problem:

$$C = \frac{5}{9}(F - 32)$$

$$C = \frac{5}{9}(59 - 32)$$

$$C = \frac{5}{9}(27)$$

$$= \frac{135}{9} = 15 \text{ degrees Celsius}$$

Drill: Measurement

1. A brick walkway measuring 3 feet by 11 feet is to be built. The bricks measure 4 inches by 6 inches. How many bricks will it take to complete the walkway?

    (A) 132   (B) 198   (C) 330   (D) 1927   (E) 4752

2. A wall to be papered is three times as long as it is wide. The total area to be covered is 192 ft². Wallpaper comes in rolls that are 2 feet wide by 8 feet long. How many rolls will it take to cover the wall?

    (A) 8   (B) 12   (C) 16   (D) 24   (E) 32

3. A bottle of medicine containing 2 kg is to be poured into smaller containers that hold 8 grams each. How many of these smaller containers can be filled from the 2 kg bottle?

    (A) 0.5   (B) 1   (C) 5   (D) 50   (E) 250

Estimation

*   **EXAMPLE**

    Jim is hosting a pizza party for 11 of his close friends. He wants to serve each guest a mini-pizza. Mini-pizzas cost $6.79 each. Estimate the total cost.

    Round 11 to 10. Round $6.79 to $7.00. Now, multiply $7 times 10. The estimated cost is $70.00.

    Note: The exact cost is $74.69.

- **EXAMPLE**

The chart below shows the number of fishing lures a factory produced annually over a 6-year period.

Year	Fishing Lures
2000	6,257
2001	10,374
2002	5,890
2003	12,125
2004	9,642
2005	13,092

Estimate the total number of fishing lures produced from 2000 through 2005.

First, round each number to the thousands. Then, add the rounded numbers in order to find the estimate.

$$6,000 + 10,000 + 6,000 + 12,000 + 10,000 + 13,000 = 57,000 \text{ lures}$$

Note: The actual number of lures is 57,380.

PROBLEM

A rectangular duck pond (43 feet by 47 feet) is on a lot that measures 108 feet by 96 feet. The rest of the lot is a flower garden. Estimate the size of the flower garden in square feet.

SOLUTION

First, estimate the area of the duck pond. Round 47 to 50, and round 43 to 40. Now, multiply: $50 \times 40 = 2,000$. The area of the duck pond is about 2,000 square feet. Now, calculate the area of the lot. Round 96 to 100, and 108 to 100. Multiply: $100 \times 100 = 10,000$. In order to find the approximate area of the flower garden, subtract the area of the duck pond from the area of the lot. $10,000 - 2,000 = 8,000$. The flower garden is about 8,000 square feet.

Note: The actual area of the flower garden is 8,347 square feet.

PROBLEM

Mr. Taylor drove his car to the gas station to fill it up. By the time he got there, the gas tank was empty. The total cost to fill up his gas tank was $31.45. Gasoline costs $1.46 per gallon. Estimate how many gallons Mr. Taylor's gas tank holds.

SOLUTION

Round $31.45 to $30.00 and $1.46 to $1.50. Divide: $30 \div 1.5 = 20$ gallons.

Note: The actual number of gallons that the tank holds is 21.54.

PROBLEM

A rancher owns 26,450 acres of land. According to the results from a recent geological survey and soil analysis, 38% of the land is farmable. Estimate the number of farmable acres.

SOLUTION

Round 26,450 to 25,000. Round 38% to 40%, which is 0.4 in decimal form. Then, multiply $25,000 \times 0.4 = 10,000$ acres.

Note: The actual number is 10,051 acres.

KNOWLEDGE OF MEASUREMENT DRILL

ANSWER KEY

Drill: Measurement

1. (B)
2. (B)
3. (E)

Competency 3: Knowledge of Geometry and Spatial Sense

Points, Lines, and Angles

Geometry is built upon a series of undefined terms. These terms are those we accept as known in order to define other undefined terms.

A) **Point:** Although we represent points on paper with small dots, a point has no size, thickness, or width.

B) **Line:** A line is a series of adjacent points that extends indefinitely. A line can be either curved or straight; however, unless otherwise stated, the term "line" refers to a straight line.

C) **Plane:** A plane is a collection of points lying on a flat surface, that extends indefinitely in all directions.

If A and B are two points on a line, then the **line segment** AB is the set of points on that line between A and B and including A and B, which are called **endpoints**. The line segment is referred to as $\overline{AB}$.

A **ray** is a series of points that lie to one side of a single endpoint.

PROBLEM

How many lines can be found that contain (a) one given point (b) two given points (c) three given points?

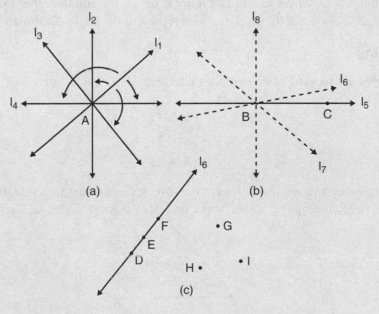

(a)

(b)

(c)

SOLUTION

(a)   *Given one point A,* there are an infinite number of distinct lines that contain the given point. To see this, consider line l_1 passing through point A. By rotating l_1 around A like the hands of a clock, we obtain different lines l_2, l_3, etc. Since we can rotate l_1 in infinitely many ways, there are infinitely many lines containing A. Note that three or more lines (or rays or segments) are called concurrent if there exists one point common to all of them, that is, if they all intersect at the same point.

(b)   *Given two distinct points B and C,* there is one and only one distinct line. To see this, consider all the lines containing point B; l_5, l_6, l_7, and l_8. Only l_5 contains both points B and C. Thus, there is only one line containing both points B and C. Since there is always at least one line containing two distinct points and never more than one, the line passing through the two points is said to be *determined* by the two points.

(c)   *Given three distinct points,* there may be one line or none. If a line exists that contains the three points, such as D, E, and F, then the points are said to be **colinear**. If no such line exists — as in the case of points G, H, and I, then the points are said to be **noncolinear**.

Intersecting Lines and Angles

An **angle** is a collection of points that is the union of two rays having the same endpoint. An angle such as the one illustrated below can be referred to in any of the following ways:

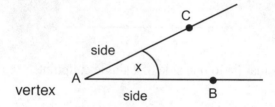

A)   by a capital letter which names its **vertex** (common endpoint), i.e., $\angle A$;

B)   by a lowercase letter or number placed inside the angle, i.e., $\angle x$;

C)   by three capital letters, where the middle letter is the vertex and the other two letters are not on the same ray, i.e., $\angle CAB$ or $\angle BAC$, both of which represent the angle illustrated in the figure.

Types of Angles

A)   **Vertical angles** are formed when two lines intersect. These angles are equal.

B)   **Adjacent angles** are two angles with a common vertex and a common side, but no common interior points. In the following figure, $\angle DAC$ and $\angle BAC$ are adjacent angles. $\angle DAB$ and $\angle BAC$ are not.

C)   A **right angle** is an angle whose measure is 90°.

D)   An **acute angle** is an angle whose measure is larger than 0° but less than 90°.

E)   An **obtuse angle** is an angle whose measure is larger than 90° but less than 180°.

F)   A **straight angle** is an angle whose measure is 180°. Such an angle is, in fact, a straight line.

G)   A **reflex angle** is an angle whose measure is greater than 180° but less than 360°.

H)   **Complementary angles** are two angles, the sum of the measures of which equals 90°.

I)   **Supplementary angles** are two angles, the sum of the measures of which equals 180°.

J)   **Congruent angles** are angles of equal measure.

PROBLEM

In the figure, we are given $x = \dfrac{-b}{a}$ and triangle ABC. We are told that the measure of $\angle 1$ is five times the measure of $\angle 2$. Determine the measures of $\angle 1$ and $\angle 2$.

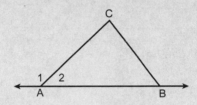

SOLUTION

Since $\angle 1$ and $\angle 2$ are adjacent angles whose non-common sides lie on a straight line, they are supplementary. As supplements, their measures must sum to 180°.

If we let x = the measure of $\angle 2$, then, $5x$ = the measure of $\angle 1$.

To determine the respective angle measures, set $x + 5x = 180$ and solve for x. $6x = 180$. Therefore, $x = 30$ and $5x = 150$.

Therefore, the measure of $\angle 1 = 150$ degrees and the measure of $\angle 2 = 30$ degrees.

PROBLEM

Measure the angle below. Determine if the angle is obtuse or acute.

SOLUTION

Step 1 is to measure the angle by placing the center of the protractor on the vertex of the angle. Side *BC* of the angle should now be aligned with the straight edge of the protractor.

Step 2 is to follow side *AB* from the vertex toward the numbers on the curved edge of the protractor. Read the value where side *AB* crosses the numbers. This is the measure of ∠*ABC*.

The correct answer is 135 degrees. Since ∠*ABC* is larger than 90 degrees, the angle is obtuse.

PROBLEM

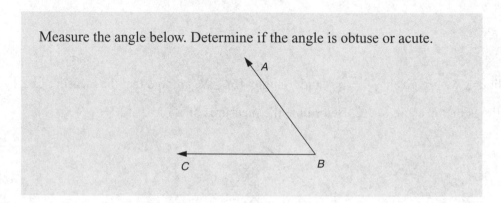

Measure the angle below. Determine if the angle is obtuse or acute.

SOLUTION

Step 1 is to measure the angle by placing the center of the protractor on the vertex of the angle. Side *BC* of the angle should now be aligned with the straight edge of the protractor.

Step 2 is to follow side *AB* from the vertex toward the numbers on the curved edge of the protractor. Read the value where side *AB* crosses the numbers. This is the measure of ∠*ABC*.

The correct answer is 58 degrees. Since ∠*ABC* is smaller than 90 degrees, the angle is acute.

PROBLEM

Measure the angles below. Determine if the angles are complementary.

SOLUTION

Step 1 is to measure ∠ABC by placing the center of the protractor on the vertex of the angle. Side BC of the angle should now be aligned with the straight edge of the protractor.

Step 2 is to follow side AB from the vertex toward the numbers on the curved edge of the protractor. Read the value where side AB crosses the numbers. The measure of ∠ABC is 50 degrees.

Step 3 is to measure ∠CBD by placing the center of the protractor on the vertex of the angle. Side BD of the angle should now be aligned with the straight edge of the protractor.

Step 4 is to follow side CB from the vertex toward the numbers on the curved edge of the protractor. Read the value where side AB crosses the numbers. The measure of ∠CBD is 30 degrees.

Complementary angles are angles that sum to 90 degrees. Since ∠ABC and ∠CBD do not have a sum of 90, the angles are not complementary.

PROBLEM

The angles in the figure below are supplementary. If ∠MNO is 117 degrees, what is the measurement of ∠ONP?

SOLUTION

It is known that the sum of supplementary angles equals 180 degrees. If ∠MNO equals 117 degrees, then ∠ONP equals 180 minus 117.

The correct answer is ∠ONP is 63 degrees.

PROBLEM

Measure the angles below. Determine if the angles are congruent.

SOLUTION

Step 1 is to measure ∠*ABC* by placing the center of the protractor on the vertex of the angle. Side *BC* of the angle should now be aligned with the straight edge of the protractor.

Step 2 is to follow side *AB* from the vertex toward the numbers on the curved edge of the protractor. Read the value where side *AB* crosses the numbers. The measure of ∠*ABC* is 70 degrees.

Step 3 is to measure ∠*PQR* by placing the center of the protractor on the vertex of the angle. Side *QR* of the angle should now be aligned with the straight edge of the protractor.

Step 4 is to follow side *PQ* from the vertex toward the numbers on the curved edge of the protractor. Read the value where side *PQ* crosses the numbers. The measure of ∠*PQR* is 70 degrees.

Congruent angles are angles that are equal in measurement. Since ∠*ABC* and ∠*PQR* are equal, the angles are congruent.

PROBLEM

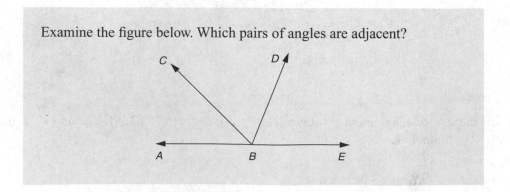

Examine the figure below. Which pairs of angles are adjacent?

SOLUTION

Adjacent angles are angles that share a common side. The adjacent angles are ∠*ABC* and ∠*CBD*, ∠*ABD* and ∠*DBE*, ∠*CBD* and ∠*DBE*, ∠*ABC* and ∠*CBE*.

Perpendicular Lines

Two lines are said to be **perpendicular** if they intersect and form right angles. The symbol for perpendicular (or, is therefore perpendicular to) is y; $= 7 \cdot$ is perpendicular to $y =$ is written $y = -5 \frac{1}{2}$.

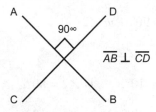

$\overline{AB} \perp \overline{CD}$

PROBLEM

Given straight lines $\overline{AB}$ and $\overline{CD}$ intersecting at point P, $\overline{PR} \perp \overline{AB}$ and the measure of ∠*APD* is 170°, find the measures of ∠1, ∠2, ∠3, and ∠4. (See figure below.)

SOLUTION

This problem will involve making use of several of the properties of supplementary and vertical angles, as well as perpendicular lines.

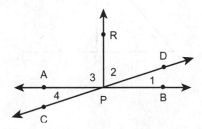

∠*APD* and ∠1 are adjacent angles whose non-common sides lie on a straight line, $\overline{AB}$. Therefore, they are supplements and their measures sum to 180°.

$$m \angle APD + m \angle 1 = 180°.$$

We know $m \angle APD = 170°$. Therefore, by substitution, $170° + m \angle 1 = 180°$. This implies $m \angle 1 = 10°$.

$\angle 1$ and $\angle 4$ are vertical angles because they are formed by the intersection of two straight lines, $\overline{CD}$ and $\overline{AB}$, and their sides form two pairs of opposite rays. As vertical angles, they are, by theorem, of equal measure. Since $m\ \angle 1 = 10°$, then $m\ \angle 4 = 10°$.

Since $\overline{PR} \perp \overline{AB}$, at their intersection the angles formed must be right angles. Therefore, $\angle 3$ is a right angle and its measure is 90°. $m\ \angle 3 = 90°$.

The figure shows us that $\angle APD$ is composed of $\angle 3$ and $\angle 2$. Since the measure of the whole must be equal to the sum of the measures of its parts, $m\ \angle APD = m\ \angle 3 + m\ \angle 2$. We know the $m\ \angle APD = 170°$ and $m\ \angle 3 = 90°$; therefore, by substitution, we can solve for $m\ \angle 2$, our last unknown.

$$170° = 90° + m\ \angle 2$$

$$80° = m\ \angle 2$$

Therefore, $m\ \angle 1 = 10°, \quad m\ \angle 2 = 80°,$

                 $m\ \angle 3 = 90°, \quad m\ \angle 4 = 10°.$

PROBLEM

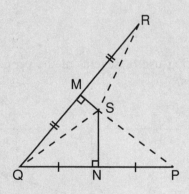

In the accompanying figure, $\overline{SM}$ is the perpendicular bisector of $\overline{QR}$, and $\overline{SN}$ is the perpendicular bisector of $\overline{QP}$. Prove that SR = SP.

SOLUTION

Every point on the perpendicular bisector of a segment is equidistant from the endpoints of the segment.

Since point S is on the perpendicular bisector of $\overline{QR}$,

      $SR = SQ$ (1)

Also, since point S is on the perpendicular bisector of $\overline{QP}$,

$$SQ = SP \qquad (2)$$

Because quantities equal to the same quantity are equal to each other, we have:

$$SR = SP. \qquad (3)$$

Parallel Lines

Two lines are called **parallel lines** if, and only if, they are in the same plane (coplanar) and do not intersect. The symbol for parallel, or is parallel to, is $\|$; $\overline{AB}$ is parallel to $\overline{CD}$ is written $\overline{AB} \| \overline{CD}$.

The distance between two parallel lines is the length of the perpendicular segment from any point on one line to the other line.

$$l_1 \| l_2$$

Given a line l and a point P not on line l, there is one and only one line through point P that is parallel to line l.

Any two coplanar lines are either intersecting lines or parallel lines.

If two (or more) lines are perpendicular to the same line, then they are parallel to each other.

If $l_1 \perp l_0$ and $l_2 \perp l_0$.

then $l_1 \| l_2$

If two lines are cut by a transversal so that alternate interior angles are equal, the lines are parallel.

If $\angle\alpha = \angle\beta$

then $l_1 \| l_2$

If two lines are parallel to the same line, then they are parallel to each other.

If $l_1 \parallel l_0$ and $l_2 \parallel l_0$

then $l_1 \parallel l_2$

If a line is perpendicular to one of two parallel lines, then it is perpendicular to the other line, too.

If $l_1 \parallel l_2$ and $l_0 \perp l_1$

then $l_0 \perp l_2$

If two lines being cut by a transversal form congruent corresponding angles, then the two lines are parallel.

If $\angle\alpha = \angle\beta$,

then $l_1 \parallel l_2$

If two lines being cut by a transversal form interior angles on the same side of the transversal that are supplementary, then the two lines are parallel.

If $m\angle\alpha + m\angle\beta = 180°$

then $l_1 \parallel l_2$

If a line is parallel to one of two parallel lines, it is also parallel to the other line.

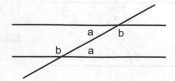

If $l_1 \parallel l_2$ and $l_0 \parallel l_1$

then $l_0 \parallel l_2$

If two parallel lines are cut by a transversal, then:

A) The alternate interior angles are congruent.

B)   The corresponding angles are congruent.

C)   The consecutive interior angles are supplementary.

D)   The alternate exterior angles are congruent.

PROBLEM

Given: $\angle 2$ is supplementary to $\angle 3$.

Prove: $l_1 \parallel l_2$.

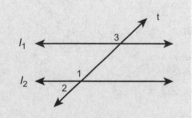

SOLUTION

Given two lines intercepted by a transversal, if a pair of corresponding angles are congruent, then the two lines are parallel. In this problem, we will show that since $\angle 1$ and $\angle 2$ are supplementary and $\angle 2$ and $\angle 3$ are supplementary, $\angle 1$ and $\angle 3$ are congruent. Since corresponding angles $\angle 1$ and $\angle 3$ are congruent, it follows $l_1 \parallel l_2$.

Statement		**Reason**
1.	$\angle 2$ is supplementary to $\angle 3$.	1. Given.
2.	$\angle 1$ is supplementary to $\angle 2$.	2. Two angles that form a linear pair are supplementary.
3.	$\angle 1 \cong \angle 3$	3. Angles supplementary to the same angle are congruent.
4.	$l_1 \parallel l_2$.	4. Given two lines intercepted by a transversal, if a pair of corresponding angles are congruent, then the two lines are parallel.

PROBLEM

> If line $\overline{AB}$ is parallel to line $\overline{CD}$ and line $\overline{EF}$ is parallel to line $\overline{GH}$, prove that $m \angle 1 = m \angle 2$.
>
>

SOLUTION

To show $\angle 1 \cong \angle 2$, we relate both to $\angle 3$. Because $\overline{EF} \parallel \overline{GH}$, corresponding angles 1 and 3 are congruent. Since $\overline{AB} \parallel \overline{CD}$, corresponding angles 3 and 2 are congruent. Because both $\angle 1$ and $\angle 2$ are congruent to the same angle, it follows that $\angle 1 \cong \angle 2$.

Statement		**Reason**
1.	$\overline{EF} \parallel \overline{GH}$	1. Given.
2.	$m \angle 1 = m \angle 3$	2. If two parallel lines are cut by a transversal, corresponding angles are of equal measure.
3.	$\overline{AB} \parallel \overline{CD}$	3. Given.
4.	$m \angle 2 = m \angle 3$	4. If two parallel lines are cut by a transversal, corresponding angles are equal in measure.
5.	$m \angle 1 = m \angle 2$	5. If two quantities are equal to the same quantity, they are equal to each other.

Drill: Lines and Angles

Intersection Lines

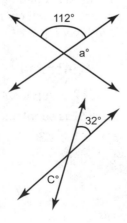

1. Find a.

    (A) 38°   (B) 68°   (C) 78°

    (D) 90°   (E) 112°

2. Find c.

    (A) 32°   (B) 48°   (C) 58°

    (D) 82°   (E) 148°

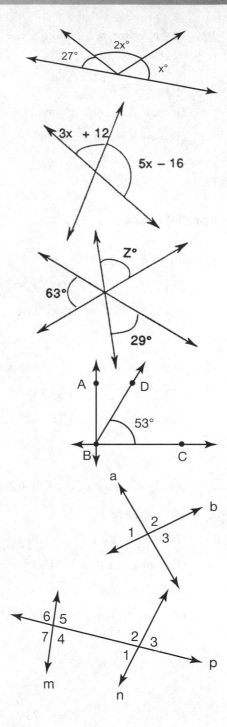

3. Determine x.

   (A) 21°   (B) 23°   (C) 51°

   (D) 102°   (E) 153°

4. Find x.

   (A) 8   (B) 11.75   (C) 21

   (D) 23   (E) 32

5. Find z.

   (A) 29°   (B) 54°   (C) 61°

   (D) 88°   (E) 92°

Perpendicular Lines

6. $\overline{BA} \perp \overline{BC}$ and $m \angle DBC = 53$. Find $m \angle ABD$.

   (A) 27°   (B) 33°   (C) 37°

   (D) 53°   (E) 90°

7. $m \angle 1 = 90°$. Find $m \angle 2$.

   (A) 80°   (B) 90°   (C) 100°

   (D) 135°   (E) 180°

8. If $n \perp p$, which of the following statements is true?

   (A) $\angle 1 \cong \angle 2$

   (B) $\angle 4 \cong \angle 5$

   (C) $m \angle 4 + m \angle 5 > m \angle 1 + m \angle 2$

   (D) $m \angle 3 > m \angle 2$

   (E) $m \angle 4 = 90°$

9. $\overline{CD} \perp \overline{EF}$ If $m \angle 1 = 2x$, $m \angle 2 = 30°$, and $m \angle 3 = x$, find x.

   (A) 5°   (B) 10°   (C) 12°

   (D) 20°   (E) 25°

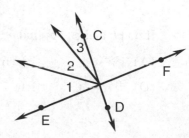

10. In the figure, $p \perp t$ and $q \perp t$. Which of the following statements is false?

    (A) $\angle 1 \cong \angle 4$

    (B) $\angle 2 \cong \angle 3$

    (C) $m\angle 2 + m\angle 3 = m\angle 4 + m\angle 6$

    (D) $m\angle 5 + m\angle 6 = 180°$

    (E) $m\angle 2 > m\angle 5$

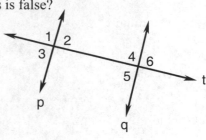

Parallel Lines

11. If $a \mid\mid b$, find z.

    (A) 26°   (B) 32°   (C) 64°

    (D) 86°   (E) 116°

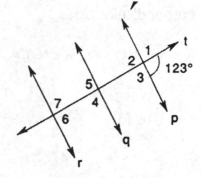

12. In the figure, $p \mid\mid q \mid\mid r$. Find $m\angle 7$.

    (A) 27°   (B) 33°   (C) 47°

    (D) 57°   (E) 64°

13. If $m \mid\mid n$, which of the following statements is false?

    (A) $\angle 2 \cong \angle 5$

    (B) $\angle 3 \cong \angle 6$

    (C) $m\angle 4 + m\angle 5 = 180°$

    (D) $\angle 2 \cong \angle 8$

    (E) $m\angle 7 + m\angle 3 = 180°$

14. If $r \mid\mid s$, find $m\angle 2$.

    (A) 17°   (B) 27°   (C) 43°

    (D) 67°   (E) 73°

15. If $a \mid\mid b$ and $c \mid\mid d$, find $m\angle 5$.

    (A) 55°   (B) 65°   (C) 75°

    (D) 95°   (E) 125°

Triangles

A closed three-sided geometric figure is called a **triangle**. The points of the intersection of the sides of a triangle are called the **vertices** of the triangle.

The **perimeter** of a triangle is the sum of the measures of the sides of the triangle.

A triangle with no equal sides is called a **scalene** triangle.

A triangle having at least two equal sides is called an **isosceles** triangle. The third side is called the **base** of the triangle.

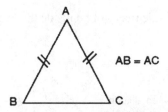

A side of a triangle is a line segment whose endpoints are the vertices of two angles of the triangle.

An interior angle of a triangle is an angle formed by two sides and includes the third side within its collection of points.

An equilateral triangle is a triangle having three equal sides. $AB = AC = BC$

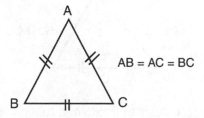

A triangle with an obtuse angle (greater than 90°) is called an **obtuse triangle**.

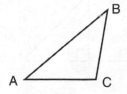

An **acute triangle** is a triangle with three acute angles (less than 90°).

A triangle with a right angle is called a **right triangle**. The side opposite the right angle in a right triangle is called the hypotenuse of the right triangle. The other two sides are called arms or legs of the right triangle.

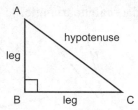

An **altitude,** or **height,** of a triangle is a line segment from a vertex of the triangle perpendicular to the opposite side.

Note: For an obtuse triangle, the altitude may not be inside the triangle.

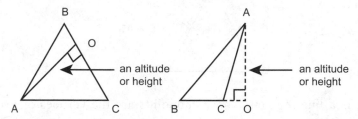

A line segment connecting a vertex of a triangle and the midpoint of the opposite side is called a **median** of the triangle.

A line that bisects and is perpendicular to a side of a triangle is called a **perpendicular bisector** of that side.

An **angle bisector** of a triangle is a line that bisects an angle and extends to the opposite side of the triangle.

The line segment that joins the midpoints of two sides of a triangle is called a midline of the triangle.

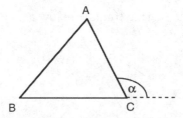

An exterior angle of a triangle is an angle formed outside a triangle by one side of the triangle and the extension of an adjacent side.

A triangle whose three interior angles have equal measure is said to be equiangular.

PROBLEM

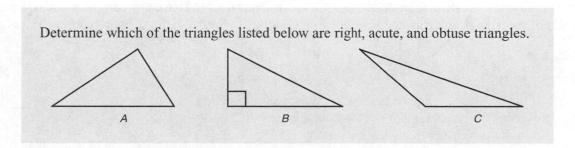

Determine which of the triangles listed below are right, acute, and obtuse triangles.

SOLUTION

Triangle *A* is an acute triangle. An acute triangle is a triangle comprised of three acute angles. Triangle *B* is a right triangle. A right triangle is a triangle with a right angle. Triangle *C* is an obtuse triangle. An obtuse triangle is a triangle with one obtuse angle.

Chapter 3   *FTCE General Knowledge Test*

PROBLEM

Determine which of the triangles listed below are scalene, isosceles, and equilateral.

  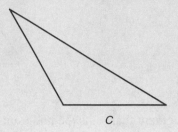

SOLUTION

Triangle *A* is an equilateral triangle. An equilateral triangle is a triangle with three congruent sides. Triangle *B* is an isosceles triangle. An isosceles triangle is a triangle with at least two congruent sides. Therefore, an equilateral triangle is also a type of isosceles triangle. Triangle *C* is a scalene triangle. *A* scalene triangle is a triangle with no congruent sides.

PROBLEM

Determine if the sides of the scalene triangle below are equal.

SOLUTION

The triangle is a scalene triangle. Since a scalene triangle does not have any congruent sides, none of the sides of the triangle are equal.

PROBLEM

If the measure of the vertex angle of an isosceles triangle exceeds the measurement of each base angle by 30°, find the value of each angle of the triangle.

SOLUTION

We know that the sum of the values of the angles of a triangle is 180°. In an isosceles triangle, the angles opposite the congruent sides (the base angles) are, themselves, congruent and of equal value.

Therefore,

(1)   Let x = the measure of each base angle.

(2)   Then $x + 30$ = the measure of the vertex angle.

We can solve for x algebraically because the sum of all the measures will be 180°.

$$x + x + (x + 30) = 180$$
$$3x + 30 = 180$$
$$3x \quad = 150$$
$$x \quad = 50$$

Therefore, the base angles each measure 50°, and the vertex angle measures 80°.

PROBLEM

Prove that the base angles of an isosceles right triangle measure 45°.

SOLUTION

As drawn in the figure, $\triangle ABC$ is an isosceles right triangle with base angles BAC and BCA. The sum of the measures of the angles of any triangle is 180°. For $\triangle ABC$, this means

$$m \angle BAC + m \angle BCA + m \angle ABC = 180° \tag{1}$$

But $m \angle ABC = 90°$ because $\triangle ABC$ is a right triangle. Furthermore, $m \angle BCA = m \angle BAC$, since the base angles of an isosceles triangle are congruent. Using these facts in equation   (1)

$$m \angle BAC + m \angle BCA + 90° = 180°$$
or $$2m \angle BAC = 2m \angle BCA = 90°$$
or $$m \angle BAC = m \angle BCA = 45°.$$

Therefore, the base angles of an isosceles right triangle measure 45°.

The area of a triangle is given by the formula $A = \frac{1}{2} bh$, where b is the length of a base, which can be any side of the triangle and h is the corresponding height of the triangle, which is the perpendicular line segment from the vertex opposite the base to the base itself.

$A = \frac{1}{2} bh$

$A = \frac{1}{2} (10)(3)$

$A = 15$

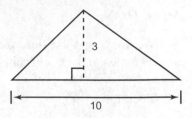

The area of a right triangle is found by taking $\frac{1}{2}$ the product of the lengths of its two arms.

$A = \frac{1}{2}(5)(12)$

$A = 30$

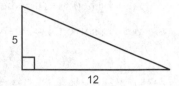

Similar Triangles

The measures of the angles of a pair of similar triangles are equal in a one-to-one fashion. Therefore, a triangle whose angles are 30°, 60°, and 90° is similar to every other triangle with those angle measurements, even though the sides of the two triangles may be different. The sides, however, are proportional, meaning they correspond to one another. The following figure shows two similar triangles, but one is three times the size of the other, so the corresponding sides are three times as long (even though the angles remain the same).

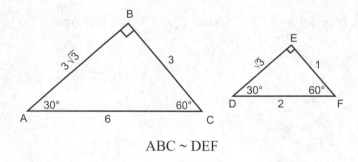

ABC ~ DEF

The sign for similar is ~ and the corresponding angles are listed in the same order: ∠A = ∠D, ∠B = ∠E, and ∠C = ∠F.

Drill: Triangles

Angle Measures

1.   In △ *PQR*, ∠*Q* is a right angle. Find *m* ∠*R*.

(A) 27°   (B) 33°   (C) 54°

(D) 67°   (E) 157°

2. Δ *MNO* is isosceles. If the vertex angle, ∠*N*, has a measure of 96°, find the measure of ∠*M*.

   (A) 21°   (B) 42°   (C) 64°

   (D) 84°   (E) 96°

3. Find *x*.

   (A) 15°   (B) 25°   (C) 30°

   (D) 45°   (E) 90°

4. Find *m* ∠1.

   (A) 40   (B) 66   (C) 74

   (D) 114   (E) 140

5. Δ *ABC* is a right triangle with a right angle at *B*. Δ *BDC* is a right triangle with right angle ∠*BDC*. If *m* ∠*C* = 36, find *m* ∠*A*.

   (A) 18   (B) 36   (C) 54

   (D) 72   (E) 180

Similar Triangles

6. The two triangles shown are similar. Find *b*.

   (A) 2 2/3   (B) 3   (C) 4

   (D) 16   (E) 24

7. The two triangles shown are similar. Find *m* ∠1.

   (A) 48   (B) 53   (C) 74

   (D) 127   (E) 180

8. The two triangles shown are similar. Find *a* and *b*.

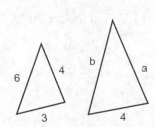

   (A) 5 and 10   (B) 4 and 8   (C) 4 2/3 and 7 1/3

   (D) 5 and 8   (E) 5 1/3 and 8

9. The perimeter of $\triangle LXR$ is 45 and the perimeter of $\triangle ABC$ is 27. If $LX = 15$, find the length of AB.

(A) 9   (B) 15   (C) 27

(D) 45   (E) 72

10. Find b.

(A) 9   (B) 15   (C) 20

(D) 45   (E) 60

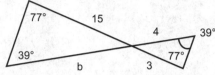

Area

11. Find the area of $\triangle MNO$.

(A) 22   (B) 49   (C) 56

(D) 84   (E) 112

12. Find the area of $\triangle PQR$.

(A) 31.5   (B) 38.5   (C) 53

(D) 77   (E) 82.5

13. Find the area of $\triangle STU$.

(A) $4\sqrt{2}$ (B) $8\sqrt{2}$ (C) $12\sqrt{2}$

(D) $16\sqrt{2}$ (E) $32\sqrt{2}$

14. Find the area of $\triangle ABC$.

(A) 54 cm^2 (B) 81 cm^2 (C) 108 cm^2

(D) 135 cm^2 (E) 180 cm^2

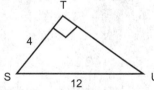

15. Find the area of $\triangle XYZ$.

(A) 20 cm^2 (B) 50 cm^2 (C) $50\sqrt{2}$ cm^2

(D) 100 cm^2 (E) 200 cm^2

Change in Linear Dimension

PROBLEM

Given triangle *ABC*, if angle *A* was made smaller, and *AB* and *AC* stay the same length, what would happen to *CB*?

SOLUTION

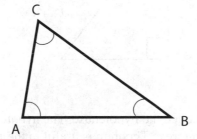

The length of line *CB* gets shorter.

PROBLEM

Given triangle *ABC*, if angle *A* was made larger and *AB* and *AC* stay the same length, what would happen to *CB*?

SOLUTION

The length of line *CB* gets longer.

The Pythagorean Theorem

The Pythagorean Theorem refers to right triangles. A right triangle is a triangle that has a right angle. A right angle measures 90 degrees. The Pythagorean Theorem tells you that $a^2 + b^2 = c^2$.

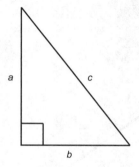

a and *b* are called legs, and *c* is called the hypotenuse. The hypotenuse is the side of the triangle that is opposite the right angle. The Pythagorean Theorem is useful in the following way: Given the length of any two sides of a right triangle, you can figure out the length of the third.

PROBLEM

In a right triangle, one leg is 3 inches and the other leg is 4 inches. What is the length of the hypotenuse?

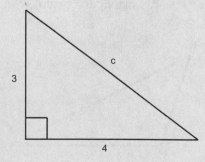

SOLUTION

$$a^2 + b^2 = c^2$$
$$3^2 + 4^2 = c^2$$
$$9 + 16 = c^2$$
$$25 = c^2$$
$$c = \sqrt{25} = 5 \text{ inches}$$

PROBLEM

If one leg of a right triangle is 6 inches, and the hypotenuse is 10 inches, what is the length of the other leg?

SOLUTION

First, write down the equation for the Pythagorean Theorem. Next, plug the information you are given into the equation. The hypotenuse c is equal to 10 and one of the legs b is equal to 6. Solve for a.

$$a^2 + b^2 = c^2$$
$$a^2 + 6^2 = 10^2$$
$$a^2 + 36 = 100$$
$$a^2 = 100 - 36$$
$$a^2 = 64$$
$$a = \sqrt{64} = 8 \text{ inches}$$

PROBLEM

What is the value of a in the triangle shown below?

SOLUTION

In order to answer this question, you need to use the Pythagorean Theorem: $a^2 + b^2 = c^2$, where a and b are the legs and c is the hypotenuse. The hypotenuse is the side opposite the right angle. The present problem is asking you to find the value of the missing leg, a.

$$a^2 + b^2 = c^2$$
$$a^2 + 12^2 = 13^2$$
$$a^2 + 144 = 169$$
$$a^2 = 169 - 144$$
$$a^2 = 25$$
$$a = \sqrt{25} = 5$$

Polygons (Convex)

A **polygon** is a figure with the same number of sides as angles.

An **equilateral polygon** is a polygon all of whose sides are of equal length.

An **equiangular polygon** is a polygon all of whose angles are of equal measure.

A **regular polygon** is a polygon that is both equilateral and equiangular.

PROBLEM

Each interior angle of a regular polygon contains 120°. How many sides does the polygon have?

120°   60°

SOLUTION

At each vertex of a polygon, the exterior angle is supplementary to the interior angle, as shown in the diagram. The sum of all exterior angles always sums to 360°, no matter how many sides the polygon has; however, the sum of the interior angles varies.

Since we are told that the interior angles measure 120 degrees, we can deduce that the exterior angle measures 60°.

Each exterior angle of a regular polygon of n sides measure 360°/n degrees. We know that each exterior angle measures 60°, and, therefore, by setting 360°/n equal to 60°, we can determine the number of sides in the polygon. The calculation is as follows:

$$\frac{360°}{n} = 60°$$
$$60°n = 360°$$
$$n = 6$$

Therefore, the regular polygon, with interior angles of 120°, has 6 sides. It is called a hexagon.

The area of a regular polygon can be determined by using the **apothem** and **radius** of the polygon. The apothem (a) of a regular polygon is the segment from the center of the polygon perpendicular to a side of the polygon. The radius (r) of a regular polygon is the segment joining any vertex of a regular polygon with the center of that polygon.

(1) All radii of a regular polygon are congruent.

(2) The radius of a regular polygon is congruent to a side.

(3) All apothems of a regular polygon are congruent.

The **area** of a regular polygon equals one-half the product of the length of the apothem and the perimeter.

$$\text{Area} = \frac{1}{2}\, a \times p$$

PROBLEM

Find the area of the regular pentagon whose radius is 8 and whose apothem is 6.

SOLUTION

If the radius is 8, the length of a side is also 8. Therefore, the perimeter of the pentagon is $5 \times 8 = 40$.

$$A = \frac{1}{2}\, a \times p$$
$$A = \frac{1}{2}\, (6)\,(40)$$
$$A = 120$$

PROBLEM

Find the area of a regular hexagon if one side has length 6.

SOLUTION

Since the length of a side equals 6, the radius also equals 6 and the perimeter equals 36. The base of the right triangle formed by the radius and apothem is half the length of a side, or 3. Using the Pythagorean theorem, you can find the length of the apothem.

$$a^2 + b^2 = c^2$$
$$a^2 + (3)^2 = (6)^2$$
$$a^2 = 36 - 9$$
$$a^2 = 27$$
$$a = 3\sqrt{3}$$

The apothem equals $3\sqrt{3}$. Therefore, the area of the hexagon is

$$A = \tfrac{1}{2}\, a \times p$$
$$= \tfrac{1}{2}(3\sqrt{3})(36)$$
$$= 54\sqrt{3}$$

Drill: Polygons

1. Find the measure of an interior angle of a regular pentagon.

    (A) 55   (B) 72   (C) 90   (D) 108   (E) 540

2. Find the measure of an exterior angle of a regular octagon.

    (A) 40   (B) 45   (C) 135   (D) 540   (E) 1080

3. Find the sum of the measures of the exterior angles of a regular triangle.

    (A) 90   (B) 115   (C) 180   (D) 250   (E) 360

4. Find the area of a square with a perimeter of 12 cm.

    (A) 9 cm²   (B) 12 cm²   (C) 48 cm²   (D) 96 cm²   (E) 144 cm²

5. A regular triangle has sides of 8 mm. If the apothem is $4\sqrt{3}$ mm, find the area of the triangle.

    (A) $12\sqrt{3}$ cm²   (B) 24 cm²   (C) $24\sqrt{3}$ cm²

    (D) 48 cm²   (E) $48\sqrt{3}$ cm²

6. Find the area of a regular hexagon with sides of 4 cm.

    (A) $12\sqrt{3}$ cm²   (B) 24 cm²   (C) $24\sqrt{3}$ cm²

    (D) 48 cm²   (E) $48\sqrt{3}$ cm²

7. Find the area of a regular decagon with sides of length 6 cm and an apothem of length 9.2 cm.

    (A) 55.2 cm²   (B) 60 cm²   (C) 138 cm²

    (D) 138.3 cm²   (E) 276 cm²

8. The perimeter of a regular heptagon (7-gon) is 36.4 cm. Find the length of each side.

    (A) 4.8 cm   (B) 5.2 cm   (C) 6.7 cm   (D) 7 cm   (E) 10.4 cm

9. The apothem of a regular quadrilateral is 4 in. Find the perimeter.

    (A) 12 in   (B) 16 in   (C) 24 in   (D) 32 in   (E) 64 in

10. A regular triangle has a perimeter of 18 cm; a regular pentagon has a perimeter of 30 cm; a regular hexagon has a perimeter of 33 cm. Which figure (or figures) have sides with the longest measure?

    (A) regular triangle

    (B) regular triangle and regular pentagon

    (C) regular pentagon

    (D) regular pentagon and regular hexagon

    (E) regular hexagon

Quadrilaterals

A **quadrilateral** is a polygon with four sides.

Parallelograms

A **parallelogram** is a quadrilateral whose opposite sides are parallel.

Two angles that have their vertices at the endpoints of the same side of a parallelogram are called **consecutive angles**. ∠A and ∠B are consecutive angles. So are ∠B and ∠D, ∠D and ∠C, and ∠C and ∠A.

The perpendicular segment connecting any point of a line containing one side of the parallelogram to the line containing the opposite side of the parallelogram is called the **altitude**, or **height**, of the parallelogram.

A diagonal of a polygon is a line segment joining any two non-consecutive vertices. The diagonals of a parallelogram bisect each other.

BE = ED, AE = EC

The area of a parallelogram is given by the formula $A = bh$ where b is the base and h is the height drawn perpendicular to that base.

$$A = bh$$
$$A = (10)(3)$$
$$A = 30$$

Rectangles

A rectangle is a parallelogram with right angles.

The diagonals of a rectangle are equal.

If the diagonals of a parallelogram are equal, the parallelogram is a rectangle.

If a quadrilateral has four right angles, it is a rectangle.

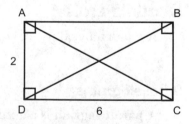

The area of a rectangle is given by the formula $A = lw$ where l is the length and w is the width.

$$A = lw$$
$$A = (3)(10)$$
$$A = 30$$

Rhombi (plural of rhombus)

A rhombus is a parallelogram with all sides equal.

The diagonals of a rhombus are perpendicular to each other.

The diagonals of a rhombus bisect the angles of the rhombus.

If the diagonals of a parallelogram are perpendicular, the parallelogram is a rhombus.

If a quadrilateral has four equal sides, then it is a rhombus.

A parallelogram is a rhombus if either diagonal of the parallelogram bisects the angles of the vertices it joins.

The area of a rhombus is ½ the product of the lengths of the diagonals.

Squares

A square is a rhombus with a right angle.

A square is an equilateral and equiangular quadrilateral.

A square has all the properties of parallelograms and rectangles.

A rectangle is a square if two consecutive sides are congruent.

A rhombus is a square if one of its interior angles is a right angle.

In a square, the measure of either diagonal can be calculated by multiplying the length of any side by the square root of 2.

$$AD = AB\sqrt{2}$$

The area of a square is given by the formula $A = s^2$ where s is the side of the square. Since all sides of a square are equal, it does not matter which side is used.

$A = s^2$

$A = 6^2$

$A = 36$

The area of a square can also be found by taking $\frac{1}{2}$ the product of the length of the diagonal squared.

$$A = \tfrac{1}{2}\, d^2$$

$$A = \tfrac{1}{2}\, (8)^2$$

$$A = 32$$

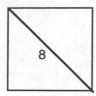

Trapezoids

A **trapezoid** is a quadrilateral with two and only two sides parallel. The parallel sides of a trapezoid are called **bases**.

The **median** of a trapezoid is the line joining the midpoints of the non-parallel sides.

The median of a trapezoid is parallel to the bases and equal to one-half their sum.

The perpendicular segment connecting any point in the line containing one base of the trapezoid to the line containing the other base is the **altitude**, or **height**, of the trapezoid.

An **isosceles trapezoid** is a trapezoid whose non-parallel sides are equal. A pair of angles including only one of the parallel sides is called **a pair of base angles**.

The base angles of an isosceles trapezoid are equal.

The diagonals of an isosceles trapezoid are equal.

The opposite angles of an isosceles trapezoid are supplementary.

Area Review

Triangle $A = \frac{1}{2}bh$

Rectangle $A = lw$

Parallelogram $A = bh$

Trapezoid $A = \frac{1}{2}h(b_1 + b_2)$

Rhombus $A = \frac{1}{2}d_1 d_2$

PROBLEM

Prove that all pairs of consecutive angles of a parallelogram are supplementary.

SOLUTION

We must prove that the pairs of angles $\angle BAD$ and $\angle ADC$, $\angle ADC$ and $\angle DCB$, $\angle DCB$ and $\angle CBA$, and $\angle CBA$ and $\angle BAD$ are supplementary. (This means that the sum of their measures is 180°.)

Because $ABCD$ is a parallelogram, $\overline{AB} \parallel \overline{CD}$. $\angle BAD$ and $\angle ADC$ are therefore consecutive interior angles formed when parallel lines AB and CD are cut by transversal AD. Since the consecutive interior angles formed by 2 parallel lines and a transversal are supplementary, $\angle BAD$ and $\angle ADC$ are supplementary. Similarly, $\angle CBA$ and $\angle DCB$ are supplementary. Since $\angle AD \parallel \angle BC$, a similar argument shows that $\angle ADC$ and $\angle DCB$ are supplementary, as are $\angle CBA$ and $\angle BAD$.

PROBLEM

In the accompanying figure, $\triangle ABC$ is given to be an isosceles right triangle with $\angle ABC$ a right angle and $AB \cong BC$. Line segment $\overline{BD}$, which bisects $\overline{CA}$, is extended to E, so that $\overline{BD} \cong \overline{DE}$. Prove $BAEC$ is a square.

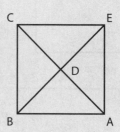

SOLUTION

A square is a rectangle in which two consecutive sides are congruent. This definition will provide the framework for the proof in this problem. We will prove that $BAEC$ is a parallelogram that is specifically a rectangle with consecutive sides congruent, namely a square.

	Statement		**Reason**
1.	$\overline{BD} \cong \overline{DE}$	1.	Given.
2.	$\overline{AD} \cong \overline{DC}$	2.	$\overline{BD}$ bisects $\overline{CA}$.
3.	$BAEC$ is a parallelogram	3.	If diagonals of a quadrilateral bisect each other, then the quadrilateral is a parallelogram.
4.	$\angle ABC$ is a right angle	4.	Given.
5.	$BAEC$ is a rectangle	5.	A parallelogram, one of whose angles is a right angle, is a rectangle.
6.	$AB \cong BC$	6.	Given.
7.	$BAEC$ is a square	7.	If a rectangle has two congruent consecutive sides, then the rectangle is a square.

PROBLEM

Calculate the area of the trapezoid below.

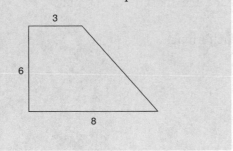

SOLUTION

Step 1 is to write the formula for the area of a trapezoid.

$$A = \frac{1}{2}h(b_1 + b_2) \text{ , where } b_1 \text{ and } b_2 \text{ are the bases}$$

Step 2 is to substitute the known values into the formula.

$$A = \frac{1}{2}(6)(3 + 8)$$

Step 3 is to solve the equation.

$$A = 33$$

The correct answer is that the area of the trapezoid is 33.

PROBLEM

Calculate the area of the rhombus below.

SOLUTION

Step 1 is to write the formula for the area of a rhombus.

$$A = \frac{1}{2}(d_1)(d_2) \text{, where } d_1 \text{ and } d_2 \text{ are the diagonals of the rhombus}$$

Step 2 is to substitute the known values into the formula.

$$A = \frac{1}{2}(5)(4)$$

Step 3 is to solve the equation.

$$A = 10$$

The correct answer is that the area of the rhombus is 10.

Drill: Quadrilaterals

Parallelograms, Rectangles, Rhombi, Squares, Trapezoids

1. In parallelogram $WXYZ$, $WX = 14$, $WZ = 6$, $ZY = 3x + 5$, and $XY = 2y - 4$. Find x and y.

    (A) 3 and 5   (B) 4 and 5   (C) 4 and 6

    (D) 6 and 10   (E) 6 and 14

2. Quadrilateral $ABCD$ is a parallelogram. If $m \angle B = 6x + 2$ and $m \angle D = 98$, find x.

    (A) 12   (B) 16   (C) 16 2/3

    (D) 18   (E) 20

3. Find the area of parallelogram $STUV$.

    (A) 56   (B) 90   (C) 108

    (D) 162   (E) 180

4. Find the area of parallelogram $MNOP$.

    (A) 19   (B) 32   (C) $32\sqrt{3}$

    (D) 44   (E) $44\sqrt{3}$

5. Find the perimeter of rectangle *PQRS*, if the area is 84 in².

(A) 31 in   (B) 38 in   (C) 40 in

(D) 44 in   (E) 121 in

6. In rectangle *ABCD*, *AD* = 6 cm and *DC* = 8 cm. Find the length of the diagonal *AC*.

(A) 10 cm   (B) 12 cm   (C) 20 cm

(D) 28 cm   (E) 48 cm

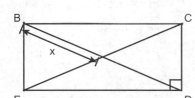

7. Find the area of rectangle *UVXY*.

(A) 17 cm²   (B) 34 cm²   (C) 35 cm²

(D) 70 cm²   (E) 140 cm²

8. Find *x* in rectangle *BCDE* if the diagonal *EC* is 17 mm.

(A) 6.55 mm   (B) 8 mm   (C) 8.5 mm

(D) 17 mm   (E) 34 mm

9. In rhombus *DEFG*, *DE* = 7 cm. Find the perimeter of the rhombus.

(A) 14 cm   (B) 28 cm   (C) 42 cm

(D) 49 cm   (E) 56 cm

10. In rhombus *RHOM*, the diagonal $\overline{RO}$ is 8 cm and the diagonal $\overline{HM}$ is 12 cm. Find the area of the rhombus.

(A) 20 cm²   (B) 40 cm²   (C) 48 cm²

(D) 68 cm²   (E) 96 cm²

11. In rhombus *GHIJ*, *GI* = 6 cm and *HJ* = 8 cm. Find the length of *GH*.

(A) 3 cm   (B) 4 cm   (C) 5 cm

(D) $4\sqrt{3}$ cm   (E) 14 cm

12. In rhombus *CDEF*, *CD* is 13 mm and *DX* is 5 mm.
Find the area of the rhombus.

(A) 31 mm²   (B) 60 mm²   (C) 78 mm²

(D) 120 mm²   (E) 260 mm²

13. Quadrilateral *ATUV* is a square. If the perimeter of the square is 44 cm, find the length of $\overline{AT}$.

(A) 4 cm   (B) 11 cm   (C) 22 cm   (D) 30 cm   (E) 40 cm

14. The area of square *XYZW* is 196 cm².
Find the perimeter of the square.

(A) 28 cm   (B) 42 cm   (C) 56 cm

(D) 98 cm   (E) 196 cm.

15. In square *MNOP*, *MN* is 6 cm. Find the length of diagonal $\overline{MO}$.

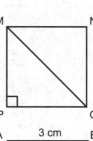

(A) 6 cm   (B) $6\sqrt{2}$ cm   (C) $6\sqrt{3}$ cm

(D) $6\sqrt{6}$ cm   (E) 12 cm

16. In square *ABCD*, *AB* = 3 cm. Find the area of the square.

(A) 9 cm²   (B) 12 cm²   (C) 15 cm²

(D) 18 cm²   (E) 21 cm²

17. *ABCD* is an isosceles trapezoid. Find the perimeter.

(A) 21 cm   (B) 27 cm   (C) 30 cm

(D) 50 cm   (E) 54 cm

18. Find the area of trapezoid *MNOP*.

(A) $(17+3\sqrt{3})$ mm²

(B) 33/2 mm²

(C) $33\sqrt{3}/2$ mm²

(D) 33 mm²

(E) $33\sqrt{3}$ mm²

19. Trapezoid *XYZW* is isosceles. If $m \angle W = 58°$ and $m \angle Z = 4x - 6°$, find *x*.

    (A) 8   (B) 12   (C) 13

    (D) 16   (E) 58

Circles

A **circle** is a set of points in the same plane equidistant from a fixed point called its center. Circles are named by their centers, so the figure to the right is O.

A **radius** of a circle is a line segment drawn from the center of the circle to any point on the circle.

A portion of a circle is called an **arc** of the circle.

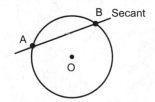

A line that intersects a circle in two points is called a **secant.**

A line segment joining two points on a circle is called a **chord** of the circle.

A chord that passes through the center of the circle is called a **diameter** of the circle.

The line passing through the centers of two (or more) circles is called the **line of centers**.

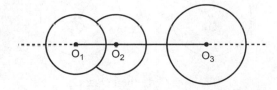

An angle whose vertex is on the circle and whose sides are chords of the circle is called an **inscribed angle**.

Inscribed angles, ∠BAC

An angle whose vertex is at the center of a circle and whose sides are radii is called a **central angle.**

The measure of a minor arc is the measure of the central angle that intercepts that arc.

$$\alpha = \text{central angle}$$

$$m\widehat{AB} = \alpha = m\angle AOB$$

The distance from a point P to a given circle is the distance from that point to the point where the circle intersects with a line segment with endpoints at the center of the circle and point P. The distance of point P to the diagrammed circle (above right) with center O is the line segment PB.

A line that has one and only one point of intersection with a circle is called a tangent to that circle, while their common point is called a **point of tangency**.

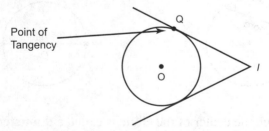

Congruent circles are circles whose radii are congruent.

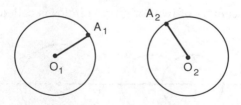

If $O_1A_1 \cong O_2A_2$, then $O_1 \cong O_2$.

The measure of a semicircle is 180°.

A **circumscribed circle** is a circle passing through all the vertices of a polygon.

Circles that have the same center and unequal radii are called **concentric circles**.

Circumscribed Circle

Concentric Circles

The **circumference** of a circle is given by $2\pi r$ or πd, and the **area** of a circle is given by πr^2, where r is the radius, d is the diameter, and π (pi) is 3.14, or 22/7.

$$C = \pi d = 2\pi r$$
$$A = \pi r^2$$

PROBLEM

Using the figure below, determine the length of the line segment *CB*.

$\overline{AB} = 12$

SOLUTION

If a chord is perpendicular to the diameter as in the above figure, then the diameter bisects the chord. Since the length of the chord is 12, the line segment *CB* is 6.

PROBLEM

Given that the coordinates of the diameter of a circle are (1, 1) and (6, 6), what is the radius of the circle?

SOLUTION

Step 1 is to use the distance formula to calculate the diameter.

$$D = \sqrt{(6-1)^2 + (6-1)^2}$$

$$D = \sqrt{25 + 25} = \sqrt{50} = 5\sqrt{2}$$

Step 2 is to divide the diameter by 2 to obtain the radius.

$$r = \frac{5\sqrt{2}}{2} = 2.5\sqrt{2}$$

$$\sqrt{2} = 1.414,$$

$$r = 3.535$$

The correct answer is $r = 3.535$.

PROBLEM

The radius of a circle is $y + 2$. Give the length of the diameter.

SOLUTION

Step 1 is to write the equation for calculating the diameter of a circle.

$D = 2r$, where r is the radius

Step 2 is to substitute the value of the radius into the equation.

$$D = 2(y + 2)$$

Step 3 is to solve the equation.

$$D = 2y + 4$$

The correct answer is the diameter $= 2y + 4$.

PROBLEM

A and B are points on circle Q such that $\triangle AQB$ is equilateral. If length of side $AB = 12$, find the length of arc AB.

SOLUTION

To find the arc length of $\overset{\frown}{AB}$, we must find the measure of the central angle $\angle AQB$ and the measure of the radius $\overline{QA}$. $\angle AQB$ is an interior angle of the equlateral triangle ΔAQB. Therefore, $m \angle AQB = 60°$. Similarly, in the equilateral ΔAQB, $AQ = AB = QB = 12$. Given the radius, r, and the central angle, n, the arc length is given by $n/360 \times 2\pi r$. Therefore, by substitution, $60/360 \times 2\pi \times 12 = \frac{1}{6} \times 2\pi \times 12 = 4\pi$. Therefore, the length of $\overset{\frown}{AB} = 4\pi$.

PROBLEM

In circle O, the measure of $\overset{\frown}{AB}$ is 80°.
Find the measure of $\angle A$.

SOLUTION

The accompanying figure shows that $\overset{\frown}{AB}$ is intercepted by central angle AOB. By definition, we know that the measure of the central angle is the measure of its intercepted arc. In this case,

$$m \overset{\frown}{AB} = m \angle AOB = 80°.$$

Radius $\overline{OA}$ and radius $\overline{OB}$ are congruent and form two sides of ΔOAB. By a theorem, the angles opposite these two congruent sides must, themselves, be congruent. Therefore, $m \angle A = m \angle B$.

The sum of the measures of the angles of a triangle is 180°. Therefore,

$$m \angle A + m \angle B + m \angle AOB = 180°.$$

Since $m \angle A = m \angle B$, we can write

$$m \angle A + m \angle A + 80° = 180°$$

$$\text{or } 2m \angle A = 100°$$

$$\text{or } m \angle A = 50°.$$

Therefore, the measure of $\angle A$ is 50°.

PROBLEM

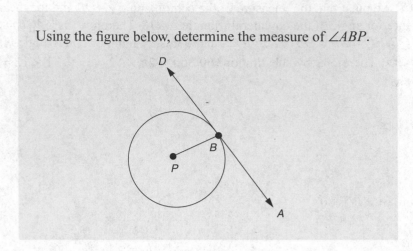

Using the figure below, determine the measure of ∠*ABP*.

SOLUTION

Step 1 is to recognize that line *AD* is tangent to Circle *P*.

In Step 2, since line *AD* is tangent to Circle *P*, ∠*ABP* must be a right angle.

The correct answer is 90 degrees.

PROBLEM

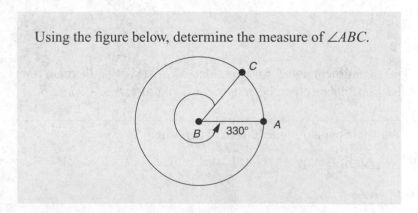

Using the figure below, determine the measure of ∠*ABC*.

SOLUTION

Since the angle of the arc is given, and a circle is 360 degrees, the measure of ∠*ABC* must be 360 minus the angle of the arc.

$$360 - 330 = 30$$

The correct answer is 30 degrees.

Drill: Circles

Circumference, Area, Concentric Circles

1. Find the circumference of circle A if its radius is 3 mm.

    (A) 3π mm   (B) 6π mm   (C) 9π mm   (D) 12π mm   (E) 15π mm

2. The circumference of circle H is 20π cm. Find the length of the radius.

    (A) 10 cm   (B) 20 cm   (C) 10π cm   (D) 15π cm   (E) 20π cm

3. The circumference of circle A is how many millimeters larger than the circumference of circle B?

    (A) 3   (B) 6   (C) 3π

    (D) 6π (E) 7π

4. If the diameter of circle X is 9 cm and if $\pi = 3.14$, find the circumference of the circle to the nearest tenth.

    (A) 9 cm   (B) 14.1 cm   (C) 21.1 cm   (D) 24.6 cm   (E) 28.3 cm

5. Find the area of circle I.

    (A) 22 mm^2 (B) 121 mm^2 (C) 121π mm^2

    (D) 132 mm^2 (E) 132π mm^2

6. The diameter of circle Z is 27 mm. Find the area of the circle.

    (A) 91.125 mm^2 (B) 182.25 mm^2 (C) 191.5π mm^2

    (D) 182.25π mm^2 (E) 729 mm^2

7. The area of circle B is 225π cm^2. Find the length of the diameter of the circle.

    (A) 15 cm   (B) 20 cm   (C) 30 cm   (D) 20π cm   (E) 25π cm

8. The area of circle X is 144π mm^2 while the area of circle Y is 81π mm^2. Write the ratio of the radius of circle X to that of circle Y.

    (A) $3 : 4$ (B) $4 : 3$ (C) $9 : 12$ (D) $27 : 12$ (E) $18 : 24$

9. The circumference of circle *M* is 18π cm. Find the area of the circle.

   (A) 18π cm²   (B) 81 cm²   (C) 36 cm²   (D) 36π cm²   (E) 81π cm²

10. In two concentric circles, the smaller circle has a radius of 3 mm while the larger circle has a radius of 5 mm. Find the area of the shaded region.

   (A) 2π mm²   (B) 8π mm²   (C) 13π mm²

   (D) 16π mm²   (E) 26π mm²

11. The radius of the smaller of two concentric circles is 5 cm while the radius of the larger circle is 7 cm. Determine the area of the shaded region.

   (A) 7π cm²   (B) 24π cm²   (C) 25π cm²

   (D) 36π cm²   (E) 49π cm²

12. Find the measure of arc *MN* if *m* ∠*MON* = 62°.

   (A) 16°   (B) 32°   (C) 59°

   (D) 62°   (E) 124°

13. Find the measure of arc *AXC*.

   (A) 150°   (B) 160°   (C) 180°

   (D) 270°   (E) 360°

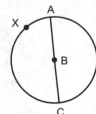

14. If arc *MXP* = 236°, find the measure of arc *MP*.

   (A) 62°   (B) 124°   (C) 236°

   (D) 270°   (E) 360°

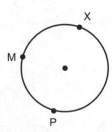

15. In circle *S*, major arc *PQR* has a measure of 298°. Find the measure of the central angle ∠*PSR*.

   (A) 62°   (B) 124°   (C) 149°

   (D) 298°   (E) 360°

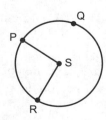

16. Find the measure of arc *XY* in circle *W*.

    (A) 40°   (B) 120°   (C) 140°

    (D) 180°   (E) 220°

17. Find the area of the sector shown.

    (A) 4 cm²   (B) 2π cm²   (C) 16 cm²

    (D) 8π cm²   (E) 16π cm²

18. Find the area of the shaded region.

    (A) 10   (B) 5π   (C) 25

    (D) 20π   (E) 25π

19. Find the area of the sector shown.

    (A) $\dfrac{9\pi \text{ mm}^2}{4}$ (B) $\dfrac{9\pi \text{ mm}^2}{2}$ (C) 18 mm²

    (D) 6π mm²   (E) 9π mm²

20. If the area of the square is 100 cm², find the area of the sector.

    (A) 10π cm²   (B) 25 cm²   (C) 25π cm²

    (D) 100 cm²   (E) 100π cm²

PROBLEM

Calculate the circumference of a circle that has a radius of 12 inches.

SOLUTION

Step 1 is to write the formula for the circumference of a circle.

circumference = 2π*r*

Step 2 is to substitute the known values into the equation. Pi (π) is approximately 3.14.

The radius is 12.

circumference = 2(3.14)12

Step 3 is to solve the equation.

$$circumference = 75.4$$

The correct answer is that the circumference = 75.4 inches.

PROBLEM

Calculate the area of a circle that has a diameter of 10 meters.

SOLUTION

Step 1 is to write the formula for the area of a circle.

$$A = \pi r^2$$

Step 2 is to substitute the known values into the equation. Pi is approximately 3.14. The diameter of the circle is 10 meters, so the radius is 5 meters.

$$A = (3.14)(5)^2$$

Step 3 is to solve the equation.

$$A = 78.5$$

The correct answer is that the area of the circle is 78.5 m².

Solids

Solid geometry is the study of figures that consist of points not all in the same plane.

Prisms

A solid with lateral faces and bases that are congruent polygons is called a **prism**. If the congruent polygons and lateral faces are all rectangles, it is called a **rectangular solid**.

The surface area of a prism is the sum of the areas of all the faces. The area of each face is referred to as a lateral area.

The volume of a prism equals the area of the base (*B*) times the height (*h*).

$$V = Bh$$

The volume of a rectangular solid is equal to the product of its length, width, and height.

$$V = lwh$$

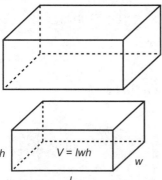

PROBLEM

What are the dimensions of a solid cube whose surface area is numerically equal to its volume?

SOLUTION

The surface area of a cube of edge length a is equal to the sum of the areas of its 6 faces. Since a cube is a regular polygon, all 6 faces are congruent. Each face of a cube is a square of edge length a. Hence, the surface area of a cube of edge length a is

$$S = 6a^2.$$

The volume of a cube of edge length a is

$$V = a^3.$$

We require that $S = V$, or that

$$6a^2 = a^3 \quad \text{or} \quad a = 6$$

Hence, if a cube has edge length 6, its surface area will be numerically equal to its volume.

PROBLEM

Calculate the volume of a rectangular solid that has a length of 5, a height of 1.5, and a width of 4.

SOLUTION

Step 1 is to write the formula for the volume of a rectangular solid.

$$V = l \times w \times h$$

Step 2 is to substitute the known values into the formula.

$$V = 5 \times 4 \times 1.5$$

Step 3 is to solve the equation.

$$V = 30$$

The correct answer is that the volume of the rectangular solid $= 30$.

Spheres

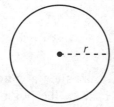

A solid for which every point on the surface is the same distance from the center point is called a **sphere**.

The surface area of a sphere is

$$A = 4\pi r^2$$

The volume of a sphere is

$$V = \frac{4}{3}\pi r^3$$

PROBLEM

Calculate the volume of a sphere that has a radius of 2 meters.

SOLUTION

Step 1 is to write the formula for the volume of a sphere.

$$V = \frac{4}{3}\pi r^3$$

Step 2 is to substitute the known values into the equation. Pi is approximately 3.14 and the radius is 2 meters.

$$V = \frac{4}{3}(3.14)(2)^3$$

Step 3 is to solve the equation.

$$V = 33.49 \text{ or } \sim 33.5$$

The correct answer is that the volume of the sphere is 33.5 m³.

Pyramid

The figure formed when the vertices of a plane polygon (called the base) are joined by line segments to a point not in the same plane is called a **pyramid**.

The surface area of a pyramid equals the sum of areas of all faces.

The volume of a pyramid or cone equals $\frac{1}{3}$ times the Area of the Base (B) times the height (h).

$$V = \frac{1}{3} Bh$$

Cone

A "pyramid" with a circular base is called a **cone**. The distance from any point on the circular base to the point of the cone is called the slant height.

The surface area of a cone is given by

$$A = \pi rs + \pi r^2$$

The volume of a cone is given by

$$V = \frac{1}{3}\pi r h$$

Cylinder

A solid with bases that are congruent circles is called a **cylinder**.

The surface area of a cylinder equals the sum of the areas of the bases and the rectangular "wrap".

$$A = 2(\pi r^2) + 2(\pi r)h$$

The volume of a cylinder equals the Area of the Base (B) times the height (h).

$$V = Bh$$

PROBLEM

Calculate the volume of a pyramid that has a height of 3 feet. The area of the base of the pyramid was calculated to be 15 square feet.

SOLUTION

Step 1 is to write the formula for the volume of a pyramid.

$$V = \frac{1}{3}Bh,$$ where B is the area of the base of the pyramid

Step 2 is to substitute the known values into the formula.

$$V = \frac{1}{3}(15)(3)$$

Step 3 is to solve the equation.

$$V = 15$$

The correct answer is that the volume of the pyramid is 15 cubic feet.

PROBLEM

Calculate the volume of the cone below.

SOLUTION

Step 1 is to write the formula for the volume of a cone.

$$V = \frac{1}{3}\pi r^2 h$$

Step 2 is to substitute the known values into the equation.

$$V = \frac{1}{3}(3.14)(2)^2(6)$$

Step 3 is to solve the equation.

$$V = 25.12$$

The correct answer is that the volume of the cone is 25.12.

PROBLEM

Calculate the volume of the cylinder below.

SOLUTION

Step 1 is to write the formula for the volume of a cylinder.

$$V = \pi r^2 h$$

Step 2 is to substitute the known values into the formula.

$$V = \pi(2)^2(11) = 3.14(4)(11)$$

Step 3 is to solve the equation.

$$V = 138.16$$

The correct answer is that the volume is 138.16 m³.

PROBLEM

Calculate the total area of the cone below. Round to the nearest square meter.

SOLUTION

Step 1 is to write the formula for the total area of a cone.

$$A = \pi rs + \pi r^2, \text{ where } s \text{ is the slant height, or the surface length of the cone.}$$

Step 2 is to substitute the known values into the formula.

$$A = \pi(2)(5) + \pi(2)^2$$

Step 3 is to solve the equation.

$$A = 10\pi + 4\pi = 14\pi = 14(3.14)$$
$$A = 44$$

The correct answer is 44 m².

Drill: Solids

1. Find the surface area of the rectangular prism shown.

    (A) 138 cm²   (B) 336 cm²   (C) 381 cm²

    (D) 426 cm²   (E) 540 cm²

2. Find the volume of the rectangular storage tank shown.

(A) 24 m³   (B) 36 m³   (C) 38 m³   (D) 42 m³   (E) 45 m³

3. The lateral area of a cube is 100 cm². Find the length of an edge of the cube.

(A) 4 cm   (B) 5 cm   (C) 10 cm   (D) 12 cm   (E) 15 cm

Ratio and Proportion

Ratio

The results of observation or measurement often must be compared with some standard value in order to have any meaning. For example, to say that a man can read 400 words per minute has little meaning as it stands. However, when his rate is compared to the 250 words per minute of the average reader, one can see that he reads considerably faster than the average reader. How much faster? To find out, his rate is divided by the average rate, as follows:

$$\frac{400}{250} = \frac{8}{5}$$

Thus, for every 5 words read by the average reader, this man reads 8.

When the relationship between two numbers is shown in this way, they are compared as a **ratio**. A ratio is a comparison of two quantities. It is the quotient obtained by dividing the first number of a comparison by the second.

Since a ratio is also a fraction, all the rules that govern fractions may be used in working with ratios. Thus, the terms may be reduced, increased, simplified, and so forth, according to the rules for fractions.

Proportion

Closely allied with the study of ratio is the subject of proportion. A **proportion** is nothing more than an equation in which the members are ratios. In other words, when two ratios are set equal to each other, a proportion is formed. The proportion may be written in three different ways, as in the following examples:

15:20 : : 3:4

15:20 = 3:4

$$\frac{15}{20} = \frac{3}{4}$$

The last two forms are the most common. All these forms are read, "15 is to 20 as 3 is to 4." In other words, 15 has the same ratio to 20 as 3 has to 4.

One reason for the extreme importance of proportions is that if any three of the terms are given, the fourth may be found by solving a simple equation. In science, many chemical and physical relations are expressed as proportions. Consequently, a familiarity with proportions will provide one method for solving many applied problems. It is evident from the last form shown, $\frac{15}{20} = \frac{3}{4}$, that a proportion is really a fractional equation. Therefore, all the rules for fractional equations apply.

In a proportion $A : B = C : D$, or as a fraction, $\frac{A}{B} = \frac{C}{D}$, A and D are called the **extremes** (they are all the extreme outsides of the ratio) and B and C are called the **means**.

To solve for one of the means or extremes, **cross-multiply**, which means the product of the means equals the product of the extremes, or $AD = BC$.

PROBLEM

Express the following phrases as a ratio of students in Mrs. Polly's class to students in Mr. Smith's:

Mrs. Polly teaches 30 students.

Mr. Smith teaches 10 students.

SOLUTION

Step 1 is to write the phrase in the following format:

      30 students:10 students

Step 2 is to reduce the ratio to its lowest terms, if possible. To do this, write out each number as a product of its primes and find the greatest common divisor (GCD).

$$30 = 5 \times 6 \qquad 10 = 5 \times 2$$
$$\quad\, = 5 \times 3 \times 2$$

The GCD is 5×2, or 10.

Next, divide each number by the GCD.

$$\frac{30}{10} = 3 \qquad \frac{10}{10} = 1$$

Step 3 is to rewrite the ratio.

> 3 students:1 student

The correct answer is 3 students:1 student.

PROBLEM

Express the following phrases as a ratio of Robin's apples to Tim's apples:

Robin has 5 apples.

Tim has 3 apples.

SOLUTION

Step 1 is to write the phrase in the following format:

> 5 apples:3 apples

Step 2 is to reduce the ratio to its lowest terms, if possible. To do this, write out each number as a product of its primes and find the greatest common divisor (GCD).

$$5 = 5 \times 1 \qquad 3 = 3 \times 1$$

Since there is no GCD, the ratio is already reduced to its lowest terms.

The correct answer is 5 apples:3 apples.

PROBLEM

Express the following phrases as a ratio of cats to dogs:

21 cats are in the house.

7 dogs are in the house.

SOLUTION

Step 1 is to write the phrase in the following format:

> 21 cats:7 dogs

Step 2 is to reduce the ratio to its lowest terms, if possible. To do this, write out each number as a product of its primes and find the greatest common divisor (GCD).

$$21 = 7 \times 3 \qquad 7 = 7 \times 1$$

The GCD is 7.

Next, divide each number by the GCD.

$$\frac{21}{7} = 3 \qquad \frac{7}{7} = 1$$

Step 3 is to rewrite the ratio.

3 cats:1 dog

The correct answer is 3 cats:1 dog.

PROBLEM

Sandy has to walk 1 kilometer to get to school. John has to walk 400 meters to get to school. What is the ratio (in meters) of the distance walked by Sandy to that walked by John?

SOLUTION

Step 1 is to write the phrase in the following format:

1 kilometer:400 meters

Step 2 is to convert kilometers to meters.

1 kilometer = 1,000 meters

Step 3 is to rewrite the problem in meters.

1,000 meters:400 meters

Step 4 is to reduce the ratio to its lowest terms, if possible. To do this, write out each number as a product of its primes and find the greatest common divisor (GCD).

$$1,000 = 10 \times 10 \times 10 \qquad\qquad 400 = 40 \times 10$$
$$= 5 \times 2 \times 5 \times 2 \times 5 \times 2 \qquad\qquad = 4 \times 10 \times 10$$
$$= 2 \times 2 \times 5 \times 2 \times 5 \times 2$$

The GCD is 200 or $2 \times 5 \times 2 \times 5 \times 2$.

Next, divide each number by the GCD.

$$\frac{1,000}{200} = 5 \qquad \frac{400}{200} = 2$$

Step 5 is to rewrite the ratio.

5 meters:2 meters

The correct answer is 5 meters:2 meters.

PROBLEM

Express the following phrase as a ratio of dollars lost to dollars invested:

Stockbroker Brian lost $3 for every $6 invested.

SOLUTION

Step 1 is write the phrase in the following format:

$3:$6

Step 2 is to reduce the ratio to its lowest terms, if possible. To do this, write out each number as a product of its primes and find the greatest common divisor (GCD).

$$3 = 3 \times 1 \qquad\qquad 6 = 3 \times 2$$

The GCD is 3.

Next, divide each number by the GCD.

$$\frac{3}{3} = 1 \qquad \frac{6}{3} = 2$$

Step 3 is to rewrite the ratio.

1:2

The correct answer is 1 lost : 2 invested.

PROBLEM

Express the following fraction as a ratio: $\frac{54}{63}$.

SOLUTION

Step 1 is to rewrite the fraction in the following format:

$$\frac{54}{63} = 54 : 63$$

Step 2 is to simplify, if possible. To do this, write out each number as a product of its primes and find the greatest common divisor (GCD).

$$54 = 9 \times 6 \qquad\qquad 63 = 9 \times 7$$
$$\quad = 3 \times 3 \times 3 \times 2 \qquad\quad = 3 \times 3 \times 7$$

The GCD is 9.

Next, divide each number by the GCD.

$$\frac{54}{9} = 6 \qquad \frac{63}{9} = 7$$

Step 3 is to rewrite the ratio.

6:7

The correct answer is 6:7.

PROBLEM

Express the following fraction as a ratio: $\frac{8}{5}$.

SOLUTION

Step 1 is to rewrite the fraction in the following format:

$$\frac{8}{5} = 8:5$$

Step 2 is to simplify, if possible. To do this, write out each number as a product of its primes and find the greatest common divisor (GCD).

$$8 = 4 \times 2 \qquad 5 = 5 \times 1$$
$$= 2 \times 2 \times 2$$

Since there is no GCD, the ratio is already reduced to its lowest terms.

Step 3 is to rewrite the ratio.

8:5

The correct answer is 8:5.

PROBLEM

Express the following ratio as a fraction:

60:12.

SOLUTION

Step 1 is to determine the numerator and denominator.

The left side of the ratio becomes the numerator: 60.

The right side of the ratio becomes the denominator: 12.

Step 2 is to rewrite the ratio as a fraction.

$$60:12 = \frac{60}{12}$$

Step 3 is to simplify, if possible. To do this, write out each number as a product of its primes and find the greatest common divisor (GCD).

$$60 = 6 \times 10 \qquad\qquad 12 = 6 \times 2$$
$$= 6 \times 5 \times 2 \qquad\qquad = 3 \times 2 \times 2$$
$$= 3 \times 2 \times 5 \times 2$$

The GCD is 12.

Next, divide each number by the GCD.

$$\frac{60}{12} = 5 \qquad \frac{12}{12} = 1$$

Step 4 is to rewrite the fraction.

$$\frac{5}{1}$$

The correct answer is $\frac{5}{1}$.

PROBLEM

Express the following ratio as a fraction:

11:33.

SOLUTION

Step 1 is to determine the numerator and denominator.

The left side of the ratio becomes the numerator: 11.

The right side of the ratio becomes the denominator: 33.

Step 2 is to rewrite the ratio as a fraction.

$$11:33 = \frac{11}{33}$$

Step 3 is to simplify, if possible. To do this, write out each number as a product of its primes and find the greatest common divisor (GCD).

$$11 = 11 \times 1 \qquad 33 = 11 \times 3$$

The GCD is 11.

Next, divide each number by the GCD.

$$\frac{11}{11} = 1 \qquad \frac{33}{11} = 3$$

Step 4 is to rewrite the fraction.

$$\frac{1}{3}$$

The correct answer is $\frac{1}{3}$.

PROBLEM

Find the solution to the proportion below.
$$\frac{3}{7} = \frac{?}{21}$$

SOLUTION

Step 1 is to put the proportion $\frac{A}{B} = \frac{C}{D}$ in the following format, $AD = BC$:

$$3(21) = 7C$$

Step 2 is to rewrite the proportion.

$$63 = 7C$$

Step 3 is to find the missing integer that solves the proportion. To do this, divide both sides by 7, the coefficient of C.

$$\frac{63}{7} = \frac{7C}{7}$$

Step 4 is to rewrite the proportion.

$$9 = C$$

The solution is 9.

CHECK

Write the original problem

$$\frac{3}{7} = \frac{?}{21}$$

Substituting 9 for ?,

$$\frac{3}{7} = \frac{9}{21}$$

Next, put the proportion in the following format

$$AD = BC \qquad 3(21) = 9(7)$$

Solve both sides of the proportion.

$$3(21) = 63 \qquad 9(7) = 63$$

Solution "9" checks out correctly.

PROBLEM

Find the solution to the proportion below.
$$\frac{?}{45} = -\frac{2}{5}$$

SOLUTION

Step 1 is to put the proportion $\frac{A}{B} = \frac{C}{D}$ in the following format, $AD = BC$:

$$A(5) = -2(45)$$

Step 2 is to solve the right side of the proportion.

$$-2(45) = -90$$

Step 3 is to rewrite the proportion.

$$A(5) = -90$$

Step 4 is to find the missing integer that solves the proportion. To do this, divide both sides by 5, the coefficient of A.

$$\frac{?(5)}{5} = ? \qquad -\frac{90}{5} = -18$$

Step 5 is to rewrite the proportion.

$$? = -18$$

The solution is −18.

CHECK

$$\frac{?}{45} = -\frac{2}{5}$$

Substituting −18 for ?,

$$-\frac{18}{45} = -\frac{2}{5}$$

Next, put the proportion in the following format.

$$AD = BC \qquad -18(5) = -2(45)$$

Solve both sides of the proportion.

$$-18(5) = -90 \qquad -2(45) = -90$$

Solution "−18" checks out correctly.

PROBLEM

A chemist is preparing a chemical solution. She needs to add 3 parts sodium and 2 parts zinc to a flask of chlorine. If she has already placed 300 grams of sodium into the flask, how much zinc must she now add?

SOLUTION

Step 1 is to determine the ratio of sodium and zinc.

3 parts sodium, 2 parts zinc = 3:2

Step 2 is to write the problem as a proportion.

$$\frac{3}{2} = \frac{300}{?}$$

Step 3 is to put the proportion in the following format:

$$AD = BC \qquad 3(?) = 2(300)$$

Step 4 is to solve the right side of the proportion.

$$2(300) = 600$$

Step 5 is to rewrite the proportion.

$$3(?) = 600$$

Step 6 is to find the missing integer that solves the proportion. To do this, divide both sides by the known extreme, 3.

$$\frac{3(?)}{3} = ? \qquad \frac{600}{3} = 200$$

Step 7 is to rewrite the proportion.

$$? = 200$$

The solution is 200 grams of zinc.

PROBLEM

An automobile dealer has to sell 3.5 cars for every 1 truck to achieve the optimum profit. This year, it is estimated that 3,500 cars will be sold. How many trucks must he sell to achieve the optimum profit?

SOLUTION

Step 1 is to determine the ratio of cars to trucks.

3.5 cars:1 truck = 3.5:1

Make both sides of the ratio an integer. To do this, multiply both sides of the ratio by 2.

2(3.5):2(1) = 7:2

Step 2 is to write the problem as a proportion.

$$\frac{7}{2} = \frac{3,500}{?}$$

Step 3 is to put the proportion in the following format:

$AD = BC$ $7(?) = 2(3,500)$

Step 4 is to solve the right side of the proportion.

2(3,500) = 7,000

Step 5 is to rewrite the proportion.

7(?) = 7,000

Step 6 is to find the missing integer that solves the proportion. To do this, divide both sides by the known extreme, 7.

$$\frac{7(?)}{7} = ? \qquad \frac{7,000}{7} = 1,000$$

Step 7 is to rewrite the proportion.

? = 1,000

The solution is 1,000 trucks.

PROBLEM

Centralville's town council voted on a bill that would increase taxes. To pass the bill, 75% of the council has to vote for the bill. If all 56 council members voted, how many members would it take to pass the bill? If 30 members voted to pass the bill, will taxes be increased?

SOLUTION

Step 1 is to determine the ratio. Remember that fractions can also express ratios.

$$75\% = \frac{75}{100}$$

$$\frac{75}{100} = \frac{3}{4}$$

Step 2 is to write the problem as a proportion.

$$\frac{3}{4} = \frac{?}{56}$$

Step 3 is to put the proportion in the following format:

$$AD = BC \qquad 3(56) = 4(?)$$

Step 4 is to solve the left side of the proportion.

$$3(56) = 168$$

Step 5 is to rewrite the proportion.

$$168 = 4(?)$$

Step 6 is to find the missing integer that solves the proportion. To do this, divide both sides by the known mean, 4.

$$\frac{4(?)}{4} = ? \qquad \frac{168}{4} = 42$$

Step 7 is to rewrite the proportion.

$$? = 42$$

The solution is that 42 votes are needed to pass the bill.

Step 8 is to determine if taxes will be increased.

$$30 < 42$$

Since only 30 council members voted for the bill, taxes will not be increased.

PROBLEM

A baker is making a new recipe for chocolate chip cookies. He decides that for every 6 cups of flour, he needs to add 1 cup of sugar. He puts 30 cups of flour and 2 cups of sugar into the batter. How much more sugar does he need?

SOLUTION

Step 1 is to determine the ratio of flour to sugar.

6 cups flour, 1 cup sugar = 6:1

Step 2 is to write the problem as a proportion.

$$\frac{6}{1} = \frac{30}{?}$$

Step 3 is to put the proportion in the following format:

$$AD = BC \qquad 6(?) = 1(30)$$

Step 4 is to solve the right side of the proportion.

$$1(30) = 30$$

Step 5 is to rewrite the proportion.

$$6(?) = 30$$

Step 6 is to find the missing integer that solves the proportion. To do this, divide both sides by the known extreme, 6.

$$\frac{6(?)}{6} = ? \qquad \frac{30}{6} = 5$$

Step 7 is to rewrite the proportion.

$$? = 5$$

The solution is that 5 cups of sugar must be added to the batter.

Step 8 is to determine how many more cups of sugar are needed, since 2 cups have already been added.

$$5 - 2 = 3$$

The baker must still add 3 cups.

PROBLEM

Interest Rates

Stacey, a stockbroker, is developing a portfolio for her client. She chooses a stock that will earn her client 8% interest. If her client invests $25,000, how much interest will be earned?

SOLUTION

Step 1 is to determine the ratio of interest earned per dollar invested. Remember that fractions can also express ratios.

$$8\% = \frac{8}{100}$$

Step 2 is to divide both parts of the fraction by the GCD to simplify the expression.

$$8 = 2 \times 4 \qquad 100 = 10 \times 10$$
$$= 2 \times 2 \times 2 \qquad = 5 \times 2 \times 5 \times 2$$

The GCD is 4; divide both parts of he fraction by 4.

$$\frac{8}{4} = 2 \qquad \frac{100}{4} = 25$$

The new ratio is $\frac{2}{25}$.

Step 3 is to write the problem as a proportion.

$$\frac{2}{25} = \frac{?}{25,000}$$

Step 4 is to put the proportion in the following format:

$$AD = BC \qquad 2(25,000) = ?(25)$$

Step 5 is to solve the left side of the proportion.

$$2(25,000) = 50,000$$

Step 6 is to rewrite the proportion.

$$50,000 = ?(25)$$

Step 7 is to find the missing integer that solves the proportion. To do this, divide both sides by the known mean, 25.

$$\frac{50,000}{25} = 2,000 \qquad \frac{?(25)}{25} = ?$$

Step 8 is to rewrite the proportion.

$$2,000 = ?$$

The solution is that $2,000 of interest will be earned.

PROBLEM

> Marina grew 4 inches during the last 10 months. If Michael grew at a proportional rate to Marina, how long did it take him to grow 1 inch?

SOLUTION

Step 1 is to determine the ratio of inches grown to months for Marina.

4 inches per 10 months = 4:10

Step 2 is to write the problem as a proportion, using the same rate for Michael to grow 1 inch.

$$\frac{4}{10} = \frac{1}{?}$$

Step 3 is to put the proportion in the following format:

$$AD = BC \qquad 4(?) = 1(10)$$

Step 4 is to solve the right side of the proportion.

$$1(10) = 10$$

Step 5 is to rewrite the proportion.

$$4(?) = 10$$

Step 6 is to find the missing integer that solves the proportion. To do this, divide both sides by the known extreme, 4.

$$\frac{4(?)}{4} = ? \qquad \frac{10}{4} = \frac{5}{2}$$

Step 7 is to rewrite the proportion.

$$? = \frac{5}{2}$$

Step 8 is to convert 5/2 to a mixed number.

$$\frac{5}{2} = 2\frac{1}{2}$$

The correct answer is $2\frac{1}{2}$ months.

PROBLEM

Mr. Miller owns a Christmas tree farm. Every year he plants 270 seedlings. During the summer, for every 9 seedlings he plants, 1 dies. How many seedlings survive after the summer?

SOLUTION

Step 1 is to determine the ratio of seedlings that live to those that die.

9 seedlings live, 1 seedling dies = 9:1

Step 2 is to write the problem as a proportion.

$$\frac{9}{1} = \frac{270}{?}$$

Step 3 is to put the proportion in the following format:

$AD = BC$ $9(?) = 1(270)$

Step 4 is to solve the right side of the proportion.

$1(270) = 270$

Step 5 is to rewrite the proportion.

$9(?) = 270$

Step 6 is to find the missing integer that solves the proportion. To do this, divide both sides by the known extreme, 9.

$$\frac{9(?)}{9} = ?   \frac{270}{9} = 30$$

Step 7 is to rewrite the proportion.

$? = 30$

So 30 seedlings die.

Step 8 is to determine the number of seedlings that survive after the summer.

total seedlings − seedlings that die = surviving seedlings

$270 - 30 = 240$

The correct answer is that 240 seedlings survive after the summer.

PROBLEM

Elena works as a traveling salesperson for Knives Incorporated. Each year, she increases the number of customers proportionally (5:1). If in her first year she started with 100 customers, how many does she have by the end of the second year?

SOLUTION

Step 1 is to write the problem as a proportion.

$$\frac{5}{1} = \frac{?}{100}$$

Step 2 is to put the proportion in the following format:

$AD = BC$ $5(100) = 1(?)$

Step 3 is to solve the left side of the proportion.

$5(100) = 500$

Step 4 is to rewrite the proportion.

$500 = 1(?)$, or Elena adds 500 new customers in the first year.

Step 5 is to add the number of new customers to the original number of customers.

$100 + 500 = 600$

Therefore, after her first year, Elena has 600 customers. Repeat the above steps for the second year.

Step 6 is to rewrite the problem as a proportion.

$$\frac{5}{1} = \frac{?}{600}$$

Step 7 is to put the proportion in the following format:

$AD = BC$ $5(600) = 1(?)$

Step 8 is to solve the left side of the proportion.

$5(600) = 3,000$

Step 9 is to rewrite the proportion.

$3,000 = ?(1)$

Step 10 is to find the missing integer that solves the proportion. To do this, divide both sides by the known mean, 1.

$$\frac{3,000}{1} = 3,000 \qquad \frac{?(1)}{1} = ?$$

Step 11 is to rewrite the proportion.

3,000 = ?, or Elena adds 3,000 new customers the second year.

Step 12 is to add the number of new customers to the number of customers acquired during the first year.

$$600 + 3,000 = 3,600$$

The correct answer is 3,600 customers.

Coordinate Geometry, Plotting, and Graphing

The rectangular coordinate system, having vertical and horizontal lines meeting each other at right angles and thus forming a rectangular grid, is often called the Cartesian coordinate system. It is named after the French philosopher and mathematician, René Descartes, who invented it. The vertical line is usually labeled with the capital letter y and called the y-axis. The horizontal line is usually labeled with the capital letter x and called the x-axis. The point where the x- and y-axes intersect is called the **origin**.

Above the origin, numbers measured along or parallel to the y-axis are positive; below the origin they are negative. To the right of the origin, numbers measured along or parallel to the x-axis are positive; to the left they are negative.

A point anywhere on the graph may be located by two numbers (x, y), one showing the distance of the point from the y-axis, and the other showing the distance of the point from the x-axis. We call the numbers that indicate the position of a point **coordinates**.

PROBLEM

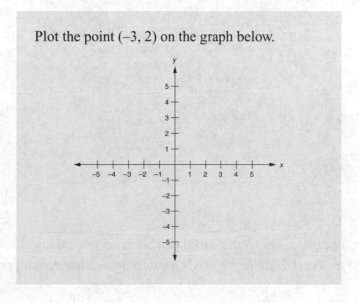

Plot the point (−3, 2) on the graph below.

SOLUTION

Step 1 is to find the point -3 along the x-axis. Draw a dashed vertical line through that point.

Step 2 is to find the point 2 along the y-axis. Draw a dashed horizontal line through that point.

Step 3 is to plot the point where the two dashed lines intersect with a solid circle. This is the point $(-3, 2)$.

The solution is the point shown in the following figure:

PROBLEM

Plot the points $(x_1, y_1) = (1, 2)$ and $(x_2, y_2) = (-4, -5)$ on the graph below. Draw a line connecting the points.

SOLUTION

Step 1 is to find the point 1 along the x-axis. Draw a dashed vertical line through that point.

Step 2 is to find the point 2 along the y-axis. Draw a dashed horizontal line through that point.

Step 3 is to plot the point where the two dashed lines intersect with a solid circle. This is the point (1, 2), shown in the figure below.

Step 4 is to find the point –4 along the *x*-axis. Draw a dashed vertical line through that point.

Step 5 is to find the point –5 along the *y*-axis. Draw a dashed horizontal line through that point.

Step 6 is to plot the point where the two dashed lines intersect with a solid circle. This is the point (–4, –5), shown in the figure below.

Step 7 is to draw a straight line connecting the two points, as shown in the figure below.

Given a line containing points (x_1, y_1) and (x_2, y_2)

- The slope of a line measures how much the *y*-value changes for every increase in the *x*-axis. It is calculated by:

$$\text{slope} = \frac{y_2 - y_1}{x_2 - x_1}$$

Note that the slopes of parallel lines will be the same. The slopes of perpendicular lines are negative reciprocals of each other.
The equation for any straight line can be written in the form

$$y = mx + b$$

where *m* is the slope and *b* is the y-intercept of the line. This is called the slope-intercept form of the equation.

- The distance between two points on a line is given by:

$$\sqrt{(x_2 - x_1)^2 + (y_2 - y_1)^2}$$

- The midpoint between two points on a line is given by:

$$\left(\frac{x_1 + x_2}{2}, \frac{y_1 + y_2}{2} \right)$$

Graphs of Functions

• **EXAMPLE**

The equation $y = 2x + 3$ is the equation of a line with a slope equal to 2. This means that for every one-unit change in x, the y measurement goes up 2 units. The number 3 in this equation is called the y-intercept. The y-intercept is the point where the line crosses the y-axis. The y-intercept is the value of y when x equals 0.

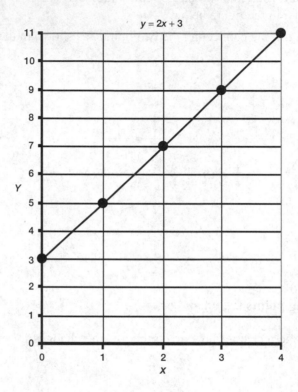

PROBLEM

Examine the figure below for this problem. What is Point A? Does Line a pass through Point A? Where does Line a intercept the x-axis?

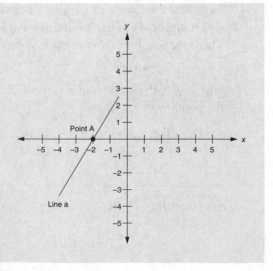

SOLUTION

Point A is the point (–2, 0). The graph illustrates that the coordinates for Point A are (–2, 0).

Line a does pass through Point A. This can be seen by looking at the graph. Since Line a passes through the point (–2, 0), it must pass through Point A.

Use the graph to see where the line crosses the x-axis. This will be where Line a intercepts the x-axis, which is at the point (–2, 0). The y-coordinate will always be 0 when a line intercepts the x-axis.

PROBLEM

A line contains the points (–6, 3) and (–3, 6). What is the slope of the line?

SOLUTION

Step 1 is to use the coordinates in the formula for the slope of a line. The formula is

$$\frac{(y_2 - y_1)}{(x_2 - x_1)}.$$

$$\text{slope} = \frac{6 - 3}{-3 - (-6)}$$

Step 2 is to solve the formula to obtain the slope.

$$\text{slope} = \frac{6 - 3}{-3 + 6} = \frac{3}{3} = 1$$

The slope of the line is 1.

PROBLEM

Line a contains the points (–1, 4) and (4, 6). Line b contains the points (5, 2) and (–3, –3). Are the two lines parallel?

SOLUTION

Step 1 is to calculate the slope for Line a. The formula for the slope of a line is

$$\frac{(y_2 - y_1)}{(x_2 - x_1)}.$$

$$\frac{6-4}{4-(-1)}=\frac{2}{5}$$

Step 2 is to calculate the slope for Line b. The formula for the slope of a line is $\frac{(y_2-y_1)}{(x_2-x_1)}$.

$$\frac{-3-2}{-3-5}=\frac{-5}{-8}=\frac{5}{8}$$

Parallel lines have the same slope. Since the slope of Line a does not equal the slope of Line b, the lines cannot be parallel.

PROBLEM

Line a contains the points (–2, –2) and (6, 4). Line b contains the points (0, 4) and (3, 0). Are the two lines perpendicular?

SOLUTION

Step 1 is to calculate the slope for Line a. The formula for the slope of a line is $\frac{(y_2-y_1)}{(x_2-x_1)}$.

$$\frac{4-(-2)}{6-(-2)}=\frac{4+2}{6+2}=\frac{6}{8}=\frac{3}{4}$$

Step 2 is to calculate the slope for Line b. The formula for the slope of a line is $\frac{(y_2-y_1)}{(x_2-x_1)}$.

$$\frac{0-4}{3-0}=-\frac{4}{3}$$

Two lines are perpendicular if the slope of one line (m) equals the negative reciprocal of the other $\left(\frac{-1}{m}\right)$. Since the slope of Line a is $\frac{3}{4}$ and the slope of Line b is $\frac{-4}{3}$, the lines are perpendicular.

PROBLEM

Use the graph below to calculate the slope of Line a.

SOLUTION

Step 1 is to find two points that are intersected by Line a.

$(-4, 1)$ and $(-1, -3)$

Step 2 is to use the formula for the slope of a line to calculate the slope of Line a. The formula is $\dfrac{(y_2 - y_1)}{(x_2 - x_1)}$.

$$\text{slope} = \frac{-3 - 1}{-1 - (-4)}$$

Step 3 is to solve the formula to obtain the slope.

$$\text{slope} = \frac{-3 - 1}{-1 - (-4)} = \frac{-4}{3}$$

The slope of the line is $-\dfrac{4}{3}$.

PROBLEM

Put the following equation in slope–intercept form.

$$y + 2x = 12$$

SOLUTION

Step 1 is to isolate the variable y. To do this, subtract $2x$ from both sides of the equation.

$$y + 2x - 2x = 12 - 2x$$

Step 2 is to simplify the left side of the equation.

$$y + 2x - 2x = y$$

Step 3 is to simplify the right side of the equation.

$$12 - 2x = 12 - 2x$$

Step 4 is to rewrite the equation.

$$y = 12 - 2x$$

Step 5 is to rewrite the equation to be in the form $y = mx + b$, where m is the slope and b is the y-intercept.

$$y = -2x + 12$$

The correct answer is $y = -2x + 12$.

PROBLEM

Find the slope of the following equation.

$$\frac{1}{2}y - \frac{1}{4}x - 4 = 0$$

SOLUTION

Step 1 is to first isolate the term $\frac{1}{2}y$ by subtracting $\left(-\frac{1}{4}x - 4\right)$ from each side (remember that substracting a negative makes it a positive):

$$\frac{1}{2}y - \frac{1}{4}x - 4 = 0$$

$$\frac{1}{2}y = \frac{1}{4}x + 4$$

Step 2 is to multiply both sides of the equation by 2. This will isolate the variable y and put the equation in slope–intercept form.

$$y = \frac{1}{2}x + 8$$

Step 3 is to find the slope of the line. The coefficient of x is the slope.

$$m = \frac{1}{2}$$

The correct answer is $m = \frac{1}{2}$.

PROBLEM

Graph the equation $\frac{1}{2}y = x - 1$.

SOLUTION

Step 1 is to put the equation in slope–intercept form by multiplying both sides by 2.

$$\frac{1}{2}y = x - 1$$

$$y = 2x - 2$$

Step 2 is to choose two arbitrary values of x. Log the values in a chart. Use the values of x to obtain values for y.

x	y
0	−2
3	4

Step 3 is to use the x and y values to plot points. Note that there are many different possible points. However, the graph should look the same.

$(0, -2)$ and $(3, 4)$

Step 4 is to use the points to graph the line.

PROBLEM

Graph the equation $\dfrac{1}{4}y = \dfrac{1}{2}x - 1$.

SOLUTION

Step 1 is to put the equation in slope–intercept form.

$$\frac{1}{4}y = \frac{1}{2}x - 1$$

$$y = 2x - 4$$

Step 2 is to choose two arbitrary values of x. Log the values in a chart. Use the values of x to obtain values for y.

x	y
0	−4
2	0

Step 3 is to use the x and y values to plot points. Note that there are many different possible points. However, the graph should look the same.

$$(0, -4) \text{ and } (2, 0)$$

Step 4 is to use the points to graph the line.

Drill: Coordinate Geometry

1.   Which point shown has the coordinates (−3, 2)?

   (A) A   (B) B   (C) C

   (D) D   (E) E

2.   Name the coordinates of point A.

   (A) (4, 3)   (B) (3, −4)   (C) (3, 4)

   (D) (−4, 3)   (E) (4, −3)

3.   Which point shown has the coordinates (2.5, −1)?

   (A) M   (B) N   (C) P

   (D) Q   (E) R

4.   The correct *x*-coordinate for point *H* is what number?

   (A) 3   (B) 4   (C) −3

   (D) −4   (E) −5

5. The correct *y*-coordinate for point *R* is what number?

    (A) −7   (B) 2   (C) −2

    (D) 7   (E) 8

6. Find the distance between (4, −7) and (−2, −7).

    (A) 4   (B) 6   (C) 7   (D) 14   (E) 15

7. Find the distance between (3, 8) and (5, 11).

    (A) 2   (B) 3   (C) $\sqrt{13}$ (D) $\sqrt{15}$ (E) $3\sqrt{3}$

8. How far from the origin is the point (3, 4)?

    (A) 3   (B) 4   (C) 5   (D) $5\sqrt{3}$ (E) $4\sqrt{5}$

9. Find the distance between the point (−4, 2) and (3, −5).

    (A) 3   (B) $3\sqrt{3}$ (C) 7   (D) $7\sqrt{2}$ (E) $7\sqrt{3}$

10. The distance between points *A* and *B* is 10 units. If *A* has coordinates (4, −6) and *B* has coordinates (−2, *y*), determine the value of *y*.

    (A) −6   (B) −2   (C) 0   (D) 1   (E) 2

11. Find the midpoint between the points (−2, 6) and (4, 8).

    (A) (3, 7)   (B) (1, 7)   (C) (3, 1)   (D) (1, 1)   (E) (−3, 7)

12. Find the coordinates of the midpoint between the points (−5, 7) and (3, −1).

    (A) (−4, 4)   (B) (3, −1)   (C) (1, −3)   (D) (−1, 3)   (E) (4, −4).

13. What is the *y*-coordinate of the midpoint of segment $\overline{AB}$ if *A* has coordinates (−3, 7) and *B* has coordinates (−3, −2)?

    (A) 5/2   (B) 3   (C) 7/2   (D) 5   (E) 15/2

14. One endpoint of a line segment is (5, −3). The midpoint is (−1, 6). What is the other endpoint?

    (A) (7, 3)   (B) (2, 1.5)   (C) (−7, 15)   (D) (−2, 1.5)   (E) (−7, 12)

15. The point (–2, 6) is the midpoint for which of the following pair of points?

    (A)   (1, 4) and (–3, 8)   (B)   (–1, –3) and (5, 9)

    (C)   (1, 4) and (5, 9)   (D)   (–1, 4) and (3, –8)

    (E)   (1, 3) and (–5, 9)

Scaled Drawings

A scaled drawing is a drawing of an object that is proportional to the size of the actual object. Scaled drawings are based on a certain scale of conversion. If you know this scale, you can determine the measurements of the actual objects.

- **EXAMPLE**

The scaled drawing of a volleyball court shown below is drawn using the scale 1 centimeter is equal to 2 meters.

Calculate the area of this volleyball court in square meters.

In the scaled drawing, length is equal to 9 centimeters and width is equal to 4.5 centimeters. The scale is "1 centimeter is equal to 2 meters." So, the length is 18 meters and the width is 9 meters. To find area, multiply length times width: $18 \times 9 = 162$. The volleyball court is 162 square meters.

- **EXAMPLE**

1 inch equals 24 feet in the scaled drawing of a tennis court (shown below).

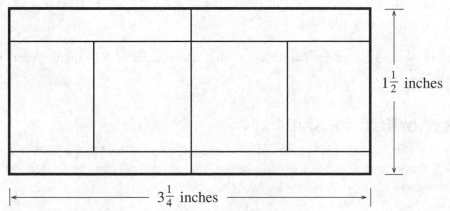

Calculate the length of this tennis court in feet.

In the scaled drawing, length is equal to $\frac{1}{3}$ inches (in decimal form, 3.25 inches). The scale is "1 inch equals 24 feet." In order to find the length in feet, multiply the number of inches times 24: $3.25 \times 24 = 78$ feet.

PROBLEM

In the scaled drawing of a soccer field below, 1 centimeter (cm) = 10 meters.

What is the area of the Penalty Box in square meters (not including the Goal Box)?

SOLUTION

First, calculate the large area that includes both the Penalty Box and the Goal Box. 4 cm represents 40 meters, and 2 cm represents 20 meters. $40 \times 20 = 800$ square meters.

Second, calculate the area of the Goal Box. 2 centimeters represents 20 meters, and 1 cm represents 10 meters. $20 \times 10 = 200$ square meters.

Finally, to find the area of Penalty Box alone, subtract the smaller area from the larger area. $800 - 200 = 600$ square meters.

Spatial Sense/Relationships

In representing a three-dimensional object we make use of a method that is universally understood. This method is a standardized technique, often referred to as orthographic projection, which represents an object in a series of views projected onto planes.

Figure 1 shows the relationships among the three principal planes that define and/or represent the object. The method shown allows three-dimensional objects to be represented by two-dimensional views.

Fig. 1 — The Principal Projection Planes.

PROBLEM

Given Fig. 2, draw the front, top, and right side views of the object.

Fig. 2

SOLUTION

Front View   **Top View**   **Side View**

PROBLEM

From the drawing given in Fig. 3, draw the front, top, and right side views.

Fig. 3

SOLUTION

Front View

Top View

Side View

PROBLEM

Given the numbered drawing shown in Fig. 4, draw and number the corners of the top, front, and right side views of the object.

Fig. 4

SOLUTION

In order to draw the different views asked for in the problem, first determine which planes are horizontal and which planes are vertical (refer to Fig. 4). For example, planes 1-2-15-12-13-14 and 7-8-9-10 are horizontal planes, whereas planes 6-7-10-13-12-11 and 4-1-14-9-8-5 are vertical. Keep in mind that a vertical plane will appear as a line in the top view while a horizontal plane will appear as a line in the front and side views. To draw the top view, for example, first draw the horizontal plane 1-2-15-12-13-14. The horizontal plane 7-8-9-10 lies directly below it. This means that lines 8-9 and 9-10 of the lower plane appear to be on the same lines as lines 1-14 and 14-13 as seen from the top. Therefore, plane 7-8-9-10 can be drawn by using lines 1-14 and 14-13 as references. The same type of analysis can be made for both the front and right side views. Notice that this problem would be made more complicated had inclined planes been included in the given drawing. Had this been the case, the lines representing the inclined planes would have to be located by using horizontal and vertical planes for reference.

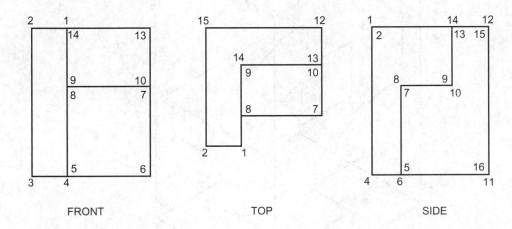

FRONT   TOP   SIDE

PROBLEM

Draw the front, top, and right views of the object represented in Fig. 5. Use the "Glass Box" method.

Fig. 5

SOLUTION

The "Glass Box" method of drawing the projections of an object makes use of an imaginary box that surrounds the given object. The box is placed so that the faces of the "glass box" are parallel to the principal sides of the given object. When the "glass box" has been properly placed, each of the faces of the object is projected perpendicularly to the corresponding face of the "glass box." Figure 6 shows what the "glass box" looks like after all the sides of the object have been projected. Figure 7 shows the three required views.

Fig. 6

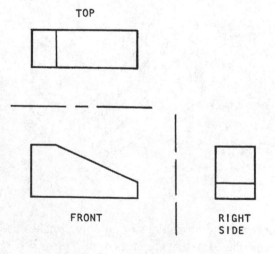

Fig. 7

Drill: Spatial Sense/Relationships

1. Fig. 8 is a top view of a combination of stacked cubes. Numbers in the squares correspond to the number of cubes in the stacks below the top plane. Which one of the configurations—A, B, C, or D—corresponds to the top view? (The designation "Front" merely shows which side of each figure is considered the front side; you are looking for a top view.)

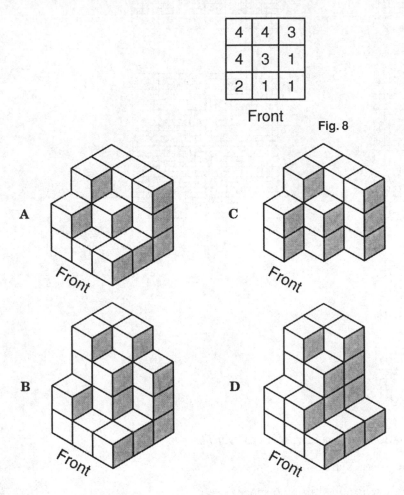

4	4	3
4	3	1
2	1	1

Front

Fig. 8

A   C

B   D

2. The triangle in Fig. 9 is reflected across the y-axis. Which one of the configurations, A to E, is the result?

Fig. 9

A.

D.

B.

E.

C.

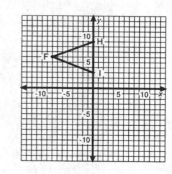

3.   In Fig. 10, which transformation will map ΔABC onto ΔDEF?

A.   Reflect ΔABC over the y-axis and shift up 6 spaces.

B.   Reflect ΔABC over the x-axis and shift up 6 spaces.

C.   Reflect ΔABC over the y-axis and shift down 6 spaces.

D.   Reflect ΔABC over the y-axis, reflect over the x-axis, and shift down 4 spaces.

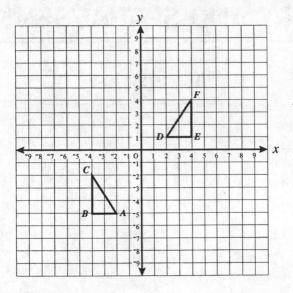

Fig. 10

4. Fig. 11 is constructed from cube blocks. Which drawing—A, B, C, or D—represents the top view of the structure? (The designation "Front" merely shows which side of each figure is considered the front side; you are looking for a top view.)

Fig. 11

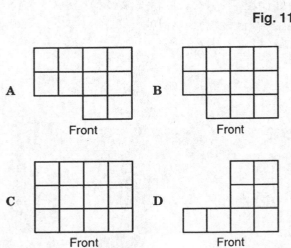

A
Front

B
Front

C
Front

D
Front

GEOMETRY AND SPATIAL SENSE DRILLS

ANSWER KEY

Drill: Lines and Angles

1. (B)	4. (D)	7. (B)	10. (E)	13. (B)
2. (A)	5. (D)	8. (A)	11. (C)	14. (E)
3. (C)	6. (C)	9. (D)	12. (D)	15. (A)

Drill: Triangles

1. (D)	4. (E)	7. (B)	10. (C)	13. (D)
2. (B)	5. (C)	8. (E)	11. (C)	14. (A)
3. (C)	6. (A)	9. (A)	12. (B)	15. (B)

Drill: Regular Polygons

1. (D)	3. (E)	5. (E)	7. (E)	9. (D)
2. (B)	4. (A)	6. (C)	8. (B)	10. (B)

Drill: Quadrilaterals

1. (A)	5. (C)	9. (B)	13. (B)	17. (B)
2. (B)	6. (A)	10. (C)	14. (C)	18. (C)
3. (D)	7. (D)	11. (C)	15. (B)	19. (D)
4. (E)	8. (C)	12. (D)	16. (A)	

Drill: Circles

1. (B)	5. (C)	9. (E)	13. (C)	17. (B)
2. (A)	6. (D)	10. (D)	14. (B)	18. (D)
3. (D)	7. (C)	11. (B)	15. (A)	19. (A)
4. (E)	8. (B)	12. (D)	16. (C)	20. (C)

Drill: Solids

1. (D)
2. (B)
3. (C)

Drill: Coordinate Geometry

1. (C)	4. (D)	7. (C)	10. (E)	13. (A)
2. (E)	5. (A)	8. (C)	11. (B)	14. (C)
3. (B)	6. (B)	9. (D)	12. (D)	15. (E)

Drill: Spatial Sense/Relationships

1. (B)	3. (A)
2. (D)	4. (B)

Competency 4: Knowledge of Algebraic Thinking

Analyze and Generalize Patterns

In algebra, letters or variables are used to represent numbers. A **variable** is defined as a placeholder, which can take on any of several values at a given time. A **constant**, on the other hand, is a symbol that takes on only one value at a given time. A **term** is a constant, a variable, or a combination of constants and variables. For example: 7.76, $3x$, xyz, $5 \,{}^z/_x$, and $(0.99)x^2$ are all terms. If a term is a combination of constants and variables, the constant part of the term is referred to as the **coefficient** of the variable. If a variable is written without a coefficient, the coefficient is assumed to be 1.

- **EXAMPLES**

$3x^2$	y^3
coefficient: 3	coefficient: 1
variable: x	variable: y

An **expression** is a collection of one or more terms. If the number of terms is greater than 1, the expression is said to be the sum of the terms.

- **EXAMPLES**

$$9, 9xy, 6x + \frac{x}{3}, 8yz - 2x$$

An algebraic expression consisting of only one term is called a **monomial**; of two terms is called a **binomial**; of three terms is called a **trinomial**. In general, an algebraic expression consisting of two or more terms is called a **polynomial**.

Laws for Working with Polynomials

Commutative Laws

The commutative law states that the sum or product of two or more terms or factors is the same regardless of the order in which they are arranged.

Addition

The algebraic form of the commutative law for addition is as follows:

$$a + b + c = a + c + b = c + b + a$$

Multiplication

The algebraic form of the commutative law for multiplication is as follows:

$$abc = acb = cba$$

Associative Laws

The associative laws of addition and multiplication refer to the grouping (association) of terms and factors in a mathematical expression.

Addition

The algebraic form of the associative law for addition is as follows:

$$a + b + c = (a + b) + c = a + (b + c)$$

The sum of three or more addends is the same regardless of the manner in which the addends are grouped.

Multiplication

The algebraic form of the associative law for multiplication is as follows:

$$a \times b \times c = (a \times b) \times c = a \times (b \times c)$$

The product of three or more factors is the same regardless of the manner in which the factors are grouped.

Distributive Law

The distributive law refers to the distribution of factors among the terms of an additive expression. The algebraic form of this law is as follows:

$$a(b + c + d) = ab + ac + ad$$

If the sum of two or more quantities is multiplied by a third quantity, the product is found by applying the multiplier to each of the original quantities separately and summing the resulting expressions.

PROBLEM

Which of the following statements illustrates the Commutative Property of Addition?

a) $12 + 24 = 12 + x$ c) $10x + 12y = 12y + 10x$

b) $69 + 3x = 3(x - 23)$ d) $2(2 + 3) = 10$

SOLUTION

The correct answer is statement c. Statement c correctly illustrates the Commutative Property of Addition. This property states that order is not relevant when performing addition. In statement c,

$10x + 12y = 12y + 10x$, both sides of the equation will be equal, showing that order is not relevant in addition. Statements a, b, and d do not illustrate the Commutative Property of Addition.

PROBLEM

Using the Commutative Property of Addition, fill in the missing part of the equation below.

$$78 + (95 - 2) = ?$$

SOLUTION

The Commutative Property of Addition states that order is not relevant in addition. The format for this property is shown below.

$$A + B = B + A$$

Step 1 is to determine what terms represent A and B in the given equation.

A represents 78

B represents $(95 - 2)$

Step 2 is to rewrite the missing part of the given equation using the values for A and B.

$$78 + (95 - 2) = (95 - 2) + 78$$

The correct answer is $78 + (95 - 2) = (95 - 2) + 78$.

PROBLEM

Which of the following statements illustrates the Commutative Property of Multiplication?

a) $xy = x + y$

c) $35(2) = \dfrac{70}{1}$

b) $2x(-45y) = -45y(2x)$

d) $52 = 25$

SOLUTION

The correct answer is statement b. Statement b correctly illustrates the Commutative Property of Multiplication. This property states that order is not relevant when performing multiplication. In statement b, $2x(-45y) = -45y(2x)$, both sides of the equation will be equal, showing that order is not relevant in multiplication. Statements a, c, and d do not illustrate the Commutative Property of Multiplication.

PROBLEM

Using the Commutative Property of Multiplication, fill in the missing part of the equation below.

$$8\left(\frac{10}{12}\right) = ?$$

SOLUTION

The Commutative Property of Multiplication states that order is not relevant in multiplication. The format for this property is shown below.

$$A(B) = B(A)$$

Step 1 is to determine what terms represent A and B in the given equation.

A represents 8

B represents $\left(\dfrac{10}{12}\right)$

Step 2 is to rewrite the missing part of the given equation using the values for A and B.

$$8\left(\frac{10}{12}\right) = \left(\frac{10}{12}\right)8$$

The correct answer is $8\left(\dfrac{10}{12}\right) = \left(\dfrac{10}{12}\right)8$.

PROBLEM

Which of the following statements illustrates the Associative Property of Addition?

a) $(8x + 2) + 5y = 8x + (2 + 5y)$

b) $85 + 2 = 85y + 2y$

c) $\left(\dfrac{165}{5}\right) + 4x = \dfrac{(165 + 4x)}{5}$

d) $(5x - 2) + 20 = 20 + 5x - 2$

SOLUTION

The correct answer is statement a. Statement a correctly illustrates the Associative Property of Addition. This property states that grouping of terms is not relevant when performing addition. In statement a,

$(8x + 2) + 5y = 8x + (2 + 5y)$, both sides of the equation will be equal, showing that grouping of terms is not relevant in addition. Statements b, c, and d do not illustrate the Associative Property of Addition.

PROBLEM

Using the Associative Property of Addition, fill in the missing part of the equation below.

$$(4x + 2y) + z = ?$$

SOLUTION

The Associative Property of Addition states that grouping is not relevant in addition. The format for this property is shown below. Notice that the order is the same, but the parentheses have changed position.

$$(A + B) + C = A + (B + C)$$

Step 1 is to determine what terms represent A, B, and C in the given equation.

A represents $4x$

B represents $2y$

C represents z

Step 2 is to rewrite the missing part of the given equation using the values for A, B, and C.

$$(4x + 2y) + z = 4x + (2y + z)$$

The correct answer is $(4x + 2y) + z = 4x + (2y + z)$.

PROBLEM

Which of the following statements illustrates the Associative Property of Multiplication?

a) $3(xy) = 3x + y$ c) $72y(3) - 25 = 8(9)y - 5(5)$

b) $100(xy) = (100x)y$ d) $10y = 5(2) + y$

SOLUTION

The correct answer is statement b. Statement b correctly illustrates the Associative Property of Multiplication. This property states that grouping of terms is not relevant when performing multiplication. In statement b, $100(xy) = (100x)y$, both sides of the equation will be equal, showing that grouping is not relevant in multiplication. Statements a, c, and d do not illustrate the Associative Property of Multiplication.

PROBLEM

Using the Associative Property of Multiplication, fill in the missing part of the equation below.

$$8(x \times 3y) = ?$$

SOLUTION

The Associative Property of Multiplication states that grouping is not relevant in multiplication. The format for this property is shown below. Notice that the order is the same, but the parentheses have changed position.

$$A(BC) = AB(C)$$

Step 1 is to determine what terms represent A, B, and C in the given equation.

    A represents 8

    B represents x

    C represents $3y$

Step 2 is to rewrite the missing part of the given equation using the values for A, B, and C.

$$8(x \times 3y) = (8x)3y$$

The correct answer is $8(x \times 3y) = (8x)3y$.

PROBLEM

Which of the following statements illustrates the Distributive Property?

a) $10(x - y) = 10x - 10y$ c) $\dfrac{5}{8x(8y)}(3) = \dfrac{5x}{y} + 3$

b) $3x + 11y = 3(x + 11y)$ d) $x(y)(z) = x + y + z$

SOLUTION

The correct answer is statement a. Statement a correctly illustrates the Distributive Property. This property states that multiplying (or distributing) terms in parentheses will not change the solution. In statement a, $10(x - y) = 10x - 10y$, both sides of the equation will be equal, showing that multiplying term-by-term will not change the solution. Statements b, c, and d do not illustrate the Distributive Property.

PROBLEM

> Use the Distributive Property to solve the following problem.
> $$-(9y - 5)$$

SOLUTION

The Distributive Property is shown in the format below.

$$A(B + C) = AB + AC$$

Step 1 is to determine what terms represent A, B, and C in the given equation.

A represents -1 (shown as "$-$")

B represents $9y$

C represents -5

Step 2 is to perform the multiplication operation.

$$AB = -(9y) = -9y$$
$$AC = -(-5) = 5$$

Step 3 is to rewrite the problem.

$$-(9y - 5) = -9y + 5$$

The answer is $-9y + 5$.

PROBLEM

> Use the Distributive Property to solve the following problem.
> $$x(y + 2x)$$

SOLUTION

The Distributive Property is shown in the format below.

$$A(B + C) = AB + AC$$

Step 1 is to determine what terms represent A, B, and C in the given equation.

A represents x

B represents y

C represents $2x$

Step 2 is to perform the multiplication operation.

$$AB = x(y) = xy$$
$$AC = x(2x) = 2x^2$$

Step 3 is to rewrite the problem.

$$x(y + 2x) = xy + 2x^2$$

The answer is $xy + 2x^2$.

PROBLEM

Simplify the following expression.

$$\frac{1}{2}x + \frac{3}{4}x + \frac{3}{2}x$$

SOLUTION

Step 1 is to group like terms. Since all the terms contain the variable x, all the terms in the expression are like terms. To make the problem easier, group the terms with the denominator "2" together.

$$\left(\frac{1}{2}x + \frac{3}{2}x\right) + \frac{3}{4}x$$

Step 2 is to perform the operation inside the parentheses.

$$\frac{1}{2}x + \frac{3}{2}x = \frac{4}{2}x = 2x$$

Step 3 is to rewrite the problem.

$$2x + \frac{3}{4}x$$

Step 4 is to perform the addition operation.

$$2x + \frac{3}{4}x = \frac{8}{4}x + \frac{3}{4}x = \frac{11}{4}x$$

The correct answer is $\frac{11}{4}x$.

PROBLEM

Simplify the following expression.

$$\frac{14y}{7} + 15 - 5y + 2$$

SOLUTION

Step 1 is to group like terms. Group the terms containing the variable y together. Group the constants together.

$$\left(\frac{14y}{7} - 5y\right) + (15 + 2)$$

Step 2 is to perform the operation inside the parentheses.

$$\left(\frac{14y}{7} - 5y\right) = 2y - 5y$$

$$2y - 5y = -3y$$

Step 3 is to rewrite the problem.

$$-3y + (15 + 2)$$

Step 4 is to perform the operation inside the parentheses.

$$15 + 2 = 17$$

Step 5 is to rewrite the problem.

$$-3y + 17$$

Since the remaining terms are not like terms, the problem cannot be simplified any further.

The correct answer is $-3y + 17$.

PROBLEM

Simplify the following expression.
$$3x^2 - 7 - 2x^2 + y$$

SOLUTION

Step 1 is to group like terms. Group the terms containing the variable x^2 together. Group the terms containing the variable y together. Group the constants together.

$$(3x^2 - 2x^2) + y - 7$$

Step 2 is to perform the operation inside the parentheses.

$$3x^2 - 2x^2 = x^2$$

Step 3 is to rewrite the problem.

$$x^2 + y - 7$$

Since the remaining terms are not like terms, the problem cannot be simplified any further.

The correct answer is $x^2 + y - 7$.

PROBLEM

> Simplify the following expression.
> $$3(2x^2 + 6x - 1) + 2(5x + 1) + 4x^2$$

SOLUTION

Step 1 is to use the Distributive Property to rewrite the terms in the problem.

$$3(2x^2 + 6x - 1) = 3(2x^2) + 3(6x) - 3(1)$$

$$2(5x + 1) = 2(5x) + 2(1)$$

Step 2 is to perform the operations for each term.

$$3(2x^2) + 3(6x) - 3(1) = 6x^2 + 18x - 3$$

$$2(5x) + 2(1) = 10x + 2$$

Step 3 is to rewrite the problem.

$$6x^2 + 18x - 3 + 10x + 2 + 4x^2$$

Step 4 is to group the like terms. Group the terms with the variable x^2 together. Group the terms with the variable x together. Group the constants together.

$$(6x^2 + 4x^2) + (18x + 10x) + (-3 + 2)$$

Step 5 is to perform the operations inside the parentheses.

$$6x^2 + 4x^2 = 10x^2$$

$$18x + 10x = 28x$$

$$-3 + 2 = -1$$

Step 6 is to rewrite the problem.

$$10x^2 + 28x - 1$$

Since the remaining terms are not like terms, the problem cannot be simplified any further.

The correct answer is $10x^2 + 28x - 5$.

Operations with Polynomials

A) Addition of polynomials is achieved by combining like terms, or terms that differ only in their numerical coefficients. For example,

$$P(x) = (x^2 - 3x + 5) + (4x^2 + 6x - 3)$$

Note that the parentheses are used to distinguish the two polynomials.

By using the commutative and associative laws, we can rewrite $P(x)$ as:

$$P(x) = (x^2 + 4x^2) + (6x - 3x) + (5 - 3)$$

This is called grouping like terms together.

Using the distributive law, $ab + ac = a(b + c)$, yields:

$$(1 + 4)x^2 + (6 - 3)x + (5 - 3)$$
$$= 5x^2 + 3x + 2$$

B) **Subtraction of two polynomials** is achieved by first changing the signs of all the terms in the expression that is being subtracted and then adding this result to the other expression. For example,

$$(5x^2 + 4y^2 + 3z^2) - (4xy + 7y^2 - 3z^2 + 1)$$
$$= 5x^2 + 4y^2 + 3z^2 - 4xy - 7y^2 + 3z^2 - 1$$
$$= 5x^2 + (4y^2 - 7y^2) + (3z^2 + 3z^2) - 4xy - 1$$
$$= 5x^2 + (-3y^2) + 6z^2 - 4xy - 1$$

C) **Multiplication of two or more polynomials** is achieved by using the laws of exponents, the rules of signs, and the commutative and associative laws of multiplication. Begin by multiplying the coefficients and then multiply the variables according to the laws of exponents. For example,

$$(y^2)\,(5)\,(6y^2)\,(yz)\,(2z^2)$$
$$= (1)\,(5)\,(6)\,(1)\,(2)\,(y^2)\,(y^2)\,(yz)\,(z^2)$$
$$= 60[(y^2)\,(y^2)\,(y)]\,[(z)\,(z^2)]$$
$$= 60(y^5)\,(z^3)$$
$$= 60y^5z^3$$

D) **Multiplication of a polynomial by a monomial** is achieved by multiplying each term of the polynomial by the monomial and combining the results. For example,

$$(4x^2 + 3y)\,(6xz^2)$$
$$= (4x^2)(6xz^2) + (3y)\,(6xz^2)$$
$$= 24x^3z^2 + 18xyz^2$$

E) **Multiplication of a polynomial by a polynomial** is achieved by multiplying each of the terms of one polynomial by each of the terms of the other polynomial and combining the result. For example,

$$(5y + z + 1)\,(y^2 + 2y)$$
$$= [(5y)\,(y^2) + (5y)\,(2y)] + [(z)\,(y^2) + (z)\,(2y)] + [(1)\,(y^2) + (1)\,(2y)]$$

$$= (5y^3 + 10y^2) + (y^2z + 2yz) + (y^2 + 2y)$$
$$= (5y^3) + (10y^2 + y^2) + (y^2z) + (2yz) + (2y)$$
$$= 5y^3 + 11y^2 + y^2z + 2yz + 2y$$

F) **Division of a monomial by a monomial** is achieved by first dividing the constant coefficients and the variable factors separately, and then multiplying these quotients. For example,

$$6xyz^2 \div 2y^2z$$
$$= \left(\frac{6}{2}\right)\left(\frac{x}{1}\right)\left(\frac{y}{y^2}\right)\left(\frac{z^2}{z}\right)$$
$$= 3xy^{-1}z$$
$$= \frac{3xz}{y}$$

G) **Division of a polynomial by a polynomial** is achieved by following the given procedure, called long division:

    Step 1: The terms of both polynomials are arranged in order of ascending or descending powers of one variable.

    Step 2: The first term of the dividend is divided by the first term of the divisor, which gives the first term of the quotient.

    Step 3: This first term of the quotient is multiplied by the entire divisor and the result is subtracted from the dividend.

    Step 4: Using the remainder obtained from Step 3 and the next term in the dividend polynomial as the new dividend, repeat Steps 2 and 3 until the remainder is zero or the degree of the remainder is less than the degree of the divisor.

    Step 5: The result is written as follows:

$$\frac{dividend}{divisor} = quotient + \frac{remainder}{divisor}$$

$$divisor \neq 0$$

For example, $(2x^2 + x + 6) \div (x + 1)$

$$
\begin{array}{r}
2x \;\; - 1 \\
(x+1)\overline{)2x^2 + x + 6} \\
\underline{-(2x^2 + 2x)} \\
-x + 6 \\
\underline{-(-x - 1)} \\
7
\end{array}
$$

The result is $(2x^2 + x + 6) \div (x + 1) = 2x - 1 + \dfrac{7}{x+1}$

Drill: Operations with Polynomials

Addition

DIRECTIONS: Add the following polynomials.

1. $9a^2b + 3c + 2a^2b + 5c =$

    (A) $19a^2bc$ (B) $11a^2b + 8c$ (C) $11a^4b^2 + 8c^2$

    (D) $19a^4b^2c^2$ (E) $12a^2b + 8c^2$

2. $14m^2n^3 + 6m^2n^3 + 3m^2n^3 =$

    (A) $20m^2n^3$ (B) $23m^6n^9$ (C) $23m^2n^3$

    (D) $32m^6n^9$ (E) $23m^8n^{27}$

3. $3x + 2y + 16x + 3z + 6y =$

    (A) $19x + 8y$ (B) $19x + 11yz$ (C) $19x + 8y + 3z$

    (D) $11xy + 19xz$ (E) $30xyz$

4. $(4d^2 + 7e^3 + 12f) + (3d^2 + 6e^3 + 2f) =$

    (A) $23d^2e^3f$ (B) $33d^2e^2f$ (C) $33d^4e^6f^2$

    (D) $7d^2 + 13e^3 + 14f$ (E) $23d^2 + 11e^3f$

5. $3ac^2 + 2b^2c + 7ac^2 + 2ac^2 + b^2c =$

    (A) $12ac^2 + 3b^2c$ (B) $14ab^2c^2$ (C) $11ac^2 + 4ab^2c$

    (D) $15ab^2c^2$ (E) $15a^2b^4c^4$

Subtraction

DIRECTIONS: Subtract the following polynomials.

6. $14m^2n - 6m^2n =$

    (A) $20m^2n$ (B) $8m^2n$ (C) $8m$

    (D) 8 (E) $8m^4n^2$

7. $3x^3y^2 - 4xz - 6x^3y^2 =$

    (A) $-7x^2y^2z$ (B) $3x^3y^2 - 10x^4y^2z$ (C) $-3x^3y^2 - 4xz$

    (D) $-x^2y^2z - 6x^3y^2$ (E) $-7xyz$

8. $9g^2 + 6h - 2g^2 - 5h =$

    (A) $15g^2h - 7g^2h$ (B) $7g^4h^2$ (C) $11g^2 + 7h$

    (D) $11g^2 - 7h^2$ (E) $7g^2 + h$

9. $7b^3 - 4c^2 - 6b^3 + 3c^2 =$

    (A) $b^3 - c^2$ (B) $-11b^2 - 3c^2$ (C) $13b^3 - c$

    (D) $7b - c$ (E) 0

10. $11q^2r - 4q^2r - 8q^2r =$

    (A) $22q^2r$ (B) q^2r (C) $-2q^2r$

    (D) $-q^2r$ (E) $2q^2r$

Multiplication

DIRECTIONS: Multiply the following polynomials.

---

11. $5p^2t \times 3p^2t =$

    (A) $15p^2t$ (B) $15p^4t$ (C) $15p^4t^2$

    (D) $8p^2t$ (E) $8p^4t^2$

12. $(2r + s)\,14r =$

    (A) $28rs$ (B) $28r^2 + 14sr$ (C) $16r^2 + 14rs$

    (D) $28r + 14sr$ (E) $17r^2s$

13. $(4m + p)\,(3m - 2p) =$

    (A) $12m^2 + 5mp + 2p^2$ (B) $12m^2 - 2mp + 2p^2$ (C) $7m - p$

    (D) $12m - 2p$ (E) $12m^2 - 5mp - 2p^2$

14. $(2a + b)\,(3a^2 + ab + b^2) =$

    (A) $6a^3 + 5a^2b + 3ab^2 + b^3$ (B) $5a^3 + 3ab + b^3$ (C) $6a^3 + 2a^2b + 2ab^2$

    (D) $3a^2 + 2a + ab + b + b^2$ (E) $6a^3 + 3a^2b + 5ab^2 + b^3$

15. $(6t^2 + 2t + 1)\,3t =$

   (A) $9t^2 + 5t + 3$ (B) $18t^2 + 6t + 3$ (C) $9t^3 + 6t^2 + 3t$

   (D) $18t^3 + 6t^2 + 3t$ (E) $12t^3 + 6t^2 + 3t$

Division

> **DIRECTIONS**: Divide the following polynomials.

16. $(x^2 + x - 6) \div (x - 2) =$

   (A) $x - 3$ (B) $x + 2$ (C) $x + 3$

   (D) $x - 2$ (E) $2x + 2$

17. $24b^4c^3 \div 6b^2c =$

   (A) $3b^2c^2$ (B) $4b^4c^3$ (C) $4b^3c^2$

   (D) $4b^2c^2$ (E) $3b^4c^3$

18. $(3p^2 + pq - 2q^2) \div (p + q) =$

   (A) $3p + 2q$ (B) $2q - 3p$ (C) $3p - q$

   (D) $2q + 3p$ (E) $3p - 2q$

19. $(y^3 - 2y^2 - y + 2) \div (y - 2) =$

   (A) $(y - 1)^2$ (B) $y^2 - 1$ (C) $(y + 2)(y - 1)$

   (D) $(y + 1)^2$ (E) $(y + 1)(y - 2)$

20. $(m^2 + m - 14) \div (m + 4) =$

   (A) $m - 2$ (B) $m - 3 + \dfrac{-2}{m + 4}$ (C) $m - 3 + \dfrac{4}{m + 4}$

   (D) $m - 3$ (E) $m - 2 + \dfrac{-3}{m + 4}$

Interpret Algebraic Expressions

To factor a polynomial completely is to find the prime factors of the polynomial.

The following concepts are important while factoring or simplifying expressions.

   1. The factors of an algebraic expression consist of two or more algebraic expressions that, when multiplied together, produce the given algebraic expression.

2. **A prime factor** is a polynomial with no factors other than itself and 1.

3. The **least common multiple (LCM)** for an algebraic expression is the smallest quantity divisible by every term in the algebraic expression. The least common numerical coefficients for each of the given expressions will be a factor.

4. **The greatest common factor (GCF)** for an algebraic expression is the largest factor that is common to all terms in the algebraic expressions. The greatest common factor is the polynomial of highest degree and the largest numerical coefficient that is a factor of all the given expressions.

Some important formulae, useful for factoring polynomials, are listed below.

$$a(c + d) = ac + ad$$
$$(a + b)(a - b) = a^2 - b^2$$
$$(a + b)(a + b) = (a + b)^2 = a^2 + 2ab + b^2$$
$$(a - b)(a - b) = (a - b)^2 = a^2 - 2ab + b^2$$
$$(x + a)(x + b) = x^2 + (a + b)x + ab$$
$$(ax + b)(cx + d) = acx^2 + (ad + bc)x + bd$$
$$(a + b)(c + d) = ac + bc + ad + bd$$
$$(a + b)(a + b)(a + b) = (a + b)^3 = a^3 + 3a^2b + 3ab^2 + b^3$$
$$(a - b)(a - b)(a - b) = (a - b)^3 = a^3 - 3a^2b + 3ab^2 - b^3$$
$$(a - b)(a^2 + ab + b^2) = a^3 - b^3$$
$$(a + b)(a^2 - ab + b^2) = a^3 + b^3$$
$$(a + b + c)^2 = a^2 + b^2 + c^2 + 2ab + 2ac + 2bc$$
$$(a - b)(a^3 + a^2b + ab^2 + b^3) = a^4 - b^4$$
$$(a - b)(a^4 + a^3b + a^2b^2 + ab^3 + b^4) = a^5 - b^5$$
$$(a - b)(a^5 + a^4b + a^3b^2 + a^2b^3 + ab^4 + b^5) = a^6 - b^6$$
$$(a - b)(a^{n-1} + a^{n-2}b + a^{n-3}b^2 + \ldots + ab^{n-2} + b^{n-1}) = a^n - b^n$$

where n is any positive integer (1, 2, 3, 4, …).

$$(a + b)(a^{n-1} - a^{n-2}b + a^{n-3}b^2 - \ldots - ab^{n-2} + b^{n-1}) = a^n + b^n$$

where n is any positive odd integer (1, 3, 5, 7, …).

The procedure for factoring an algebraic expression completely is as follows:

Step 1: First find the greatest common factor if there is any. Then examine each remaining factor for common factors.

Step 2: Continue factoring the factors obtained in Step 1 until all factors other than monomial factors are prime.

• **EXAMPLE**

Factoring $4 - 16x^2$,
$$4 - 16x^2 = 4(1 - 4x^2) = 4(1 + 2x)(1 - 2x)$$

PROBLEM

Express each of the following as a single term.

    (A) $3x^2 + 2x^2 - 4x^2$ (B) $5axy^2 - 7axy^2 - 3xy^2$

SOLUTION

    (A)   Factor x^2 in the expression.

$$3x^2 + 2x^2 - 4x^2 = (3 + 2 - 4)x^2 = 1x^2 = x^2.$$

    (B)   Factor xy^2 in the expression and then factor a.

$$
\begin{aligned}
5axy^2 - 7axy^2 - 3xy^2 &= (5a - 7a - 3)xy^2 \\
&= [(5 - 7)a - 3]xy^2 \\
&= (-2a - 3)xy^2.
\end{aligned}
$$

PROBLEM

Simplify $\dfrac{\dfrac{1}{x-1} - \dfrac{1}{x-2}}{\dfrac{1}{x-2} - \dfrac{1}{x-3}}$.

SOLUTION

Simplify the expression in the numerator by using the addition rule:

$$\frac{a}{b} + \frac{c}{d} = \frac{ad + bc}{bd}$$

Notice bd is the Least Common Denominator (LCD). We obtain

$$\frac{(x-2)-(x-1)}{(x-1)(x-2)} = \frac{-1}{(x-1)(x-2)}$$

in the numerator.

Repeat this procedure for the expression in the denominator:

$$\frac{(x-3)-(x-2)}{(x-2)(x-3)} = \frac{-1}{(x-2)(x-3)}$$

We now have

$$\frac{\dfrac{-1}{(x-1)(x-2)}}{\dfrac{-1}{(x-2)(x-3)}},$$

which is simplified by inverting the fraction in the denominator and multiplying it by the numerator, cancelling like terms

$$\frac{-1}{(x-1)\cancel{(x-2)}} \times \frac{\cancel{(x-2)}(x-3)}{-1} = \frac{x-3}{x-1}$$

Factoring

PROBLEM

Factor the following expression.

$$x^2 - x^3 + x^4$$

SOLUTION

Step 1 is to find the greatest common factor (GCF) for x^2, x^3, and x^4. When looking for the GCF for the coefficients, the coefficient for each term is 1, so 1 is the GCF.

Step 2 is to find the term with the lowest exponent of the same variable, x.

x^2 has the lowest exponent.

Step 3 is to divide each term by x^2.

$$\frac{x^2}{x^2} = 1$$

$$-\frac{x^3}{x^2} = -x$$

$$\frac{x^4}{x^2} = x^2$$

Step 4 is to rewrite the problem. Place the lowest exponent outside of the parentheses.

$$x^2(x^2 - x + 1)$$

The correct answer is $x^2(x^2 - x + 1)$.

PROBLEM

Factor the following expression.

$6x^3y + 8x^2y - 4xy$

SOLUTION

Step 1 is to find the greatest common factor (GCF) for $6x^3y$, $8x^2y$, and $4xy$. When looking for the GCF for a variable, use only the coefficients. List all factors for each.

$$6 = (1, 2, 3, 6)$$

$$8 = (1, 2, 4, 8)$$

$$4 = (1, 2, 4)$$

The GCF is 2.

Step 2 is to divide each term by the GCF.

$$\frac{6x^3y}{2} = 3x^3y$$

$$\frac{8x^2y}{2} = 4x^2y$$

$$\frac{-4xy}{2} = -2xy$$

Step 3 is to rewrite the problem. Place the GCF outside of the parentheses.

$2(3x^3y + 4x^2y - 2xy)$

Step 4 is to find the term with the lowest exponent of the same variable xy.

$2xy$ has the lowest exponent.

Step 5 is to divide each term by xy.

$$\frac{3x^3y}{xy} = 3x^2$$

$$\frac{4x^2y}{xy} = 4x$$

$$\frac{-2xy}{xy} = -2$$

Step 6 is to rewrite the problem. Place the lowest exponent outside of the parentheses.

$xy(2)(3x^2 + 4x - 2)$

Step 7 is to multiply the GCF and the lowest exponent.

$$xy(2) = 2xy$$

The correct answer is $2xy(3x^2 + 4x - 2)$.

PROBLEM

> Factor the following expression.
> $$8x^3 - 2x^2 + 9x - 3y$$

SOLUTION

To solve this problem, the expression must be factored by grouping.

Step 1 is to group the first two terms and the last two terms together.

$$(8x^3 - 2x^2) + (9x - 3y)$$

Step 2 is to determine how each group will be factored.

Group 1 has a GCF of 2. Also, the variable x^2 can be factored since it appears in both terms.

Group 2 has a GCF of 3. The variables are different so they have no GCF.

Step 3 is to factor each group.

$$8x^3 - 2x^2 = 2x^2(4x - 1)$$
$$9x - 3y = 3(3x - y)$$

Step 4 is to rewrite the problem.

$$2x^2(4x - 1) + 3(3x - y)$$

The correct answer is $2x^2(4x - 1) + 3(3x - y)$.

Drill: Simplifying Algebraic Expressions

1. $16b^2 - 25z^2 =$

   (A) $(4b - 5z)^2$ (B) $(4b + 5z)^2$ (C) $(4b - 5z)(4b + 5z)$

   (D) $(16b - 25z)^2$ (E) $(5z - 4b)(5I + 4b)$

2. $x^2 - 2x - 8 =$

   (A) $(x - 4)^2$ (B) $(x - 6)(x - 2)$ (C) $(x + 4)(x - 2)$

   (D) $(x - 4)(x + 2)$ (E) $(x - 4)(x - 2)$

3. $2c^2 + 5cd - 3d^2 =$

   (A) $(c - 3d)(c + 2d)$ (B) $(2c - d)(c + 3d)$ (C) $(c - d)(2c + 3dI)$

   (D) $(2c + d)(c + 3d)$ (E) Not possible

4. $4t^3 - 20t =$

   (A) $4t(t^2 - 5)$ (B) $4t^2(t - 20)$ (C) $4t(t + 4)(t - 5)$

   (D) $2t(2t^2 - 10)$ (E) Not possible

5. $x^2 + xy - 2y^2 =$

   (A) $(x - 2y)(x + y)$ (B) $(x - 2y)(x - y)$ (C) $(x + 2y)(x + y)$

   (D) $(x + 2y)(x - y)$ (E) Not possible

6. $5b^2 + 17bd + 6d^2 =$

   (A) $(5b + d)(b + 6d)$ (B) $(5b + 2d)(b + 3d)$ (C) $(5b - 2d)(b - 3d)$

   (D) $(5b - 2d)(b + 3d)$ (E) Not possible

7. $x^2 + x + 1 =$

   (A) $(x + 1)^2$ (B) $(x + 2)(x - 1)$. (C) $(x - 2)(x + 1)$

   (D) $(x + 1)(x - 1)$ (E) Not possible

8. $3z^3 + 6z^2 =$

   (A) $3(z^3 + 2z^2)$ (B) $3z^2(z + 2)$ (C) $3z(z^7 + 2z)$

   (D) $z^2(3z + 6)$ (E) $3z^2(1 + 2z)$

9. $m^2p^2 + mpg - 6g^2 =$

   (A) $(mp + 3g)(mp - 2g)$ (B) $mp(mp - 2q)(mp + 3q)$

   (C) $mpq(1 - 6q)$ (D) $(mp + 2q)(mp + 3q)$

   (E) Not possible

10. $2h^3 + 2h^2t - 4ht^2 =$

    (A) $2(h^3 - t)(h + t)$ (B) $2h(h - 2t)^2$ (C) $4h(ht - t^2)$

    (D) $2h(h + t) - 4ht^2$ (E) $2h(h + 2t)(h - t)$

Solve Equations and Inequalities

An **equation** is defined as a statement that two separate expressions are equal.

A **solution** to an equation containing a single variable is a number that makes the equation true when it is substituted for the variable. For example, in the equation $3x = 18$, 6 is the solution since $3(6) = 18$. Depending on the equation, there can be more than one solution. Equations with the same solutions are said to be **equivalent equations**. An equation without a solution is said to have a solution set that is the **empty** or **null** set, represented by ϕ.

A) Replacing an expression within an equation by an equivalent expression will result in a new equation with solutions equivalent to the original equation. Sometimes this replacement helps in finding the solution.

Suppose we are given the equation

$$3x + y + x + 2y = 15.$$

By combining like terms, for the left side we get

$$3x + y + x + 2y = 4x + 3y.$$

Since these two expressions are equivalent, we can substitute the simpler form into the equation to get

$$4x + 3y = 15$$

B) Performing the same operation to both sides of an equation by the same expression will result in a new equation that is equivalent to the original equation.

Addition or subtraction

$$y + 6 = 10$$

We can add (-6) to both sides

$$y + 6 + (-6) = 10 + (-6)$$

to get $y + 0 = 10 - 6$, or $y = 4$

Multiplication or division

$$3x = 6$$

$$\frac{3x}{3} = \frac{6}{3}$$

$$x = 2$$

$3x = 6$ is equivalent to $x = 2$.

Raising to a power

This can be applied to positive, negative, and fractional powers.

$$x^2 = 3y^4$$

If we raise both sides to the $^{1}\!/_{2}$ power, which is the same as taking the square root, we get

$$(x^2)^{1/2} = (3y^4)^{1/2}$$
$$x = \pm\sqrt{3}\,y^2$$

The **reciprocals** of both sides of an equation are equivalent to the original equation. *Note*: The reciprocal of zero is undefined.

$$\frac{1}{x} = \frac{2}{3y+7}$$
$$x = \frac{3y+7}{2}$$

PROBLEM

> Solve for x, justifying each step.
> $3x - 8 = 7x + 8$

SOLUTION

$$3x - 8 = 7x + 8$$

Add 8 to both sides: $3x - 8 + 8 = 7x + 8 + 8$

Additive inverse property: $3x + 0 = 7x + 16$

Additive identity property: $3x = 7x + 16$

Add $(-7x)$ to both sides: $3x - 7x = 7x + 16 - 7x$

Commute: $-4x = 7x - 7x + 16$

Additive inverse property: $-4x = 0 + 16$

Additive identity property: $-4x = 16$

Divide both sides by -4: $\dfrac{-4x}{-4} = \dfrac{16}{-4}$

$$x = -4$$

Check: Replacing x with (-4) in the original equation:

$$3x - 8 = 7x + 8$$

$$3(-4) - 8 = 7(-4) + 8$$

$$-12 - 8 = -28 + 8$$

$$-20 = -20$$

Linear Equations

A linear equation with one unknown is one that can be put into the form $ax + b = 0$, where a and b are constants, $a \neq 0$.

To solve a linear equation means to transform it in the form $x = \dfrac{-b}{a}$.

A) If the equation has unknowns on both sides of the equality, it is convenient to put similar terms on the same sides. Refer to the following example.

$$4x + 3 = 2x + 9$$
$$4x + 3 - 2x = 2x + 9 - 2x$$
$$(4x - 2x) + 3 = (2x - 2x) + 9$$
$$2x + 3 = 0 + 9$$
$$2x + 3 - 3 = 0 + 9 - 3$$
$$2x = 6$$
$$\frac{2x}{2} = \frac{6}{2}$$
$$x = 3$$

B) If the equation appears in fractional form, it is necessary to transform it, using cross-multiplication, and then use the procedure in A, to obtain the solution. Remember that cross-multiplication of $\dfrac{A}{B} = \dfrac{C}{D}$ yields $AD = BC$.

$$\frac{3x + 4}{3} \quad\times\quad \frac{7x + 2}{5}$$

By using cross-multiplication we would obtain:

$$3(7x + 2) = 5(3x + 4).$$

This is equivalent to:

$$21x + 6 = 15x + 20,$$

which can be solved as in A.

$$21x + 6 = 15x + 20$$
$$21x - 15x + 6 = 15x - 15x + 20$$
$$6x + 6 - 6 = 20 - 6$$
$$6x = 14$$
$$x = \frac{14}{6} = \frac{2 \times 7}{2 \times 3}$$
$$x = \frac{7}{3}$$

C) If there are radicals in the equation, it is necessary to square both sides and then apply A.

$$\sqrt{3x+1}=5$$
$$(\sqrt{3x+1})^2=5^2$$
$$3x+1=25$$
$$3x+1-1=25-1$$
$$3x=24$$
$$x=\frac{24}{3}=\frac{3\times 8}{3\times 1}$$
$$x=8$$

PROBLEM

Solve the equation $2(x+3)=(3x+5)-(x-5)$.

SOLUTION

We transform the given equation to an equivalent equation in which we can easily recognize the solution set.

$$2(x+3)=(3x+5)-(x-5)$$

Distribute: $\qquad\qquad\qquad\qquad\qquad 2x+6=3x+5-x+5$

Combine terms: $\qquad\qquad\qquad\qquad 2x+6=2x+10$

Subtract $2x$ from both sides: $\qquad\qquad\quad 6=10$

Since $6=10$ is not a true statement. There is no real number x that will make the original equation true. The equation is said to be inconsistent and the solution set is ϕ, the empty set.

PROBLEM

Solve the equation $2(\frac{2}{3}y+5)+2(y+5)=130$.

SOLUTION

The procedure for solving this equation is as follows:

Distribute: $\qquad\qquad\qquad\qquad\qquad \frac{4}{3}y+10+2y+10=130$

Combine like terms: $\qquad\qquad\qquad\qquad \frac{4}{3}y+2y+20=130$

Subtract 20 from both sides: $\qquad\qquad\qquad \frac{4}{3}y+2y=110$

Clear fractions by multiplying both sides by 3: $3(\frac{4}{3}y + 2y) = 3(110)$

Use the distributive property: $4y + 6y = 330$

Combine like terms: $10y = 330$

Divide both sides by 10: $y = 33$

Check: Replace y with 33 in the original equation.

$$2(\frac{2}{3}(33) + 5) + 2(33 + 5) = 130$$
$$2(22 + 5) + 2(38) = 130$$
$$2(27) + 76 = 130$$
$$54 + 76 = 130$$
$$130 = 130$$

Therefore, the solution to the given equation is $y = 33$.

Drill: Linear Equations

DIRECTIONS: Solve for *x*.

1. $4x - 2 = 10$
    (A) −1   (B) 2   (C) 3   (D) 4   (E) 6

2. $7z + 1 - z = 2z - 7$
    (A) −2   (B) 0   (C) 1   (D) 2   (E) 3

3. $\frac{1}{3}b + 3 = \frac{1}{2}b$
    (A) $\frac{1}{2}$ (B) 2   (C) $3\frac{3}{5}$ (D) 6   (E) 18

4. $0.4p + 1 = 0.7p - 2$
    (A) 0.1   (B) 2   (C) 5   (D) 10   (E) 12

5. $4(3x + 2) - 11 = 3(3x - 2)$
    (A) −3   (B) −1   (C) 2   (D) 3   (E) 7

Two Linear Equations

Equations of the form $ax + by = c$, where a, b, c are constants and $a, b \neq 0$ are called **linear equations** with two unknown variables.

A system of linear equations is **consistent** if there is only one solution for the system.

A system of linear equations is **inconsistent** if it does not have any solutions.

There are several ways to solve systems of linear equations with two variables.

Method 1: **Addition or subtraction**—If necessary, multiply the equations by numbers that will make the coefficients of one unknown in the resulting equations numerically equal. If the signs of equal coefficients are the same, subtract the equations; otherwise, add them.

The result is one equation with one unknown. Solve it and substitute the value into the other equation to find the value of the other unknown.

Method 2: **Substitution**—Find the value of one unknown in terms of the other. Substitute this value in the other equation and solve.

Method 3: **Graph**—Graph both equations. The point of intersection of the drawn lines is a simultaneous solution for the equations and its coordinates correspond to the answer that would be found analytically. If the lines are parallel, they never intersect, and the equations have no simultaneous solution.

Dependent equations are equations that represent the same line; therefore, every point on the line of the graph of one equation is a solution for the other equation. Since there is an infinite number of points on a line, there is an infinite number of simultaneous solutions. An example of a pair of dependent equations is:

$$\begin{cases} 2x + y = 8 \\ 4x + 2y = 16 \end{cases}$$

- **EXAMPLE**

Find the point of intersection of the graphs of the equations.

$$x + y = 3$$
$$3x - 2y = 14$$

To solve these linear equations, solve for y in terms of x. The equations will be in the form $y = mx + b$, where m is the slope and b is the intercept on the y-axis.

Subtract x from both sides of the first equation:

$$x + y = 3$$
$$y = 3 - x$$

Subtract $3x$ from both sides of the second equation: $3x - 2y = 14$

Divide by -2: $-2y = 14 - 3x$

$$y = -7 + \frac{3}{2}x$$

The graphs of the linear functions, $y = 3 - x$ and $y = 7 + \frac{3}{2}x$ can be determined by plotting only two points. For example, for $y = 3 - x$, let $x = 0$, then $y = 3$. Let $x = 1$, then $y = 2$. The two points on this first line are $(0, 3)$ and $(1, 2)$. For $y = -7 + \frac{3}{2}x$, let $x = 0$, then $y = -7$. Let $x = 1$, then, $y = -5\frac{1}{2}$. The two points on this second line are $(0, -7)$ and $(1, -5\frac{1}{2})$.

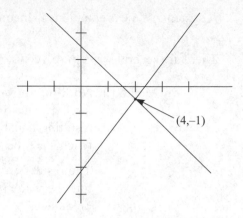

$(4,-1)$

AB is the graph of the first equation, and CD is the graph of the second equation. The point of intersection P of the two graphs is the only point on both lines. The coordinates of P satisfy both equations and represent the desired solution of the problem. From the graph, P seems to be the point $(4, -1)$. These coordinates satisfy both equations, and hence are the exact coordinates of the point of intersection of the two lines.

To show that $(4, -1)$ satisfies both equations, substitute this point into both equations.

$$x + y = 3 \qquad\qquad 3x - 2y = 14$$
$$4 + (-1) = 3 \qquad\qquad 3(4) - 2(-1) = 14$$
$$4 - 1 = 3 \qquad\qquad 12 + 2 = 14$$
$$3 = 3 \qquad\qquad 14 = 14$$

Note: To solve the original equations algebraically, multiply the first equation by 2, and add the equations to eliminate the variable y.

$$
\begin{array}{r}
2x + 2y = 6 \\
3x - 2y = 14 \\
\hline
5x \phantom{{}+2y} = 20
\end{array}
$$

Solve for x to obtain $x = 4$. Substitute this into $y = 3 - x$ to get $y = 3 - 4 = -1$. So the solution is $x = 4$, $y = -1$

- **EXAMPLE**

Solve the equations $2x + 3y = 6$ and $4x + 6y = 7$ simultaneously.

We have two equations and two unknowns,

$$2x + 3y = 6 \qquad (1)$$

and

$$4x + 6y = 7 \qquad (2)$$

There are several methods to solve this problem. We have chosen to multiply each equation by a different number so that when the two equations are added, one of the variables drops out. Thus,

Multiply equation (1) by 2: $\qquad\qquad\qquad 4x + 6y = 12 \qquad\qquad\qquad\qquad$ (3)

Multiply equation (2) by -1: $\qquad\qquad \underline{-4x - 6y = -7} \qquad\qquad\qquad\qquad$ (4)

Add equations (3) and (4): $\qquad\qquad\qquad\quad 0 = 5$

We obtain a peculiar result!

Actually, what we have shown in this case is that if there were a simultaneous solution to the given equations, then 0 would equal 5. But the conclusion is impossible; therefore there can be no simultaneous solution to these two equations, hence no point satisfying both.

The straight lines which are the graphs of these equations must be parallel if they never intersect, but not identical, which can be seen from the graph of these equations.

• **EXAMPLE**

Solve the equations $2x + 3y = 6$ and $y = -\left(\dfrac{2x}{3}\right) + 2$ simultaneously.

We have two equations and two unknowns.

$$2x + 3y = 6 \qquad\qquad\qquad (1)$$

and

$$y = -\left(\frac{2x}{3}\right) + 2 \qquad\qquad\qquad (2)$$

There are several methods of solution for this problem. Since equation (2) already gives us an expression for y, we use the method of substitution. Substitute: $-(2x/3) + 2$ for y in the first equation:

$$2x + 3\left(-\frac{2x}{3} + 2\right) = 6$$

Distribute: $2x - 2x + 6 = 6$

$$6 = 6$$

Apparently we have gotten nowhere! The result $6 = 6$ is true, but indicates no solution. Actually, our work shows that no matter what real number x is, if y is determined by the second equation, then the first equation will always be satisfied.

The reason for this peculiarity may be seen if we take a closer look at the equation $y = -\left(\dfrac{2x}{3}\right) + 2$. Multiply both sides by 3 to get $3y = -2x + 6$, which is equivalent to $2x + 3y = 6$.

In other words, the two equations are equivalent. Any pair of values of x and y that satisfies one satisfies the other.

It is hardly necessary to verify that in this case the graphs of the given equations are identical lines, and that there are an infinite number of simultaneous solutions of these equations.

Three Linear Equations

A system of three linear equations in three unknowns is solved by eliminating one unknown from any two of the three equations and solving these two equations for the two remaining unknowns. After finding these two unknowns, substitute them in any of the equations to find the third unknown.

PROBLEM

Solve the system

$2x + 3y - 4z = -8$	(1)
$x + y - 2z = -5$	(2)
$7x - 2y + 5z = 4$	(3)

SOLUTION

We cannot eliminate any variable from any two of these equations by a single multiplication. However, both x and z may be eliminated from equations 1 and 2 by multiplying equation (2) by -2. Then we get

$2x + 3y - 4z = -8$	(1)
$-2x - 2y + 4z = 10$	(4)

By addition, we have $y = 2$. Although we may now eliminate either x or z from another pair of equations, we can more conveniently substitute $y = 2$ in equations (2) and (3) to get two equations with two variables. Thus, making the substitution $y = 2$ in equations (2) and (3), we have

$x - 2z = -7$	(5)
$7x + 5z = 8$	(6)

We then multiply equation (5) by 5 and multiply (6) by 2 to eliminate z, and add the two new equations to get $x = -1$. We substitute $x = -1$ in either equation (5) or (6) to find z.

$$-1 - 2z = -7, \text{ or } z = 3.$$

The solution of the system is thus $x = -1$, $y = 2$, and $z = 3$. Check by substitution.

PROBLEM

Solve for x and y.

$x + 2y = 8$	(1)
$3x + 4y = 20$	(2)

SOLUTION

Solve equation (1) for x in terms of y: $x = 8 - 2y$ (3)

Substitute $(8 - 2y)$ for x in (2): $3(8 - 2y) + 4y = 20$ (4)

Solve equation (4) for y as follows:

Distribute: $24 - 6y + 4y = 20$

Combine like terms and then subtract 24 from both sides:

$$24 - 2y = 20$$
$$24 - 24 - 2y = 20 - 24$$
$$-2y = -4$$

Divide both sides by -2: $y = 2$

Substitute 2 for y into equation (1): $x + 2(2) = 8$
$$x = 4$$

Thus, our solution is $x = 4$, $y = 2$.

Check: Substitute $x = 4$, $y = 2$ into equations (1) and (2):

$$4 + 2(2) = 8$$
$$8 = 8$$
$$3(4) + 4(2) = 20$$
$$20 = 20$$

PROBLEM

Solve algebraically.

$4x + 2y = -1$	(1)
$5x - 3y = 7$	(2)

SOLUTION

We arbitrarily choose to eliminate x first.

Multiply (1) by 5:	$20x + 10y = -5$	(3)
Multiply (2) by -4:	$-20x + 12y = -28$	(4)
Add (3) and (4):	$22y = -33$	(5)
Divide (5) by 22:	$y = -\dfrac{33}{22} = -\dfrac{3}{2}$	

To find x, substitute $y = -\frac{3}{2}$ in either of the original equations. If we use equation (1), we obtain

$$4x + 2(-\tfrac{3}{2}) = -1,$$

$$4x - 3 = -1,$$

$$4x = 2,$$

$$x = \tfrac{1}{2}$$

The solution $(\frac{1}{2}, -\frac{3}{2})$ should be checked in both equations of the given system.

Replacing $(\frac{1}{2}, -\frac{3}{2})$ in equation (1):

$$4x + 2y = -1$$
$$4(\tfrac{1}{2}) + 2(-\tfrac{3}{2}) = -1$$
$$\tfrac{4}{2} - 3 = -1$$
$$2 - 3 = -1$$
$$-1 = -1$$

Replacing $(\frac{1}{2}, -\frac{3}{2})$ in equation (2):

$$5x - 3y = 7$$
$$5(\tfrac{1}{2}) - 3(-\tfrac{3}{2}) = 7$$
$$\tfrac{5}{2} + \tfrac{9}{2} = 7$$
$$\tfrac{14}{2} = 7$$
$$7 = 7$$

Note: Instead of eliminating x from the two given equations, we could have eliminated y by multiplying equation (1) by 3, multiplying equation (2) by 2, and then adding the two derived equations.

Drill: Two Linear Equations

DIRECTIONS: Find the solution set for each pair of equations.

1. $3x + 4y = -2$
    $x - 6y = -8$

    (A) $(2, -1)$ (B) $(1, -2)$ (C) $(-2, -1)$

    (D) $(1, 2)$ (E) $(-2, 1)$

2. $2x + y = -10$
    $-2x - 4y = 4$

    (A) $(6, -2)$ (B) $(-6, 2)$ (C) $(-2, 6)$

    (D) $(2, 6)$ (E) $(-6, -2)$

3. $6x + 5y = -4$
    $3x - 3y = 9$

    (A) $(1, -2)$ (B) $(1, 2)$ (C) $(2, -1)$

    (D) $(-2, 1)$ (E) $(-1, 2)$

4. $4x + 3y = 9$
    $2x - 2y = 8$

    (A) $(-3, 1)$ (B) $(1, -3)$ (C) $(3, 1)$

    (D) $(3, -1)$ (E) $(-1, 3)$

5. $x + y = 7$
    $x = y - 3$

    (A) $(5, 2)$ (B) $(-5, 2)$ (C) $(2, 5)$

    (D) $(-2, 5)$ (E) $(2, -5)$

6. $5x + 6y = 4$
    $3x - 2y = 1$

(A) $(3, 6)$ (B) $\left(\dfrac{1}{2}, \dfrac{1}{4}\right)$ (C) $(-3, 6)$

(D) $(2, 4)$ (E) $\left(\dfrac{1}{3}, \dfrac{3}{2}\right)$

7. $x - 2y = 7$

$x + y = -2$

(A) $(-2, 7)$ (B) $(3, -1)$ (C) $(-7, 2)$
(D) $(1, -3)$ (E) $(1, -2)$

8. $4x + 3y = 3$

$-2x + 6y = 3$

(A) $\left(\dfrac{1}{2}, \dfrac{2}{3}\right)$ (B) $(-0.3, 0.6)$ (C) $\left(\dfrac{2}{3}, -1\right)$

(D) $(-0.2, 0.5)$ (E) $(0.3, 0.6)$

9. $4x - 2y = -14$

$8x + y = 7$

(A) $(0, 7)$ (B) $(2, -7)$ (C) $(7, 0)$

(D) $(-7, 2)$ (E) $(0, 2)$

10. $6x - 3y = 1$

$-9x + 5y = -1$

(A) $(1, -1)$ (B) $\left(\dfrac{2}{3}, 1\right)$ (C) $\left(1, \dfrac{2}{3}\right)$

(D) $(-1, 1)$ (E) $\left(\dfrac{2}{3}, -1\right)$

Quadratic Equations

A second degree equation in x of the type $ax^2 + bx + c = 0$, $a \neq 0$, a, b and c are real numbers, is called a **quadratic equation**.

To solve a quadratic equation is to find values of x that satisfy $ax^2 + bx + c = 0$. These values of x are called solutions, or roots, of the equation.

A quadratic equation has a maximum of two roots. Methods of solving quadratic equations:

A) **Direct solution:** Given $x^2 - 9 = 0$.

We can solve directly by isolating the variable x.

$$x^2 = 9$$

$$x = \pm 3$$

B) **Factoring:** Given a quadratic equation $ax^2 + bx + c = 0$, $a, b, c \neq 0$, to factor means to express it as the product $a(x - r_1)(x - r_2) = 0$, where r_1 and r_2 are the two roots.

Some helpful hints to remember are

a) $r_1 + r_2 = -\dfrac{b}{a}$.

b) $r_1 r_2 = \dfrac{c}{a}$.

For example, given $x^2 - 5x + 4 = 0$.

Since

$$r_1 + r_2 = -\frac{b}{a} = -\frac{(-5)}{1} = 5,$$

the possible solutions are two numbers that sum to 5, or (3, 2), (4, 1), and (5, 0). Also, the solution must satisfy

$$r_1 r_2 = \frac{c}{a} = \frac{4}{1} = 4.$$

This equation is thus satisfied only by the second pair (4, 1), so $r_1 = 4$, $r_2 = 1$, and the factored form is

$$(x - 4)(x - 1) = 0.$$

If the coefficient of x^2 is not 1, it is necessary to divide the equation by this coefficient and then factor.

For example, given $2x^2 - 12x + 16 = 0$.

Dividing by 2, we obtain

$$x^2 - 6x + 8 = 0.$$

Since

$$r_1 + r_2 = -\frac{b}{a} = 6,$$

the possible solutions are (6, 0), (5, 1), (4, 2), and (3, 3). Also $r_1 r_2 = 8$, so the only possible answer is (4, 2) and the expression $x^2 - 6x + 8 = 0$ can be factored as $(x - 4)(x - 2)$.

C) **Completing the squares:** If it is difficult to factor the quadratic equation using the previous method, we can complete the squares.

Given $x^2 - 12x + 8 = 0$.

We know that the two roots added up should be 12 because

$$r_1 + r_2 = -\frac{b}{a} = \frac{-(-12)}{1} = 12.$$

The possible roots are (12, 0), (11, 1), (10, 2), (9, 3), (8, 4), (7, 5), and (6, 6).

But none of these satisfy $r_1 r_2 = 8$, so we cannot use factoring (B).

To complete the square, it is necessary to isolate the constant term,

$$x^2 - 12x = -8.$$

To complete the square, take ½ the coefficient of x, square it and add it to both sides.

$$x^2 - 12x + \left(\frac{-12}{2}\right)^2 = -8 + \left(\frac{-12}{2}\right)^2$$
$$x^2 - 12x + 36 = -8 + 36 = 28$$

Now we can use the previous method to factor the left side.

$$r_1 + r_2 = 12, r_1 r_2 = 36$$

is satisfied by the pair (6, 6), so we have

$$(x - 6)^2 = 28.$$

Now extract the root of both sides and solve for x.

$$(x - 6) = \pm\sqrt{28} = \pm 2\sqrt{7}$$
$$\text{or} \qquad x = \pm 2\sqrt{7} + 6$$

So the roots are

$$x = 2\sqrt{7} + 6, \; x = -2\sqrt{7} + 6.$$

PROBLEM

Factor the following trinomial.
$$2x^2 + 9x + 4$$

SOLUTION

Trinomials are in the format $ax^2 + bx + c$. Determine what terms represent a, b, and c in the given equation.

$$a = 2 \qquad b = 9 \qquad c = 4$$

Since the coefficient for x^2 does not equal 1, use the following steps.

Step 1 is to list pairs of factors for a and c.

$$a = (2, 1)$$

$$c = (2, 2) (4, 1)$$

Step 2 is to find factors of 4 that equal b when multiplied by factors of a and added. The factors can be made negative if necessary.

$$4(2) + 1(1) = 9$$

Step 3 is to put the factors in the following format. The numbers in parentheses become coefficients of x.

$$(2x + 1)(x + 4)$$

Step 4 is to verify the answer by using the First–Outer–Inner–Last (FOIL) method:

The **First** terms are $2x$ and x, yielding $2x(x)$

The **Outer** terms are $2x$ and 4, yielding $8(x)$

The **Inner** terms are 1 and x, yielding x

The **Last** terms are 1 and 4, yielding 4

Thus

$$(2x + 1)(x + 4) = 2x(x) + 8(x) + x + 4$$
$$= 2x^2 + 9x + 4$$

The correct answer is $(2x + 1)(x + 4)$.

PROBLEM

Solve the equation $x^2 + 8x + 15 = 0$.

SOLUTION

Since

$$(x + r_1) (x + r_2) = x^2 + (r_1 + r_2) x + r_1 r_2,$$

we may factor the given equation, by finding numbers r_1 and r_2 such that $r_1 + r_2 = 8$, and $r_1 r_2 = 15$.

Check all pairs of numbers whose product is 15: 1 and 15, 5 and 3.

$1 + 15 = 16$, and $3 + 5 = 8$; therefore, the two numbers are 5 and 3.

Hence, $x^2 + 8x + 15 = 0$ is equivalent to

$$0 = x^2 + (3 + 5)x + 3 \times 5 = (x + 3)(x + 5)$$

Either $x + 5 = 0$ or $x + 3 = 0$ since for the product of these two factors to be zero, one of the factors must be zero. Hence, $x = -5$, or $x = -3$, and the solution set is $x = \{-5, -3\}$.

This means $x = -5$ *or* $x = -3$; certainly $x = -5$ and $x = -3$ cannot both be true at the same time. Check that both these numbers do actually satisfy the given equations and hence are solutions.

Check: Replacing x by (-5) in the original equation:

$$x^2 + 8x + 15 = 0$$

$$(-5)^2 + 8(-5) + 15 = 0$$

$$25 - 40 + 15 = 0$$

$$-15 + 15 = 0$$

$$0 = 0$$

Replacing x by (-3) in the original equation:

$$x^2 + 8x + 15 = 0$$

$$(-3)^2 + 8(-3) + 15 = 0$$

$$9 - 24 + 15 = 0$$

$$-15 + 15 = 0$$

$$0 = 0$$

PROBLEM

Solve the following equations by factoring.

(1) $2x^2 + 3x = 0$ (2) $y^2 - 2y - 3 = y - 3$

(3) $z^2 - 2z - 3 = 0$ (4) $2m^2 - 11m - 6 = 0$

SOLUTION

(1) $2x^2 + 3x = 0$. Factor out the common factor of x from the left side of the given equation.

$$x(2x + 3) = 0$$

Whenever a product $ab = 0$, where a and b are any two numbers, either $a = 0$ or $b = 0$. Then, either

$$x = 0 \text{ or } 2x + 3 = 0$$

$$2x = -3$$

$$x = -\frac{3}{2}$$

Hence, the solution set to the original equation $2x^2 + 3x = 0$ is $\left\{ -\frac{3}{2}, 0 \right\}$

(2) $y^2 - 2y - 3 = y - 3$. Subtract $(y - 3)$ from both sides of the given equation:

$$y^2 - 2y - 3 - (y - 3) = y - 3 - (y - 3)$$

$$y^2 - 2y - 3 - y + 3 = y - 3 - y + 3$$

$$y^2 - 2y - 3 - y + 3 = y - 3 - y + 3$$

$$y^2 - 3y = 0$$

Factor out a common factor of y from the left side of this equation:

$$y(y - 3) = 0$$

Thus, $y = 0$ or $y - 3 = 0$, so $y = 3$.

Therefore, the solution set to the original equation $y^2 - 2y - 3 = y - 3$ is $\{0, 3\}$.

(3) $z^2 - 2z - 3 = 0$. Factor the original equation into a product of two polynomials.

$$z^2 - 2z - 3 = (z - 3)(z + 1) = 0$$

Hence,

$$(z - 3)(z + 1) = 0; \text{ and } z - 3 = 0 \text{ or } z + 1 = 0,$$

which means $\qquad z = 3 \quad$ or $\quad z = -1$.

Therefore, the solution set to the original equation $z^2 - 2z - 3 = 0$ is $\{-1, 3\}$.

(4) $2m^2 - 11m - 6 = 0$. Factor the original equation into a product of two polynomials.

$$2m^2 - 11m - 6 = (2m + 1)(m - 6) = 0$$

Thus,

$$2m + 1 = 0 \quad \text{or} \quad m - 6 = 0$$

which means $2m = -1 \quad$ or $\quad m = 6$

$$\text{or} \qquad\qquad m = -\frac{1}{2} \quad \text{or} \quad m = 6.$$

Therefore, the solution set to the original equation $2m^2 - 11m - 6 = 0$ is $\left\{ -\frac{1}{2}, 6 \right\}$.

Drill: Quadratic Equations

DIRECTIONS: Solve for all values of x.

1. $x^2 - 2x - 8 = 0$

    (A) 4 and -2 (B) 4 and 8   (C) 4

    (D) -2 and 8   (E) -2

2. $x^2 + 2x - 3 = 0$

    (A) -3 and 2   (B) 2 and 1   (C) 3 and 1

    (D) -3 and 1   (E) -3

3. $x^2 - 7x = -10$

    (A) -3 and 5   (B) 2 and 5   (C) 2

    (D) -2 and -5 (E) 5

4. $x^2 - 8x + 16 = 0$

    (A) 8 and 2   (B) 1 and 16   (C) 4

    (D) -2 and 4   (E) 4 and -4

5. $3x^2 + 3x = 6$

    (A) 3 and -6 (B) 2 and 3   (C) -3 and 2

    (D) 1 and -3 (E) 1 and -2

6. $x^2 + 7x = 0$

    (A) 7   (B) 0 and -7 (C) -7

    (D) 0 and 7   (E) 0

7. $x^2 - 25 = 0$

    (A) 5   (B) 5 and -5 (C) 15 and 10

    (D) -5 and 10   (E) -5

8. $2x^2 + 4x = 16$

    (A)   2 and −2   (B)   8 and −2   (C)   4 and 8

    (D)   2 and −4   (E)   2 and 4

9. $6x^2 - x - 2 = 0$

    (A)   2 and 3   (B) $\dfrac{1}{2}$ and $\dfrac{1}{3}$ (C) $-\dfrac{1}{2}$ and $\dfrac{2}{3}$

    (D) $\dfrac{2}{3}$ and 3   (E)   2 and $-\dfrac{1}{3}$

10. $12x^2 + 5x = 3$

    (A) $\dfrac{1}{3}$ and $-\dfrac{1}{4}$ (B)   4 and −3   (C)   4 and $\dfrac{1}{6}$

    (D) $\dfrac{1}{3}$ and −4   (E) $-\dfrac{3}{4}$ and $\dfrac{1}{3}$

Absolute Value Equations

Recall that the absolute value of a, $|\,a\,|$, is defined as

$$|\,a\,| = a \text{ when } a > 0,$$

$$|\,a\,| = -a \text{ when } a < 0,$$

$$|\,a\,| = 0 \text{ when } a = 0.$$

When the definition of absolute value is applied to an equation, the quantity within the absolute value symbol is considered to have two values, either positive or negative before the absolute value is taken. As a result, each absolute value equation actually contains two separate equations.

When evaluating equations containing absolute values, proceed as follows:

· **EXAMPLE**

$|\,5 - 3x\,| = 7$ is valid if either

$$
\begin{array}{ll}
5 - 3x = 7 \quad \text{or} \quad & 5 - 3x = -7 \\
-3x = 2 & -3x = -12 \\
x = -\dfrac{2}{3} & x = 4
\end{array}
$$

The solution set is therefore $x = (-\!\tfrac{2}{3}, 4)$.

Remember, the absolute value of a number cannot be negative. So, for the equation $|5x+4|=-3$, there would be no solution.

• **EXAMPLE**

Solve for x in $|2x-6|=|4-5x|$.

There are four possibilities here. Each term, $2x-6$ and $4-5x$, can be either positive or negative. The four possibilities are:

$$2x-6=4-5x \tag{1}$$

$$-(2x-6)=4-5x \tag{2}$$

$$2x-6=-(4-5x) \tag{3}$$

$$-(2x-6)=-(4-5x) \tag{4}$$

Equations (2) and (3) result in the same solution, as do equations (1) and (4). Therefore, it is necessary to solve only for equations (1) and (2). This gives

$$2x-6=4-5x \qquad \text{or} \qquad -(2x-6)=4-5x$$
$$7x=10 \qquad\qquad\qquad -2x+6=4-5x$$
$$x=\frac{10}{7} \qquad\qquad\qquad\qquad x=-\frac{2}{3}$$

The solution set is $(^{10}\!/_7, -^2\!/_3)$.

Drill: Absolute Value Equations

DIRECTIONS: Find the appropriate solutions.

1. $|4x-2|=6$

(A) -2 and -1 (B) -1 and 2 (C) 2

(D) $\frac{1}{2}$ and -2 (E) No solution

2. $\left|3-\frac{1}{2}y\right|=-7$

(A) -8 and 20 (B) 8 and -20 (C) 2 and -5

(D) 4 and -2 (E) No solution

3. $2|x+7|=12$

    (A) -13 and -1 (B) -6 and 6 (C) -1 and 13

    (D) 6 and -13 (E) No solution

4. $|5x|-7=3$

    (A) 2 and 4 (B) $\dfrac{4}{5}$ and 3 (C) -2 and 2

    (D) 2 (E) No solution

5. $\left|\dfrac{3}{4}m\right|=9$

    (A) 24 and -16 (B) $\dfrac{4}{27}$ and $-\dfrac{4}{3}$ (C) $\dfrac{4}{3}$ and 12

    (D) -12 and 12 (E) No solution

Inequalities

An inequality is a statement where the value of one quantity or expression is greater than ($>$), less than ($<$), greater than or equal to ($\geq$), less than or equal to ($\leq$), or not equal to ($\neq$) that of another.

- **EXAMPLE**

    $5>4$

The expression above means that the value of 5 is greater than the value of 4.

A **conditional inequality** is an inequality whose validity depends on the values of the variables in the sentence. That is, certain values of the variables will make the sentence true, and others will make it false.

    $3-y>3+y$

is a conditional inequality for the set of real numbers, since it is true for any replacement less than zero and false for all others.

    $x+5>x+2$

is an **absolute inequality** for the set of real numbers, meaning that for any real value x, the expression on the left is greater than the expression on the right.

    $5y<2y+y$

is inconsistent for the set of non-negative real numbers. For any y greater than 0 the sentence is always false. A sentence is inconsistent if it is always false when its variables assume allowable values.

The solution of a given inequality in one variable x consists of all values of x for which the inequality is true.

The graph of an inequality in one variable is represented by either a ray or a line segment on the real number line.

The endpoint is not a solution if the variable is strictly less than or greater than a particular value.

•   **EXAMPLE**

$$x > 2$$

2 is not a solution and should be represented as shown with an open circle at 2.

The endpoint is a solution if the variable is either (1) less than or equal to or (2) greater than or equal to a particular value.

•   **EXAMPLE**

$$5 > x \geq 2$$

In this case 2 is a solution and should be represented as shown.

Properties of Inequalities

If x and y are real numbers, then one and only one of the following statements is true.

$$x > y, x = y, \text{ or } x < y.$$

This is the order property of real numbers.

If a, b, and c are real numbers, the following are true:

A)   If $a < b$ and $b < c$, then $a < c$.

B)   If $a > b$ and $b > c$, then $a > c$.

This is the **transitive property of inequalities**.

If a, b, and c are real numbers and $a > b$, then $a + c > b + c$ and $a - c > b - c$. This is the **addition property of inequality**.

Two inequalities are said to have the same **sense** if their signs of inequality point in the same direction.

The sense of an inequality remains the same if both sides are multiplied or divided by the same positive real number.

- **EXAMPLE**

$$4 > 3$$

If we multiply both sides by 5, we will obtain

$$4 \times 5 > 3 \times 5$$
$$20 > 15$$

The sense of the inequality does not change.

The sense of an inequality becomes opposite, however, if each side is multiplied or divided by the same negative real number.

- **EXAMPLE**

$$4 > 3$$

If we multiply both sides by -5, we would obtain

$$4 \times -5 < 3 \times -5$$
$$-20 < -15$$

The sense of the inequality becomes opposite.

If $a > b$ and a, b, and n are positive real numbers, then

$$a^n > b^n \text{ and } a^{-n} < b^{-n}.$$

If $x > y$ and $q > p$, then $x + q > y + p$.

If $x > y > 0$ and $q > p > 0$, then $xq > yp$.

Inequalities that have the same solution set are called **equivalent inequalities**.

PROBLEM

Solve the inequality $2x + 5 > 9$.

SOLUTION

Add -5 to both sides:	$2x + 5 + (-5) > 9 + (-5)$
Additive inverse property:	$2x > 9 + (-5)$
Combine terms:	$2x > 4$

Multiply both sides by $\frac{1}{2}$:

$$\frac{1}{2}(2x) > \frac{1}{2} \times 4$$

$$x > 2$$

The solution set is

$$X = \{x \mid 2x + 5 > 9\}$$
$$= \{x \mid x > 2\}$$

(that is, all x such that x is greater than 2).

PROBLEM

> Solve the inequality $4x + 3 < 6x + 8$.

SOLUTION

In order to solve the inequality $4x + 3 < 6x + 8$, we must find all values of x that make it true. To do this, we wish to obtain x alone on one side of the inequality.

Add -3 to both sides:

$$
\begin{array}{r}
4x + 3 < 6x + 8 \\
-3 \qquad -3 \\
\hline
4x < 6x + 5
\end{array}
$$

Add $-6x$ to both sides:

$$
\begin{array}{r}
4x < \;\; 6x + 5 \\
-6x \;\; -6x \\
\hline
-2x < \;\;\; 5
\end{array}
$$

In order to obtain x alone we must divide both sides by (-2). Recall that dividing an inequality by a negative number reverses the inequality sign, hence

$$\frac{-2x}{-2} > \frac{5}{-2},$$

or $\qquad\qquad x > -\tfrac{5}{2}.$

Thus, our solution is $\{x : x > -\tfrac{5}{2}\}$ (the set of all x such that x is greater than $-\tfrac{5}{2}$).

PROBLEM

Put the following inequality in slope–intercept form.

$$y + 5x > 22$$

SOLUTION

Step 1 is to isolate the variable y. To do this, subtract $5x$ from both sides of the inequality.

$$y + 5x - 5x > 22 - 5x$$

Step 2 is to simplify the left side of the inequality.

$$y + 5x - 5x = y$$

Step 3 is to simplify the right side of the inequality.

$$22 - 5x = 22 - 5x$$

Step 4 is to rewrite the inequality.

$$y > 22 - 5x$$

Step 5 is to rewrite the inequality in the form $y > mx + b$, where m is the slope and b is the y–intercept.

$$y > -5x + 22$$

The correct answer is $y > -5x + 22$.

PROBLEM

Graph the inequality $4y \leq 4x - 4$.

SOLUTION

Step 1 is to put the inequality in y slope–intercept form by dividing both sides of the equation by 4.

$$4y \leq 4x - 4$$

$$y \leq x - 1$$

Step 2 is to choose two arbitrary values of x. Log the values in a chart the same as for equalities. Use the values of x to obtain values for y. These points actually solve the equality $y = x - 1$.

x	y
0	−1
2	1

Step 3 is to use the x and y values to plot points. Note that there are many different possible points. However, the graph should look the same.

$$(0, -1) \text{ and } (2, 1)$$

Step 4 is to use the points to graph the line. Notice that a solid line connects the points. The points along the line satisfy the inequality because the sign $\leq$ includes the "equal" points. The points in the shaded region also satisfy the inequality.

PROBLEM

Graph the inequality $y + 3x \geq 0$.

SOLUTION

Step 1 is to put the inequality in y slope–intercept form by adding $-3x$ to both sides.

$$y + 3x \geq 0$$

$$y \geq -3x$$

Step 2 is to choose two arbitrary values of x. Log the values in a chart the same as for equalities. Use the values of x to obtain values for y. These points actually solve the equality $y = -3x$.

x	y
0	0
−3	9

Step 3 is to use the x and y values to plot points. Note that there are many different possible points. However, the graph should look the same.

(0, 0) and (−3, 9)

Step 4 is to use the points to graph the line. Notice that a solid line connects the points. The points along the line satisfy the inequality because ≥ includes "equal" points, and the points in the shaded region satisfy the inequality.

PROBLEM

Graph the inequality $-y > x + 5$.

SOLUTION

Step 1 is to put the inequality in slope–intercept form by multiplying both sides by −1. Multiplying an inequality by a negative number changes the inequality sign to its opposite.

$-y > x + 5$

$y < -x - 5$

Step 2 is to choose two arbitrary values of x. Log the values in a chart the same as for equalities. Use the values of x to obtain values for y. This will actually solve the equality $y = -x - 5$.

x	y
0	−5
−5	0

Step 3 is to use the x and y values to plot points. Note that there are many different possible points. However, the graph should look the same.

$$(0, -5) \text{ and } (-5, 0)$$

Step 4 is to use the points to graph a line. Notice that a dashed line connects the points here. The points along the line do not satisfy the inequality because the sign is >, not ≥. Only the points in the shaded region satisfy the inequality.

Drill: Inequalities

> **DIRECTIONS**: Find the solution set for each inequality.

1. $3m + 2 < 7$

    (A) $m \geq \dfrac{5}{3}$ (B) $m \leq 2$ (C) $m < 2$

    (D) $m > 2$ (E) $m < \dfrac{5}{3}$

2. $\dfrac{1}{2}x - 3 \leq 1$

    (A) $-4 \leq x \leq 8$ (B) $x \geq -8$ (C) $x \leq 8$

    (D) $2 \leq x \leq 8$ (E) $x \geq 8$

3. $-3p + 1 \geq 16$

    (A) $p \geq -5$ (B) $p \geq \dfrac{-17}{3}$ (C) $p \leq \dfrac{-17}{3}$

    (D) $p \leq -5$ (E) $p \geq 5$

4. $-6 < \dfrac{2}{3}r + 6 \le 2$

    (A) $-6 < r \le -3$ (B) $-18 < r \le -6$ (C) $r \ge -6$

    (D) $-2 < r \le -\dfrac{4}{3}$ (E) $r \le -6$

5. $0 < 2 - y < 6$

    (A) $-4 < y < 2$ (B) $-4 < y < 0$ (C) $-4 < y < -2$

    (D) $-2 < y < 4$ (E) $0 < y < 4$

Word Problems

One of the main problems students have in mathematics involves solving word problems. The secret to solving these problems is being able to convert words into numbers and variables in the form of an algebraic equation.

The easiest way to approach a word problem is to read the question and ask yourself what you are trying to find. This unknown quantity can be represented by a variable.

Next, determine how the variable relates to the other quantities in the problem. More than likely, these quantities can be explained in terms of the original variable. If not, a separate variable may have to be used to represent a quantity.

Using these variables and the relationships determined among them, an equation can be written. Solve for a particular variable and then plug this number in for each relationship that involves this variable in order to find any unknown quantities.

The key to converting word problems into mathematical problems is attention to *reasonableness*, with the choice of operations most crucial to success. Often, individual words and phrases translate into numbers and operation symbols, and making sure that the translations are reasonable is important. Consider this word problem:

Roberto babysat for the Yagers one evening. They paid him $5 just for coming over to their house, plus $7 for every hour of sitting. How much was he paid if he babysat for 4 hours?

"Plus" indicates addition, and "for every hour" suggests multiplication. Thus, the computational work can be set up like this: $5 + (7 \times 4)$ = Roberto's earnings. It would have been unreasonable to use a multiplication symbol in place of the addition sign. He earned $5 *plus* $7 for each of 4 hours.

Last, re-read the problem to be sure that you have answered the questions correctly and fully.

- **EXAMPLE**

Find two consecutive odd integers whose sum is 36.

Let x = the first odd integer

Let $x + 2$ = the second odd integer

The sum of the two numbers is 36. Therefore,

$$x + (x + 2) = 36$$

Simplifying,

$$2x + 2 = 36$$
$$2x + 2 + (-2) = 36 + (-2)$$
$$2x = 34$$
$$x = 17$$

Plugging 17 in for x, we find the second odd integer = $(x + 2) = (17 + 2) = 19$. Therefore, we find that the two consecutive odd integers whose sum is 36 are 17 and 19, respectively.

Drill: Algebraic Word Problems

DIRECTIONS: Solve the following word problems algebraically.

1. The sum of two numbers is 41. One number is one less than twice the other. Find the larger of the two numbers.

    (A) 13   (B) 14   (C) 21   (D) 27   (E) 41

2. The sum of two consecutive integers is 111. Find the value of the smaller integer.

    (A) 55   (B) 56   (C) 58   (D) 111   (E) 112

3. The difference between two integers is 12. The sum of the two integers is 2. Find both integers.

    (A) 7 and 5   (B) 7 and −5   (C) −7 and 5   (D) 2 and 12   (E) −2 and 12

Rate

One of the formulas you will use for rate problems will be

Rate × Time = Distance

PROBLEM

> If a plane travels five hours from New York to California at a speed of 600 miles per hour, how many miles does the plane travel?

SOLUTION

Using the formula rate × time = distance, multiply 600 mph × 5 hours = 3,000 miles.

The average rate at which an object travels can be solved by dividing the total distance traveled by the total amount of time.

PROBLEM

> On a 40-mile bicycle trip, Cathy rode half the distance at 20 mph and the other half at 10 mph. What was Cathy's average speed on the bike trip?

SOLUTION

First you need to break down the problem. On half of the trip, which would be 20 miles, Cathy rode 20 mph. Using the rate formula,

$$\frac{\text{distance}}{\text{rate}} = \text{time},$$

you would compute that it took

$$\frac{20 \text{ miles}}{20 \text{ miles per hour}} = 1 \text{ hour}$$

to travel the first 20 miles. During the second 20 miles, Cathy traveled at 10 miles per hour, which would take

$$\frac{20 \text{ miles}}{10 \text{ miles per hour}} = 2 \text{ hours}$$

Thus, the average speed Cathy traveled would be 40 miles in 3 hours, or $\frac{40}{3} = 13.3$ miles per hour.

In solving for some rate problems you can use cross multiplication involving ratios to solve for x.

PROBLEM

If 2 pairs of shoes cost $52, then what is the cost of 10 pairs of shoes at this rate?

SOLUTION

$$\frac{2}{52} = \frac{10}{x}, \ 2x = 52 \times 10, \ x = \frac{520}{2}, \ x = \$260$$

Drill: Rate

DIRECTIONS: Solve to find the rate.

1. Two towns are 420 miles apart. A car leaves the first town traveling toward the second town at 55 mph. At the same time, a second car leaves the other town and heads toward the first town at 65 mph. How long will it take for the two cars to meet?

    (A) 2 hr   (B) 3 hr   (C) 3.5 hr   (D) 4 hr   (E) 4.25 hr

2. A camper leaves the campsite walking due east at a rate of 3.5 mph. Another camper leaves the campsite at the same time but travels due west. In two hours the two campers will be 15 miles apart. What is the walking rate of the second camper?

    (A) 2.5 mph   (B) 3 mph   (C) 3.25 mph   (D) 3.5 mph   (E) 4 mph

3. A bicycle racer covers a 75-mile training route to prepare for an upcoming race. If the racer could increase his speed by 5 mph, he could complete the same course in three-fourths of the time. Find his average speed.

    (A) 15 mph   (B) 15.5 mph   (C) 16 mph   (D) 18 mph   (E) 20 mph

Work

In work problems, one of the basic formulas is

$$\frac{1}{x} + \frac{1}{y} = \frac{1}{z}$$

where x and y represent the number of hours it takes two objects or people to complete the work and z is the total number of hours when both are working together.

PROBLEM

> Otis can seal and stamp 400 envelopes in 2 hours while Elizabeth seals and stamps 400 envelopes in 1 hour. In how many hours can Otis and Elizabeth, working together, complete a 400-piece mailing at these rates?

SOLUTION

$$\frac{1}{2} + \frac{1}{1} = \frac{1}{z}$$

$$\frac{1}{2} + \frac{2}{2} = \frac{3}{2}$$

$$\frac{3}{2} = \frac{1}{z}$$

$$3z = 2$$

$z = \frac{2}{3}$ of an hour, or 40 minutes, working together, Otis and Elizabeth can seal and stamp 400 envelopes in 40 minutes.

Drill: Work

> **DIRECTIONS:** Solve to find the amount of work.

1. It takes Marty 3 hours to type the address labels for his club's newsletter. It takes Pat only $2\frac{1}{4}$ hours to type the same amount of labels. How long would it take them working together to complete the address labels?

    (A) $\frac{7}{9}$ hr
    (B) $1\frac{2}{7}$ hr
    (C) $1\frac{4}{5}$ hour
    (D) $2\frac{5}{8}$ hr
    (E) $5\frac{1}{4}$ hr

2. It takes Troy 3 hours to mow his family's large lawn. With his little brother's help, he can finish the job in only 2 hours. How long would it take the little brother to mow the entire lawn alone?

    (A) 4 hr
    (B) 5 hr
    (C) 5.5 hr
    (D) 6 hr
    (E) 6.75 hr

3. A tank can be filled by one inlet pipe in 15 minutes. It takes an outlet pipe 75 minutes to drain the tank. If the outlet pipe is left open by accident, how long would it take to fill the tank?

    (A) 15.5 min
    (B) 15.9 min
    (C) 16.8 min
    (D) 18.75 min
    (E) 19.3 min

ALGEBRAIC THINKING DRILLS

ANSWER KEY

Drill: Operations with Polynomials

1. (B)	5. (A)	9. (A)	13. (E)	17. (D)
2. (C)	6. (B)	10. (D)	14. (A)	18. (E)
3. (C)	7. (C)	11. (C)	15. (D)	19. (B)
4. (D)	8. (E)	12. (B)	16. (C)	20. (B)

Drill: Simplifying Algebraic Expressions

1. (C)	3. (B)	5. (D)	7. (A)	9. (A)
2. (D)	4. (A)	6. (B)	8. (B)	10. (E)

Drill: Linear Equations

1. (C)	4. (D)
2. (A)	5. (B)
3. (E)	

Drill: Two Linear Equations

1. (E)	3. (A)	5. (C)	7. (D)	9. (A)
2. (B)	4. (D)	6. (B)	8. (E)	10. (B)

Drill: Quadratic Equations

1. (A)	3. (B)	5. (E)	7. (B)	9. (C)
2. (D)	4. (C)	6. (B)	8. (D)	10. (E)

Drill: Absolute Value Equations

1. (B)	4. (C)
2. (E)	5. (D)
3. (A)	

Drill: Inequalities

1. (E)	4. (B)
2. (C)	5. (A)
3. (D)	

Drill: Algebraic Word Problems

1. (D)
2. (A)
3. (B)

Drill: Rate

1. (C)
2. (E)
3. (A)

Drill: Work

1. (B)
2. (D)
3. (D)

Competency 5: Knowledge of Data Analysis and Probability

Data Interpretation

Some problems test the ability to apply information given in graphs and tables.

PROBLEM

In which year was the least number of bushels of wheat produced? (See figure below.)

SOLUTION

By inspection of the graph, we find that the shortest bar representing wheat production is the one representing the wheat production for 1993. Thus, the least number of bushels of wheat was produced in 1993.

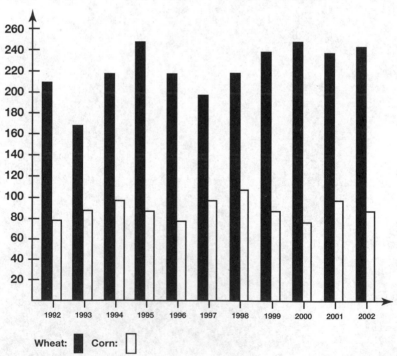

Number of bushels (to the nearest 5 bushels) of wheat and corn produced by farm RQS from 1992 - 2002.

Wheat: ■   Corn: ☐

PROBLEM

What was the ratio of wheat production in 2002 to that of 1992?

SOLUTION

From the graph representing wheat production, the number of bushels of wheat produced in 1992 is equal to 210 bushels. This number can be found by locating the bar on the graph representing wheat production in 1992 and then drawing a horizontal line from the top of that bar to the vertical axis. The point where this horizontal line meets the vertical axis represents the number of bushels of wheat produced in 1992. This number on the vertical axis is 210. Similarly, the graph indicates that the number of bushels of wheat produced in 2002 is equal to 245 bushels.

Thus, the ratio of wheat production in 2002 to that of 1992 is 245 to 210, which can be written as $^{245}/_{210}$. Changing this ratio to its simplest form yields

$$\frac{245}{210} = \frac{5 \times 7 \times 7}{2 \times 3 \times 5 \times 7}$$
$$= \frac{7}{2 \times 3}$$
$$= \frac{7}{6} \text{ or } 7:6$$

Interpretation of Graphic Information Questions

Graphs, charts, and tables may play a large part on the test, and you should be familiar with them. More than likely, you will encounter at least one passage that is accompanied by some form of graphic information. You will then be required to answer any question(s) based on the interpretation of the information presented in the graph, chart, or table.

Graphs are used to produce visual aids for sets of information. Often, the impact of quantities and statistics is diminished by an overabundance of tedious numbers. A graph helps a reader rapidly visualize or organize irregular information, as well as trace long periods of decline or increase. The following is a guide to reading three principal graphic forms.

Line Graphs

IMMIGRATION TO THE UNITED STATES 1820–1930

Source: Immigration and Naturalization Service of the U.S. Dept. of Justice

Line graphs are used to track multiple elements of one or more subjects. One element is usually a time factor, over whose span the other element increases, decreases, or remains static. The lines that compose such graphs are connected points that are displayed on the chart through each integral stage. For example, look at the given immigration graph.

The average number of immigrants from 1820 to 1830 is represented at one point; the average number of immigrants from 1831 to 1840 is represented at the next. The line that connects these points is used only to ease the visual gradation between the points. It is not meant to give a strictly accurate representation for every year between the two decades. If this were so, the line would hardly be straight, even progression from year to year. The sharp directness of the lines reveals otherwise. The purpose of the graph is to plot the average increases or decreases from point to point. When dealing with more than one subject, a line graph must use either differently colored lines (or different types of lines if the graph is black-and-white). In the graph, the dark bold line represents immigration from Northwestern Europe; the broken line represents immigration from Southeastern Europe.

To read a line graph, find the point of change that interests you. For example, if you want to trace immigration from Northwestern Europe from 1861 to 1870, you would find the position of the dark line on that point. Next, trace the position to the vertical information on the chart. In this instance, one would discover that approximately 2 million immigrants arrived from Northwestern Europe in the period of time from 1861 to 1870. If wishing to discover when the number of immigrants reached 4 million you would read across from 4 million on the vertical side of the graph, and see that this number was reached in 1881–1890 from Northwestern Europe, and somewhere over the two decades from 1891 to 1910 from Southeastern Europe.

Bar Graphs

Bar graphs are also used to plot two dynamic elements of a subject. However, unlike a line graph, the bar graph usually deals with only one subject. The exception to this is when the graph is three-dimensional, and the bars take on the dimension of depth. However, because we will be dealing with only two-dimensional graphs, we will be working only with a single subject. The other difference between a line and a bar graph is that a bar graph usually calls for a single element to be traced in terms of another, whereas a line graph usually plots either of the two elements with equal interest. For example, in the following bar graph, inflation and deflation are being marked over a span of years.

INFLATION
Inflation is a rise in the general level of prices.
Deflation is a decline in the general level of prices.

Percentage points are assigned to each year's level of prices, and that percentage decreases (deflation) from 1980 to 1981, and from 1981 to 1982. The price level is static from 1982 to 1983. The price level then increases (inflation) from 1983 to 1984. Therefore, it is obvious that the bar graph is read strictly in terms of the changes exhibited over a period of time or against some other element. Conversely, a line graph is used to plot two dynamic elements of equal interest to the reader (e.g., either number of immigrants or the particular decade in question, as we saw in the sample line graph).

To read a bar graph, simply begin with the element at the base of a bar and trace the bar to its full length. Once reaching its length, cross-reference the other element of information that match the length of the bar.

Pie Charts

Pie charts differ greatly from line or bar graphs. Pie charts are used to help a reader visualize percentages of information with many elements to the subject. An entire "pie" represents 100 percent of a given quantity of information. The pie is then sliced into measurements that correspond to their respective shares of the 100 percent. For example, in the pie chart that follows, Myrna's rent occupies a slice greater than any other in the pie, because no other element equals or exceeds 25 percent of Myrna's monthly budget.

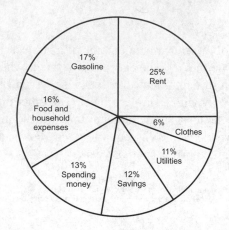

To read a pie chart, choose the element of the subject that interests you and compare its size to those of the other elements. In cases where the elements are similar in size, do not assume that they are equal. The exact percentage of the element will be listed within that slice of the chart. For example, Myrna's utilities, savings, and spending money all appear similar in size, but it is clear when reading the chart that each possesses a different value.

Reading Tables

Tables are useful because they can present large bodies of information within a confined area. To read a table, cross-reference the column headings that run horizontally across the top of the table with the row headings that run vertically down the left side of the table. Scanning the table for the overall information within it is usually done by reading line by line, as if reading regular text, while referring to the appropriate headings of the table to interpret the information listed. Note that some tables possess horizontal subheadings, which further ease the separation of different areas of information.

Effects of Common Drugs				
Drug	**Psychological Dependence**	**Physical Dependence**	**Physical Withdrawal Effects**	**Development of Tolerance**
Depressants				
Alcohol	Mild to very strong	Very strong	Severe/dangerous	Minimal
Barbiturates	Develops slowly	Develops slowly	Death possible	Minimal
Narcotics				
Opiates (heroin, morphine)	Very strong Develops rapidly	Rapid/increases with dosage	Frightening symptoms but not dangerous	Very high; goes down quickly after withdrawal (danger if user returns to original dose)

Effects of Common Drugs (*Continued*)				
Drug	**Psychological Dependence**	**Physical Dependence**	**Physical Withdrawal Effects**	**Development of Tolerance**
Stimulants				
Amphetamines	Strong	Not in formal sense, but body seeks "rush"	Mild	Extremely high
Cocaine	Very strong	None	None (can cause heart spasms and instant death even if healthy)	None
Crack	Strong	Strong	Mild	High
Psychedelics				
LSD	Unpredictable	None	None	Extremely high
Marijuana	Mild to strong	Some, in high doses	None	None (some for high doses)

To use the preceding table, simply choose a particular drug, and then find the appropriate information needed about that drug through the headings listed at the top of the table. For example, according to this table, the physical withdrawal effects of amphetamines, a stimulant drug, are mild.

Helpful Hints

You should approach any graphic information you encounter as a key to a larger body of information in abbreviated form. Be sure to use the visual aids of the graphics (e.g., the size of slices on pie charts) as aids only; do not ignore the written information listed on the graph, table, or other visual aid.

Note especially the title and headings so that you know exactly what you are looking at. Also, be aware of the source of the information, where applicable. Know what each element of the graphic information represents; this will help you compare how drastic or subtle any changes are, and over what span of time they take place. Be sure you realize what the actual numbers represent, whether it is dollars, so many thousands of people, millions of shares, and so forth. Finally, note the way in which the graphic information relates to the text it seeks to illustrate; know in what ways the graphic information supports the arguments of the author of the given passage.

Drill: Data Interpretation

DIRECTIONS: Determine the correct response from the information provided.

Amount of Scholarship Money Awarded to Graduating Seniors
West High — 1981 – 1990

1. What was the approximate amount of scholarship money awarded in 1985?

   (A) $150,000   (B) $155,000   (C) $165,000

   (D) $175,000   (E) $190,000

2. By how much did the scholarship money increase between 1987 and 1988?

   (A) $25,000   (B) $30,000   (C) $50,000

   (D) $55,000   (E) $75,000

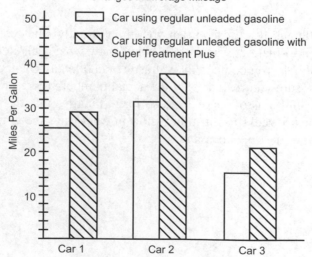

Changes in Average Mileage

3. By how much did the mileage increase for Car 2 when the new product was used?

    (A) 5 mpg   (B) 6 mpg   (C) 7 mpg

    (D) 10 mpg   (E) 12 mpg

4. Which car's mileage increased the most in this test?

    (A) Car 1   (B) Car 2   (C) Car 3

    (D) Cars 1 and 2   (E) Cars 2 and 3

5. According to the bar graph, if your car averages 25 mpg, what mileage might you expect with the new product?

    (A) 21 mpg   (B) 30 mpg   (C) 31 mpg

    (D) 35 mpg   (E) 37 mpg

Sample Family Budget

Auto – 15%

Food – 25%

Medical Insurance – 6%

Miscellaneous – 8%

Clothing – 8%

Housing – 30%

Gifts/Charity – 8%

6. Using the budget shown, a family with an income of $4,500 a month would plan to spend what amount on housing?

    (A) $900   (B) $1125   (C) $1350

    (D) $1470   (E) $1560

7. In this sample family budget, how does the amount spent on an automobile compare to the amount spent on housing?

    (A) $\dfrac{1}{3}$ (B) $\dfrac{1}{2}$ (C) $\dfrac{2}{3}$

    (D) $1\dfrac{1}{2}$ (E) 2

8. A family with a monthly income of $3,720 spends $375 a month on clothing. By what amount do they exceed the sample budget?

(A) $3.00

(B) $15.60

(C) $30.00

(D) $77.40

(E) $95.25

CALORIE CHART — BREADS

Bread	Amount	Calories
French Bread	2 oz	140
Bran Bread	1 oz	95
Whole Wheat Bread	1 oz	115
Oatmeal Bread	0.5 oz	55
Raisin Bread	1 oz	125

9. One dieter eats two ounces of French bread. A second dieter eats two ounces of bran bread. The second dieter has consumed how many more calories than the first dieter?

(A) 40

(B) 45

(C) 50

(D) 55

(E) 65

10. One ounce of whole wheat bread has how many more calories than an ounce of oatmeal bread?

(A) 5

(B) 15

(C) 60

(D) 75

(E) 125

Statistical Concepts

The term *data* refers to numerical information acquired by counting or measuring. The number of students in a class, their test scores on the ISAT, and their individual heights are all examples of data.

Data can be represented in *discrete* or *continuous* form, depending on what they represent. If data are discrete, they have gaps between them. A bar graph is a common way to depict discrete data. Discrete data are generally obtained from counting rather than by measuring. Continuous data are usually represented by an unbroken line on a graph, and they are usually obtained by measuring rather than counting.

Here is a list of statistical concepts that are useful in interpreting data:

mean   The mean is the sum of a set of numbers divided by the quantity of numbers n in the set. It gives the *average value* of a data set.

range   The range is the measure of spread (*variation*); it is the difference between the largest value and the smallest value in a set of data.

sample survey   This is a survey of a population not really true made by taking a sample judged to be representative of that population. Use of a random mechanism for choosing the sample is essential for validity and believability.

spread of data   Also called **variation**, the spread of data describes the degree to which data are spread out around their center. Useful measures of spread include the standard deviation and range.

standard deviation   This is the most commonly used expression of spread, or variation, of data. The higher the standard deviation, the higher the degree of spread around the center of the data (that is, the data are more inconsistent with each other).

median   The median is the center value in a set of numbers: there are an equal number of values above and below it.

percentiles   Percentiles are the measures of where a piece of data stands in relation to the other data in its set. Perhaps best known from standardized tests, percentiles tell how many other data are lower in value. For instance, a test taker might have a raw score of 82% (that is, 82% of the answers correct) but rank in the 91st percentile, meaning that 90% of all test takers received lower raw scores. The median occurs at the 50th percentile.

frequency distributions   These represent the probability that a statistic of interest will fall in a certain interval; for example, the height of a person chosen at random may follow the *normal distribution*. Following are some samples of kinds of distributions, with location of the means and medians indicated:

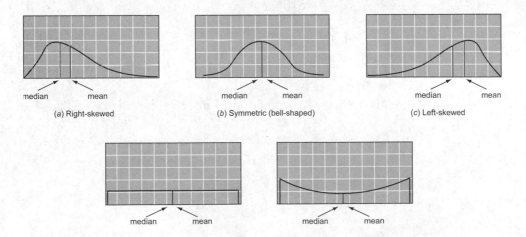

Distribution (b) in the figure is the well-known normal, or bell-shaped, curve on which tests are often said to be graded. Assuming that these graphs represent test scores, notice that more scores fall in the middle in the normal distribution than on the high or low ends. In the right-skewed distribution, shown in (a), more of the scores are low, and in the left-skewed distribution of (c), more of the scores are high. The distribution in (d) shows that all the scores are distributed equally from high to low, and (e) shows a distribution in which most scores were either high or low, with very few being average. Notice that in (a), the right-skewed distribution, the mean is higher than the median, and in (c) the median is higher than the mean.

Mean, Median, Mode—Measures of Central Tendency

Mean

The mean is the arithmetic average. It is the sum of the variables divided by the total number of variables. For example, the mean of 4, 3, and 8 is

$$\frac{4+3+8}{3} = \frac{15}{3} = 5$$

PROBLEM

Find the mean salary for four company employees who make $5/hr, $8/hr, $12/hr, and $15/hr.

SOLUTION

The mean salary is the average.

$$\frac{\$5 + \$8 + \$12 + \$15}{4} = \frac{\$40}{4} = \$10/hr$$

PROBLEM

Find the mean length of five fish with lengths of 7.5 in., 7.75 in., 8.5 in., 8.5 in., and 8.25 in.

SOLUTION

The mean length is the average length.

$$\frac{7.5 + 7.75 + 8.5 + 8.5 + 8.25}{5} = \frac{40.5}{5} = 8.1 \text{ in}$$

Median

The median is the middle value in a set when there is an odd number of values, which leaves an equal number of values larger and smaller than the median. When the set is an even number of values, the average of the two middle values is the median. Note that to find the median, the set must be in order by size. For example:

The median of (2, 3, 5, 8, 9) is 5.

The median of (2, 3, 5, 9, 10, 11) is $\dfrac{5+9}{2}$ =7.

Mode

The mode is the most frequently occurring value in the set of values. For example, the mode of 4, 5, 8, 3, 8, 2 would be 8 because it occurs twice whereas the other values occur only once.

PROBLEM

For this series of observations, find the mean, median, and mode: 500, 600, 800, 800, 900, 900, 900, 900, 900, 1,000, 1,100

SOLUTION

The mean is the value obtained by adding all the measurements and dividing by the number of measurements.

$$\text{mean} = \frac{500+600+800+800+900+900+900+900+900+1,000+1,100}{11}$$
$$= \frac{9,300}{11} = 845.45$$

The median is the value appearing in the middle of the ordered set of numbers. We have 11 values, so here the sixth, 900, is the median.

The mode is the value that appears most frequently. That is also 900, which appears five times.

All three of these numbers are measures of central tendency. They describe the "middle" or "center" of the data.

PROBLEM

Nine rats run through a maze. The time each rat took to traverse the maze is recorded, and these times (in minutes) are listed below.

1 min, 2.5 min, 3 min, 1.5 min, 2 min, 1.25 min, 1 min, .9 min, 30 min

Which of the three measures of central tendency would be the most appropriate in this case?

SOLUTION

We will calculate the three measures of central tendency and then compare them to determine which would be the most appropriate in describing these data.

The mean is the sum of the values listed divided by the number of values. In this case

$$\frac{1+2.5+3+1.5+2+1.25+1+.9+30}{9}=\frac{43.15}{9}=4.79$$

The median is the "middle number" in an array of the values from the lowest to the highest.

0.9, 1.0, 1.0, 1.25, 1.5, 2.0, 2.5, 3.0, 30.0

The median is the fifth value in this ordered array or 1.5. There are four values larger than 1.5 and four values smaller than 1.5.

The mode is the most frequently occurring value in the sample. In this data set the mode is 1.0.

mean = 4.79

median = 1.5

mode = 1.0

The mean is not appropriate here. Only one rat took more than 4.79 minutes to run the maze and this rat took 30 minutes. We see that the mean has been distorted by this one large value.

The median or mode seems to describe this data set better and would be more appropriate to use.

Drill: Measures of Central Tendency

Mean

DIRECTIONS: Find the mean of each set of numbers.

1. 18, 25, and 32

    (A) 3   (C) 50   (E) 150
    (B) 25   (D) 75

2. $\frac{4}{9}, \frac{2}{3}$, and $\frac{5}{6}$

    (A) $\frac{11}{18}$ (C) $\frac{41}{54}$ (E) $\frac{54}{18}$

    (B) $\frac{35}{54}$ (D) $\frac{35}{18}$

3. 97, 102, 116, and 137

   (A) 40   (C) 109   (E) 116

   (B) 102   (D) 113

4. 12, 15, 18, 24, and 31

   (A) 18   (C) 20   (E) 100

   (B) 19.3   (D) 25

5. 7, 4, 6, 3, 11, and 14

   (A) 5   (C) 7   (E) 8

   (B) 6.5   (D) 7.5

Median

DIRECTIONS: Find the median value of each set of numbers.

---

6. 3, 8, and 6

   (A) 3   (C) 8   (E) 20

   (B) 6   (D) 17

7. 19, 15, 21, 27, and 12

   (A) 19   (C) 21   (E) 94

   (B) 15   (D) 27

8. $1\frac{2}{3}, 1\frac{7}{8}, 1\frac{3}{4}$, and $1\frac{5}{6}$

   (A) $1\frac{30}{48}$ (C) $1\frac{3}{4}$ (E) $1\frac{21}{24}$

   (B) $1\frac{2}{3}$ (D) $1\frac{19}{24}$

9. 29, 18, 21, and 35

   (A) 29   (C) 21   (E) 25

   (B) 18   (D) 35

10. 8, 15, 7, 12, 31, 3, and 28

    (A) 7   (B) 11.6   (C) 12

    (D) 14.9   (E) 104

Mode

DIRECTIONS: Find the mode(s) of each set of numbers.

---

11. 1, 3, 7, 4, 3, and 8

   (A) 1   (B) 3   (C) 7   (D) 4   (E) None

12. 12, 19, 25, and 42

   (A) 12   (B) 19   (C) 25   (D) 42   (E) None

13. 16, 14, 12, 16, 30, and 28

   (A) 6   (B) 14   (C) 16   (D) $19.\overline{3}$ (E) None

14. 4, 3, 9, 2, 4, 5, and 2

   (A) 3 and 9   (B) 5 and 9   (C) 4 and 5   (D) 2 and 4   (E) None

15. 87, 42, 111, 116, 39, 111, 140, 116, 97, and 111

   (A) 111   (B) 116   (C) 39   (D) 140   (E) None

Probability and Statistics

Probability theory provides models for chance variations. The *probability* of any event occurring is equal to the number of desired outcomes divided by the number of all possible events. Thus, the probability of blindly pulling a green ball out of a hat (in this case the desired outcome) if the hat contains two green and five yellow balls, is $\frac{2}{7}$ (about 29%). *Odds* are related to probability, but are different. The odds that any given event *will* occur is the ratio of the probability that the event will occur to the probability that the event *will not* occur (typically expressed as a ratio). In the example here, the odds that a green ball will be drawn are 2:5.

Statistics is the branch of mathematics that involves collecting, analyzing, and interpreting data, organizing data to describe them usefully, then drawing conclusions and making decisions. Statistics builds on probability, and typically studies "populations," meaning quantifiable groups of things. Trends and patterns not otherwise noticed may be revealed via statistics.

One key statistical concept is that of *standard deviation*. The standard deviation of a set of values tells how "tightly" all of the values are clustered around the mean of the set. When values are tightly clustered near the mean, the standard deviation is small. If values are widespread the standard deviation is large. Here is one way to find the standard deviation of a set. Consider the set

   6   8   14   5   6   5   5

First find the mean (7).

Next, find the difference of each value in the set and the mean (ignoring negative signs). This gives 1, 1, 7, 2, 1, 2, and 2.

Now, square each of those values, giving 1, 1, 49, 4, 1, 4, and 4.

Next take the sum of those squares (64) and divide the sum by the number of values ($\frac{64}{7} = 9.14$).

Finally, take the square root of 9.14, giving a standard deviation of 3.02. Think of 3.02 as the amount that the values in the set "typically" vary from the center.

Permutation, Combination, and Probability

Permutation refers to the method of finding the number of ways n things can be arranged taking r at a time. The formula is $P(n, r) = \dfrac{n!}{(n-r)!}$.

The mathematical symbol ! (looks like an exclamation mark) means multiplying a whole number by each of its preceding whole numbers, down to 1. Therefore, $4! = 4 \times 3 \times 2 \times 1$. Symbolically, $n! = n \times (n-1) \times (n-2) \times (n-3) \dots 1$,

PROBLEM

Evaluate each of the following symbols:

(a) $5!$ (b) $\dfrac{7!}{4!}$ (c) $P(6,2)$ (d) $P(9,2)$

SOLUTION

(a) $5! = 5 \times 4 \times 3 \times 2 \times 1 = 120$

(b) $\dfrac{7!}{4!} = \dfrac{7 \times 6 \times 5 \times \cancel{4!}}{\cancel{4!}} = 210$

(c) $P(n,r) = \dfrac{n!}{(n-r)!}$

$P(6,2) = \dfrac{6!}{(6-2)!} = \dfrac{6!}{4!} = \dfrac{6 \times 5 \times \cancel{4!}}{\cancel{4!}} = 30$

(d) Similarly

$P(9,2) = \dfrac{9!}{(9-2)!} = \dfrac{9!}{7!} = \dfrac{9 \times 8 \times \cancel{7!}}{\cancel{7!}} = 72$

PROBLEM

Calculate the number of permutations of the letters a, b, c, d taken two at a time.

SOLUTION

The first of the two letters may be taken in 4 ways (a, b, c, or d). The second letter may therefore be selected from the remaining three letters in 3 ways. By the fundamental principle, the total number of ways of selecting two letters is equal to the product of the number of ways of selecting each letter. Hence

$$P(4,2) = 4 \times 3 = 12$$

The list of these permutations is:

ab	ba	ca	da
ac	bc	cb	db
ad	bd	cd	dc

PROBLEM

In how many ways may 3 books be placed next to each other on a shelf?

SOLUTION

We construct a pattern of 3 boxes to represent the places where the 3 books are to be placed next to each other on the shelf:

Since there are 3 books, the first place may be filled in 3 ways. There are then 2 books left, so that the second place may be filled in 2 ways. There is only 1 book left to fill the last place. Hence our boxes take the following form:

3	2	1

The Fundamental Principle of Counting states that if one thing can be done in a different ways and, when it is done in any one of these ways, a second thing can be done in b different ways, and a third thing can be done in c ways, ... then all the things in succession can be done in $a \times b \times c$ ... different ways. Thus the books can be arranged in $3 \times 2 \times 1 = 6$ ways.

This can also be seen using the following approach. Since the arrangement of books on the shelf is important, this is a permutation problem. Recalling the general formula for the number of pemutations of n things taken r at a time, $_nP_r = n!/(n-r)!$, we replace n by 3 and r by 3 to obtain

$$_3P_3 = \frac{3!}{(3-3)!} = \frac{3!}{0!} = \frac{3\times2\times1}{1} = 6$$

PROBLEM

Candidates for 3 different political offices are to be chosen from a list of 10 people. In how many ways may this be done?

SOLUTION

There are 10 choices for the first office, and to go with each choice there are 9 choices for the second office, and to go with each of these there are 8 choices for the third office. The Fundamental Principle of Counting states that if one thing can be done in a different ways, a second thing can be done in b different ways, and a third thing can be done in c different ways ..., then all the things in succession can be done in $a \times b \times c \ldots$ different ways. Hence, there are $10 \times 9 \times 8 = 720$ ways of choosing the officers.

This can also be seen using the following approach. Since the arrangement of candidates on each slate is important (each arrangement represents people running for different political offices), this is a permutation problem. Recalling the general formula for the number of permutations of n things taken r at a time, $_nP_r = n!/(n-r)!$, we replace n by 10 and r by 3 to obtain

$$_{10}P_3 = \frac{10!}{(10-3)!} = \frac{10!}{7!} = \frac{10\times9\times8\times\cancel{7}!}{\cancel{7}!} = 720$$

PROBLEM

In how many ways may a party of four women and four men be seated at a round table if the women and men are to occupy alternate seats?

SOLUTION

If we consider the seats indistinguishable, then this is a problem in circular permutations, as opposed to linear permutations. In the standard linear permutations approach, each chair is distinguishable from the others. Thus, if a woman is seated first, she may be chosen 4 ways, then a man seated next to her may be chosen 4 ways, the next woman can be chosen 3 ways and the man next to her can be chosen 3 ways, and so on. Our diagram to the linear approach shows the number of ways each seat can be occupied.

| 4 | 4 | 3 | 3 | 2 | 2 | 1 | 1 |

By the Fundamental Principle of Counting there are thus $4 \times 4 \times 3 \times 3 \times 2 \times 2 \times 1 \times 1 = 576$ ways to seat the people.

However, if the seats are indistinguishable, so long as each person has the same two people on each side, the seating arrangement is considered the same. Thus, we may suppose one person, say a woman, is seated in a particular place, and then arrange the remaining three women and four men relative to her. Because of the alternate seating scheme, there are three possible places for the remaining three women, so that there are $3! = 6$ ways of seating them. There are four possible places for the four men, hence there are $4! = 24$ ways in which the men may be seated. Hence the total number of arrangements is $6 \times 24 = 144$. In general, the formula for circular permutations of n things and n other things that are alternating is $(n-1)!n!$. In our case, we have

$$(4-1)!4! = 3!4! = 3 \times 2 \times 4 \times 3 \times 2 = 144.$$

Combination refers to the method of finding the number of ways of arranging n things taken r at a time when the order within the arrangements is not important. The formula is $C(n, r) = \dfrac{n!}{r!(n-r)!}$.

PROBLEM

Evaluate each of the following symbols:

(a)   C(6,3)   (b)   C(18,16)

SOLUTION

The general formula for the number of combinations of n different things taken r at a time,

$$C(n,r) = \frac{n!}{r!(n-r)!}:$$

(a) $C(6,3) = \dfrac{6!}{3!(6-3)!} = \dfrac{6!}{3!3!} = \dfrac{\cancel{6} \times 5 \times 4 \times \cancel{3}!}{\cancel{3} \times \cancel{2} \times 1 \times \cancel{3}!} = 20$

(b) $C(18,16) = \dfrac{18!}{16!(18-16)!} = \dfrac{18!}{16!2!} = \dfrac{\overset{9}{\cancel{18}} \times 17 \times \cancel{16}!}{\cancel{2} \times 1 \times \cancel{16}!} = 153$

Note: that the numerator and denominator of the fractions are first divided by the larger factorial in the denominator.

PROBLEM

In how many different ways may a pair of dice fall?

SOLUTION

The Fundamental Principle of Counting states that if one thing can be done in a different ways, and when it is done in any one of these ways, a second thing can be done in b different ways, then both things in succession can be done in $a \times b$ different ways. A die has 6 sides, thus it may land in any of six ways. Since each die may land in 6 ways, by the Fundamental Principle both dice may fall in $6 \times 6 = 36$ ways. We can verify this result by enumerating all the possible ordered pairs of dice throws:

1,1	1,2	1,3	1,4	1,5	1,6
2,1	2,2	2,3	2,4	2,5	2,6
3,1	3,2	3,3	3,4	3,5	3,6
4,1	4,2	4,3	4,4	4,5	4,6
5,1	5,2	5,3	5,4	5,5	5,6
6,1	6,2	6,3	6,4	6,5	6,6

PROBLEM

In how many ways can we select a committee of 3 from a group of 10 people?

SOLUTION

The arrangement or order of people chosen is unimportant. Thus this is a combination problem. Recalling the general formula for the number of combinations of n different things taken r at a time,

$C(n,r) = \dfrac{n!}{r!(n-r)!}$, the number of committees of 3 from a group of 10 people is

$$C(10,3) = \frac{10!}{3!(10-3)!} = \frac{10!}{3!7!} = \frac{10 \times^3 \cancel{9} \times^4 \cancel{8} \times \cancel{7}!}{\cancel{3} \times \cancel{2} \times 1 \times \cancel{7}!} = 120$$

PROBLEM

How many baseball teams of nine members can be chosen from among twelve boys, without regard to the position played by each member?

SOLUTION

Since there is no regard to position, this is a combination problem (if order or arrangement had been important, it would have been a permutation problem). The general formula for the number of combinations of n things taken r at a time is $C(n,r) = \dfrac{n!}{r!(n-r)!}$.

We have to find the number of combinations of 12 things taken 9 at a time. Hence, we have

$$C(12,9) = \frac{12!}{9!(12-9)!} = \frac{12!}{9!3!} = \frac{12 \times 11 \times 10 \times \cancel{9}!}{3 \times 2 \times 1 \times \cancel{9}!} = 220$$

Therefore, there are 220 possible teams.

PROBLEM

A man and his wife decide to entertain 24 friends by giving 4 dinners with 6 guests each. In how many ways can the first group be chosen?

Dinner Party

SOLUTION

In the first group, we are considering one dinner and there are 6 people out of 24 friends to be invited. We must find the number of ways to choose 6 out of 24. We are dealing with combinations. To select r things out of n objects, we use the definition of combinations:

$$C(n,r) = \binom{n}{r} = \frac{n!}{r!(n-r!)}$$

$$C(24,6) = \binom{24}{6} = \frac{24!}{6!18!} = \frac{24 \times 23 \times 22 \times 21 \times 20 \times 19 \times 18\,!}{6!18!}$$

$$= \frac{24 \times 23 \times 22 \times 21 \times 20 \times 19}{6 \times 5 \times 4 \times 3 \times 2 \times 1}$$

$$= 134{,}596$$

PROBLEM

Bridge Club

A lady has 12 friends. She wishes to invite 3 of them to a bridge party. How many times can she entertain without having the same 3 people again?

SOLUTION

Since no reference has been made to order or arrangement (for example, the order in which the guests arrive or their seating at the bridge table), the problem is one of combinations rather than permutations. Recall the general formula for the number of combinations of n different things taken r at a time, $C(n,r)$

$= \dfrac{n!}{r!(n-r)!}$. Thus, the number of ways of selecting 3 friends from 12 is

$$C(12,3) = \frac{12!}{3!(12-3)!} = \frac{12!}{3!9!} = \frac{\overset{4}{\cancel{12}} \times 11 \times \overset{5}{\cancel{10}} \times \cancel{9}!}{\cancel{3} \times \cancel{2} \times 1 \times \cancel{9}!} = 220$$

Thus, the lady can entertain 220 times without having the same 3 people.

Probability refers to the method of calculating the likelihood that an event will take place. Probability is expressed as a ratio between 0 and 1.

Probability is used for prediction when we cannot predict with certainty that an event will or will not take place.

Probabilities can be expressed in the form of fractions, decimals, or percents.

PROBLEM

What is the probability of throwing a "six" with a single die?

SOLUTION

The die may land in any of 6 ways:

1,   2,   3,   4,   5,   6

The probability of throwing a six,

$$P(6) = \frac{\text{number of ways to get a six}}{\text{number of ways the die may land}}$$

Thus $P(6) = \dfrac{1}{6}$.

PROBLEM

A deck of playing cards is thoroughly shuffled and a card is drawn from the deck. What is the probability that the card drawn is the ace of diamonds?

SOLUTION

The probability of an event occurring is

$$P = \frac{\text{the number of ways the event can occur}}{\text{the number of possible outcomes}}$$

In our case there is one way the event can occur, for there is only one ace of diamonds, and there are 52 possible outcomes (for there are 52 cards in the deck). Hence, the probability that the card drawn is the ace of diamonds is 1/52.

PROBLEM

A box contains 7 red, 5 white, and 4 black balls. What is the probability of your drawing at random one red ball? One black ball?

SOLUTION

There are $7 + 5 + 4 = 16$ balls in the box. The probability of drawing one red ball,

$$P(R) = \frac{\text{number possible ways of drawing a red ball}}{\text{number of ways of drawing any ball}}$$

$$P(R) = \frac{7}{16}.$$

Similarly, the probability of drawing one black ball

$$P(B) = \frac{\text{number possible ways of drawing a black ball}}{\text{number of ways of drawing any ball}}$$

Thus,

$$P(B) = \frac{4}{16} = \frac{1}{4}.$$

PROBLEM

Calculate the probability of the Dodgers' winning the world series if the Yankees have won the first three games.

SOLUTION

We assume the probability of each team winning any specific game is 1/2. The only way the Dodgers can win is if they can take the next four games. Since the games can be considered independent events,

$$P(DDDD) = \frac{1}{2} \times \frac{1}{2} \times \frac{1}{2} \times \frac{1}{2} \text{ by the multiplication rule.}$$

$$P(DDDD) = \left(\frac{1}{2}\right)^4 = \frac{1}{16}$$

PROBLEM

A bag contains 4 white balls, 6 black balls, 3 red balls, and 8 green balls. If one ball is drawn from the bag, find the probability that it will be either white or green.

SOLUTION

The probability that it will be either white or green is: P(a white ball or a green ball) = P(a white ball) + P(a green ball). This is true because if we are given two mutually exclusive events A or B, then P(A or B) = P(A) + P(B). Note that two events, A and B, are mutually exclusive events if their intersection is the null or empty set. In this case, the intersection of choosing a white ball and of choosing a green ball is the empty set. There are no elements in common.

$$P(\text{a white ball}) = \frac{\text{number of ways to choose a white ball}}{\text{number of ways to select a ball}}$$

$$= \frac{4}{21}$$

$$P(\text{a green ball}) = \frac{\text{number of ways to choose a green ball}}{\text{number of ways to select a ball}}$$

$$= \frac{8}{21}$$

Thus,

$$P(\text{a white ball or a green ball}) = \frac{4}{21} + \frac{8}{21} = \frac{12}{21} = \frac{4}{7}.$$

PROBLEM

A penny is to be flipped 3 times. What is the probability there will be 2 heads and 1 tail?

SOLUTION

We start this problem by constructing a set of all possible outcomes:

We can have heads on all 3 tosses:	(HHH)	
heads on first 2 tosses, tails on the third:	(HHT)	(1)
heads on first toss, tails on next two:	(HTT)	
etc.:	(HTH)	(2)
	(THH)	(3)
	(THT)	
	(TTH)	
	(TTT)	

Hence there are eight possible outcomes (2 possibilities on first toss × 2 on second × 2 on third = $2 \times 2 \times 2 = 8$). We assume that these outcomes are all equally likely and assign the probability 1/8 to each. Now we look for the set of outcomes that produce 2 heads and 1 tail. We see there are 3 such outcomes out of the 8 possibilities (numbered (1), (2), (3) in our listing). Hence the probability of 2 heads and 1 tail is 3/8.

Trees

A list of all possible outcomes from an experiment is called a sample space. A tree diagram is helpful in determining these possible outcomes.

- **EXAMPLE**

You flip a coin and you roll a six-sided die. Construct a tree diagram showing all possible outcomes from this experiment.

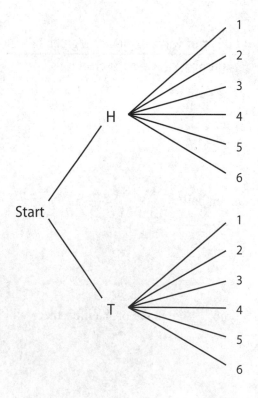

The sample space for this experiment looks like this:

{H1, H2, H3, H4, H5, H6, T1, T2, T3, T4, T5, T6}

There are twelve possible outcomes of this experiment.

- **EXAMPLE**

    You flip a coin three times. Construct a tree diagram showing all the possible outcomes of this experiment.

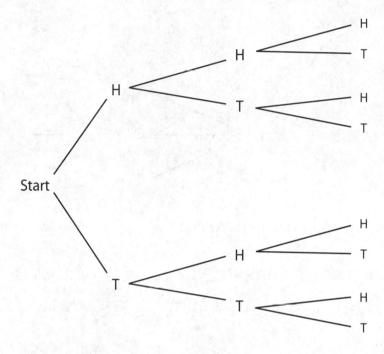

The sample space for this experiment looks like this:

{HHH, HHT, HTH, HTT, THH, THT, TTH, TTT}

There are eight possible outcomes of this experiment.

PROBLEM

There is a special at the school cafeteria: you can get a hamburger or a veggie-burger along with your choice of one topping and one drink. The choices look like this:

Hamburger (H)	Lettuce (L)	Soda (S)
Veggie-burger (V)	Onion (O)	Juice (J)
	Tomato (T)	

What does a tree diagram of the cafeteria special look like?

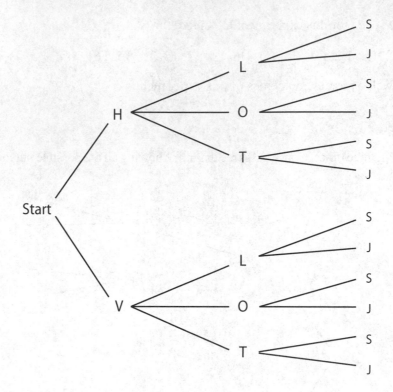

The sample space for this experiment looks like this:

{HLS, HLJ, HOS, HOJ, HTS, HTJ, VLS, VLJ, VOS, VOJ, VTS, VTJ}

There are twelve possible outcomes of this experiment.

Iteration

Iteration means a repetition. In mathematics, iteration refers to the repetition of an operation. The output from this function can be used as the input for the next iteration.

- **EXAMPLE**

Using the formula given below, calculate the value of the third iteration, if the starting number is 4.

$$\frac{x}{2} + 4 =$$

$$\frac{4}{2} + 4 = 6$$

$$\frac{6}{2} + 4 = 7$$

one iteration

$$\frac{7}{2} + 4 = 7.5 \qquad \text{two iterations}$$

$$\frac{7.5}{2} + 4 = 7.75 \qquad \text{three iterations}$$

- **EXAMPLE**

  Using the formula given below, calculate the value of the fourth iteration, if the starting number is 0.

  $$3x - 1 =$$
  $$3(0) - 1 = -1$$
  $$3(-1) - 1 = -4 \qquad \text{one iteration}$$
  $$3(-4) - 1 = -13 \qquad \text{two iterations}$$
  $$3(-13) - 1 = -40 \qquad \text{three iterations}$$
  $$3(-40) - 1 = -121 \qquad \text{four iterations}$$

- **EXAMPLE**

  Using the formula given below, calculate the value of the second iteration, if the starting number is 1.

  $$x^2 + x =$$
  $$1^2 + 1 = 2$$
  $$2^2 + 2 = 6 \qquad \text{one iteration}$$
  $$6^2 + 6 = 42 \qquad \text{two iterations}$$

PROBLEM

Using the equation $2x + x + 1$, what is the value of the third iteration, if the starting number is 5?

SOLUTION

$$2x + x + 1$$
$$2(5) + 5 + 1 = 16$$
$$2(16) + 16 + 1 = 49 \qquad \text{one iteration}$$
$$2(49) + 49 + 1 = 148 \qquad \text{two iterations}$$
$$2(148) + 148 + 1 = 445 \qquad \text{three iterations}$$

PROBLEM

Using the formula $\dfrac{x+3}{2} =$, what is the value of the third iteration, if the starting number is 1?

SOLUTION

$$\frac{x+3}{2} =$$

$$\frac{1+3}{2} = 2$$

$$\frac{2+3}{2} = 2.5 \qquad \text{one iteration}$$

$$\frac{2.5+3}{2} = 2.75 \qquad \text{two iterations}$$

$$\frac{2.75+3}{2} = 2.875 \qquad \text{three iterations}$$

Recursion

A recursive function is a procedure that calls a simpler version of itself to arrive at a solution.

- **EXAMPLE**

The factorial function is an example of recursion. The factorial of a positive integer n, is written $n!$ This is the product of all positive integers from 1 up to and including n.

$$6! = 6 \times 5 \times 4 \times 3 \times 2 \times 1 = 720$$
$$5! = 5 \times 4 \times 3 \times 2 \times 1 = 120$$
$$4! = 4 \times 3 \times 2 \times 1 = 24$$
$$3! = 3 \times 2 \times 1 = 6$$
$$2! = 2 \times 1 = 2$$
$$1! = 1 \times 1 = 1$$
$$0! = 1$$

PROBLEM

> What does 8! equal?

SOLUTION

$$8! = 8 \times 7 \times 6 \times 5 \times 4 \times 3 \times 2 \times 1 = 40{,}320$$

Growth

Growth is an increase in size or quantity over time. There are many different types of growth, depending on what you want to measure.

- **EXAMPLE**

When a person puts money into a savings account, many banks pay compound interest. Compound interest is defined as earning interest on both the principal and on the interest previously accrued. The formula for compound interest is:

$$A = P(1 + r)^n$$

where

P is the principal (the money you start with)

r is the annual rate of interest in decimal form

n is the number of years you leave your money in the bank

A is the total amount of money you will have after n years, if interest is compounded once a year.

For example, if a person deposits $1,000 into a savings account that pays an interest rate of 5% compounded annually, how much money will be in this account after 2 years?

$$A = P(1 + r)^n$$

$$= 1{,}000(1 + 0.05)^2$$

$$= 1{,}000(1.05)^2$$

$$= 1{,}000(1.1025)$$

$$= \$1{,}102.50$$

- **EXAMPLE**

Exponential growth is when growth starts off slowly, but quickly increases. Bacteria are known to show exponential growth. Let's say that bacteria can divide in two about every 20 minutes. If you start off with 1 bacterium, calculate the number you will have at the end of 6 hours.

Since there are three 20-minute periods in an hour, you need $6 \times 3 = 18$ bacteria divisions starting from the single bacterium.

$1 \rightarrow 2 \rightarrow 4 \rightarrow 8 \rightarrow 16 \rightarrow 32 \rightarrow 64 \rightarrow 128 \rightarrow 256 \rightarrow 512 \rightarrow 1,024 \rightarrow 2,048 \rightarrow 4,096 \rightarrow 8,192 \rightarrow$ $16,384 \rightarrow 32,768 \rightarrow 65,536 \rightarrow 131,072 \rightarrow 262,144$

At the end of six hours, there will be 262,144 bacteria.

- **EXAMPLE**

Graph the function $y = y = \frac{1}{2}x^2$.

When creating a graph, first make two columns and label the first column x and the second column y. Then, under the x column, put in the values 0, 1, −1, 3, and −3. Next, calculate the y values for each x value by plugging the x value into the equation. Finally, plot the (x, y) points on the graph and connect the points. Note: This curve is called a parabola.

x	y
0	0
1	0.5
−1	0.5
3	4.5
−3	4.5

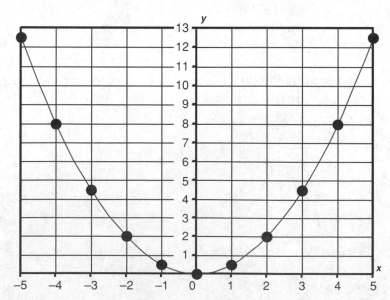

Note: In order to create a more detailed graph of this function, additional x values of 2, −2, 4, −4, 5, and −5 were used in the above graph.

DATA ANALYSIS DRILLS

Drill: Data Interpretation

1. (D)	3. (B)	5. (B)	7. (B)	9. (C)
2. (E)	4. (E)	6. (C)	8. (D)	10. (A)

Drill: Measures of Central Tendency

1. (B)	4. (C)	7. (A)	10. (C)	13. (C)
2. (D)	5. (D)	8. (D)	11. (B)	14. (D)
3. (D)	6. (B)	9. (E)	12. (E)	15. (A)

English Language Skills

Overview

This review offers comprehensive coverage of Florida's required competencies and provides 21 drills that will help build your English language skills. On the FTCE-GKT, you will have 40 minutes to complete the 40-question section, which covers the following:

- conceptual and organizational skills
- word choice skills
- sentence structure skills
- grammar, spelling, capitalization, and punctuation skills

Competency 1: Conceptual and Organizational Skills

Skill 1: Identify Logical Order in a Written Passage

The unit of work for revising is the paragraph. After you have read a passage, spend some time reviewing the passage by looking to see whether the author needed to indent for paragraphs anywhere. If so, make a proofreader's mark to indicate to the reader that you think a paragraph should start-here. Check to see whether the author should add anything that would make the point of view more convincing. Be sure to check for useful transitions to keep up the flow and maintain the focus of ideas. If the paragraphs are out of order, add that paragraph and indicate with a number or some other mark where you want it to go.

Skill 2: Identify Irrelevant Sentences

Identify content that does not contribute to the purpose of a passage or provides irrelevent or illogical information.

- Either/Or—The writer assumes that only two opposing possibilities may be attained: "Either _____, or this _____."

- Oversimplification—The writer simplifies the subject: "The rich only want one thing."

- Begging the question—The writer assumes she has proven something (often counterintuitive) that may need to be proven to the reader: "The death penalty actually increases, rather than deters, violent crime."

- Ignoring the issue—The writer argues against the truth of an issue due to its conclusion: "John is a good boy and, therefore, did not rob the store."

- Arguing against a person, not an idea—The writer argues that somebody's idea has no merit because he is immoral or personally stupid: "Eric will fail out of school because he is not doing well in gym class."

- Non sequitur—The writer leaps to the wrong conclusion: "Jake is from Canada; he must play hockey."

- Drawing the wrong conclusion from a sequence—The author attributes the outcome to the wrong reasons: "Betty married at a young age to an older man and now has three children and is therefore a housewife."

Competency 2: Word Choice Skills

Skill 1: Choose Appropriate Word or Expression in Context

Consider this sentence: The high school *principal* resigned for two *principal* reasons. If you think that the second *principal* is the wrong word (that it should be *principle*), think again. This usage is correct. You may be asked about words that are commonly confused and misused, as well as the use of words based on their grammatical appropriateness in a sentence, such as the distinction between *principal* and *principle*, *fewer* and *less*, and *lie* and *lay*. Here are some commonly confused pairs:

principal—as an adjective, most important; as a noun, the chief authority.

principle—always a noun: a fundamental law. "We hold these principles to be self-evident."

affect—usually a verb, meaning to *influence*; sometimes a noun, with a specific meaning in psychology. "Her performance was adversely affected by the heat."

effect—usually a noun, meaning something that results from something else; occasionally a verb, meaning *to cause to come into being*. "The heat had no effect on his performance." "Her persistence helped to effect the new zoning ordinance."

Skill 2: Recognize Commonly Confused or Misused Words or Phrases

It is important to understand the meanings of all words—not just the ones you are asked to define. A good vocabulary is a strength that can help you perform well on all sections of this test. The following information will build your skills in determining the meanings of words.

Similar Forms and Sounds

The complex nature of language sometimes makes reading difficult. Words often become confusing when they have similar forms and sounds. Indeed the author may have a correct meaning in mind, but an incorrect word choice can alter the meaning of the sentence or even make it totally illogical.

NO: Martha was always part of that *cliché.*

YES: Martha was always part of that *clique.*

(A *cliché* is a trite or hackneyed expression; a *clique* is an exclusive group of people.)

NO: The minister spoke of the soul's *immorality.*

YES: The minister spoke of the soul's *immortality.*

(*Immorality* means wickedness; *immortality* means imperishable or unending life.)

NO: Where is the nearest *stationary* store?

YES: Where is the nearest *stationery* store?

(*Stationary* means immovable; *stationery* is paper used for writing.)

Below are groups of words that are often confused because of their similar forms and sounds.

1. accent – *v.* – to stress or emphasize (You must *accent* the last syllable.)

   ascent – *n.* – a climb or rise (John's *ascent* of the mountain was dangerous.)

   assent – *n.* – consent; compliance (We need your *assent* before we can go ahead with the plans.)

2. accept – *v.* – to take something offered (She *accepted* the gift.)

   except – *prep.* – other than; but (Everyone was included in the plans *except* him.)

3. advice – *n.* – opinion given as to what to do or how to handle a situation (Her sister gave her *advice* on what to say at the interview.)

   advise – *v.* – to counsel (John's guidance counselor *advised* him on which colleges to apply to.)

4. affect – *v.* – to influence (Mary's suggestion did not *affect* me.)

   effect – 1. *v.* – to cause to happen (The plan was *effected* with great success.); 2. *n.* – result (The *effect* of the medicine is excellent.)

5. allusion – *n.* – indirect reference (In the poem, there are many biblical *allusions*.)

illusion – *n.* – false idea or conception; belief or opinion not in accord with the facts (Greg was under the *illusion* that he could win the race after missing three weeks of practice.)

6. already – *adv.* – previously (I had *already* read that novel.)

all ready – *adv.* + *adj.* – prepared (The family was *all ready* to leave on vacation.)

7. altar – *n.* – table or stand used in religious rites (The priest stood at the *altar*.)

alter – *v.* – to change (Their plans were *altered* during the strike.)

8. capital – 1. *n.* – a city where the government meets (The senators had a meeting in Albany, the *capital* of New York.); 2. money used in business (They had enough *capital* to develop the industry.)

capitol – *n.* – building in which the legislature meets (Senator Brown gave a speech at the *capitol* in Washington.)

9. choose – *v.* – to select (Which camera did you *choose*?)

chose – (past tense, *choose*) (Susan *chose* to stay home.)

10. cite – *v.* – to quote (The student *cited* evidence from the text.)

site – *n.* – location (They chose the *site* where the house would be built.)

11. clothes – *n.* – garments (Because she got caught in the rain, her *clothes* were wet.)

cloths – *n.* – pieces of material (The *cloths* were used to wash the windows.)

12. coarse – *adj.* – rough; unrefined (Sandpaper is *coarse*.)

course – 1. *n.* – path of action (She did not know what *course* would solve the problem.); 2. passage (We took the long *course* to the lake.); 3. series of studies (We both enrolled in the physics *course*.); 4. part of a meal (She served a five *course* meal.)

13. consul – *n.* – a person appointed by the government to live in a foreign city and represent the citizenry and business interests of his native country there (The *consul* was appointed to Naples, Italy.)

council – *n.* – a group used for discussion, advisement (The *council* decided to accept his letter of resignation.)

counsel – *v.* – to advise (Tom *counsels* Jerry on tax matters.)

14. decent – *adj.* – proper; respectable (He was very *decent* about the entire matter.)

descent – 1. *n.* – moving down (In Dante's *Inferno,* the *descent* into Hell was depicted graphically.); 2. ancestry (He is of Irish *descent*.)

15. device – 1. *n.* – plan; scheme (The *device* helped her win the race.); 2. invention (We bought a *device* that opens the garage door automatically.)

devise – *v.* – to contrive (He *devised* a plan so John could not win.)

16. emigrate – *v.* – to go away from a country (Many Japanese *emigrated* from Japan in the late 1800s.)

    immigrate – *v.* – to come into a country (Her relatives *immigrated* to the United States after World War I.)

17. eminent – *n.* – prominent (He is an *eminent* member of the community.)

    imminent – *adj.* – impending (The decision is *imminent.*)

    immanent – *adj.* – existing within (Maggie believed that religious spirit is *immanent* in human beings.)

18. fair – 1. *adj.* – beautiful (She was *a fair* maiden.); 2. just (She tried to be *fair.*); 3. *n* – festival (There were many games at the *fair.*)

    farc – *n.* – amount of moncy paid for transportation (Thc city proposcd that the subway *fare* be raised.)

19. forth – *adv.* – onward (The soldiers moved *forth* in the blinding snow.)

    fourth – *n., adj.* – 4th (She was the *fourth* runner-up in the beauty contest.)

20. its – possessive form of *it* (Our town must improve *its* roads.)

    it's – contraction of "it is" (*It's* time to leave the party.)

21. later – *adj., adv.* – at a subsequent date (We will take a vacation *later* this year.)

    latter – *n.* – second of the two (Susan can visit Monday or Tuesday. The *latter*, however, is preferable.)

22. lead – 1. *n.* – (led) a metal (The handgun was made of *lead.*); 2. *v.t.* – (leed) to show the way (The camp counselor *leads* the way to the picnic grounds.)

    led – past tense of *lead* (#2 above) (The dog *led* the way.)

23. loose – *adj.* – free; unrestricted (The dog was let *loose* by accident.)

    lose – *v.* – to suffer the loss of (He was afraid he would *lose* the race.)

24. moral – 1. *adj.* – virtuous (She is a *moral* woman with high ethical standards.); 2. *n.* – lesson taught by a story, incident, etc. (Most fables end with a *moral.*)

    morale – *n.* – mental condition (After the team lost the game, their *morale* was low.)

25. of – *prep.* – from (She is *of* French descent.)

    off – *adj.* – away; at a distance (The television fell *off* the table.)

26. passed – *v.* – having satisfied some requirement (He *passed* the test.)

    past – 1. *adj.* – gone by or elapsed in time (His *past* deeds got him in trouble.); 2. *n.* – a period of time gone by (His *past* was shady.); 3. *prep.* – beyond (She ran *past* the house.)

27. personal – *adj.* – private (Jack was unwilling to discuss his childhood; it was too *personal*.)

    personnel – *n.* – staff (The *personnel* at the department store was made up of young adults.)

28. principal – *n.* – head of a school (The *principal* addressed the graduating class.)

    principle – *n.* – the ultimate source, origin, or cause of something; a law, truth (The *principles* of physics were reviewed in class today.)

29. prophecy – *n.* – prediction of the future (His *prophecy* that he would become a doctor came true.)

    prophesy – *v.* – to declare or predict (He *prophesied* that we would win the lottery.)

30. quiet – *adj.* – still; calm (At night all is *quiet*.)

    quite – *adv.* – really; truly (She is *quite* a good singer.)

    quit – *v.* – to free oneself (Peter had little time to spare so he *quit* the chorus.)

31. respectfully – *adv.* – with respect, honor, esteem (He declined the offer *respectfully*.)

    respectively – *adv.* – in the order mentioned (Jack, Susan and Jim, who are members of the club, were elected president, vice president, and secretary *respectively*.)

32. stationary – *adj.* – immovable (The park bench is *stationary*.)

    stationery – *n.* – paper used for writing (The invitations were printed on yellow *stationery*.)

33. straight – *adj.* – not curved (The road was *straight*.)

    strait – 1. *adj.* – restricted; narrow; confined (The patient was put in a *strait* jacket.); 2. *n.* – narrow waterway (He sailed through the *Straits* of Magellan.)

34. than – *conj.* – used most commonly in comparisons (Maggie is older *than* I.)

    then – *adv.* – soon afterward (We lived in Boston, *then* we moved to New York.)

35. their – possessive form of *they* (That is *their* house on Tenafly Drive.)

    they're – contraction of "they are" (*They're* leaving for California next week.)

    there – *adv.* – at that place (Who is standing *there* under the tree?)

36. to – *prep.* – in the direction of; toward; as (She made a turn *to* the right on Norman Street.)

    too – 1. *adv.* – more than enough (She served *too* much for dinner.); 2. also (He is going to Maine *too*.)

    two – *n.* – 2; one and one (We have *two* pet rabbits.)

37. weather – *n.* – the general condition of the atmosphere (The *weather* is expected to be clear on Sunday.)

    whether – *conj.* – if it be a case or fact (We don't know *whether* the trains are late.)

38. who's – contraction of "who is" or "who has" (*Who's* willing to volunteer for the night shift?)

    whose – possessive form of *who* (*Whose* book is this?)

39. your – possessive form of *you* (Is this *your* seat?)

    you're – contraction of you and are (I know *you're* going to do well on the test.)

Multiple Meanings

In addition to words that sound alike, you must be careful when dealing with words that have multiple meanings. For example:

> The boy was thrilled that his mother gave him a piece of chewing *gum*.

> Dentists advise people to floss their teeth to help prevent *gum* disease.

As you can see, one word can have different meanings depending on the context in which it is used.

Connotation and Denotation

Language can become even more complicated. Not only can a single word have numerous definitions and subtle meanings, it may also take on added meanings through implication. The **connotation** is the idea suggested by its place near or association with other words or phrases. The **denotation** of a word is the direct explicit meaning.

Connotation

Sometimes, you will be asked to tell the meaning of a word in the context of the paragraph. You may not have seen the word before, but from your understanding of the writer's intent, you should be able to figure out what it is s/he's after. For example, read the following paragraph:

> Paris is a beautiful city, perhaps the most beautiful on earth. Long, broad avenues are lined with seventeenth- and eighteenth-century apartments, office buildings, and cafes. Flowers give the city a rich and varied look. The bridges and the river lend an air of lightness and grace to the whole urban landscape.

1. In this paragraph, "rich" most nearly means

    (A) wealthy.

    (B) polluted.

    (C) colorful.

    (D) dull.

If you chose "colorful" you would be right. Although "rich" literally means "wealthy" (that is its *denotation*, its literal meaning), here the writer means more than the word's literal meaning, and seems to be highlighting the variety and color that the flowers add to the avenues, that is, richness in a figurative sense.

The writer is using a non-literal meaning, or *connotation* that we associate with the word "rich" to show what s/he means. When we think of something "rich," we usually also think of abundance, variety, color, and not merely numbers.

Denotation

Determining the denotation of a word is different from determining a word's connotation. Read this paragraph:

> Many soporifics are on the market to help people sleep. Take a glass of water and two *Sleepeze* and you get the "zzzzz" you need. *Sominall* supposedly helps you get the sleep you need so you can go on working. With *Morpho*, your head hits the pillow and you're asleep before the light goes out.

1.   From this paragraph, a "soporific" is probably

   (A)   a drug that stimulates you to stay awake.

   (B)   a kind of sleeping bag.

   (C)   a kind of bed.

   (D)   a drug that helps you sleep.

What is a soporific? You can figure out what it means by looking at what is said around it. People take these "soporifics" to go to sleep, not to wake up. So it can't be (A). You can't take two beds and a glass of water to go to sleep, either. So, it can't be (C). Anyway, you might be able to identify what a soporific is because you recognize the brand names used as examples. So, it must be some sort of pill that you take to sleep. Well, pills are usually drugs of some kind. Therefore, the answer is (D).

Vocabulary Builder

Although the context in which a word appears can help you determine the meaning of the word, one sure-fire way to know a definition is to learn it. By studying the following lists of words and memorizing their definition(s), you will be better equipped to answer Reading Section questions that deal with word meanings.

To benefit most from this vocabulary list, study the words and their definitions, then answer all of the drill questions making sure to check your answers with the answer key that appears at the end of the review.

Group 1

abstract – *adj.* – not easy to understand; theoretical

acclaim – *n.* – loud approval; applause

acquiesce – *v.* – agree or consent to an opinion

adamant – *adj.* – not yielding; firm

adversary – *n.* – an enemy; foe

advocate – 1. *v.* – to plead in favor of; 2. *n.* – supporter; defender

aesthetic – *adj.* – showing good taste; artistic

alleviate – *v.* – to lessen or make easier

aloof – *adj.* – distant in interest; reserved; cool

altercation – *n.* – controversy; dispute

altruistic – *adj.* – unselfish

amass – *v.* – to collect together; accumulate

ambiguous – *adj.* – not clear; uncertain; vague

ambivalent – *adj.* – undecided

ameliorate – *v.* – to make better; to improve

amiable – *adj.* – friendly

amorphous – *adj.* – having no determinate form

anarchist – *n.* – one who believes that a formal government is unnecessary

antagonism – *n.* – hostility; opposition

apathy – *n.* – lack of emotion or interest

appease – *v.* – to make quiet; to calm

apprehensive – *adj.* – fearful; aware; conscious

arbitrary – *adj.* – based on one's preference or whim

arrogant – *adj.* – acting superior to others; conceited

articulate – 1. *v.* – to speak distinctly; 2. *adj.* – eloquent; fluent; 3. *adj.* – capable of speech; 4. *v.* – to hinge; to connect; 5. *v.* – to convey; to express effectively

Drill 1

> **DIRECTIONS:** Match each word in the left column with the word in the right column that is most *opposite* in meaning.

	Word				**Match**		
1.	___ articulate	6.	___ abstract	A.	hostile	F.	disperse
2.	___ apathy	7.	___ acquiesce	B.	concrete	G.	enthusiasm
3.	___ amiable	8.	___ arbitrary	C.	selfish	H.	certain
4.	___ altruistic	9.	___ amass	D.	reasoned	I.	resist
5.	___ ambivalent	10.	___ adversary	E.	ally	J.	incoherent

> **DIRECTIONS:** Match each word in the left column with the word in the right column that is most *similar* in meaning.

	Word				**Match**		
11.	___ adamant	14.	___ antagonism	A.	afraid	D.	insistent
12.	___ aesthetic	15.	___ altercation	B.	disagreement	E.	hostility
13.	___ apprehensive			C.	tasteful		

Group 2

assess – *v.* – to estimate the value of

astute – *adj.* – cunning; sly; crafty

atrophy – *v.* – to waste away through lack of nutrition

audacious – *adj.* – fearless; bold

augment – *v.* – to increase or add to; to make larger

austere – *adj.* – harsh; severe; strict

authentic – *adj.* – real; genuine; trustworthy

authoritarian – *adj.* – acting as a dictator; demanding obedience

banal – *adj.* – common; petty; ordinary

belittle – *v.* – to make small; to think lightly of

benefactor – *n.* – one who helps others; a donor

benevolent – *adj.* – kind; generous

benign – *adj.* – mild; harmless

biased – *adj.* – prejudiced; influenced; not neutral

blasphemous – *adj.* – irreligious; away from acceptable standards

blithe – *adj.* – happy; cheery; merry

brevity – *n.* – briefness; shortness

candid – *adj.* – honest; truthful; sincere

capricious – *adj.* – changeable; fickle

caustic – *adj.* – burning; sarcastic; harsh

censor – *v.* – to examine and delete objectionable material

censure – *v.* – to criticize or disapprove of

charlatan – *n.* – an imposter; fake

coalesce – *v.* – to combine; come together

collaborate – *v.* – to work together; cooperate

Drill 2

DIRECTIONS: Match each word in the left column with the word in the right column that is most *opposite* in meaning.

Word			Match			
1. ___ augment	6. ___ authentic	A. permit		F. malicious		
2. ___ biased	7. ___ candid	B. religious		G. neutral		
3. ___ banal	8. ___ belittle	C. praise		H. mournful		
4. ___ benevolent	9. ___ blasphemous	D. diminish		I. unusual		
5. ___ censor	10. ___ blithe	E. dishonest		J. ersatz		

DIRECTIONS: Match each word in the left column with the word in the right column that is most *similar* in meaning.

Word		Match		
11. ___ collaborate	14. ___ censure	A. harmless	D. cooperate
12. ___ benign	15. ___ capricious	B. cunning	E. criticize
13. ___ astute		C. changeable	

Group 3

compatible – *adj.* – in agreement; harmonious

complacent – *adj.* – content; self-satisfied; smug

compliant – *adj.* – yielding; obedient

comprehensive – *adj.* – all-inclusive; complete; thorough

compromise – *v.* – to settle by mutual adjustment

concede – 1. *v.* – to acknowledge; admit; 2. to surrender; to abandon one's position

concise – *adj.* – in few words; brief; condensed

condescend – *v.* – to come down from one's position or dignity

condone – *v.* – to overlook; to forgive

conspicuous – *adj.* – easy to see; noticeable

consternation – *n.* – amazement or terror that causes confusion

consummation – *n.* – the completion; finish

contemporary – *adj.* – living or happening at the same time; modern

contempt – *n.* – scorn; disrespect

contrite – *adj.* – regretful; sorrowful

conventional – *adj.* – traditional; common; routine

cower – *v.* – crouch down in fear or shame

defamation – *n.* – any harm to a name or reputation; slander

deference – *n.* – a yielding to the opinion of another

deliberate – 1. *v.* – to consider carefully; weigh in the mind; 2. *adj.* – intentional

denounce – *v.* – to speak out against; condemn

depict – *v.* – to portray in words; present a visual image

deplete – *v.* – to reduce; to empty

depravity – *n.* – moral corruption; badness

deride – *v.* – to ridicule; laugh at with scorn

Drill 3

DIRECTIONS: Match each word in the left column with the word in the right column that is most *opposite* in meaning.

Word		Match	
1. ___ deplete	6. ___ condone	A. unintentional	F. support
2. ___ contemporary	7. ___ conspicuous	B. disapprove	G. beginning
3. ___ concise	8. ___ consummation	C. invisible	H. ancient
4. ___ deliberate	9. ___ denounce	D. respect	I. virtue
5. ___ depravity	10. ___ contempt	E. fill	J. verbose

DIRECTIONS: Match each word in the left column with the word in the right column that is most *similar* in meaning.

Word		Match	
11. ___ compatible	14. ___ comprehensive	A. portray	D. thorough
12. ___ depict	15. ___ complacent	B. content	E. common
13. ___ conventional		C. harmonious	

Group 4

desecrate – *v.* – to violate a holy place or sanctuary

detached – *adj.* – separated; not interested; standing alone

deter – *v.* – to prevent; to discourage; hinder

didactic – 1. *adj.* – instructive; 2. dogmatic; preachy

digress – *v.* – stray from the subject; wander from topic

diligence – *n.* – hard work

discerning – *adj.* – distinguishing one thing from another

discord – *n.* – disagreement; lack of harmony

discriminating – 1. *v.* – distinguishing one thing from another; 2. *v.* – demonstrating bias; 3. *adj.* – able to distinguish disdain – 1. *n.* – intense dislike; 2. *v.* – look down upon; scorn

disparage – *v.* – to belittle; undervalue

disparity – *n.* – difference in form, character, or degree

dispassionate – *adj.* – lack of feeling; impartial

disperse – *v.* – to scatter; separate

disseminate – *v.* – to circulate; scatter

dissent – *v.* – to disagree; differ in opinion

dissonance – *n.* – harsh contradiction

diverse – *adj.* – different; dissimilar

document – 1. *n.* – official paper containing information; 2. *v.* – to support; substantiate; verify

dogmatic – *adj.* – stubborn; biased; opinionated

dubious – *adj.* – doubtful; uncertain; skeptical; suspicious

eccentric – *adj.* – odd; peculiar; strange

efface – *v.* – wipe out; erase

effervescence – 1. *n.* – liveliness; spirit; enthusiasm; 2. bubbliness

egocentric – *adj.* – self-centered

Drill 4

DIRECTIONS: Match each word in the left column with the word in the right column that is most *opposite* in meaning.

	Word				Match		
1.	___ detached	6.	___ dubious	A.	agree	F.	respect
2.	___ deter	7.	___ diligence	B.	certain	G.	compliment
3.	___ dissent	8.	___ disdain	C.	lethargy	H.	sanctify
4.	___ discord	9.	___ desecrate	D.	connected	I.	harmony
5.	___ efface	10.	___ disparage	E.	assist	J.	restore

DIRECTIONS: Match each word in the left column with the word in the right column that is most *similar* in meaning.

Word   **Match**

11. ___ effervescence   14. ___ document   A. stubborn   D. liveliness

12. ___ dogmatic   15. ___ eccentric   B. distribute   E. odd

13. ___ disseminate   C. substantiate

Group 5

elaboration – *n.* – the act of clarifying or adding details

eloquence – *n.* – the ability to speak well

elusive – *adj.* – hard to catch; difficult to understand

emulate – *v.* – to imitate; copy; mimic

endorse – *v.* – support; to approve of; recommend

engender – *v.* – to create; bring about

enhance – *v.* – to improve; compliment; make more attractive

enigma – *n.* – mystery; secret; perplexity

ephemeral – *adj.* – temporary; brief; short-lived

equivocal – *adj.* – doubtful; uncertain

erratic – *adj.* – unpredictable; strange

erroneous – *adj.* – untrue; inaccurate; not correct

esoteric – *adj.* – incomprehensible; obscure

euphony – *n.* – pleasant sound

execute –1. *v.* – put to death; kill; 2. to carry out; fulfill

exemplary – *adj.* – serving as an example; outstanding

exhaustive – *adj.* – thorough; complete

expedient – *adj.* – helpful; practical; worthwhile

expedite – *v.* – speed up

explicit – *adj.* – specific; definite

cxtol – *v.* – praise; commend

extraneous – *adj.* – irrelevant; not related; not essential

facilitate   *v.*   makc casicr; simplify

fallacious – *adj.* – misleading

fanatic – *n.* – enthusiast; extremist

Drill 5

DIRECTIONS: Match each word in the left column with the word in the right column that is most *opposite* in meaning.

Word   ### Match

1. ___ extraneous	6. ___ erratic	A.	incomplete	F.	eternal
2. ___ ephemeral	7. ___ explicit	B.	delay	G.	condemn
3. ___ exhaustive	8. ___ euphony	C.	dependable	H.	relevant
4. ___ expedite	9. ___ elusive	D.	comprehensible	I.	indefinite
5. ___ erroneous	10. ___ extol	E.	dissonance	J.	accurate

DIRECTIONS: Match each word in the left column with the word in the right column that is most *similar* in meaning.

Word   ### Match

11. ___ endorse	14. ___ fallacious	A.	enable	D.	worthwhile
12. ___ expedient	15. ___ engender	B.	recommend	E.	deceptive
13. ___ facilitate		C.	create		

Group 6

fastidious – *adj.* – fussy; hard to please

fervent – *n.* – passionate; intense

fickle – *adj.* – changeable; unpredictable

fortuitous – *adj.* – accidental; happening by chance; lucky

frivolity – *n.* – giddiness; lack of seriousness

fundamental – *adj.* – basic; necessary

furtive – *adj.* – secretive; sly

futile – *adj.* – worthless; unprofitable

glutton – *n.* – overeater

grandiose – *adj.* – extravagant; flamboyant

gravity – *n.* – seriousness

guile – *n.* – slyness; deceit

gullible – *adj.* – easily fooled

hackneyed – *adj.* – commonplace; trite

hamper – *v.* – interfere with; hinder

haphazard – *adj.* – disorganized; random

hedonistic – *adj.* – pleasure seeking

heed – *v.* – obey; yield to

heresy – *n.* – opinion contrary to popular belief

hindrance – *n.* – blockage; obstacle

humility – *n.* – lack of pride; modesty

hypocritical – *adj.* – two-faced; deceptive

hypothetical – *adj.* – assumed; uncertain

illuminate – *v.* – make understandable

illusory – *adj.* – unreal; false; deceptive

Drill 6

DIRECTIONS: Match each word in the left column with the word in the right column that is most *opposite* in meaning.

	Word				Match		
1.	___ heresy	6.	___ fervent	A.	predictable	F.	beneficial
2.	___ fickle	7.	___ fundamental	B.	dispassionate	G.	orthodoxy
3.	___ illusory	8.	___ furtive	C.	simple	H.	organized
4.	___ frivolity	9.	___ futile	D.	extraneous	I.	candid
5.	___ grandiose	10.	___ haphazard	E.	real	J.	seriousness

DIRECTIONS: Match each word in the left column with the word in the right column that is most *similar* in meaning.

	Word				Match		
11.	___ glutton	14.	___ hackneyed	A.	hinder	D.	overeater
12.	___ heed	15.	___ hindrance	B.	obstacle	E.	obey
13.	___ hamper			C.	trite		

Group 7

immune – *adj.* – protected; unthreatened by

immutable – *adj.* – unchangeable; permanent

impartial – *adj.* – unbiased; fair

impetuous – 1. *adj.* – rash; impulsive; 2. forcible; violent

implication – *n.* – suggestion; inference

inadvertent – *adj.* – not on purpose; unintentional

incessant – *adj.* – constant; continual

incidental – *adj.* – extraneous; unexpected

inclined – 1. *adj.* – apt to; likely to; 2. angled

incoherent – *adj.* – illogical; rambling

incompatible – *adj.* – disagreeing; disharmonious

incredulous – *adj.* – unwilling to believe; skeptical

indifferent – *adj.* – unconcerned

indolent – *adj.* – lazy; inactive

indulgent – *adj.* – lenient; extravagant

inevitable – *adj.* – sure to happen; unavoidable

infamous – *adj.* – having a bad reputation; notorious

infer – *v.* – form an opinion; conclude

initiate – 1. *v.* – begin; admit into a group; 2. *n.* – a person who is in the process of being admitted into a group

innate – *adj.* – natural; inborn

innocuous – *adj.* – harmless; innocent

innovate – *v.* – introduce a change; depart from the old

insipid – *adj.* – uninteresting; bland

instigate – *v.* – start; provoke

intangible – *adj.* – incapable of being touched; immaterial

Drill 7

DIRECTIONS: Match each word in the left column with the word in the right column that is most *opposite* in meaning.

Word			Match		
1. ___ immutable	6. ___ innate	A. intentional	F. changeable
2. ___ impartial	7. ___ incredulous	B. articulate	G. avoidable
3. ___ inadvertent	8. ___ inevitable	C. gullible	H. harmonious
4. ___ incoherent	9. ___ intangible	D. material	I. learned
5. ___ incompatible	10. ___ indolent	E. biased	J. energetic

DIRECTIONS: Match each word in the left column with the word in the right column that is most *similar* in meaning.

Word			Match		
11. ___ impetuous	14. ___ instigate	A. lenient	D. conclude
12. ___ incidental	15. ___ indulgent	B. impulsive	E. extraneous
13. ___ infer		C. provoke	

Group 8

ironic – *adj.* – contradictory; inconsistent; sarcastic

irrational – *adj.* – not logical

jeopardy – *n.* – danger

kindle – *v.* – ignite; arouse

languid – *adj.* – weak; fatigued

laud – *v.* – to praise

lax – *adj.* – careless; irresponsible

lethargic – *adj.* – lazy; passive

levity – *n.* – silliness; lack of seriousness

lucid – 1. *adj.* – shining; 2. easily understood

magnanimous – *adj.* – forgiving; unselfish

malicious – *adj.* – spiteful; vindictive

marred – *adj.* – damaged

meander – *v.* – wind on a course; go aimlessly

melancholy – *n.* – depression; gloom

meticulous – *adj.* – exacting; precise

minute – *adj.* – extremely small; tiny

miser – *n.* – penny pincher; stingy person

mitigate – *v.* – alleviate; lessen; soothe

morose – *adj.* – moody; despondent

negligence – *n.* – carelessness

neutral – *adj.* – impartial; unbiased

nostalgic – *adj.* – longing for the past; filled with bittersweet memories

novel – *adj.* – new

Drill 8

DIRECTIONS: Match each word in the left column with the word in the right column that is most *opposite* in meaning.

	Word				Match		
1.	___ irrational	6.	___ magnanimous	A.	extinguish	F.	ridicule
2.	___ kindle	7.	___ levity	B.	jovial	G.	kindly
3.	___ meticulous	8.	___ minute	C.	selfish	H.	sloppy
4.	___ malicious	9.	___ laud	D.	logical	I.	huge
5.	___ morose	10.	___ novel	E.	seriousness	J.	stale

DIRECTIONS: Match each word in the left column with the word in the right column that is most *similar* in meaning.

	Word				Match		
11.	___ ironic	14.	___ jeopardy	A.	lessen	D.	carelessness
12.	___ marred	15.	___ negligence	B.	damaged	E.	danger
13.	___ mitigate			C.	sarcastic		

Group 9

nullify – *v.* – cancel; invalidate

objective – 1. *adj.* – open-minded; impartial; 2. *n.* – goal

obscure – *adj.* – not easily understood; dark

obsolete – *adj.* – out of date; passe

ominous – *adj.* – threatening

optimism – *n.* – hope for the best; seeing the good side

orthodox – *adj.* – traditional; accepted

pagan – 1. *n.* – polytheist; 2. *adj.* – polytheistic

partisan – 1. *n.* – supporter; follower; 2. *adj.* – biased; one sided

perceptive – *adj.* – full of insight; aware

peripheral – *adj.* – marginal; outer

pernicious – *adj.* – dangerous; harmful

pessimism – *n.* – seeing only the gloomy side; hopelessness

phenomenon – 1. *n.* – miracle; 2. occurrence

philanthropy – *n.* – charity; unselfishness

pious – *adj.* – religious; devout; dedicated

placate – *v.* – pacify

plausible – *adj.* – probable; feasible

pragmatic – *adj.* – matter-of-fact; practical

preclude – *v.* – inhibit; make impossible

predecessor – *n.* – one who has occupied an office before another

prodigal – *adj.* – wasteful; lavish

prodigious – *adj.* – exceptional; tremendous

profound – *adj.* – deep; knowledgeable; thorough

profusion – *n.* – great amount; abundance

Drill 9

DIRECTIONS: Match each word in the left column with the word in the right column that is most *opposite* in meaning.

Word			Match		
1. ___ objective	6. ___ plausible	A. scantiness	F. minute		
2. ___ obsolete	7. ___ preclude	B. assist	G. anger		
3. ___ placate	8. ___ prodigious	C. mundane	H. pessimism		
4. ___ profusion	9. ___ profound	D. biased	I. modern		
5. ___ peripheral	10. ___ optimism	E. improbable	J. central		

DIRECTIONS: Match each word in the left column with the word in the right column that is most *similar* in meaning.

Word		Match	
11. ___ nullify	14. ___ pernicious	A. invalidate	D. threatening
12. ___ ominous	15. ___ prodigal	B. follower	E. harmful
13. ___ partisan		C. lavish	

Group 10

prosaic – *adj.* – tiresome; ordinary

provincial – *adj.* – regional; unsophisticated

provocative – 1. *adj.* – tempting; 2. irritating

prudent – *adj.* – wise; careful; prepared

qualified – *adj.* – experienced; indefinite

rectify – *v.* – correct

redundant – *adj.* – repetitious; unnecessary

refute – *v.* – challenge; disprove

relegate – *v.* – banish; put to a lower position

relevant – *adj.* – of concern; significant

remorse – *n.* – guilt; sorrow

reprehensible – *adj.* – wicked; disgraceful

repudiate – *v.* – reject; cancel

rescind – *v.* – retract; discard

resignation – 1. *n.* – quitting; 2. submission

resolution – *n.* – proposal; promise; determination

respite – *n.* – recess; rest period

reticent – *adj.* – silent; reserved; shy

reverent – *adj.* – respectful

rhetorical – *adj.* – having to do with verbal communication

rigor – *n.* – severity

sagacious – *adj.* – wise; cunning

sanguine – 1. *adj.* – optimistic; cheerful; 2. red

saturate – *v.* – soak thoroughly; drench

scanty – *adj.* – inadequate; sparse

Drill 10

DIRECTIONS: Match each word in the left column with the word in the right column that is most *opposite* in meaning.

Word			Match		
1. ___ provincial	6. ___ remorse	A. inexperienced	F. affirm
2. ___ reticent	7. ___ repudiate	B. joy	G. extraordinary
3. ___ prudent	8. ___ sanguine	C. pessimistic	H. sophisticated
4. ___ qualified	9. ___ relevant	D. unrelated	I. forward
5. ___ relegate	10. ___ prosaic	E. careless	J. promote

DIRECTIONS: Match each word in the left column with the word in the right column that is most *similar* in meaning.

Word			Match		
11. ___ provocative	14. ___ rescind	A. drench	D. severity
12. ___ rigor	15. ___ reprehensible	B. tempting	E. blameworthy
13. ___ saturate		C. retract	

Group 11

scrupulous – *adj.* – honorable; exact

scrutinize – *v.* – examine closely; study

servile – *adj.* – slavish; groveling

skeptic – *n.* – doubter

slander – *v.* – defame; maliciously misrepresent

solemnity – *n.* – seriousness

solicit – *v.* – ask; seek

stagnant – *adj.* – motionless; uncirculating

stanza – *n.* – group of lines in a poem having a definite pattern

static – *adj.* – inactive; changeless

stoic – *adj.* – detached; unruffled; calm

subtle – *adj.* – understated

superficial – *adj.* – on the surface; narrow-minded; lacking depth

superfluous – *adj.* – unnecessary; extra

surpass – *v.* – go beyond; outdo

sycophant – *n.* – flatterer

symmetry – *n.* – correspondence of parts; harmony

taciturn – *adj.* – reserved; quiet; secretive

tedious – *adj.* – time-consuming; burdensome; uninteresting

temper – *v.* – soften; pacify; compose

tentative – *adj.* – not confirmed; indefinite

thrifty – *adj.* – economical; pennywise

tranquility – *n.* – peace; stillness; harmony

trepidation – *n.* – apprehension; uneasiness

trivial – *adj.* – unimportant; small; worthless

Drill 11

> **DIRECTIONS:** Match each word in the left column with the word in the right column that is most *opposite* in meaning.

Word				Match			
1. ___ scrutinize	6. ___ tentative	A. frivolity	F. skim
2. ___ skeptic	7. ___ thrifty	B. enjoyable	G. turbulent
3. ___ solemnity	8. ___ tranquility	C. prodigal	H. active
4. ___ static	9. ___ solicit	D. chaos	I. believer
5. ___ tedious	10. ___ stagnant	E. give	J. confirmed

> **DIRECTIONS:** Match each word in the left column with the word in the right column that is most *similar* in meaning.

Word				Match			
11. ___ symmetry	14. ___ subtle	A. understated	D. fear
12. ___ superfluous	15. ___ trepidation	B. unnecessary	E. flatterer
13. ___ sycophant		C. balance	

Group 12

tumid – *adj.* – swollen; inflated

undermine – *v.* – weaken; ruin

uniform – *adj.* – consistent; unvaried; unchanging

universal – *adj.* – concerning everyone; existing everywhere

unobtrusive – *adj.* – inconspicuous; reserved

unprecedented – *adj.* – unheard of; exceptional

unpretentious – *adj.* – simple; plain; modest

vacillation – *n.* – fluctuation

valid – *adj.* – acceptable; legal

vehement – *adj.* – intense; excited; enthusiastic

venerate – *v.* – revere

verbose – *adj.* – wordy; talkative

viable – 1. *adj.* – capable of maintaining life; 2. possible; attainable

vigorous – *adj.* – energetic; forceful

vilify – *v.* – slander

virtuoso – *n.* – highly skilled artist

virulent – *adj.* – deadly; harmful; malicious

vital – *adj.* – important; spirited

volatile – *adj.* – changeable; undependable

vulnerable – *adj.* – open to attack; unprotected

wane – *v.* – grow gradually smaller

whimsical – *adj.* – fanciful; amusing

wither – *v.* – wilt; shrivel; humiliate; cut down

zealot – *n.* – believer; enthusiast; fan

zenith – *n.* – point directly overhead in the sky

Drill 12

DIRECTIONS: Match each word in the left column with the word in the right column that is most *opposite* in meaning.

Word   **Match**

1. ___ uniform   6. ___ vigorous   A. amateur   F. support

2. ___ virtuoso   7. ___ volatile   B. trivial   G. constancy

3. ___ vital   8. ___ vacillation   C. visible   H. lethargic

4. ___ wane   9. ___ undermine   D. placid   I. wax

5. ___ unobtrusive   10. ___ valid   E. unacceptable   J. varied

---

DIRECTIONS: Match each word in the left column with the word in the right column that is most *similar* in meaning.

Word			**Match**	
11. ___ wither	14. ___ vehement	A. intense	D. possible
12. ___ whimsical	15. ___ virulent	B. deadly	E. shrivel
13. ___ viable		C. amusing	

Additional Vocabulary

The following words comprise additional vocabulary terms that may be found on the FTCE-GKT.

abandon – 1. *v.* – to leave behind; 2. *v.* – to give something up; 3. *n.* – freedom; enthusiasm; impetuosity

abase – *v.* – to degrade; humiliate; disgrace

abbreviate – *v.* – to shorten; compress; diminish

aberrant – *adj.* – abnormal

abhor – *v.* – to hate

abominate – *v.* – to loathe; to hate

abridge – 1. *v.* – to shorten; 2. to limit; to take away

absolve – *v.* – to forgive; to acquit

abstinence – *n.* – self-control; abstention; chastity

accede – *v.* – to comply with; to consent to

accomplice – *n.* – co-conspirator; partner; partner-in-crime

accrue – *v.* – collect; build up

acrid – *adj.* – sharp; bitter; foul smelling

adept – *adj.* – skilled; practiced

adverse – *adj.* – negative; hostile; antagonistic; inimical

affable – *adj.* – friendly; amiable; good-natured

aghast – 1. *adj.* – astonished; amazed; 2. horrified; terrified; appalled

alacrity – 1. *n.* – enthusiasm; fervor; 2. liveliness; sprightliness

allocate – *v.* – set aside; designate; assign

allure – 1. *v.* – to attract; entice; 2. *n.* – attraction; temptation; glamour

amiss – 1. *adj.* – wrong; awry; 2. *adv.* – wrongly; mistakenly analogy – *n.* – similarity; correlation; parallelism; simile; metaphor

anoint – 1. *v.* – to crown; ordain; 2. to smear with oil

anonymous – *adj.* – nameless; unidentified

arduous – *adj.* – difficult; burdensome

awry – 1. *adj., adv.* – crooked(ly); uneven(ly); 2. wrong; askew

baleful – *adj.* – sinister; threatening; evil; deadly

baroque – *adj.* – extravagant; ornate

behoove – *v.* – to be advantageous; to be necessary

berate – *v.* – scold; reprove; reproach; criticize

bereft – *adj.* – hurt by someone's death

biennial – 1. *adj.* – happening every two years; 2. *n.* – a plant that blooms every two years

blatant – 1. *adj.* – obvious; unmistakable; 2. crude; vulgar

bombastic – *adj.* – pompous; wordy; turgid

burly – *adj.* – strong; bulky; stocky

cache – 1. *n.* – stockpile; store; heap; 2. hiding place for goods

calamity – *n.* – disaster

cascade – 1. *n.* – waterfall; 2. *v.* – pour; rush; fall

catalyst – *n.* – anything that creates a situation in which change can occur

chagrin – *n.* – distress; shame

charisma – *n.* – appeal; magnetism; presence

chastise – *v.* – punish; discipline; admonish; rebuke

choleric – *adj.* – cranky; cantankerous

cohesion – *n.* – the act of holding together

colloquial – *adj.* – casual; common; conversational; idiomatic

conglomeration – *n.* – mixture; collection

connoisseur – *n.* – expert; authority (usually refers to a wine or food expert)

consecrate – *v.* – sanctify; make sacred; immortalize

craven – *adj.* – cowardly; fearful

dearth – *n.* – scarcity; shortage

debilitate – *v.* – deprive of strength

deign – *v.* – condescend; stoop

delineate – *v.* – to outline; to describe

demur – 1. *v.* – to object; 2. *n.* – objection; misgiving

derision – *n.* – ridicule; mockery

derogatory – *adj.* – belittling; uncomplimentary

destitute – *adj.* – poor; poverty-stricken

devoid – *adj.* – lacking; empty

dichotomy – *n.* – branching into two parts

disheartened – *adj.* – discouraged; depressed

diverge – *v.* – separate; split

docile – *adj.* – manageable; obedient

duress – *n.* – force; constraint

ebullient – *adj.* – showing excitement

educe – *v.* – draw forth

effervescence – *n.* – bubbliness; enthusiasm; animation

emulate – *v.* – to follow the example of

ennui – *n.* – boredom; apathy

epitome – *n.* – model; typification; representation

errant – *adj.* – wandering

ersatz – *adj.* – artificial

ethnic – *adj.* – native; racial; cultural

evoke – *v.* – call forth; provoke

exotic – *adj.* – unusual; striking

facade – *n.* – front view; false appearance

facsimile – *n.* – copy; reproduction; replica

fathom – *v.* – comprehend; uncover

ferret – *v.* – drive or hunt out of hiding

figment – *n.* – product; creation

finite – *adj.* – measurable; limited; not everlasting

fledgling – *n.* – inexperienced person; beginner

flinch – *v.* – wince; draw back; retreat

fluency – *n.* – smoothness of speech

flux – *n.* – current; continuous change

forbearance – *n.* – patience; self-restraint

foster – *v.* – encourage; nurture; support

frivolity – *n.* – lightness; folly; fun

frugality – *n.* – thrift

garbled – *adj.* – mixed up

generic – *adj.* – common; general; universal

germane – *adj.* – pertinent; related; to the point

gibber – *v.* – speak foolishly

gloat – *v.* – brag; glory over

guile – *n.* – slyness; fraud

haggard – *adj.* – tired looking; fatigued

hiatus – *n.* – interval; break; period of rest

hierarchy – *n.* – body of people, things, or concepts divided into ranks

homage – *n.* – honor; respect

hubris – *n.* – arrogance

ideology – *n.* – set of beliefs; principles

ignoble – *adj.* – shameful; dishonorable

imbue – *v.* – inspire; arouse

impale – *v.* – fix on a stake; stick; pierce

implement – *v.* – begin; enact

impromptu – *adj.* – without preparation

inarticulate – *adj.* – speechless; unable to speak clearly

incessant – *adj.* – uninterrupted

incognito – *adj.* – unidentified; disguised; concealed

indict – *v.* – charge with a crime

inept – *adj.* – incompetent; unskilled

innuendo – *n.* – hint; insinuation

intermittent – *adj.* – periodic; occasional

invoke – *v.* – ask for; call upon

itinerary – *n.* – travel plan; schedule; course

jovial – *adj.* – cheery; jolly; playful

juncture – *n.* – critical point; meeting

juxtapose – *v.* – place side by side

knavery – *n.* – rascality; trickery

knead – *v.* – mix; massage

labyrinth – *n.* – maze

laggard – *n.* – a lazy person; one who lags behind

larceny – *n.* – theft; stealing

lascivious – *adj.* – indecent; immoral

lecherous – *adj.* – impure in thought and act

lethal – *adj.* – deadly

liaison – *n.* – connection; link

limber – *adj.* – flexible; pliant

livid – 1. *adj.* – black-and-blue; discolored; 2. enraged; irate

lucrative – *adj.* – profitable; gainful

lustrous – *adj.* – bright; radiant

malediction – *n.* – curse; evil spell

mandate – *n.* – order; charge

manifest – *adj.* – obvious; clear

mentor – *n.* – teacher

mesmerize – *v.* – hypnotize

metamorphosis – *n.* – change of form

mimicry – *n.* – imitation

molten – *adj.* – melted

motif – *n.* – theme

mundane – *adj.* – ordinary; commonplace

myriad – *adj.* – innumerable; countless

narcissistic – *adj.* – egotistical; self-centered

nautical – *adj.* – of the sea

neophyte – *n.* – beginner; newcomer

nettle – *v.* – annoy; irritate

notorious – *adj.* – infamous; renowned

obdurate – *adj.* – stubborn; inflexible

obligatory – *adj.* – mandatory; necessary

obliterate – *v.* – destroy completely

obsequious – *adj.* – slavishly attentive; servile

obstinate – *adj.* – stubborn

occult – *adj.* – mystical; mysterious

opaque – *adj.* – dull; cloudy; nontransparent

opulence – *n.* – wealth; fortune

ornate – *adj.* – elaborate; lavish; decorated

oust – *v.* – drive out; eject

painstaking – *adj.* – thorough; careful; precise

pallid – *adj.* – sallow; colorless

palpable – *adj.* – tangible; apparent

paradigm – *n.* – model; example

paraphernalia – *n.* – equipment; accessories

parochial – *adj.* – pertaining to a parish; narrow-minded

passive – *adj.* – submissive; unassertive

pedestrian – *adj.* – mediocre; ordinary

pensive – *adj.* – reflective; contemplative

percussion – *n.* – the striking of one object against another

perjury – *n.* – the practice of lying

permeable – *adj.* – porous; allowing to pass through

perpetual – *adj.* – enduring for all time

pertinent – *adj.* – related to the matter at hand

pervade – *v.* – to occupy the whole of

petty – *adj.* – unimportant; of subordinate standing

phlegmatic – *adj.* – without emotion or interest

phobia – *n.* – morbid fear

pittance – *n.* – small allowance

plethora – *n.* – condition of going beyond what is needed; excess; over-abundance

potent – *adj.* – having great power or physical strength

privy – *adj.* – private; confidential

progeny – *n.* – children; offspring

provoke – *v.* – to stir action or feeling; arouse

pungent – *adj.* – sharp; stinging

quaint – *adj.* – old-fashioned; unusual; odd

quandary – *n.* – dilemma

quarantine – *n.* – isolation of a person to prevent spread of disease

quiescent – *adj.* – inactive; at rest

quirk – *n.* – peculiar behavior; startling twist

rabid – *adj.* – furious; with extreme anger

rancid – *adj.* – having a bad odor

rant – *v.* – to speak in a loud, pompous manner; rave

ratify – *v.* – to make valid; confirm

rationalize – *v.* – to offer reasons for; account for

raucous – *adj.* – disagreeable to the sense of hearing; harsh

realm – *n.* – an area; sphere of activity

rebuttal – *n.* – refutation

recession – *n.* – withdrawal; depression

reciprocal – *n.* – mutual; having the same relationship to each other

recluse – *n.* – solitary and shut off from society

refurbish – *v.* – to make new

regal – *adj.* – royal; grand

reiterate – *v.* – repeat; to state again

relinquish – *v.* – to let go; abandon

render – *v.* – deliver; provide; to give up a possession

replica – *n.* – copy; representation

resilient – *adj.* – flexible; capable of withstanding stress

retroaction – *n.* – an action elicited by a stimulus

reverie – *n.* – the condition of being unaware of one's surroundings; trance

rummage – *v.* – search thoroughly

rustic – *adj.* – plain and unsophisticated; homely

saga – *n.* – a legend; story

salient – *adj.* – noticeable; prominent

salvage – *v.* – rescue from loss

sarcasm – *n.* – ironic, bitter humor designed to wound

satire – *n.* – a novel or play that uses humor or irony to expose folly

saunter – *v.* – walk at a leisurely pace; stroll

savor – *v.* – to receive pleasure from; enjoy

seethe – *v.* – to be in a state of emotional turmoil; to become angry

serrated – *adj.* – having a saw-toothed edge

shoddy – *adj.* – of inferior quality; cheap

skulk – *v.* – to move secretly

sojourn – *n.* – temporary stay; visit

solace – *n.* – hope; comfort during a time of grief

soliloquy – *n.* – a talk one has with oneself (especially on stage)

somber – *adj.* – dark and depressing; gloomy

sordid – *adj.* – filthy; base; vile

sporadic – *adj.* – rarely occurring or appearing; intermittent

stamina – *n.* – endurance

steadfast – *adj.* – loyal

stigma – *n.* – a mark of disgrace

stipend – *n.* – payment for work done

stupor – *n.* – a stunned or bewildered condition

suave – *adj.* – effortlessly gracious

subsidiary – *adj.* – subordinate

succinct – *adj.* – consisting of few words; concise

succumb – *v.* – give in; yield; collapse

sunder – *v.* – break; split in two

suppress – *v.* – to bring to an end; hold back

surmise – *v.* – draw an inference; guess

susceptible – *adj.* – easily imposed; inclined

tacit – *adj.* – not voiced or expressed

tantalize – *v.* – to tempt; to torment

tarry – *v.* – to go or move slowly; delay

taut – *adj.* – stretch tightly

tenacious – *adj.* – persistently holding to something

tepid – *adj.* – lacking warmth, interest, enthusiasm; lukewarm

terse – *adj.* – concise; abrupt

thwart – *v.* – prevent from accomplishing a purpose; frustrate

timorous – *adj.* – fearful

torpid – *adj.* – lacking alertness and activity; lethargic

toxic – *adj.* – poisonous

transpire – *v.* – to take place; come about

traumatic – *adj.* – causing a violent injury

trek – *v.* – to make a journey

tribute – *n.* – expression of admiration

trite – *adj.* – commonplace; overused

truculent – *adj.* – aggressive; eager to fight

turbulence – *n.* – condition of being physically agitated; disturbance

turmoil – *n.* – unrest; agitation

tycoon – *n.* – wealthy leader

tyranny – *n.* – absolute power; autocracy

ubiquitous – *adj.* – ever present in all places; universal

ulterior – *adj.* – buried; concealed

uncanny – *adj.* – of a strange nature; weird

unequivocal – *adj.* – clear; definite

unique – *adj.* – without equal; incomparable

unruly – *adj.* – not submitting to discipline; disobedient

unwonted – *adj.* – not ordinary; unusual

urbane – *adj.* – cultured; suave

usurpation – *n.* – act of taking something for oneself; seizure

usury – *n.* – the act of lending money at illegal rates of interest

utopia – *n.* – imaginary land with perfect social and political systems

vacuous – *adj.* – containing nothing; empty

vagabond – *n.* – wanderer; one without a fixed place

vagrant – 1. *n.* – homeless person; 2. *adj.* – rambling; wandering; transient

valance – *n.* – short drapery hanging over a window frame

valor – *n.* – bravery

vantage – *n.* – position giving an advantage

vaunted – *adj.* – boasted of

velocity – *n.* – speed

vendetta – *n.* – feud

venue – *n.* – location

veracious – *adj.* – conforming to fact; accurate

verbatim – *adj.* – employing the same words as another; literal

versatile – *adj.* – having many uses; multifaceted

vertigo – *n.* – dizziness

vex – *v.* – to trouble the nerves; annoy

vindicate – *v.* – to free from charge; clear

vivacious – *adj.* – animated; gay

vogue – *n.* – modern fashion

voluble – *adj.* – fluent

waft – *v.* – move gently by wind or breeze

waive – *v.* – to give up possession or right

wanton – *adj.* – unruly; excessive

warrant – *v.* – justify; authorize

wheedle – *v.* – try to persuade; coax

whet – *v.* – sharpen

wrath – *n.* – violent or unrestrained anger; fury

wry – *adj.* – mocking; cynical

xenophobia – *n.* – fear of foreigners

yoke – *n.* – harness; collar; bond

yore – *n.* – former period of time

zephyr – *n.* – a gentle wind; breeze

Drill 13

> **DIRECTIONS:** Each of the following questions provides a given word in capitalized letters followed by five word choices. Choose the word that is *opposite* in meaning to the given word.

1. AUTHENTIC:

    (A) cheap   (B) competitive   (C) false

    (D) biased   (E) irrational

2. MISERLY:

    (A) unhappy   (B) generous   (C) optimistic

    (D) reticent   (E) golden

3. DILIGENT:

    (A) lethargic   (B) morose   (C) silly

    (D) nostalgic   (E) poor

4. PRECLUDE:

   (A) commence   (B) include   (C) produce

   (D) perpetuate   (E) enable

5. EXTOL:

   (A) criticize   (B) expedite   (C) pay

   (D) deport   (E) defer

6. DIVERSE:

   (A) solo   (B) furtive   (C) jovial

   (D) wrinkled   (E) similar

7. DISPERSE:

   (A) despair   (B) belittle   (C) renew

   (D) renege   (E) amass

8. ENDURING:

   (A) fallacious   (B) temporal   (C) dismal

   (D) minute   (E) disseminating

9. BREVITY:

   (A) gravity   (B) gluttony   (C) cowardice

   (D) authenticity   (E) verbosity

10. DEMUR:

   (A) assemble   (B) bereave   (C) approve

   (D) add   (E) ascribe

11. UNWONTED:

   (A) perceptive   (B) ordinary   (C) tepid

   (D) desirable   (E) qualified

12. CHASTISE:

   (A) repudiate   (B) immortalize   (C) endorse

   (D) virility   (E) congratulate

13. INFAMOUS:

   (A) revered   (B) resolute   (C) obscure
   (D) contiguous   (E) unknown

14. DISPASSIONATE:

   (A) resigned   (B) profound   (C) fanatical
   (D) torrid   (E) prudent

15. SCANTY:

   (A) redundant   (B) mediocre   (C) calming
   (D) profuse   (E) partisan

16. PROSAIC:

   (A) poetic   (B) unique   (C) rabid
   (D) disdainful   (E) condescending

17. DIDACTIC:

   (A) dubious   (B) imbecilic   (C) punctual
   (D) rhetorical   (E) reverent

18. COLLOQUIAL:

   (A) poetic   (B) separate   (C) formal
   (D) analogical   (E) anonymous

19. COHESIVE:

   (A) adhesive   (B) opposed   (C) smooth
   (D) adverse   (E) fragmented

20. OBLIGATORY:

   (A) promising   (B) permissible   (C) heaven
   (D) optional   (E) responsible

21. OPAQUE:

   (A) permeable   (B) similar   (C) visible
   (D) opulent   (E) translucent

22. SUNDER:

    (A) unite   (B) create noise   (C) oust

    (D) rise above   (E) freeze

23. NARCISSISTIC:

    (A) flowery   (B) detrimental   (C) gentle

    (D) modest   (E) polite

24. FOSTER:

    (A) destroy   (B) relate   (C) parent

    (D) abort   (E) revere

25. LIVID:

    (A) homeless   (B) bright   (C) calm

    (D) elusive   (E) opulent

26. SUPPRESS:

    (A) justify   (B) advocate   (C) free

    (D) level   (E) immunize

27. DESTITUTE:

    (A) organized   (B) ornate   (C) moral

    (D) wealthy   (E) obsequious

28. PAINSTAKING:

    (A) healthful   (B) sordid   (C) careless

    (D) sadistic   (E) lethal

29. PAROCHIAL:

    (A) melancholy   (B) blasphemous   (C) sporting

    (D) irreligious   (E) broad-minded

30. MANDATE:

    (A) emphasis   (B) sophism   (C) pinnacle

    (D) request   (E) meander

31. LUCID:

(A) obscure   (B) tedious   (C) calm

(D) frightening   (E) intelligent

32. IGNOBLE:

(A) brave   (B) honorable   (C) royal

(D) attentive   (E) informal

33. PERTINENT:

(A) respectful   (B) detailed   (C) dreary

(D) blatant   (E) irrelevant

34. ABSTINENCE:

(A) indulgence   (B) concurrence   (C) hedonism

(D) diligence   (E) alcoholism

35. FRUGAL:

(A) unplanned   (B) temperamental (C) regal

(D) ethical   (E) extravagant

36. FORTUITOUS:

(A) lethargic   (B) unprotected   (C) weak

(D) unlucky   (E) antagonistic

37. UNEQUIVOCAL:

(A) versatile   (B) equal   (C) noisy

(D) unclear   (E) truthful

38. CONTEMPT:

(A) respect   (B) pettiness   (C) politeness

(D) resistance   (E) compliance

39. GRAVITY:

(A) antipathy   (B) derision   (C) buoyancy

(D) eloquence   (E) effervescence

40. AUSTERE:

   (A) measurable   (B) resilient   (C) indulgent

   (D) indirect   (E) destitute

41. PASSIVE:

   (A) thoughtless   (B) supportive   (C) retentive

   (D) contemporary   (E) assertive

42. STAGNANT:

   (A) celibate   (B) active   (C) effluent

   (D) feminine   (E) polluted

43. ADVERSE:

   (A) friendly   (B) quiescent   (C) poetic

   (D) burly   (E) petty

44. CRAVEN:

   (A) difficult   (B) reptilian   (C) pungent

   (D) birdlike   (E) courageous

45. HEED:

   (A) adjust   (B) resist   (C) attend

   (D) encourage   (E) order

46. IMPARTIAL:

   (A) biased   (B) complete   (C) eternal

   (D) articulate   (E) raucous

47. VINDICATE:

   (A) remove   (B) absolve   (C) evoke

   (D) accuse   (E) ferret

48. DERISION:

   (A) elimination   (B) attention   (C) praise

   (D) entrance   (E) recession

49. REPREHENSIBLE:

   (A) released   (B) aghast   (C) awry

   (D) incidental   (E) commendable

50. RELEGATE:

   (A) promote   (B) nullify   (C) include

   (D) obliterate   (E) placate

51. VAIN:

   (A) addicted   (B) modest   (C) unscented

   (D) proud   (E) choleric

52. LAGGARD:

   (A) haggard   (B) lustrous   (C) haphazard

   (D) advanced   (E) industrious

53. LABYRINTHINE:

   (A) inconsistent   (B) amazing   (C) direct

   (D) incredulous   (E) mythological

54. SLANDER:

   (A) praise   (B) comfort   (C) discipline

   (D) risk   (E) digress

55. PITTANCE:

   (A) mound   (B) plethora   (C) quirk

   (D) grandeur   (E) phlegm

56. SOLACE:

   (A) lunation   (B) turmoil   (C) distress

   (D) valance   (E) spontaneity

57. DEFERENT:

   (A) current   (B) constructive   (C) erratic

   (D) unyielding   (E) applicant

58. FICKLE:

    (A) bland   (B) cascading   (C) caustic

    (D) dubious   (E) faithful

59. EXOTIC:

    (A) ethnic   (B) diverse   (C) realistic

    (D) mundane   (E) enigmatic

60. THWART:

    (A) imprison   (B) mystify   (C) assist

    (D) fluctuate   (E) saturate

Knowing Your Word Parts

Memorization and practice are not the only ways to learn the meanings of new words. While taking this test, you will have nothing but your own knowledge and context clues to refer to when you come into contact with unfamiliar words. Even though we have provided you with a comprehensive list of words, there is a very good chance that you will come across words that you still do not know. Therefore, you will need to study our list of prefixes, roots, and suffixes in order to be prepared. Learning the meanings of these prefixes, roots, and suffixes is essential to a strong vocabulary and, therefore, to performing well on the Reading Section, as well as the entire FTCE-GKT exam.

Prefix

Prefix	Meaning	Example
ab-, a-, abs-	away, from	absent – away, not present
		abstain – keep from doing; refrain
ad-	to, toward	adjacent – next to
		address – to direct towards
ante-	before	antecedent – going before in time
		anterior – occurring before
anti-	against	antidote – remedy to act against an evil
		antibiotic – substance that fights against bacteria
be-	over, thoroughly	bemoan – to mourn over
		belabor – to exert much labor upon
bi-	two	bisect – to divide
		biennial – happening every two years

Prefix	Meaning	Example
cata-, cat-, cath-	down	catacombs – underground passageways
		catalog – descriptive list
circum-	around	circumscribe – to draw a circle around
		circumspect – watchful on all sides
com-	with	combine – join together
		communication – to have dealing with
contra-	against	contrary – opposed
		contrast – to stand in opposition
de-	down, from, away	decline – to slope downward
		decontrol – to remove control from
di-	two	dichotomy – process of dividing into two groups or entities
		diarchy – system of government with two authorities
dis-, di-	apart, away	discern – to distinguish as separate
		digress – to turn away from the subject of attention
epi-, ep-, eph-	upon, among	epidemic – happening among a disproportionately large number of individuals
		epicycle – circle whose center moves round in the circumference of a greater circle
ex-, e-	from, out	exceed – go beyond the limit
		emit – to send forth
extra-	outside, beyond	extraordinary – beyond or outside conventional means
		extrasensory – beyond the ordinary senses
hyper-	beyond, over	hyperactive – over the normal activity level
		hypercritic – one who is critical beyond measure
hypo-	beneath, down	hypodermic – beneath the skin
		hypoglycemia – abnormally low glucose level in the blood
in-, il-, im-, ir-	not	inactive – not active
		irreversible – not reversible
in-, il-, im-, ir-	in, on, into	instill – to put in slowly
		impose – to lay on

Prefix	Meaning	Example
inter-	among, between	intercom – to exchange conversations between people
		interlude – performance given between parts in a play
intra-	within	intravenous – within a vein
		intramural – being or happening within the confines of a community, group, or institution
meta-	beyond, over, along with	metamorphosis – change over in form or nature
		metatarsus – part of foot beyond the flat of the foot
mis-	badly, wrongly	misconstrue – to interpret wrongly
		misappropriate – to use wrongly
mono-	one	monogamy – to be married to one person at a time
		monotone – a single, unvaried tone
multi-	many	multiple – of many parts
		multitude – a great number
non-	no, not	nonsense – lack of sense
		nonentity – not existing
ob-	against	obscene – offensive to modesty
		obstruct – to hinder the passage of
para-, par-	beside	parallel – continuously at equal distance apart
		parenthesis – sentence inserted within a passage
per-	through	persevere – to maintain an effort
		permeate – to pass through
poly-	many	polygon – a plane figure with many sides or angles
		polytheism – belief in existence of many gods
post-	after	posterior – coming after
		postpone – to put off till a future time
pre-	before	premature – ready before the proper time
		premonition – a previous warning
pro-	in favor of, forward	prolific – bringing forth offspring
		project – throw or cast forward

Prefix	Meaning	Example
re-	back, against	reimburse – pay back
		retract – to draw back
semi-	half	semicircle – half a circle
		semiannual – half-yearly
sub-	under	subdue – to bring under one's power
		submarine – travel under the surface of the sea
super-	above	supersonic – above the speed of sound
		superior – higher in place or position
tele-, tel-	across	telecast – transmit across a distance
		telepathy – communication between mind and mind at a distance
trans-	across	transpose – to change the position of two things
		transmit – to send from one person to another
ultra-	beyond	ultraviolet – beyond the limit of visibility
		ultramarine – beyond the sea
un-	not	undeclared – not declared
		unbelievable – not believable
uni-	one	unity – state of oneness
		unison – sounding together
with-	away, against	withhold – to hold back
		withdraw – to take away

Root

Root	Meaning	Example
act, ag	do, act, drive	activate – to make active
		agile – having quick motion
alt	high	altitude – height
		alto – lowest female singing voice
alter, altr	other, change	alternative – choice between two or more things of which just one may be picked
		altruism – living for the good of others
am, ami	love, friend	amiable – worthy of affection
		amity – friendship

Root	Meaning	Example
anim	mind, spirit	animated – spirited
		animosity – intense hostility
annu, enni	year	annual – occurring every year
		centennial – a 100-year anniversary
aqua	water	aquarium – tank for water animals and plants
		aquacade – swimming or diving exhibition
arch	principal, first	archenemy – principal enemy
		archetype – original pattern from which things are copied
aud, audit	hear	audible – capable of being heard
		audience – assembly of listeners or spectators
auto	self	automatic – self-acting
		autobiography – a story whose subject and author are one and the same
bell	war	belligerent – a nation or state waging war
		bellicose – favoring or inclined toward hostility
ben, bene	good	benign – kindly disposition
		beneficial – advantageous
bio	life	biotic – relating to life
		biology – the science of life
brev	short	abbreviate – make shorter
		brevity – shortness
cad, cas	fall	cadence – fall in voice
		casualty – loss caused by death
capit, cap	head	captain – the head or chief
		decapitate – to cut off the head
cede, ceed, cess	to go, to yield	recede – to move or fall back
		proceed – to move onward
cent	hundred	century – hundred years
		centipede – insect with a hundred legs
chron	time	chronology – science dealing with historical dates
		chronicle – register of events in order of time

Root	Meaning	Example
cide, cis	to kill, to cut	homicide – a killing of one person by another; the killer of another person
		incision – a cut
clam, claim	to shout	acclaim – receive with applause
		proclamation – announce publicly
cogn	to know	recognize – to know again
		cognition – awareness
corp	body	incorporate – combine into one body
		corpse – dead body
cred	to trust, to believe	incredible – unbelievable
		credulous – too prone to believe
cur, curr, curs	to run	current – flowing body of air or water
		excursion – short trip
dem	people	democracy – government formed for the people
		epidemic – affecting all people
dic, dict	to say	dictate – to read aloud for another to transcribe
		verdict – decision of a jury
doc, doct	to teach	docile – easily instructed
		indoctrinate – to instruct
domin	to rule	dominate – to rule
		dominion – territory of rule
duc, duct	to lead	conduct – act of guiding
		induce – to overcome by persuasion
eu	well, good	eulogy – speech or writing in praise
		euphony – pleasantness or smoothness of sound
fac, fact, fect, fic	to do, to make	factory – location of production
		fiction – something invented or imagined
fer	to bear, to carry	transfer – to move from one place to another
		refer – to direct to
fin	end, limit	infinity – unlimited
		finite – limited in quantity
flect, flex	to bend	flexible – easily bent
		reflect – to throw back
fort	luck	fortunate – lucky
		fortuitous – happening by chance

Root	Meaning	Example
fort	strong	fortify – strengthen
		fortress – stronghold
frag, fract	break	fragile – easily broken
		fracture – break
fug	flee	fugitive – fleeing
		refugee – one who flees to a place of safety
gen	class, race	engender – to breed
		generic – of a general nature in regard to all members
grad, gress	to go, to step	regress – to go back
		graduate – to divide into regular steps
gram, graph	writing	telegram – message sent by telegraph
		autograph – person's handwriting or signature
ject	to throw	projectile – capable of being thrown
		reject – to throw away
leg	law	legitimate – lawful
		legal – defined by law
leg, lig, lect	to choose, gather, read	illegible – incapable of being read
		election – the act of choosing
liber	free	liberal – favoring freedom of ideals
		liberty – freedom from restraint
log	study, speech	archaeology – study of human antiquities
		prologue – address spoken before a performance
luc, lum	light	translucent – slightly transparent
		illuminate – to light up
magn	large, great	magnify – to make larger
		magnificent – great
mal, male	bad, wrong	malfunction – to operate incorrectly
		malevolent – evil
mar	sea	marine – pertaining to the sea
		submarine – below the surface of the sea
mater, matr	mother	maternal – motherly
		matriarch – government exercised by a mother

Root	Meaning	Example
mit, miss	to send	transmit – to send from one person or place to another
		mission – the act of sending
morph	shape	metamorphosis – a changing in shape
		anthropomorphic – having a human shape
mut	change	mutable – subject to change
		mutate – to change a vowel
nat	born	innate – inborn
		native – a person born in a place
neg	deny	negative – expressing denial
		renege – to deny
nom	name	nominate – to put forward a name
		anonymous – no name given
nov	new	novel – new
		renovate – to make as good as new
omni	all	omnipotent – all powerful
		omnipresent – all present
oper	to work	operate – to work on something
		cooperate – to work with others
pass, path	to feel	pathetic – affecting the tender emotions
		passionate – moved by strong emotion
pater, patr	father	paternal – fatherly
		patriarch – government exercised by a father
ped, pod	foot	pedestrian – one who travels on foot
		podiatrist – foot doctor
pel, puls	to drive, to push	impel – to drive forward
		compulsion – irresistible force
phil	love	philharmonic – loving harmony or music
		philanthropist – one who loves and seeks to do good for others
port	carry	export – to carry out of the country
		portable – able to be carried

Root	Meaning	Example
psych	mind	psychology – study of the mind
		psychiatrist – specialist in mental disorders
quer, ques, quir, quis	to ask	inquiry – to ask about
		question – that which is asked
rid, ris	to laugh	ridiculous – laughable
		derision – to mock
rupt	to break	interrupt – to break in upon
		erupt – to break through
sci	to know	science – systematic knowledge of physical or natural phenomena
		conscious – having inward knowledge
scrib, script	to write	transcribe – to write over again
		script – text of words
sent, sens	to feel, to think	sentimental – feel great emotion
		sensitive – easily affected by changes
sequ, secut	to follow	sequence – connected series
		consecutive – following one another in unbroken order
solv, solu, solut	to loosen	dissolve – to break up
		absolute – without restraint
spect	to look at	spectator – one who watches
		inspect – to look at closely
spir	to breathe	inspire – to breathe in
		respiration – process of breathing
string, strict	to bind	stringent – binding strongly
		restrict – to restrain within bounds
stru, struct	to build	misconstrue – to interpret wrongly
		construct – to build
tang, ting, tact, tig	to touch	tangent – touching, but not intersecting
		contact – touching
ten, tent, tain	to hold	tenure – holding of office
		contain – to hold

Root	Meaning	Example
term	to end	terminate – to end
		terminal – having an end
terr	earth	terrain – tract of land
		terrestrial – existing on earth
therm	heat	thermal – pertaining to heat
		thermometer – instrument for measuring temperature
tort, tors	to twist	contortionist – one who twists violently
		torsion – act of turning or twisting
tract	to pull, to draw	attract – draw toward
		distract – to draw away
vac	empty	vacant – empty
		evacuate – to empty out
ven, vent	to come	prevent – to stop from coming
		intervene – to come between
ver	true	verify – to prove to be true
		veracious – truthful
verb	word	verbose – use of excess words
		verbatim – word for word
vid, vis	to see	video – picture phase of television
		vision – act of seeing external objects
vinc, vict, vang	to conquer	invincible – unconquerable
		victory – defeat of enemy
viv, vit	life	vital – necessary to life
		vivacious – lively
voc	to call	provocative – serving to excite or stimulate to action
		vocal – uttered by voice
vol	to wish, to will	involuntary – outside the control of will
		volition – the act of willing or choosing

Suffix

Suffix	Meaning	Example
-able, -ble	capable of	believable – capable of being believed
		legible – capable of being read
-acious, -icious, -ous	full of	vivacious – full of life
		wondrous – full of wonder
-ant, -ent	full of	eloquent – full of eloquence
		expectant – full of expectation
-ary	connected with	honorary – for the sake of honor
		disciplinary – enforcing instruction
-ate	to make	ventilate – to make public
		consecrate – to make sacred
-fy	to make	magnify – to make larger
		testify – to make witness
-ile	pertaining to, capable of	docile – capable of being managed easily
		civil – pertaining to a city or state
-ism	principle or practice	conservatism – interest in preserving or restoring
		idiotism – foolish conduct or action
-ist	doer	artist – one who creates art
		pianist – one who plays the piano
-ose	full of	verbose – full of words
		grandiose – striking, imposing
-osis	condition	neurosis – nervous condition
		psychosis – psychological condition
-tude	state	magnitude – state of greatness
		multitude – state of quantity

Figures of Speech

Figurative language helps to create imaginative and detailed writing. A figure of speech is used in the imaginative rather than the literal sense. It helps the reader to make connections between the writer's thoughts and the external world. Knowing the different types of figures of speech can help you determine the context in which a word is being used and, thereby, help you determine the meaning of that word. The following are some commonly used figures of speech.

Simile

A simile is an explicit comparison between two things. The comparison is made by using *like* or *as*.

> Her hair was *like* straw.
>
> The blanket was *as* white as snow.

Metaphor

Like the simile, the metaphor likens two things. However, *like* or *as* are not used in the comparison.

> "All the world's a stage." Shakespeare
>
> Grass is nature's blanket.

A common error is the mixed metaphor. This occurs when a writer uses two inconsistent metaphors in a single expression.

> The blanket of snow clutched the earth with icy fingers.

Hyperbole

A hyperbole is a deliberate overstatement or exaggeration used to express an idea.

> I have told you a thousand times not to play with matches.

Personification

Personification is the attribution of human qualities to an object, animal, or idea.

> The wind laughed at their attempts to catch the flying papers.

Skill 3: Recognize Diction and Tone Appropriate to a Given Audience

The denotative meaning of a word is its *literal*, dictionary definition: what the word denotes or "means." The connotative meaning of a word is what the word connotes or "suggests"; it is a meaning apart from what the word literally means. A writer should choose a word based on the tone and context of the sentence; this ensures that a word bears the appropriate connotation while still conveying some exactness in denotation. For example, a gift might be described as "cheap," but the directness of this word has a negative connotation—something cheap is something of little or no value. The word "inexpensive" has a more positive connotation, though "cheap" is a synonym for "inexpensive." Questions of this type require you to make a decision regarding the appropriateness of words and phrases for the context of a sentence.

Wordiness and Conciseness

Effective writing is concise. Wordiness, on the other hand, decreases the clarity of expression by cluttering sentences with unnecessary words.

Wordiness questions test your ability to detect redundancies (unnecessary repetitions), circumlocution (failure to get to the point), and padding with loose synonyms. Wordiness questions require you to choose sentences that use as few words as possible to convey a message clearly, economically, and effectively.

Notice the difference in impact between the first and second sentences in the following pairs:

INCORRECT: The medical exam that he gave me was entirely complete.

CORRECT: The medical exam he gave me was complete.

INCORRECT: Larry asked his friend John, who was a good, old friend, if he would join him and go along with him to see the foreign film made in Japan.

CORRECT: Larry asked his good, old friend John if he would join him in seeing the Japanese film.

INCORRECT: I was absolutely, totally happy with the present that my parents gave to me at 7 a.m. on the morning of my birthday.

CORRECT: I was happy with the present my parents gave me on the morning of my birthday.

Drill 14: Word Choice Skills

DIRECTIONS: Choose the correct option.

1.   His <u>principal</u> reasons for resigning were his <u>principles</u> of right and wrong.

   (A)   principal . . . principals

   (B)   principle . . . principals

   (C)   principle . . . principles

   (D)   No change is necessary.

2.   The book tells about Alzheimer's disease—how it <u>affects</u> the patient and what <u>effect</u> it has on the patient's family.

   (A)   effects . . . affect

   (B)   affects . . . affect

   (C)   effects . . . effects

   (D)   No change is necessary.

3. The <u>amount</u> of homeless children we can help depends on the <u>number</u> of available shelters.

    (A) number . . . number

    (B) amount . . . amount

    (C) number . . . amount

    (D) No change is necessary.

4. All students are <u>suppose to</u> pass the test before <u>achieving</u> upper-division status.

    (A) suppose to . . . acheiving

    (B) suppose to . . . being achieved

    (C) supposed to . . . achieving

    (D) No change is necessary.

5. The reason he <u>succeeded</u> is <u>because</u> he worked hard.

    (A) succeeded . . . that

    (B) seceded . . . that

    (C) succede . . . because of

    (D) No change is necessary.

DIRECTIONS: Select the sentence that clearly and effectively states the idea and has no structural errors.

---

6. (A) South of Richmond, the two roads converge together to form a single highway.

    (B) South of Richmond, the two roads converge together to form an interstate highway.

    (C) South of Richmond, the two roads converge to form an interstate highway.

    (D) South of Richmond, the two roads converge to form a single interstate highway.

7. (A) The student depended on his parents for financial support.

    (B) The student lacked the ways and means to pay for his room and board, so he depended on his parents for this kind of money and support.

    (C) The student lacked the ways and means or the wherewithal to support himself, so his parents provided him with the financial support he needed.

    (D) The student lacked the means to pay for his room and board, so he depended on his parents for financial support.

8. (A) Vincent van Gogh and Paul Gauguin were close personal friends and companions who enjoyed each other's company and frequently worked together on their artwork.

   (B) Vincent van Gogh and Paul Gauguin were friends who frequently painted together.

   (C) Vincent van Gogh was a close personal friend of Paul Gauguin's, and the two of them often worked together on their artwork because they enjoyed each other's company.

   (D) Vincent van Gogh, a close personal friend of Paul Gauguin's, often worked with him on their artwork.

9. (A) A college education often involves putting away childish thoughts, which are characteristic of youngsters, and concentrating on the future, which lies ahead.

   (B) A college education involves putting away childish thoughts, which are characteristic of youngsters, and concentrating on the future.

   (C) A college education involves putting away childish thoughts and concentrating on the future.

   (D) A college education involves putting away childish thoughts and concentrating on the future which lies ahead.

10. (A) I had the occasion to visit an Oriental pagoda while I was a tourist on vacation and visiting in Kyoto, Japan.

    (B) I visited a Japanese pagoda in Kyoto.

    (C) I had occasion to visit a pagoda when I was vacationing in Kyoto, Japan.

    (D) On my vacation, I visited a Japanese pagoda in Kyoto.

Competency 3: Sentence Structure Skills

Skill 1: Recognize Correct Placement of Modifiers

A misplaced modifier is one that is in the wrong place in the sentence. Misplaced modifiers come in all forms—words, phrases, and clauses. Sentences containing misplaced modifiers are often very comical: *Mom made me eat the spinach instead of my brother.* Misplaced modifiers, like the one in this sentence, are usually too far away from the word or words they modify. This sentence should read: *Mom made me, instead of my brother, eat the spinach.*

Modifiers like *only, nearly,* and *almost* should be placed next to the word they modify and not in front of some other word, especially a verb, that they are not intended to modify.

A modifier is misplaced if it appears to modify the wrong part of the sentence or if we cannot be certain what part of the sentence the writer intended it to modify. To correct a misplaced modifier, move the modifier next to the word it describes.

INCORRECT:	She served hamburgers to the men on paper plates.
CORRECT:	She served hamburgers on paper plates to the men.

Split infinitives also result in misplaced modifiers. Infinitives consist of the marker *to* plus the plain form of the verb. The two parts of the infinitive make up a grammatical unit that should not be split. Splitting an infinitive is placing an adverb between the *to* and the verb.

INCORRECT:	The weather service expects temperatures to not rise.
CORRECT:	The weather service expects temperatures not to rise.

Sometimes a split infinitive may be natural and preferable, though it may still bother some readers.

EXAMPLE:	Several U.S. industries expect *to* more than *triple* their use of robots within the next decade.

A squinting modifier is one that may refer to either a preceding or a following word, leaving the reader uncertain about what it is intended to modify. Correct a squinting modifier by moving it next to the word it is intended to modify.

INCORRECT:	Snipers who fired on the soldiers often escaped capture.
CORRECT:	Snipers who often fired on the soldiers escaped capture. OR
	Snipers who fired on the soldiers escaped capture often.

A dangling modifier is a modifier or verb in search of a subject: the modifying phrase (usually an *-ing* word group, an *-ed* or *-en* word group, or a *to + a verb* word group—participle phrase or infinitive phrase respectively) either appears to modify the wrong word or has nothing to modify. It is literally dangling at the beginning or the end of a sentence. The sentences often look and sound correct: *To be a student government officer, your grades must be above average.* (However, the verbal modifier has nothing to describe. Who is *to be a student government officer*? Your grades?) Questions of this type require you to determine whether a modifier has a headword or whether it is dangling at the beginning or the end of the sentence.

To correct a dangling modifier, reword the sentence by either: 1) changing the modifying phrase to a clause with a subject, or 2) changing the subject of the sentence to the word that should be modified. The following are examples of a dangling gerund, a dangling infinitive, and a dangling participle:

INCORRECT:	Shortly after leaving home, the accident occurred. Who is <u>leaving home</u>, the accident?
CORRECT:	Shortly after we left home, the accident occurred.
INCORRECT:	To get up on time, a great effort was needed. <u>To get up</u> needs a subject.
CORRECT:	To get up on time, I made a great effort.

Skill 2: Recognize Parallelism

This skill requires recognition of parallel expressions for parallel ideas. Parallel structure is used to express matching ideas. It refers to the grammatical balance of a series of any of the following:

Phrases:

The squirrel ran *along the fence, up the tree,* and *into his burrow* with a mouthful of acorns.

Adjectives:

The job market is flooded with *very talented, highly motivated,* and *well-educated* young people.

Nouns:

You will need a *notebook, pencil,* and *dictionary* for the test.

Clauses:

The children were told to decide *which toy they would keep* and *which toy they would give away.*

Verbs:

The farmer *plowed, planted,* and *harvested* his corn in record time.

Verbals:

Reading, writing, and *calculating* are fundamental skills that all of us should possess.

Correlative conjunctions:

Either you will do your homework *or* you will fail.

Repetition of structural signals:

(such as articles, auxiliaries, prepositions, and conjunctions)

> INCORRECT: I have quit my job, enrolled in school, and am looking for a reliable babysitter.
>
> CORRECT: I *have quit* my job, *have enrolled* in school, and *am looking* for a reliable babysitter.

Note: Repetition of prepositions is considered formal and is not necessary.

> You can travel *by car, by plane, or by train*; it's all up to you.

OR

> You can travel *by car, plane, or train*; it's all up to you.

When a sentence contains items in a series, check for both punctuation and sentence balance. When you check for punctuation, make sure the commas are used correctly. When you check for parallelism, make sure that the conjunctions connect similar grammatical constructions, such as all adjectives or all clauses.

Skill 3: Recognize Fragments, Comma Splices, and Run-on Sentences

A fragment is an incomplete construction that may or may not have a subject and a verb. Specifically, a fragment is a group of words pretending to be a sentence. Not all fragments appear as separate sentences, however. Often, fragments are separated by semicolons.

INCORRECT:	Traffic was stalled for ten miles on the freeway. Because repairs were being made on potholes.
CORRECT:	Traffic was stalled for ten miles on the freeway because repairs were being made on potholes.
INCORRECT:	It was a funny story; one that I had never heard before.
CORRECT:	It was a funny story, one that I had never heard before.

Comma Splices

A comma splice is the unjustifiable use of only a comma to combine what really is two separate sentences.

INCORRECT:	One common error in writing is incorrect spelling, the other is the occasional use of faulty diction.
CORRECT:	One common error in writing is incorrect spelling; the other is the occasional use of faulty diction.

Both run-on sentences and comma splices may be corrected in one of the following ways:

RUN-ON:	Neal won the award he had the highest score.
COMMA SPLICE:	Neal won the award, he had the highest score.

Separate the sentences with a period:

Neal won the award. He had the highest score.

Separate the sentences with a comma and a coordinating conjunction (*and, but, or, nor, for, yet, so*):

Neal won the award for he had the highest score.

Separate the sentences with a semicolon:

Neal won the award; he had the highest score.

Separate the sentences with a subordinating conjunction such as *although, because, since, if*:

> Neal won the award because he had the highest score.

Run-on/Fused Sentences

A run-on/fused sentence is not necessarily a long sentence or a sentence that the reader considers too long; in fact, a run-on may be two short sentences: *Dry ice does not melt it evaporates.* A run-on results when the writer fuses or runs together two separate sentences without any correct mark of punctuation separating them.

INCORRECT:	Knowing how to use a dictionary is no problem each dictionary has a section in the front of the book telling how to use it.
CORRECT:	Knowing how to use a dictionary is no problem. Each dictionary has a section in the front of the book telling how to use it.

Even if one or both of the fused sentences contains internal punctuation, the sentence is still a run-on.

INCORRECT:	Bob bought dress shoes, a suit, and a nice shirt he needed them for his sister's wedding.
CORRECT:	Bob bought dress shoes, a suit, and a nice shirt. He needed them for his sister's wedding.

Subordination, Coordination, and Predication

Suppose, for the sake of clarity, you wanted to combine the information in these two sentences to create one statement:

> I studied a foreign language. I found English quite easy.

How you decide to combine this information should be determined by the relationship you'd like to show between the two facts. *I studied a foreign language, and I found English quite easy* seems rather illogical. The **coordination** of the two ideas (connecting them with the coordinating conjunction *and*) is ineffective. Using **subordination** instead (connecting the sentences with a subordinating conjunction) clearly shows the degree of relative importance between the expressed ideas:

> After I studied a foreign language, I found English quite easy.

When using a conjunction, be sure that the sentence parts you are joining are in agreement.

INCORRECT:	She loved him dearly but not his dog.
CORRECT:	She loved him dearly but she did not love his dog.

A common mistake that is made is to forget that each member of the pair must be followed by the same kind of construction.

INCORRECT: They complimented them for their bravery and they thanked them for their being kind.

CORRECT: They complimented them for their bravery and thanked them for their kindness.

While refers to time and should not be used as a substitute for *although*, *and*, or *but*.

INCORRECT: While I'm usually interested in Fellini movies, I'd rather not go tonight.

CORRECT: Although I'm usually interested in Fellini movies, I'd rather not go tonight.

Where refers to time and should not be used as a substitute for *that*.

INCORRECT: We read in the paper where they are making great strides in DNA research.

CORRECT: We read in the paper that they are making great strides in DNA research.

After words like "reason" and "explanation", use *that*, not *because*.

INCORRECT: His explanation for his tardiness was because his alarm did not go off.

CORRECT: His explanation for his tardiness was that his alarm did not go off.

Drill 15: Sentence Structure Skills

DIRECTIONS: Choose the sentence that expresses the thought most clearly and that has no error in structure.

1.   (A)   Many gases are invisible, odorless, and they have no taste.

     (B)   Many gases are invisible, odorless, and have no taste.

     (C)   Many gases are invisible, odorless, and tasteless.

2.   (A)   Everyone agreed that she had neither the voice or the skill to be a speaker.

     (B)   Everyone agreed that she had neither the voice nor the skill to be a speaker.

     (C)   Everyone agreed that she had either the voice nor the skill to be a speaker.

3. (A) The mayor will be remembered because he kept his campaign promises and because of his refusal to accept political favors.

    (B) The mayor will be remembered because he kept his campaign promises and because he refused to accept political favors.

    (C) The mayor will be remembered because of his refusal to accept political favors and he kept his campaign promises.

4. (A) While taking a shower, the doorbell rang.

    (B) While I was taking a shower, the doorbell rang.

    (C) While taking a shower, someone rang the doorbell.

5. (A) He swung the bat, while the runner stole second base.

    (B) The runner stole second base while he swung the bat.

    (C) While he was swinging the bat, the runner stole second base.

DIRECTIONS: Choose the correct option.

---

6. Nothing grows as well in Mississippi as <u>cotton. Cotton</u> being the state's principal crop.

    (A) cotton, cotton

    (B) cotton; cotton

    (C) cotton cotton

    (D) No change is necessary.

7. It was a heartwrenching <u>movie; one</u> that I had never seen before.

    (A) movie and

    (B) movie, one

    (C) movie. One

    (D) No change is necessary.

8. Traffic was stalled for three miles on the <u>bridge. Because</u> repairs were being made.

    (A) bridge because

    (B) bridge; because

    (C) bridge, because

    (D) No change is necessary.

9. The ability to write complete sentences comes with <u>practice writing</u> run-on sentences seems to occur naturally.

  (A) practice, writing

  (B) practice. Writing

  (C) practice and

  (D) No change is necessary.

10. Even though she had taken French classes, she could not understand native French <u>speakers they</u> all spoke too fast.

  (A) speakers, they

  (B) speakers. They

  (C) speaking

  (D) No change is necessary.

Competency 4: Grammar, Spelling, Capitalization, and Punctuation Skills

Skill 1: Identify Standard Verb Forms

Verb Forms

This section covers the principal parts of some irregular verbs including troublesome verbs like *lie* and *lay*. The use of regular verbs like *look* and *receive* poses no real problem to most writers since the past and past participle forms end in *-ed*; it is the irregular forms that pose the most serious problems—for example, *seen, written,* and *begun.*

Skill 2: Identify Inappropriate Shifts in Verb Tense

Tense sequence indicates a logical time sequence.

Use present tense

in statements of universal truth:

> I learned that the sun *is* 90 million miles from the earth.

in statements about the contents of literature and other published works:

> In this book, Sandy *becomes* a nun and *writes* a book on psychology.

Use past tense

in statements concerning writing or publication of a book:

> He *wrote* his first book in 1949, and it *was published* in 1952.

Use present perfect tense

for an action that began in the past but continues into the future:

> I *have lived* here all my life.

Use past perfect tense

for an earlier action that is mentioned in a later action:

> Cindy ate the apple that she *had picked*.

(First she picked it, then she ate it.)

Use future perfect tense

for an action that will have been completed at a specific future time:

> By May, I *shall have graduated*.

Use a present participle

for action that occurs at the same time as the verb:

> *Speeding* down the interstate, I saw a cop's flashing lights.

Use a perfect participle

for action that occurred before the main verb:

> *Having read* the directions, I started the test.

Use the subjunctive mood

to express a wish or state a condition contrary to fact:

> *If it were not raining,* we could have a picnic.

in *that* clauses after verbs like *request, recommend, suggest, ask, require,* and *insist*; and after such expressions as *it is important* and *it is necessary*:

> It is necessary that all papers *be* submitted on time.

Skill 3: Identify Agreement Between Subject and Verb

Agreement is the grammatical correspondence between the subject and the verb of a sentence: *I do; we do; they do; he, she, it does.*

Every English verb has five forms, two of which are the bare form (plural) and the *-s* form (singular). Simply put, singular verb forms end in *-s*; plural forms do not.

Study these rules governing subject-verb agreement:

A verb must agree with its subject, not with any additive phrase in the sentence such as a prepositional or verbal phrase. Ignore such phrases.

> Your *copy* of the rules *is* on the desk.
>
> Ms. Craig's *record* of community service and outstanding teaching *qualifies* her for a promotion.

In an inverted sentence beginning with a prepositional phrase, the verb still agrees with its subject.

> At the end of the summer *come* the best *sales.*
>
> Under the house *are* some old Mason *jars.*

Prepositional phrases beginning with compound prepositions such as *along with, together with, in addition to,* and *as well as* should be ignored, for they do not affect subject-verb agreement.

> *Gladys Knight,* as well as the Pips, *is* riding the midnight train to Georgia.

A verb must agree with its subject, not its subject complement.

> *Taxes are* a problem.
>
> A *problem is* taxes.

When a sentence begins with an expletive such as *there, here,* or *it,* the verb agrees with the subject, not the expletive.

> Surely, there *are* several *alumni* who would be interested in forming a group.
>
> There *are* 50 *students* in my English class.
>
> There *is* a horrifying *study* on child abuse in *Psychology Today.*

Indefinite pronouns such as *each, either, one, everyone, everybody,* and *everything* are singular.

> *Somebody* in Detroit *loves* me.
>
> *Does either* [one] of you have a pencil?
>
> *Neither* of my brothers *has* a car.

Indefinite pronouns such as *several, few, both,* and *many* are plural.

> *Both* of my sorority sisters *have* decided to live off campus.
>
> *Few seek* the enlightenment of transcendental meditation.

Indefinite pronouns such as *all, some, most,* and *none* may be singular or plural depending on their referents.

> *Some* of the food *is* cold.
>
> *Some* of the vegetables *are* cold.
>
> I can think of some retorts, but *none seem* appropriate.
>
> *None* of the children *is* as sweet as Sally.

Fractions such as *one-half* and *one-third* may be singular or plural depending on the referent.

> *Half* of the mail *has* been delivered.
>
> *Half* of the letters *have* been read.

Subjects joined by *and* take a plural verb unless the subjects are thought to be one item or unit.

> *Jim* and *Tammy were* televangelists.
>
> *Earth, Wind, and Fire is* my favorite group.

In cases when the subjects are joined by *or, nor, either . . . or,* or *neither . . . nor,* the verb must agree with the subject closer to it.

> Either the teacher or the *students are* responsible.
>
> Neither the students nor the *teacher is* responsible.

Relative pronouns, such as *who, which,* or *that,* which refer to plural antecedents require plural verbs. However, when the relative pronoun refers to a singular subject, the pronoun takes a singular verb.

> She is one of the girls *who cheer* on Friday nights.
>
> She is the only cheerleader *who has* a broken leg.

Subjects preceded by *every, each,* and *many a* are singular.

> *Every* man, woman, and child *was* given a life preserver.
>
> *Each* undergraduate *is* required to pass a proficiency exam.
>
> *Many a* tear *has* to fall before one matures.

A collective noun, such as *audience, faculty, jury,* etc., requires a singular verb when the group is regarded as a whole, and a plural verb when the members of the group are regarded as individuals.

> The *jury has* made its decision.
>
> The *faculty are* preparing their grade rosters.

Subjects preceded by *the number of* or *the percentage of* are singular, while subjects preceded by *a number of* or *a percentage of* are plural.

> *The number of* vacationers in Florida *increases* every year.

> *A number of* vacationers *are* young couples.

Titles of books, companies, name brands, and groups are singular or plural depending on their meaning.

> *Great Expectations is* my favorite novel.

> The *Rolling Stones are* performing in the Super Dome.

Certain nouns of Latin and Greek origin have unusual singular and plural forms.

Singular	Plural
criterion	criteria
alumnus	alumni
datum	data
medium	media

> The *data are* available for inspection.

> The only *criterion* for membership *is* a high GPA.

Some nouns such as *deer, shrimp,* and *sheep* have the same spellings for both their singular and plural forms. In these cases, the meaning of the sentence will determine whether they are singular or plural.

> *Deer are* beautiful animals.

> The spotted *deer is* licking the sugar cube.

Some nouns like *scissors, jeans,* and *wages* have plural forms but no singular counterparts. These nouns almost always take plural verbs.

> The *scissors are* on the table.

> My new *jeans fit* me like a glove.

Words used as examples, not as grammatical parts of the sentence, require singular verbs.

> *Can't is* the contraction for "cannot."

> *Cats is* the plural form of "cat."

Mathematical expressions of subtraction and division require singular verbs, while expressions of addition and multiplication take either singular or plural verbs.

> Ten *divided* by two *equals* five.

> Five *times* two *equals* ten. OR

> Five *times* two *equal* ten.

Nouns expressing time, distance, weight, and measurement are singular when they refer to a unit and plural when they refer to separate items.

Fifty yards is a short distance.

Ten years have passed since I finished college.

Expressions of quantity are usually plural.

Nine out of ten dentists *recommend* that their patients floss.

Some nouns ending in *-ics*, such as *economics* and *ethics*, take singular verbs when they refer to principles or a field of study; however, when they refer to individual practices, they usually take plural verbs.

Ethics is being taught in the spring.

His unusual business *ethics are* what got him into trouble.

Some nouns like *measles, news,* and *calculus* appear to be plural but are actually singular in number. These nouns require singular verbs.

Measles is a very contagious disease.

Calculus requires great skill in algebra.

A verbal noun (infinitive or gerund) serving as a subject is treated as singular, even if the object of the verbal phrase is plural.

Hiding your mistakes *does* not make them go away.

To run five miles *is* my goal.

A noun phrase or clause acting as the subject of a sentence requires a singular verb.

What I need is to be loved.

Whether there is any connection between them is unknown.

Clauses beginning with *what* may be singular or plural depending on the meaning, that is, whether *what* means "the thing" or "the things."

What I want for Christmas is a new motorcycle.

What matters are Smith's ideas.

A plural subject followed by a singular appositive requires a plural verb; similarly, a singular subject followed by a plural appositive requires a singular verb.

When the girls throw a party, *they* each bring a *gift.*

The *board,* all ten members, *is* meeting today.

Drill 16: Verbs

> **DIRECTIONS: Choose the correct option.**

1. If you <u>had been concerned</u> about Marilyn, you <u>would have went</u> to greater lengths to ensure her safety.

   (A) had been concern . . . would have gone

   (B) was concerned . . . would have gone

   (C) had been concerned . . . would have gone

   (D) No change is necessary.

2. Susan <u>laid</u> in bed too long and missed her class.

   (A) lays   (C) lied

   (B) lay   (D) No change is necessary.

3. The Great Wall of China <u>is</u> fifteen hundred miles long; it <u>was built</u> in the third century B.C.

   (A) was . . . was built   (C) has been . . . was built

   (B) is . . . is built   (D) No change is necessary.

4. Joe stated that the class <u>began</u> at 10:30 a.m.

   (A) begins   (C) was beginning

   (B) had begun   (D) No change is necessary.

5. The ceiling of the Sistine Chapel <u>was</u> painted by Michelangelo; it <u>depicted</u> scenes from the Creation in the Old Testament.

   (A) was . . . depicts   (C) has been . . . depicting

   (B) is . . . depicts   (D) No change is necessary.

6. After Christmas <u>comes</u> the best sales.

   (A) has come   (C) is coming

   (B) come   (D) No change is necessary.

7. The bakery's specialty <u>are</u> wedding cakes.

    (A) is

    (B) were

    (C) be

    (D) No change is necessary.

8. Every man, woman, and child <u>were given</u> a life preserver.

    (A) have been given

    (B) had gave

    (C) was given

    (D) No change is necessary.

9. Hiding your mistakes <u>don't</u> make them go away.

    (A) doesn't

    (B) do not

    (C) have not

    (D) No change is necessary.

10. The Board of Regents <u>has recommended</u> a tuition increase.

    (A) have recommended

    (B) has recommend

    (C) had recommended

    (D) No change is necessary.

Skill 4: Identify Agreement Between Pronoun and Antecedent

These kinds of questions test your knowledge of using an appropriate pronoun to agree with its antecedent in number (singular or plural form) and gender (masculine, feminine, or neuter). An antecedent is a noun or pronoun to which another noun or pronoun refers.

Here are the two basic rules for pronoun reference-antecedent agreement:

1. Every pronoun must have a conspicuous antecedent.

2. Every pronoun must agree with its antecedent in number, gender, and person.

When an antecedent is one of dual gender like *student, singer, artist, person, citizen,* etc., use *his* or *her.* Some careful writers change the antecedent to a plural noun to avoid using the sexist, singular masculine pronoun *his*:

INCORRECT: Everyone hopes that he will win the lottery.

CORRECT: Most people hope that they will win the lottery.

Ordinarily, the relative pronoun *who* is used to refer to people, *which* to refer to things and places, *where* to refer to places, and *that* to refer to places or things. The distinction between *that* and *which* is a grammatical distinction (see the section on Word Choice Skills).

Many writers prefer to use *that* to refer to collective nouns.

        EXAMPLE: A family *that* traces its lineage is usually proud of its roots

Skill 5: Identify Inappropriate Pronoun Shifts

Many writers, especially students, are not sure when to use the reflexive case pronoun and when to use the possessive case pronoun. The rules governing the usage of the reflexive case and the possessive case are quite simple.

Use the possessive case

before a noun in a sentence:

      Our friend moved during the semester break.

      My dog has fleas, but *her* dog doesn't.

before a gerund in a sentence:

      Her running helps to relieve stress.

      His driving terrified her.

as a noun in a sentence:

      Mine was the last test graded that day.

to indicate possession:

      Karen never allows anyone else to drive *her* car.

      Brad thought the book was *his,* but it was someone else's.

Use the reflexive case

as a direct object to rename the subject:

      I kicked *myself.*

as an indirect object to rename the subject:

      Henry bought *himself* a tie.

as an object of a prepositional phrase:

      Tom and Lillie baked the pie for *themselves*.

as a predicate pronoun:

      She hasn't been *herself* lately.

Do not use the reflexive in place of the nominative pronoun:

INCORRECT:	Both Randy and *myself* plan to go.
CORRECT:	Both Randy and *I* plan to go.

INCORRECT:	*Yourself* will take on the challenges of college.
CORRECT:	*You* will take on the challenges of college.

INCORRECT:	Either James or *yourself* will paint the mural.
CORRECT:	Either James or *you* will paint the mural.

Watch out for careless use of the pronoun form:

INCORRECT:	George *hisself* told me it was true.
CORRECT:	George *himself* told me it was true.

INCORRECT:	They washed the car *theirselves.*
CORRECT:	They washed the car *themselves.*

Notice that reflexive pronouns are not set off by commas:

INCORRECT:	Mary, *herself,* gave him the diploma.
CORRECT:	Mary *herself* gave him the diploma.

INCORRECT:	I will do it, *myself.*
CORRECT:	I will do it *myself.*

Skill 6: Identify Clear Pronoun References

Pronoun reference questions require you to determine whether the antecedent is conspicuously written in the sentence or whether it is remote, implied, ambiguous, or vague, none of which results in clear writing. Make sure that every italicized pronoun has a conspicuous antecedent and that one pronoun substitutes only for another noun or pronoun, not for an idea or a sentence.

Pronoun reference problems occur

when a pronoun refers to either of two antecedents:

INCORRECT:	Joanna told Tim that *she* was getting fat.
CORRECT:	Joanna told Tim, "I'm getting fat."

when a pronoun refers to a remote antecedent:

INCORRECT: A strange car followed us closely, and *he* kept blinking his lights at us.

CORRECT: A strange car followed us closely, and its driver kept blinking his lights at us.

when *this, that,* and *which* refer to the general idea of the preceding clause or sentence rather than the preceding word:

INCORRECT: The students could not understand the pronoun reference handout, which annoyed them very much.

CORRECT: The students could not understand the pronoun reference handout, a fact which annoyed them very much.

OR   The students were annoyed because they could not understand the pronoun reference handout.

when a pronoun refers to an unexpressed but implied noun:

INCORRECT: My husband wants me to knit a blanket, but I'm not interested in it.

CORRECT: My husband wants me to knit a blanket, but I'm not interested in knitting.

when *it* is used as something other than an expletive to postpone a subject:

INCORRECT: It says in today's paper that the newest shipment of cars from Detroit, Michigan, seems to include outright imitations of European models.

CORRECT: Today's paper says that the newest shipment of cars from Detroit, Michigan, seems to include outright imitations of European models.

INCORRECT: The football game was canceled because it was bad weather.

CORRECT: The football game was canceled because the weather was bad.

when *they* or *it* is used to refer to something or someone indefinitely, and there is no definite antecedent:

INCORRECT: At the job placement office, they told me to stop wearing ripped jeans to my interviews.

CORRECT: At the job placement office, I was told to stop wearing ripped jeans to my interviews.

when the pronoun does not agree with its antecedent in number, gender, or person:

INCORRECT:	Any graduate student, if they are interested, may attend the lecture.
CORRECT:	Any graduate student, if he or she is interested, may attend the lecture.
OR	All graduate students, if they are interested, may attend the lecture.

INCORRECT:	Many Americans are concerned that the overuse of slang and colloquialisms is corrupting the language.
CORRECT:	Many Americans are concerned that the overuse of slang and colloquialisms is corrupting their language.

INCORRECT:	The Board of Regents will not make a decision about tuition increase until their March meeting.
CORRECT:	The Board of Regents will not make a decision about tuition increase until its March meeting.

when a noun or pronoun has no expressed antecedent:

INCORRECT:	In the President's address to the union, he promised no more taxes.
CORRECT:	In his address to the union, the President promised no more taxes.

Skill 7: Identify Proper Case Forms

Pronoun case questions test your knowledge of the use of nominative and objective case pronouns:

Nominative Case	Objective Case
I	me
he	him
she	her
we	us
they	them
who	whom

This review section answers the most frequently asked grammar questions: when to use *I* and when to use *me*; when to use *who* and when to use *whom*. Some writers avoid *whom* altogether, and instead of distinguishing between *I* and *me*, many writers incorrectly use *myself*.

Use the nominative case (subject pronouns)

for the subject of a sentence:

> *We* students studied until early morning for the final.
>
> Alan and *I* "burned the midnight oil," too.

for pronouns in apposition to the subject:

> Only two students, Alex and *I,* were asked to report on the meeting.

for the predicate nominative/subject complement:

> The actors nominated for the award were *she* and *I.*

for the subject of an elliptical clause:

> Molly is more experienced than *he.*

for the subject of a subordinate clause:

> Robert is the driver *who* reported the accident.

for the complement of an infinitive with no expressed subject:

> I would not want to be *he.*

Use the objective case (object pronouns)

for the direct object of a sentence:

> Mary invited *us* to her party.

for the object of a preposition:

> The books that were torn belonged to *her.*
>
> Just between you and *me,* I'm bored.

for the indirect object of a sentence:

> Walter gave a dozen red roses to *her.*

for the appositive of a direct object:

> The committee elected two delegates, Barbara and *me.*

for the object of an infinitive:

> The young boy wanted to help *us* paint the fence.

for the object of a gerund:

Enlisting *him* was surprisingly easy.

for the object of a past participle:

Having called the other students and *us,* the secretary went home for the day.

for a pronoun that precedes an infinitive (the subject of an infinitive):

The supervisor told *him* to work late.

for the complement of an infinitive with an expressed subject:

The fans thought the best player to be *him.*

for the object of an elliptical clause:

Bill tackled Joe harder than *me.*

for the object of a verb in apposition:

Charles invited two extra people, Carmen and *me,* to the party.

When a conjunction connects two pronouns or a pronoun and a noun, remove the "and" and the other pronoun or noun to determine what the correct pronoun form should be:

Mom gave ~~Tom and~~ myself a piece of cake.

Mom gave ~~Tom and~~ I a piece of cake.

Mom gave ~~Tom and~~ me a piece of cake.

Removal of these words reveals what the correct pronoun should be:

Mom gave *me* a piece of cake.

The only pronouns that are acceptable after *between* and other prepositions are: *me, her, him, them,* and *whom.* When deciding between *who* and *whom,* try substituting *he* for *who* and *him* for *whom;* then follow these easy transformation steps:

1. Isolate the *who* clause or the *whom* clause:

whom we can trust

2. Invert the word order, if necessary. Place the words in the clause in the natural order of an English sentence, subject followed by the verb:

we can trust whom

3. Read the final form with the *he* or *him* inserted:

We can trust ~~whom~~ him.

When a pronoun follows a comparative conjunction like *than* or *as,* complete the elliptical construction to help you determine which pronoun is correct.

EXAMPLE: She has more credit hours than me [do].
                She has more credit hours than I [do].

Drill 17: Pronouns

DIRECTIONS: Choose the correct option.

---

1. My friend and <u>myself</u> bought tickets for *Cats.*

    (A) I   (C) us

    (B) me   (D) No change is necessary.

2. Alcohol and tobacco are harmful to <u>whomever</u> consumes them.

    (A) whom   (C) whoever

    (B) who   (D) No change is necessary.

3. Everyone is wondering <u>whom</u> her successor will be.

    (A) who   (C) who'll

    (B) whose   (D) No change is necessary.

4. Rosa Lee's parents discovered that it was <u>her who</u> wrecked the family car.

    (A) she who   (C) her whom

    (B) she whom   (D) No change is necessary.

5. A student <u>who</u> wishes to protest <u>his or her</u> grades must file a formal grievance in the Dean's office.

    (A) that . . . their   (C) whom . . . their

    (B) which . . . his   (D) No change is necessary.

6. One of the best things about working for this company is that <u>they pay</u> big bonuses.

    (A) it pays   (C) they paid

    (B) they always pay   (D) No change is necessary.

7. Every car owner should be sure that <u>their</u> automobile insurance is adequate.

    (A) your

    (B) his or her

    (C) its

    (D) No change is necessary.

8. My mother wants me to become a teacher, but I'm not interested in <u>it</u>.

    (A) this

    (B) teaching

    (C) that

    (D) No change is necessary.

9. Since I had not paid my electric bill, <u>they</u> sent me a delinquent notice.

    (A) the power company

    (B) he

    (C) it

    (D) No change is necessary.

10. Margaret seldom wrote to her sister when <u>she</u> was away at college.

    (A) who

    (B) her

    (C) her sister

    (D) No change is necessary.

Skill 8: Identify Correct Use of Adjectives and Adverbs

Correct Usage

Adjectives are words that modify nouns or pronouns by defining, describing, limiting, or qualifying those nouns or pronouns.

Adverbs are words that modify verbs, adjectives, or other adverbs and that express such ideas as time, place, manner, cause, and degree. Use adjectives as subject complements with linking verbs; use adverbs with action verbs.

EXAMPLE:	The old man's speech was *eloquent*.	ADJECTIVE
	Mr. Brown speaks *eloquently*.	ADVERB
	Please be *careful*.	ADJECTIVE
	Please drive *carefully*.	ADVERB

Good or well

Good is an adjective; its use as an adverb is colloquial and nonstandard.

INCORRECT:	He plays *good*.
CORRECT:	He looks *good* to be an octogenarian.
	The quiche tastes very *good*.

Well may be either an adverb or an adjective. As an adjective, *well* means "in good health."

CORRECT:	He plays *well*.	ADVERB
	My mother is not *well*.	ADJECTIVE

Bad or badly

Bad is an adjective used after sense verbs such as *look, smell, taste, feel,* or *sound,* or after linking verbs (*is, am, are, was, were*).

INCORRECT:	I feel *badly* about the delay.
CORRECT:	I feel *bad* about the delay.

Badly is an adverb used after all other verbs.

INCORRECT:	It doesn't hurt very *bad*.
CORRECT:	It doesn't hurt very *badly*.

Real or really

Real is an adjective; its use as an adverb is colloquial and nonstandard. It means "genuine."

INCORRECT:	He writes *real* well.
CORRECT:	This is *real* leather.

Really is an adverb meaning "very."

INCORRECT:	This is *really* diamond.	
CORRECT:	Have a *really* nice day.	
EXAMPLE:	This is *real* amethyst.	ADJECTIVE
	This is *really* difficult.	ADVERB
	This is a *real* crisis.	ADJECTIVE
	This is *really* important.	ADVERB

Sort of and kind of

Sort of and *kind of* are often misused in written English by writers who actually mean *rather* or *somewhat*.

INCORRECT:	Jan was *kind of* saddened by the results of the test.
CORRECT:	Jan was *somewhat* saddened by the results of the test.

Skill 9: Comparisons and Superlatives

Skill 9 requires identification of appropriate comparative and superlative degree forms.

Sentences containing a faulty comparison often sound correct because their problem is not one of grammar but of logic. Read these sentences closely to make sure that like things are being compared, that the comparisons are complete, and that the comparisons are logical.

When comparing two persons or things, use the comparative, not the superlative form, of an adjective or an adverb. Use the superlative form for comparison of more than two persons or things. Use *any, other,* or *else* when comparing one thing or person with a group of which it/he or she is a part.

Most one- and two-syllable words form their comparative and superlative degrees with *-er* and *-est* suffixes. Adjectives and adverbs of more than two syllables form their comparative and superlative degrees with the addition of *more* and *most.*

Positive	Comparative	Superlative
good	better	best
old	older	oldest
friendly	friendlier	friendliest
lonely	lonelier	loneliest
talented	more talented	most talented
beautiful	more beautiful	most beautiful

A double comparison occurs when the degree of the modifier is changed incorrectly by adding both *-er* and *more* or *-est* and *most* to the adjective or adverb.

INCORRECT:　He is the *most nicest* brother.

CORRECT:　He is the *nicest* brother.

INCORRECT:　She is the *more meaner* of the sisters.

CORRECT:　She is the *meaner* sister.

Illogical comparisons occur when there is an implied comparison between two things that are not actually being compared or that cannot be logically compared.

INCORRECT:　The interest at a loan company is higher *than* a bank.

CORRECT:　The interest at a loan company is higher *than* that *at* a bank.

OR　The interest at a loan company is higher *than at a* bank.

Ambiguous comparisons occur when elliptical words (those omitted) create for the reader more than one interpretation of the sentence.

INCORRECT:　I like Mary better than you. (than you *what*?)

CORRECT:　I like Mary better than I like you.

OR　I like Mary better than you do.

Incomplete comparisons occur when the basis of the comparison (the two categories being compared) is not explicitly stated.

> INCORRECT: Skywriting is *more* spectacular.
>
> CORRECT: Skywriting is *more* spectacular *than* billboard advertising.

Do not omit the words *other, any,* or *else* when comparing one thing or person with a group of which it/he or she is a part.

> INCORRECT: Joan writes better *than any* student in her class.
>
> CORRECT: Joan writes better *than any other* student in her class.

Do not omit the second *as* of *as . . . as* when making a point of equal or superior comparison.

> INCORRECT: The University of West Florida is *as large* or larger than the University of North Florida.
>
> CORRECT: The University of West Florida is *as large as* or larger than the University of Northern Florida.

Do not omit the first category of the comparison, even if the two categories are the same.

> INCORRECT: This is one of the best, if not the best, college in the country.
>
> CORRECT: This is one of the best colleges in the country, if not the best.

The problem with the incorrect sentence is that *one of the best* requires the plural word *colleges,* not *college.*

Drill 18: Adjectives and Adverbs

DIRECTIONS: Choose the correct option.

1. Although the band performed <u>badly</u>, I feel <u>real bad</u> about missing the concert.

   (A) badly . . . real badly   (C) badly . . . very bad

   (B) bad . . . badly   (D) No change is necessary.

2. These reports are <u>relative simple</u> to prepare.

   (A) relatively simple   (C) relatively simply

   (B) relative simply   (D) No change is necessary.

3. He did <u>very well</u> on the test although his writing skills are not <u>good</u>.

   (A) real well . . . good   (C) good . . . great

   (B) very good . . . good   (D) No change is necessary.

4. Shake the medicine bottle <u>good</u> before you open it.

   (A) very good   (C) well

   (B) real good   (D) No change is necessary.

5. Though she speaks <u>fluently</u>, she writes <u>poorly</u> because she doesn't observe <u>closely</u> or think <u>clear</u>.

   (A) fluently . . . poorly . . . closely . . . clearly

   (B) fluent . . . poor . . . close . . . clear

   (C) fluently . . . poor . . . closely . . . clear

   (D) No change is necessary.

DIRECTIONS: Select the sentence that clearly and effectively states the idea and has no structural errors.

---

6. (A) Los Angeles is larger than any city in California.

   (B) Los Angeles is larger than all the cities in California.

   (C) Los Angeles is larger than any other city in California.

7. (A) Art history is as interesting as, if not more interesting than, music appreciation.

   (B) Art history is as interesting, if not more interesting than, music appreciation.

   (C) Art history is as interesting as, if not more interesting, music appreciation.

8. (A) The baseball team here is as good as any other university.

   (B) The baseball team here is as good as all the other universities.

   (C) The baseball team here is as good as any other university's.

9. (A) I like him better than you.

   (B) I like him better than I like you.

   (C) I like him better.

10. (A) You are the most stingiest person I know.

    (B) You are the most stingier person I know.

    (C) You are the stingiest person I know.

Skill 10: Identify Standard Spelling

Spelling questions test your ability to recognize misspelled words. This section reviews spelling tips and rules to help you spot incorrect spellings. Problems such as the distinction between *to* and *too* and *lead* and *led* are covered under the Word Choice Skills section of this review.

- Remember, *i* before *e* except after *c*, or when sounded as "a" as in *neighbor* and *weigh*.

- There are only three words in the English language that end in -*ceed*:

  proceed, succeed, exceed

- There are several words that end in -*cede*:

  secede, recede, concede, precede

- There is only one word in the English language that ends in -*sede*:

  supersede

Many people learn to read English phonetically; that is, by sounding out the letters of the words. However, many English words are not pronounced the way they are spelled, and those who try to spell English words phonetically often make spelling *errors*. It is better to memorize the correct spelling of English words rather than relying on phonetics to spell correctly.

Frequently Misspelled Words

The following list of words are frequently misspelled words. Study the spelling of each word by having a friend or teacher drill you on the words. Then mark down the words that you misspelled and study those select ones again. (The words appear in their most popular spellings.)

a lot	accuse	adequate	again
ability	accustomed	advantage	against
absence	ache	advantageous	aggravate
absent	achieve	advertise	aggressive
abundance	achievement	advertisement	agree
accept	acknowledge	advice	aisle
acceptable	acquaintance	advisable	all right
accident	acquainted	advise	almost
accommodate	acquire	advisor	already
accompanied	across	aerial	although
accomplish	address	affect	altogether
accumulation	addressed	affectionate	always

amateur	automobile	capitol	condition
American	autumn	captain	conference
among	auxiliary	career	confident
amount	available	careful	congratulate
analysis	avenue	careless	conquer
analyze	awful	carriage	conscience
angel	awkward	carrying	conscientious
angle	bachelor	category	conscious
annual	balance	ceiling	consequence
another	balloon	cemetery	consequently
answer	bargain	cereal	considerable
antiseptic	basic	certain	consistency
anxious	beautiful	changeable	consistent
apologize	because	characteristic	continual
apparatus	become	charity	continuous
apparent	before	chief	controlled
appear	beginning	choose	controversy
appearance	being	chose	convenience
appetite	believe	cigarette	convenient
application	benefit	circumstance	conversation
apply	benefited	citizen	corporal
appreciate	between	clothes	corroborate
appreciation	bicycle	clothing	council
approach	board	coarse	counsel
appropriate	bored	coffee	counselor
approval	borrow	collect	courage
approve	bottle	college	courageous
approximate	bottom	column	course
argue	boundary	comedy	courteous
arguing	brake	comfortable	courtesy
argument	breadth	commitment	criticism
arouse	breath	committed	criticize
arrange	breathe	committee	crystal
arrangement	brilliant	communicate	curiosity
article	building	company	cylinder
artificial	bulletin	comparative	daily
ascend	bureau	compel	daughter
assistance	burial	competent	daybreak
assistant	buried	competition	death
associate	bury	complement	deceive
association	bushes	compliment	December
attempt	business	conceal	deception
attendance	cafeteria	conceit	decide
attention	calculator	conceivable	decision
audience	calendar	conceive	decisive
August	campaign	concentration	deed
author	capital	conception	definite

delicious	ecstasy	experiment	heard
dependent	ecstatic	explanation	heavy
deposit	education	extreme	height
derelict	effect	facility	heroes
descend	efficiency	factory	heroine
descent	efficient	familiar	hideous
describe	eight	fascinate	himself
description	either	fascinating	hoarse
desert	eligibility	fatigue	holiday
desirable	eligible	February	hopeless
despair	eliminate	financial	hospital
desperate	embarrass	financier	humorous
dessert	embarrassment	flourish	hurried
destruction	emergency	forcibly	hurrying
determine	emphasis	forehead	ignorance
develop	emphasize	foreign	imaginary
development	enclosure	formal	imbecile
device	encouraging	former	imitation
dictator	endeavor	fortunate	immediately
died	engineer	fourteen	immigrant
difference	English	fourth	incidental
different	enormous	frequent	increase
dilemma	enough	friend	independence
dinner	entrance	frightening	independent
direction	envelope	fundamental	indispensable
disappear	environment	further	inevitable
disappoint	equipment	gallon	influence
disappointment	equipped	garden	influential
disapproval	especially	gardener	initiate
disapprove	essential	general	innocence
disastrous	evening	genius	inoculate
discipline	evident	government	inquiry
discover	exaggerate	governor	insistent
discriminate	exaggeration	grammar	instead
disease	examine	grateful	instinct
dissatisfied	exceed	great	integrity
dissection	excellent	grievance	intellectual
dissipate	except	grievous	intelligence
distance	exceptional	grocery	intercede
distinction	exercise	guarantee	interest
division	exhausted	guess	interfere
doctor	exhaustion	guidance	interference
dollar	exhilaration	half	interpreted
doubt	existence	hammer	interrupt
dozen	exorbitant	handkerchief	invitation
earnest	expense	happiness	irrelevant
easy	experience	healthy	irresistible

irritable
island
its
it's
itself
January
jealous
journal
judgment
kindergarten
kitchen
knew
knock
know
knowledge
labor
laboratory
laid
language
later
latter
laugh
leisure
length
lesson
library
license
light
lightning
likelihood
likely
literal
literature
livelihood
loaf
loneliness
loose
lose
losing
loyal
loyalty
magazine
maintenance
maneuver
marriage
married
marry

match
material
mathematics
measure
medicine
million
miniature
minimum
miracle
miscellaneous
mischief
mischievous
misspelled
mistake
momentous
monkey
monotonous
moral
morale
mortgage
mountain
mournful
muscle
mysterious
mystery
narrative
natural
necessary
needle
negligence
neighbor
neither
newspaper
newsstand
niece
noticeable
o'clock
obedient
obstacle
occasion
occasional
occur
occurred
occurrence
ocean
offer
often

omission
omit
once
operate
opinion
opportune
opportunity
optimist
optimistic
origin
original
oscillate
ought
ounce
overcoat
paid
pamphlet
panicky
parallel
parallelism
particular
partner
pastime
patience
peace
peaceable
pear
peculiar
pencil
people
perceive
perception
perfect
perform
performance
perhaps
period
permanence
permanent
perpendicular
perseverance
persevere
persistent
personal
personality
personnel
persuade

persuasion
pertain
picture
piece
plain
playwright
pleasant
please
pleasure
pocket
poison
policeman
political
population
portrayal
positive
possess
possession
possessive
possible
post office
potatoes
practical
prairie
precede
preceding
precise
predictable
prefer
preference
preferential
preferred
prejudice
preparation
prepare
prescription
presence
president
prevalent
primitive
principal
principle
privilege
probably
procedure
proceed
produce

professional
professor
profitable
prominent
promise
pronounce
pronunciation
propeller
prophet
prospect
psychology
pursue
pursuit
quality
quantity
quarreling
quart
quarter
quiet
quite
raise
realistic
realize
reason
rebellion
recede
receipt
receive
recipe
recognize
recommend
recuperate
referred
rehearsal
reign
relevant
relieve
remedy
renovate
repeat
repetition
representative
requirements
resemblance
resistance
resource
respectability

responsibility
restaurant
rhythm
rhythmical
ridiculous
right
role
roll
roommate
sandwich
Saturday
scarcely
scene
schedule
science
scientific
scissors
season
secretary
seize
seminar
sense
separate
service
several
severely
shepherd
sheriff
shining
shoulder
shriek
siege
sight
signal
significance
significant
similar
similarity
sincerely
site
soldier
solemn
sophomore
soul
source
souvenir
special

specified
specimen
speech
stationary
stationery
statue
stockings
stomach
straight
strength
strenuous
stretch
striking
studying
substantial
succeed
successful
sudden
superintendent
suppress
surely
surprise
suspense
sweat
sweet
syllable
symmetrical
sympathy
synonym
technical
telegram
telephone
temperament
temperature
tenant
tendency
tenement
therefore
thorough
through
title
together
tomorrow
tongue
toward
tragedy

transferred
treasury
tremendous
tries
truly
twelfth
twelve
tyranny
undoubtedly
United States
university
unnecessary
unusual
useful
usual
vacuum
valley
valuable
variety
vegetable
vein
vengeance
versatile
vicinity
vicious
view
village
villain
visitor
voice
volume
waist
weak
wear
weather
Wednesday
week
weigh
weird
whether
which
while
whole
wholly
whose
wretched

Drill 19: Spelling

DIRECTIONS: Identify the misspelled word in each set.

1. (A) probly
   (B) accommodate
   (C) acquaintance

2. (A) auxiliary
   (B) atheletic
   (C) beginning

3. (A) environment
   (B) existence
   (C) Febuary

4. (A) ocassion
   (B) occurrence
   (C) omitted

5. (A) perspiration
   (B) referring
   (C) priviledge

DIRECTIONS: Choose the correct option.

6. <u>Preceding</u> the <u>business</u> session, lunch will be served in a <u>separate</u> room.
   (A) preceeding . . . business . . . seperate
   (B) proceeding . . . bussiness . . . seperate
   (C) proceeding . . . business . . . sepcritc
   (D) No change is necessary.

7. Monte <u>inadvertently</u> left <u>several</u> of his <u>libary</u> books in the cafeteria.

    (A) inadverdently . . . serveral . . . libery

    (B) inadvertently . . . several . . . library

    (C) inadvertentely . . . several . . . librery

    (D) No change is necessary.

8. Sam wished he had more <u>liesure</u> time so he could <u>persue</u> his favorite hobbies.

    (A) leisure . . . pursue

    (B) Liesure . . . pursue

    (C) leisure . . . persue

    (D) No change is necessary.

9. One of my <u>favrite charecters</u> in <u>litrature</u> is Bilbo from *The Hobbit*.

    (A) favrite . . . characters . . . literature

    (B) favorite . . . characters . . . literature

    (C) favourite . . . characters . . . literature

    (D) No change is necessary.

10. Even <u>tho</u> Joe was badly hurt in the <u>accidant</u>, the company said they were not <u>lible</u> for damages.

    (A) though . . . accidant . . . libel

    (B) though . . . accident . . . liable

    (C) though . . . acident . . . liable

    (D) No change is necessary.

Skill 11: Identify Standard Punctuation

Commas

Commas should be placed according to standard rules of punctuation for purpose, clarity, and effect. The proper use of commas is explained in the following rules and examples:

In a series:

When more than one adjective describes a noun, use a comma to separate and emphasize each adjective. The comma takes the place of the word *and* in the series.

> the long, dark passageway
>
> another confusing, sleepless night

an elaborate, complex, brilliant plan

the old, grey, crumpled hat

Some adjective-noun combinations are thought of as one word. In these cases, the adjective in front of the adjective-noun combination needs no comma. If you inserted *and* between the adjective-noun combination, it would not make sense.

a stately oak tree

an exceptional wine glass

my worst report card

a china dinner plate

The comma is also used to separate words, phrases, and whole ideas (clauses); it still takes the place of *and* when used this way.

an apple, a pear, a fig, and a banana

a lovely lady, an elegant dress, and many admirers

She lowered the shade, closed the curtain, turned off the light, and went to bed.

The only question that exists about the use of commas in a series is whether or not one should be used before the final item. It is standard usage to do so, although many newspapers and magazines have stopped using the final comma. Occasionally, the omission of the comma can be confusing.

INCORRECT: He got on his horse, tracked a rabbit and a deer and rode on to Canton.

CORRECT: We planned the trip with Mary and Harold, Susan, Dick and Joan, Gregory and Jean and Charles.

With a long introductory phrase:

Usually if a phrase of more than five or six words or a dependent clause precedes the subject at the beginning of a sentence, a comma is used to set it off.

After last night's fiasco at the disco, she couldn't bear the thought of looking at him again.

Whenever I try to talk about politics, my wife leaves the room.

Provided you have said nothing, they will never guess who you are.

It is not necessary to use a comma with a short sentence.

In January she will go to Switzerland.

After I rest I'll feel better.

During the day no one is home.

If an introductory phrase includes a verb form that is being used as another part of speech (a *verbal*), it must be followed by a comma.

| INCORRECT: | When eating Mary never looked up from her plate. |
| CORRECT: | When eating, Mary never looked up from her plate. |

| INCORRECT: | Because of her desire to follow her faith in James wavered. |
| CORRECT: | Because of her desire to follow, her faith in James wavered. |

| INCORRECT: | Having decided to leave Mary James wrote her a letter. |
| CORRECT: | Having decided to leave Mary, James wrote her a letter. |

To separate sentences with two main ideas:

To understand this use of the comma, you need to be able to recognize compound sentences. When a sentence contains more than two subjects and verbs (clauses), and the two clauses are joined by a conjunction (*and, but, or, nor, for, yet*), use a comma before the conjunction to show that another clause is coming.

I thought I knew the poem by heart, but he showed me three lines I had forgotten.

Are we really interested in helping the children, or are we more concerned with protecting our good names?

He is supposed to leave tomorrow, but he is not ready to go.

Jim knows you are disappointed, and he has known it for a long time.

If the two parts of the sentence are short and closely related, it is not necessary to use a comma.

He threw the ball and the dog ran after it.

Jane played the piano and Michael danced.

Be careful not to confuse a sentence that has a compound verb and a single subject with a compound sentence. If the subject is the same for both verbs, there is no need for a comma.

| INCORRECT: | Charles sent some flowers, and wrote a long letter explaining why he had not been able to attend. |
| CORRECT: | Charles sent some flowers and wrote a long letter explaining why he had not been able to attend. |

| INCORRECT: | Last Thursday we went to the concert with Julia, and afterwards dined at an old Italian restaurant. |
| CORRECT: | Last Thursday we went to the concert with Julia and afterwards dined at an old Italian restaurant. |

INCORRECT:	For the third time, the teacher explained that the literacy level for high school students was much lower than it had been in previous years, and, this time, wrote the statistics on the board for everyone to see.
CORRECT:	For the third time, the teacher explained that the literacy level for high school students was much lower than it had been in previous years and this time wrote the statistics on the board for everyone to see.

In general, words and phrases that stop the flow of the sentence or are unnecessary for the main idea are set off by commas.

Abbreviations after names:

Did you invite John Paul, Jr., and his sister?

Martha Harris, Ph.D., will be the speaker tonight.

Interjections (an exclamation without added grammatical connection):

Oh, I'm so glad to see you.

I tried so hard, alas, to do it.

Hey, let me out of here.

Direct address:

Roy, won't you open the door for the dog?

I can't understand, Mother, what you are trying to say.

May I ask, Mr. President, why you called us together?

Hey, lady, watch out for that car!

Tag questions:

You're really hungry, aren't you?

Jerry looks like his father, doesn't he?

Geographical names and addresses:

The concert will be held in Chicago, Illinois, on August 12.

The letter was addressed to Mrs. Marion Heartwell, 1881 Pine Lane, Palo Alto, CA 95824.

(Note: No comma is needed before the zip code, because it is already clearly set off from the state name.)

Transitional words and phrases:

On the other hand, I hope he gets better.

In addition, the phone rang constantly this afternoon.

I'm, nevertheless, going to the beach on Sunday.

You'll find, therefore, that no one is more loyal than I am.

Parenthetical words and phrases:

You will become, I believe, a great statesman.

We know, of course, that this is the only thing to do.

In fact, I planted corn last summer.

The Mannes affair was, to put it mildly, a surprise.

Unusual word order:

The dress, new and crisp, hung in the closet.

Intently, she stared out the window.

With nonrestrictive elements:

Parts of a sentence that modify other parts are sometimes essential to the meaning of the sentence and sometimes not. When a modifying word or group of words is not vital to the meaning of the sentence, it is set off by commas. Since it does not restrict the meaning of the words it modifies, it is called "nonrestrictive." Modifiers that are essential to the meaning of the sentence are called "restrictive" and are not set off by commas.

ESSENTIAL:	The girl *who wrote the story* is my sister.
NONESSENTIAL:	My sister, *the girl who wrote the story,* has always loved to write.

ESSENTIAL:	John Milton's famous poem *Paradise Lost* tells a remarkable story.
NONESSENTIAL:	Dante's greatest work, *The Divine Comedy,* marked the beginning of the Renaissance.

ESSENTIAL:	The cup *that is on the piano* is the one I want.
NONESSENTIAL:	The cup, *which my brother gave me last year,* is on the piano.

ESSENTIAL:	The people *who arrived late* were not seated.
NONESSENTIAL:	George, *who arrived late,* was not seated.

To set off direct quotations:

Most direct quotes or quoted materials are set off from the rest of the sentence by commas.

"Please read your part more loudly," the director insisted.

"I won't know what to do," said Michael, "if you leave me."

The teacher said sternly, "I will not dismiss this class until I have silence."

Who was it who said "Do not ask for whom the bell tolls; it tolls for thee"?

Note: Commas always go inside the closing quotation mark, even if the comma is not part of the material being quoted.

Be careful not to set off indirect quotes or quotes that are used as subjects or complements.

"To be or not to be" is the famous beginning of a soliloquy in Shakespeare's *Hamlet*. (subject)

She said she would never come back. (indirect quote)

Back then my favorite poem was "Evangeline." (complement)

To set off contrasting elements:

Her intelligence, not her beauty, got her the job.

Your plan will take you a little further from, rather than closer to, your destination.

It was a reasonable, though not appealing, idea.

He wanted glory, but found happiness instead.

In dates:

Both forms of the date are acceptable.

She will arrive on April 6, 1998.

He left on 5 December 1980.

In January 1967, he handed in his resignation.

On October 22, 1992, Frank and Julie were married.

Usually, when a subordinate clause is at the end of a sentence, no comma is necessary preceding the clause. However, when a subordinate clause introduces a sentence, a comma should be used after the clause.

Some common subordinating conjunctions are:

after	so that
although	though
as	till
as if	unless
because	until
before	when
even though	whenever

if	while
inasmuch as	since

Semicolons

Questions testing semicolon usage require you to be able to distinguish between the semicolon and the comma, and the semicolon and the colon. This review section covers the basic uses of the semicolon: to separate independent clauses not joined by a coordinating conjunction, to separate independent clauses separated by a conjunctive adverb, and to separate items in a series with internal commas. It is important to be consistent; if you use a semicolon between *any* of the items in the series, you must use semicolons to separate *all* of the items in the series.

Usually, a comma follows the conjunctive adverb. Note also that a period can be used to separate two sentences joined by a conjunctive adverb. Some common conjunctive adverbs are:

accordingly	nevertheless
besides	next
consequently	nonetheless
finally	now
furthermore	on the other hand
however	otherwise
indeed	perhaps
in fact	still
moreover	therefore

Then is also used as a conjunctive adverb, but it is not usually followed by a comma.

Use the semicolon

to separate independent clauses that are not joined by a coordinating conjunction:

I understand how to use commas; the semicolon I have not yet mastered.

to separate two independent clauses connected by a conjunctive adverb:

He took great care with his work; *therefore,* he was very successful.

to combine two independent clauses connected by a coordinating conjunction if either or both of the clauses contain other internal punctuation:

Success in college, some maintain, requires intelligence, industry, and perseverance; *but* others, fewer in number, assert that only personality is important.

to separate items in a series when each item has internal punctuation:

> I bought an old, dilapidated chair; an antique table, which was in beautiful condition; and a new, ugly, blue and white rug.

> Call our customer service line for assistance: Arizona, 1-800-555-6020; New Mexico, 1-800-555-5050; California, 1-800-555-3140; or Nevada, 1-800-555-3214.

Do not use the semicolon

to separate a dependent and an independent clause:

INCORRECT:	You should not make such statements; even though they are correct.
CORRECT:	You should not make such statements even though they are correct.

to separate an appositive phrase or clause from a sentence:

INCORRECT:	His immediate aim in life is centered around two things; becoming an engineer and learning to fly an airplane.
CORRECT:	His immediate aim in life is centered around two things: becoming an engineer and learning to fly an airplane.

to precede an explanation or summary of the first clause:

Note: Although the sentence below is punctuated correctly, the use of the semicolon provides a miscue, suggesting that the second clause is merely an extension, not an explanation, of the first clause. The colon provides a better clue.

WEAK:	The first week of camping was wonderful; we lived in cabins instead of tents.
BETTER:	The first week of camping was wonderful: we lived in cabins instead of tents.

to substitute for a comma:

INCORRECT:	My roommate also likes sports; particularly football, basketball, and baseball.
CORRECT:	My roommate also likes sports, particularly football, basketball, and baseball.

to set off other types of phrases or clauses from a sentence:

> INCORRECT: Being of a cynical mind; I should ask for a recount of the ballots.
>
>   CORRECT: Being of a cynical mind, I should ask for a recount of the ballots.

> INCORRECT: The next meeting of the club has been postponed two weeks; inasmuch as both the president and vice president are out of town.
>
>   CORRECT: The next meeting of the club has been postponed two weeks, inasmuch as both the president and vice president are out of town.

Note: The semicolon is not a terminal mark of punctuation; therefore, it should not be followed by a capital letter unless the first word in the second clause ordinarily requires capitalization.

Colons

While it is true that a colon is used to precede a list, one must also make sure that a complete sentence precedes the colon. The colon signals the reader that a list, explanation, or restatement of the preceding will follow. It is like an arrow, indicating that something is to follow. The difference between the colon and the semicolon and between the colon and the period is that the colon is an introductory mark, not a terminal mark. Look at the following examples:

> The Constitution provides for a separation of powers among the three branches of government.

> **government.**   The period signals a new sentence.
>
> **government;**   The semicolon signals an interrelated sentence.
>
> **government,**   The comma signals a coordinating conjunction followed by another independent clause.
>
> **government:**   The colon signals a list.

> The Constitution provides for a separation of powers among the three branches of *government:* executive, legislative, and judicial.

Ensuring that a complete sentence precedes a colon means following these rules:

Use the colon to introduce a list (one item may constitute a list):

> I hate this one course: English.

> Three plays by William Shakespeare will be presented in repertory this summer at the University of Michigan: *Hamlet, Macbeth,* and *Othello.*

To introduce a list preceded by *as follows* or *the following*:

> The reasons he cited for his success are as follows: integrity, honesty, industry, and a pleasant disposition.

To separate two independent clauses, when the second clause is a restatement or explanation of the first:

> All of my high school teachers said one thing in particular: college is going to be difficult.

To introduce a word or word group that is a restatement, explanation, or summary of the first sentence:

> These two things he loved: an honest man and a beautiful woman.

To introduce a formal appositive:

> I am positive there is one appeal that you can't overlook: money.

To separate the introductory words from a quotation that follows, if the quotation is formal, long, or paragraphed separately:

> The actor then stated: "I would rather be able to adequately play the part of Hamlet than to perform a miraculous operation, deliver a great lecture, or build a magnificent skyscraper."

The colon should only be used after statements that are grammatically complete.

Do *not* use a colon after a verb:

| INCORRECT: | My favorite holidays are: Christmas, New Year's Eve, and Halloween. |
| CORRECT: | My favorite holidays are Christmas, New Year's Eve, and Halloween. |

Do *not* use a colon after a preposition:

| INCORRECT: | I enjoy different ethnic foods such as: Greek, Chinese, and Italian. |
| CORRECT: | I enjoy different ethnic foods such as Greek, Chinese, and Italian. |

Do *not* use a colon interchangeably with the dash:

| INCORRECT: | Mathematics, German, English: These gave me the greatest difficulty of all my studies. |
| CORRECT: | Mathematics, German, English—these gave me the greatest difficulty of all my studies. |

Information preceding the colon should be a complete sentence regardless of the explanatory information following the clause.

Do *not* use the colon before the words *for example, namely, that is,* or *for instance* even though these words may be introducing a list.

INCORRECT: We agreed to it: namely, to give him a surprise party.

CORRECT: There are a number of well-known American women writers: for example, Nikki Giovanni, Phillis Wheatley, Emily Dickinson, and Maya Angelou.

Colon usage questions test your knowledge of the colon preceding a list, restatement, or explanation. These questions also require you to be able to distinguish between the colon and the period, the colon and the comma, and the colon and the semicolon.

Apostrophes

Apostrophe questions require you to know when an apostrophe has been used appropriately to make a noun possessive, not plural. Remember the following rules when considering how to show possession.

Add '*s* to singular nouns and indefinite pronouns:

Tiffany's flowers

a dog's bark

everybody's computer

at the owner's expense

today's paper

Add '*s* to singular nouns ending in *s,* unless this distorts the pronunciation:

Delores's paper

the boss's pen

Dr. Yots' class

for righteousness' sake

Dr. Evans's office OR Dr. Evans' office

Add *an apostrophe* to plural nouns ending in *s* or *es*:

two cents' worth

ladies' night

thirteen years' experience

two weeks' pay

Add 's to plural nouns not ending in *s:*

> men's room
>
> children's toys

Add 's to the last word in compound words or groups:

> brother-in-law's car
>
> someone else's paper

Add 's to the last name when indicating joint ownership:

> Joe and Edna's home
>
> Julie and Kathy's party
>
> women and children's clinic

Add 's to both names if you intend to show ownership by each person:

> Joe's and Edna's trucks
>
> Julie's and Kathy's pies
>
> Ted's and Jane's marriage vows

Possessive pronouns change their forms *without* the addition of an apostrophe:

> her, his, hers
>
> your, yours
>
> their, theirs
>
> it, its

Use the possessive form of a noun preceding a gerund:

> His driving annoys me.
>
> My bowling a strike irritated him.
>
> Do you mind our stopping by?
>
> We appreciate your coming.

Add 's to words and initials to show that they are plural:

> no if's, and's, or but's
>
> the do's and don't's of dating
>
> three A's
>
> IRA's are available at the bank.

Add *'s* to numbers, symbols, and letters to show that they are plural:

TVs

VCRs

the 1800s

the returning POWs

Quotation Marks and Italics

These kinds of questions test your knowledge of the proper use of quotation marks with other marks of punctuation, with titles, and with dialogue. These kinds of questions also test your knowledge of the correct use of italics and underlining with titles and words used as sample words (for example, *the word is is a common verb*).

The most common use of double quotation marks (") is to set off quoted words, phrases, and sentences.

> "If everybody minded their own business," said the Duchess in a hoarse growl, "the world would go round a great deal faster than it does."
>
> "Then you would say what you mean," the March Hare went on.
>
> "I do," Alice hastily replied: "at least—at least I mean what I say—that's the same thing, you know."
>
> —from Lewis Carroll's *Alice in Wonderland*

Single quotation marks are used to set off quoted material within a quote.

> "Shall I bring 'Rime of the Ancient Mariner' along with us?" she asked her brother.
>
> Mrs. Green said, "The doctor told me, 'Go immediately to bed when you get home!'"
>
> "If she said that to me," Katherine insisted, "I would tell her, 'I never intend to speak to you again! Goodbye, Susan!'"

When writing dialogue, begin a new paragraph each time the speaker changes.

> "Do you know what time it is?" asked Jane.
>
> "Can't you see I'm busy?" snapped Mary.
>
> "It's easy to see that you're in a bad mood today!" replied Jane.

Use quotation marks to enclose words used as words (sometimes italics are used for this purpose).

> "Judgment" has always been a difficult word for me to spell.

Do you know what "abstruse" means?

"Horse and buggy" and "bread and butter" can be used either as adjectives or as nouns.

If slang is used within more formal writing, the slang words or phrases should be set off with quotation marks.

Harrison's decision to leave the conference and to "stick his neck out" by flying to Jamaica was applauded by the rest of the conference attendees.

When words are meant to have an unusual or specific significance to the reader, for instance irony or humor, they are sometimes placed in quotation marks.

For years, women were not allowed to buy real estate in order to "protect" them from unscrupulous dealers.

The "conversation" resulted in one black eye and a broken nose.

To set off titles of TV shows, poems, stories, and book chapters, use quotation marks. (Book, motion picture, newspaper, and magazine titles are underlined when handwritten and italicized when printed.)

The article "Moving South in the Southern Rain," by Jergen Smith in the *Southern News,* attracted the attention of our editor.

The assignment is "Childhood Development," Chapter 18 of *Human Behavior.*

My favorite essay by Montaigne is "On Silence."

"Happy Days" led the TV ratings for years, didn't it?

You will find Keats' "Ode to a Grecian Urn" in Chapter 3, "The Romantic Era," in Lastly's *Selections from Great English Poets.*

Errors to avoid:

Be sure to remember that quotation marks always come in pairs. Do not make the mistake of using only one set.

INCORRECT: "You'll never convince me to move to the city, said Thurman. I consider it an insane asylum."

CORRECT: "You'll never convince me to move to the city," said Thurman. "I consider it an insane asylum."

INCORRECT: "Idleness and pride tax with a heavier hand than kings and parliaments," Benjamin Franklin is supposed to have said. If we can get rid of the former, we may easily bear the latter."

CORRECT: "Idleness and pride tax with a heavier hand than kings and parliaments," Benjamin Franklin is supposed to have said. "If we can get rid of the former, we may easily bear the latter."

When a quote consists of several sentences, do not put the quotation marks at the beginning and end of each sentence; put them at the beginning and end of the entire quotation.

INCORRECT: "It was during his student days in Bonn that Beethoven fastened upon Schiller's poem." "The heady sense of liberation in the verses must have appealed to him." "They appealed to every German."—John Burke

CORRECT: "It was during his student days in Bonn that Beethoven fastened upon Schiller's poem. The heady sense of liberation in the verses must have appealed to him. They appealed to every German."—John Burke

Instead of setting off a long quote with quotation marks, if it is longer than five or six lines you may want to indent and single space it. If you do indent, do not use quotation marks.

In his *First Inaugural Address,* Abraham Lincoln appeals to the war-torn American people:

We are not enemies, but friends. We must not be enemies. Though passion may have strained, it must not break, our bonds of affection. The mystic chords of memory, stretching from every battlefield and patriot grave to every living heart and hearthstone all over this broad land, will yet swell the chorus of the Union when again touched, as surely they will be, by the better angels of our nature.

Be careful not to use quotation marks with indirect quotations.

INCORRECT: Mary wondered "if she would get over it."
CORRECT: Mary wondered if she would get over it.

INCORRECT: The nurse asked "how long it had been since we had visited the doctor's office."
CORRECT: The nurse asked how long it had been since we had visited the doctor's office.

When you quote several paragraphs, it is not sufficient to place quotation marks at the beginning and end of the entire quote. Place quotation marks at the *beginning of each paragraph,* but only at the *end of the last paragraph.* Here is an abbreviated quotation for an example:

"Here begins an odyssey through the world of classical mythology, starting with the creation of the world . . .

"It is true that themes similar to the classical may be found in any corpus of mythology . . . Even technology is not immune to the influence of Greece and Rome . . .

"We need hardly mention the extent to which painters and sculptors . . . have used and adapted classical mythology to illustrate the past, to reveal the human body, to express romantic or antiromantic ideals, or to symbolize any particular point of view."

Remember that commas and periods are *always* placed inside the quotation marks even if they are not actually part of the quote.

INCORRECT:	"Life always gets colder near the summit", Nietzsche is purported to have said, "—the cold increases, responsibility grows".
CORRECT:	"Life always gets colder near the summit," Nietzsche is purported to have said, "—the cold increases, responsibility grows."
INCORRECT:	"Get down here right away", John cried. "You'll miss the sunset if you don't."
CORRECT:	"Get down here right away," John cried. "You'll miss the sunset if you don't."
INCORRECT:	"If my dog could talk", Mary mused, "I'll bet he would say, 'Take me for a walk right this minute'."
CORRECT:	"If my dog could talk," Mary mused, "I'll bet he would say, 'Take me for a walk right this minute'."

Other marks of punctuation, such as question marks, exclamation points, colons, and semicolons, go inside the quotation marks if they are part of the quoted material. If they are not part of the quotation, however, they go outside the quotation marks. Be careful to distinguish between the guidelines for the comma and period, which always go inside the quotation marks, and those for other marks of punctuation.

INCORRECT:	"I'll always love you"! he exclaimed happily.
CORRECT:	"I'll always love you!" he exclaimed happily.
INCORRECT:	Did you hear her say, "He'll be there early?"
CORRECT:	Did you hear her say, "He'll be there early"?
INCORRECT:	She called down the stairs, "When are you going"?
CORRECT:	She called down the stairs, "When are you going?"
INCORRECT:	"Let me out"! he cried. "Don't you have any pity"?
CORRECT:	"Let me out!" he cried. "Don't you have any pity?"

Remember to use only one mark of punctuation at the end of a sentence ending with a quotation mark.

INCORRECT: She thought out loud, "Will I ever finish this paper in time for that class?".

CORRECT: She thought out loud, "Will I ever finish this paper in time for that class?"

INCORRECT: "Not the same thing a bit!", said the Hatter. "Why, you might just as well say that 'I see what I eat' is the same thing as 'I eat what I see'!".

CORRECT: "Not the same thing a bit!" said the Hatter. "Why, you might just as well say that 'I see what I eat' is the same thing as 'I eat what I see'!"

Drill 20: Punctuation

> **DIRECTIONS: Choose the correct option.**

1.   Indianola, <u>Mississippi, where B.B. King and my father grew up</u>, has a population of less than 50,000 people.

   (A) Mississippi where, B.B. King and my father grew up,

   (B) Mississippi where B.B. King and my father grew up,

   (C) Mississippi; where B.B. King and my father grew up,

   (D) No change is necessary.

2.   John Steinbeck's best known novel *The Grapes of Wrath* is the story of the <u>Joads an Oklahoma family</u> who were driven from their dustbowl farm and forced to become migrant workers in California.

   (A) Joads, an Oklahoma family

   (B) Joads, an Oklahoma family,

   (C) Joads; an Oklahoma family

   (D) No change is necessary.

3.   All students who are interested in student teaching next <u>semester, must submit an application to the Teacher Education Office.</u>

   (A) semester must submit an application to the Teacher Education Office.

   (B) semester, must submit an application, to the Teacher Education Office.

(C)　semester: must submit an application to the Teacher Education Office.

(D)　No change is necessary.

4.　Whenever you travel by <u>car, or plane, you</u> must wear a seatbelt.

(A)　car or plane you　　　　　　　(C)　car or plane, you

(B)　car, or plane you　　　　　　　(D)　No change is necessary.

5.　Wearing a seatbelt is not just a good <u>idea, it's</u> the law.

(A)　idea; it's　　　　　　　　　　(C)　idea. It's

(B)　idea it's　　　　　　　　　　(D)　No change is necessary.

6.　Senators and representatives can be reelected <u>indefinitely; a</u> president can only serve two terms.

(A)　indefinitely but a　　　　　　(C)　indefinitely a

(B)　indefinitely, a　　　　　　　(D)　No change is necessary.

7.　Students must pay a penalty for overdue library <u>books, however, there</u> is a grace period.

(A)　books; however, there　　　　(C)　books: however, there

(B)　books however, there　　　　(D)　No change is necessary.

8.　Among the states that seceded from the Union to join the Confederacy in 1860-1861 <u>were:</u> Mississippi, Florida, and Alabama.

(A)　were　　　　　　　　　　　(C)　were.

(B)　were;　　　　　　　　　　(D)　No change is necessary.

9.　The art exhibit displayed works by many famous <u>artists such as</u>: Dali, Picasso, and Michelangelo.

(A)　artists such as;　　　　　　(C)　artists. Such as

(B)　artists such as　　　　　　(D)　No change is necessary.

10.　The National Shakespeare Company will perform <u>the following plays:</u> *Othello, Macbeth, Hamlet,* and *As You Like It.*

(A)　the following plays,　　　　(C)　the following plays

(B)　the following plays;　　　　(D)　No change is necessary.

Skill 12: Identify Standard Capitalization

When a word is capitalized, it calls attention to itself. This attention should be for a good reason. There are standard uses for capital letters. In general, capitalize (1) all proper nouns, (2) the first word of a sentence, and (3) the first word of a direct quotation.

You should also capitalize

Names of ships, aircraft, spacecraft, and trains:

Apollo 13	*Mariner IV*
DC-10	S.S. *United States*
Sputnik II	Boeing 707

Names of deities:

God	Jupiter
Allah	Holy Ghost
Buddha	Venus
Jehovah	Shiva

Geological periods:

Neolithic age	Cenozoic era
late Pleistocene times	Ice Age

Names of astronomical bodies:

Mercury	Big Dipper
the Milky Way	Halley's comet
Ursa Major	North Star

Personifications:

Reliable Nature brought her promised Spring.

Bring on Melancholy in his sad might.

She believed that Love was the answer to all her problems.

Historical periods:

the Middle Ages	World War I
Reign of Terror	Great Depression
Christian Era	Roaring Twenties
Age of Louis XIV	Renaissance

Organizations, associations, and institutions:

Girl Scouts	North Atlantic Treaty Organization
Kiwanis Club	League of Women Voters

Florida Marlins   Unitarian Church

Smithsonian Institution   Common Market

Library of Congress   Franklin Glen High School

New York Philharmonic   Harvard University

Government and judicial groups:

United States Court of Appeals   Senate

Committee on Foreign Affairs   Parliament

New Jersey City Council   Peace Corps

Arkansas Supreme Court   Census Bureau

House of Representatives   Department of State

A general term that accompanies a specific name is capitalized only if it follows the specific name. If it stands alone or comes before the specific name, it is put in lowercase:

Washington State   the state of Washington

Senator Martinez   the senator from Florida

Central Park   the park

Golden Gate Bridge   the bridge

President Bush   the president of the United States

Pope Benedict   the pope

Queen Elizabeth I   the queen of England

Tropic of Capricorn   the tropics

Monroe Doctrine   the doctrine of expansion

the Mississippi River   the river

Easter Day   the day

Treaty of Versailles   the treaty

Webster's Dictionary   the dictionary

Equatorial Current   the equator

Use a capital to start a sentence:

Our car would not start.

When will you leave? I need to know right away.

Never!

Let me in! Please!

When a sentence appears within a sentence, start it with a capital letter:

> We had only one concern: When would we eat?

> My sister said, "I'll find the Monopoly game."

> He answered, "We can only stay a few minutes."

The most important words of titles are capitalized. Those words not capitalized are conjunctions (*and, or, but*) and short prepositions (*of, on, by, for*). The first and last word of a title must always be capitalized:

A Man for All Seasons	*Crime and Punishment*
Of Mice and Men	*Rise of the West*
Strange Life of Ivan Osokin	"Sonata in G Minor"
"Let Me In"	"Ode to Billy Joe"
"Rubaiyat of Omar Khayyam"	"All in the Family"

Capitalize newspaper and magazine titles:

> *U.S. News & World Report*

> *National Geographic*

> the *New York Times*

> the *Washington Post*

Capitalize radio and TV station call letters:

ABC	NBC
WNEW	WBOP
CNN	HBO

Do not capitalize compass directions or seasons:

west	north
east	south
spring	winter
autumn	summer

Capitalize regions:

the South	the Northeast
the West	Eastern Europe

BUT:	the south of France
	the east part of town

Capitalize specific military units:

the U.S. Army

the 7th Fleet

the German Navy

the 1st Infantry Division

Capitalize political groups and philosophies:

Democrat	Communist
Marxist	Nazism
Whig	Federalist
Existentialism	Transcendentalism

BUT do not capitalize systems of government or individual adherents to a philosophy:

democracy	communism
fascist	agnostic

Drill 21: Capitalization

> **DIRECTIONS: Choose the correct option.**

1. Mexico is the southernmost country in <u>North America</u>. It borders the United States on the north; it is bordered on the <u>south</u> by Belize and Guatemala.

    (A) north America . . . South

    (B) North America . . . South

    (C) North america . . . South

    (D) No change is necessary.

2. (A) Until 1989, Tom Landry was the only Coach the Dallas cowboys ever had.

    (B) Until 1989, Tom Landry was the only coach the Dallas Cowboys ever had.

    (C) Until 1989, Tom Landry was the only Coach the Dallas Cowboys ever had.

3. The <u>Northern Hemisphere</u> is the half of the <u>earth</u> that lies north of the <u>Equator.</u>

    (A) Northern hemisphere . . . earth . . . equator

    (B) Northern hemisphere . . . Earth . . . Equator

    (C) Northern Hemisphere . . . earth . . . equator

    (D) No change is necessary.

4. (A) My favorite works by Ernest Hemingway are "The Snows of Kilamanjaro," *The Sun Also Rises,* and *For Whom the Bell Tolls.*

    (B) My favorite works by Ernest Hemingway are "The Snows Of Kilamanjaro," *The Sun Also Rises,* and *For Whom The Bell Tolls.*

    (C) My favorite works by Ernest Hemingway are "The Snows of Kilamanjaro," *The Sun also Rises,* and *For whom the Bell Tolls.*

5. Aphrodite (<u>Venus in Roman Mythology</u>) was the <u>Greek</u> goddess of love.

    (A) Venus in Roman mythology . . . greek

    (B) venus in roman mythology . . . Greek

    (C) Venus in Roman mythology . . . Greek

    (D) No change is necessary.

6. The <u>Koran</u> is considered by <u>Muslims</u> to be the holy word.

    (A) koran . . . muslims   (C) Koran . . . muslims

    (B) koran . . . Muslims   (D) No change is necessary.

7. (A) The freshman curriculum at the community college includes english, a foreign language, Algebra I, and history.

    (B) The freshman curriculum at the community college includes English, a foreign language, Algebra I, and history.

    (C) The Freshman curriculum at the Community College includes English, a foreign language, Algebra I, and History.

8. At the <u>spring</u> graduation ceremonies, the university awarded more than 2,000 <u>bachelor's</u> degrees.

    (A) Spring . . . Bachelor's   (C) Spring . . . bachelor's

    (B) spring . . . Bachelor's   (D) No change is necessary.

9. The fall of the <u>Berlin wall</u> was an important symbol of the collapse of <u>Communism</u>.

    (A) berlin Wall . . . communism

    (B) Berlin Wall . . . communism

    (C) berlin wall . . . Communism

    (D) No change is necessary.

10. A photograph of <u>mars</u> was printed in <u>the *New York Times*</u>.

    (A) Mars . . . *The New York Times*

    (B) mars . . . *The New York times*

    (C) mars . . .*The New York Times*

    (D) No change is necessary.

Answer Key

Drill 1

1. (J)	4. (C)	7. (I)	10. (E)	13. (A)
2. (G)	5. (H)	8. (D)	11. (D)	14. (E)
3. (A)	6. (B)	9. (F)	12. (C)	15. (B)

Drill 2

1. (D)	4. (F)	7. (E)	10. (H)	13. (B)
2. (G)	5. (A)	8. (C)	11. (D)	14. (E)
3. (I)	6. (J)	9. (B)	12. (A)	15. (C)

Drill 3

1. (E)	4. (A)	7. (C)	10. (D)	13. (E)
2. (H)	5. (I)	8. (G)	11. (C)	14. (D)
3. (J)	6. (B)	9. (F)	12. (A)	15. (B)

Drill 4

1. (D)	4. (I)	7. (C)	10. (G)	13. (B)
2. (E)	5. (J)	8. (F)	11. (D)	14. (C)
3. (A)	6. (B)	9. (H)	12. (A)	15. (E)

Drill 5

1. (H)	4. (B)	7. (I)	10. (G)	13. (A)
2. (F)	5. (J)	8. (E)	11. (B)	14. (E)
3. (A)	6. (C)	9. (D)	12. (D)	15. (C)

Drill 6

1. (G)	4. (J)	7. (D)	10. (H)	13. (A)
2. (A)	5. (C)	8. (I)	11. (D)	14. (C)
3. (E)	6. (B)	9. (F)	12. (E)	15. (B)

Drill 7

1. (F)	4. (B)	7. (C)	10. (J)	13. (D)
2. (E)	5. (H)	8. (G)	11. (B)	14. (C)
3. (A)	6. (I)	9. (D)	12. (E)	15. (A)

Drill 8

1. (D)	4. (G)	7. (E)	10. (J)	13. (A)
2. (A)	5. (B)	8. (I)	11. (C)	14. (E)
3. (H)	6. (C)	9. (F)	12. (B)	15. (D)

Drill 9

1. (D)	4. (A)	7. (B)	10. (H)	13. (B)
2. (I)	5. (J)	8. (F)	11. (A)	14. (E)
3. (G)	6. (E)	9. (C)	12. (D)	15. (C)

Drill 10

1. (H)	4. (A)	7. (F)	10. (G)	13. (A)
2. (I)	5. (J)	8. (C)	11. (B)	14. (C)
3. (E)	6. (B)	9. (D)	12. (D)	15. (E)

Drill 11

1. (F)	4. (H)	7. (C)	10. (G)	13. (E)
2. (I)	5. (B)	8. (D)	11. (C)	14. (A)
3. (A)	6. (J)	9. (E)	12. (B)	15. (D)

Drill 12

1. (J)	4. (I)	7. (D)	10. (E)	13. (D)
2. (A)	5. (C)	8. (G)	11. (E)	14. (A)
3. (B)	6. (H)	9. (F)	12. (C)	15. (B)

Drill 13

1. (C)	13. (A)	25. (C)	37. (D)	49. (E)
2. (B)	14. (C)	26. (B)	38. (A)	50. (A)
3. (A)	15. (D)	27. (D)	39. (E)	51. (B)
4. (E)	16. (B)	28. (C)	40. (C)	52. (E)
5. (A)	17. (B)	29. (E)	41. (E)	53. (C)
6. (E)	18. (C)	30. (D)	42. (B)	54. (A)
7. (E)	19. (E)	31. (A)	43. (A)	55. (B)
8. (B)	20. (D)	32. (B)	44. (E)	56. (C)
9. (E)	21. (E)	33. (E)	45. (B)	57. (D)
10. (C)	22. (A)	34. (A)	46. (A)	58. (E)
11. (B)	23. (D)	35. (E)	47. (D)	59. (D)
12. (E)	24. (A)	36. (D)	48. (C)	60. (C)

Drill 14

1. (D)	4. (C)	7. (A)	10. (B)
2. (D)	5. (A)	8. (B)	
3. (A)	6. (C)	9. (C)	

Drill 15

1. (C)	4. (B)	7. (B)	10. (B)
2. (B)	5. (A)	8. (A)	
3. (B)	6. (A)	9. (B)	

Drill 16

1. (C)	4. (A)	7. (A)	10. (D)
2. (B)	5. (A)	8. (C)	
3. (D)	6. (B)	9. (A)	

Drill 17

1. (A)	4. (A)	7. (B)	10. (C)
2. (C)	5. (D)	8. (B)	
3. (Λ)	6. (A)	9. (A)	

Drill 18

1. (C)	4. (C)	7. (A)	10. (C)
2. (A)	5. (A)	8. (C)	
3. (D)	6. (C)	9. (B)	

Drill 19

1. (A)	4. (A)	7. (B)	10. (B)
2. (B)	5. (C)	8. (A)	
3. (C)	6. (D)	9. (B)	

Drill 20

1. (D)	4. (C)	7. (A)	10. (D)
2. (A)	5. (A)	8. (A)	
3. (A)	6. (D)	9. (B)	

Drill 21

1. (D)	4. (A)	7. (B)	10. (A)
2. (B)	5. (C)	8. (D)	
3. (C)	6. (D)	9. (B)	

Essay

Essay Writing Review

The FTCE-GKT contains one writing exercise. You will have 50 minutes to plan and write an essay on one of two topic choices. You must write on only one of the two choices of topic. Since you will have only 50 minutes to complete the essay, efficient use of your time is essential.

Your work will be scored holistically by two judges. The personal views you express will not be an issue; however, the skill with which you express those views, the logic of your arguments, and the degree to which you support your position will be very important in the scoring. Your essay will be scored both on substance and on the composition skills demonstrated.

Writing under pressure can be frustrating, but if you study this review, practice and polish your essay skills, and have a realistic sense of what to expect, you can turn problems into possibilities. The following review will show you how to plan and write a logical, coherent, and interesting essay.

Why Essays Exist

People write essays for purposes other than testing. Some of our best thinkers have written essays that we continue to read from generation to generation. Essays offer the reader a logical, coherent, and imaginative written composition showing the nature or consequences of a single controlling idea when considered from the writer's unique point of view. Writers use essays to communicate their opinion or position on a topic to readers who cannot be present during their live conversation. Writers use essays to help readers understand or learn about something that readers should or may want to know or do. Essays always express more or less directly the author's opinion, belief, position, or knowledge (backed by evidence) about the idea or object in question.

Pre-Writing/Planning

Before you begin to actually write, there are certain preliminary steps you need to take. A few minutes spent planning pays off—your final essay will be more focused, well-developed, and clearer. For a 50-minute essay, you should spend about five to ten minutes on the pre-writing process.

Skill 1: Determine the Purpose for Writing

For this test you will need to recognize and generate the elements of an excellent essay. In essence, you will be taking the principles covered in this review and utilizing them to create your own original essay. With that in mind, read carefully the standards and explanations below to prepare you for what to look for in your own essay response.

Read the essay question very carefully and ask yourself the following questions:

- What is the meaning of the topic statement?

- Is the question asking me to persuade the reader of the validity of a certain opinion?

- Do I agree or disagree with the statement? What will be my thesis (main idea)?

- What kinds of examples can I use to support my thesis? Explore personal experiences, historical evidence, current events, and literary subjects.

Skill 2: Formulate a Thesis or Statement of Main Idea

In academic writing, two purposes dominate essays:

1. Persuasion through argumentation using one, some, or all of the logical patterns described here.

2. Informing and educating through analysis and using one, some, or all of the logical patterns described here.

All of an essay's organizational strategies may be used to argue in writing. The author offers reasons and/or evidence so an audience will be inclined to believe the position that the author presents about the idea under discussion. Writers use seven basic strategies to organize information and ideas in essays to help prove their point (thesis). All of these strategies might be useful in arguing for an idea and persuading a reader to see the issue the writer's way. Your job is to use strategies that are appropriate to demonstrate your thesis. For example, you may wish to use comparison and contrast to demonstrate that one thing or idea is better or worse than another.

The following seven steps can be used to prove a thesis:

Seven Steps to Prove a Thesis

1. Show how a *process* or procedure does or should work, step by step, in time.

2. *Compare or contrast* two or more things or ideas to show important differences or similarities.

3. *Identify a problem* and then explain how to solve it.

4. *Analyze* into its components, or *classify* by its types or categories an idea or thing to show how it is put together, how it works, or how it is designed.

5. *Explain* why something happens to produce a particular result or set of results.

6. *Describe* the particular individual characteristics, beauty and features of a place, person(s), time, or idea.

7. *Define* what a thing is or what an idea means.

Depending upon the purpose of the essay, one pattern tends to dominate the discussion question. (For example, the writer might use *description* and *explanation* to define the varied meanings of "love.")

Skill 3: Organize Ideas and Details Effectively

Decide how many paragraphs you will write. In a 30-minute exercise, you will probably have time for no more than four or five paragraphs. In such a format, the first paragraph will be the introduction, the next two or three will develop your thesis with specific examples, and the final paragraph should be a strong conclusion.

The Introduction

The focus of your introduction should be the thesis statement. This statement allows your reader to understand the point and direction of your essay. The statement identifies the central idea of your essay and should clearly state your attitude about the subject. It will also dictate the basic content and organization of your essay. If you do not state your thesis clearly, your essay will suffer.

The thesis is the heart of the essay. Without it, readers won't know what your major message or central idea is in the essay.

The thesis must be something that can be argued or needs to be proven, not just an accepted fact. For example, "Animals are used every day in cosmetic and medical testing" is a fact—it needs no proof. But if the writer says, "Using animals for cosmetic and medical testing is cruel and should be stopped," we have a point that must be supported and defended by the writer.

The thesis can be placed in any paragraph of the essay, but in a short essay, especially one written for evaluative exam purposes, the thesis is most effective when placed in the last sentence of the opening paragraph.

Consider the following sample question:

ESSAY TOPIC:

   "That government is best which governs least."

ASSIGNMENT:

Do you agree or disagree with this statement? Choose a specific example from current events, personal experience, or your reading to support your position.

After reading the topic statement, decide if you agree or disagree. If you agree with this statement, your thesis statement could be the following:

> "Government has the right to protect individuals from interference but no right to extend its powers and activities beyond this function."

This statement clearly states the writer's opinion in a direct manner. It also serves as a blueprint for the essay. The remainder of the introduction should give two or three brief examples that support your thesis.

Supporting Paragraphs

The next two or three paragraphs of your essay will elaborate on the supporting examples you gave in your introduction. Each paragraph should discuss only one idea. Like the introduction, each paragraph should be coherently organized, with a topic sentence and supporting details.

The topic sentence is to each paragraph what the thesis statement is to the essay as a whole. It tells the reader what you plan to discuss in that paragraph. It has a specific subject and is neither too broad nor too narrow. It also establishes the author's attitude and gives the reader a sense of the direction in which the writer is going. An effective topic sentence also arouses the reader's interest.

Although it may occur in the middle or at the end of the paragraph, the topic sentence usually appears at the beginning of the paragraph. Placing it at the beginning is advantageous because it helps you stay focused on the main idea.

The remainder of each paragraph should support the topic sentence with examples and illustrations. Each sentence should progress logically from the previous one and be centrally connected to your topic sentence. Do not include any extraneous material that does not serve to develop your thesis.

Conclusion

Your conclusion should briefly restate your thesis and explain how you have shown it to be true. Since you want to end your essay on a strong note, your conclusion should be concise and effective.

Do not introduce any new topics that you cannot support. If you were watching a movie that suddenly shifted plot and characters at the end, you would be disappointed or even angry. Similarly, conclusions must not drift away from the major focus and message of the essay. Make sure your conclusion is clearly on the topic and represents your perspective without any confusion about what you really mean and believe. The reader will respect you for staying true to your intentions.

The conclusion is your last chance to grab and impress the reader. You can even use humor, if appropriate, but a dramatic close will remind the reader you are serious, even passionate, about what you believe.

Skill 4: Provide Adequate, Relevant Supporting Material

You may employ any one of the seven steps previously listed to prove any thesis that you maintain is true. You may also call on evidence from one or all of the four following kinds of evidence to support the thesis of your essay. Identify which kind(s) of evidence you can use to prove the points of your essay. In test situations, most essayists use anecdotal evidence or analogy to explain, describe, or prove a thesis. But if you know salient facts or statistics, don't hesitate to call upon them.

1. **Hard data** (facts, statistics, scientific evidence, research)—documented evidence that has been verified to be true.

2. **Anecdotal evidence**—stories from the writer's own experience and knowledge that illustrate a particular point or idea.

3. **Expert opinions**—assertions or conclusions, usually by authorities, about the matter under discussion.

4. **Analogies**—show a resemblance between one phenomenon and another.

Skill 5: Use Effective Transitions

Transitions are like the links of a bracelet, holding the beads or major points of your essay together. They help the reader follow the smooth flow of your ideas and show a connection between major and minor ideas. Transitions are used either at the beginning of a paragraph, or to show the connections among ideas within a single paragraph. Without transitions, you will jar the reader and distract him from your true ideas.

Here are some typical transitional words and phrases:

Linking similar ideas

again	for example	likewise
also	for instance	moreover
and	further	nor
another	furthermore	of course
besides	in addition	similarly
equally important	in like manner	too

Linking dissimilar/contradictory ideas

although	however	on the other hand
and yet	in spite of	otherwise
as if	instead	provided that
but	nevertheless	still
conversely	on the contrary	yet

Indicating cause, purpose, or result

as	for	so
as a result	for this reason	then
because	hence	therefore
consequently	since	thus

Indicating time or position

above	before	meanwhile
across	beyond	next
afterwards	eventually	presently
around	finally	second
at once	first	thereafter
at the present time	here	thereupon

Indicating an example or summary

as a result	in any event	in other words
as I have said	in brief	in short
for example	in conclusion	on the whole
for instance	in fact	to sum up

Skill 6: Demonstrate Mature Command of Language

Common Writing Errors

The four writing errors most often made by beginning writers are run-ons (also known as fused sentences), fragments, lack of subject-verb agreement, and incorrect use of the object:

1. **Run-ons:** "She swept the floor it was dirty" is a run-on, because the pronoun "it" stands as a noun subject and starts a new sentence. A period or semicolon is needed after "floor."

2. **Fragments:** "Before Jimmy learned how to play baseball" is a fragment, even though it has a subject and verb (Jimmy learned). The word "before" fragmentizes the clause, and the reader needs to know what happened before Jimmy learned how to play baseball.

3. **Problems with subject-verb agreement:** "Either Maria or Robert are going to the game" is incorrect because either Maria is going or Robert is going, but not both. The sentence should say, "Either Maria or Robert is going to the game."

4. **Incorrect object:** Probably the most common offender in this area is saying "between you and I," which sounds correct, but isn't. "Between" is a preposition that takes the objective case "me." The correct usage is "between you and me."

The FTCE-GKT test graders also cite lack of thought and development, misspellings, incorrect pronouns or antecedents, and lack of development as frequently occurring problems. Finally, keep in mind that clear, coherent handwriting always works to your advantage. Readers will appreciate an essay they can read with ease.

Five Words Weak Writers Overuse

Weak and beginning writers overuse the vague pronouns "you, we, they, this, and it" often without telling exactly who or what is represented by the pronoun.

1. Beginning writers often shift to second person **"you,"** when the writer means "a person." This shift confuses readers and weakens the flow of the essay. Although "you" is commonly accepted in creative writing, journalism, and other arenas, in a short, formal essay, it is best to avoid "you" altogether.

2. **"We"** is another pronoun that should be avoided. If by "we" the writer means "Americans," "society," or some other group, then he or she should say so.

3. **"They"** is often misused in essay writing, because it is overused in conversation: "I went to the doctor, and they told me to take some medicine." Tell the reader who "they" are.

4. **"This"** is usually used incorrectly without a referent: "She told me she received a present. This sounded good to me." This what? This idea? This news? This present? Be clear—don't make your readers guess what you mean. The word "this" should be followed by a noun or referent.

5. **"It"** is a common problem among weak writers. To what does "it" refer? Your readers don't appreciate vagueness, so take the time to be clear and complete in your expression of ideas.

Use Your Own Vocabulary

Is it a good idea to use big words that sound good in the dictionary or thesaurus, but that you don't really use or understand? No. So whose vocabulary should you use? Your own. You will be most comfortable with your own level of vocabulary.

This "comfort zone" doesn't give you license to be informal in a formal setting or to violate the rules of standard written English, but if you try to write in a style that is not yours, your writing will be awkward and lack a true voice.

You should certainly improve and build your vocabulary at every opportunity, but remember: you should not attempt to change your vocabulary level at this point.

Avoid the Passive Voice

In writing, the active voice is preferable because it is emphatic and direct. A weak passive verb leaves the doer unknown or seemingly unimportant. However, the passive voice is essential when the action of the verb is more important than the doer, when the doer is unknown, or when the writer wishes to place the emphasis on the receiver of the action rather than on the doer.

Skill 7: Avoid Inappropriate Use of Slang, Jargon, and Clichés

The requirements for informal spoken English are much more relaxed than the rigid rules for "standard written English." While slang, colloquialisms, and other informal expressions are acceptable and sometimes very appropriate in casual speech, they are inappropriate in academic and business writing. More often than not, writers, especially student writers, do not make a distinction between the two: they use the same words, grammar, and sentence structure from their everyday speech in their college papers, albeit unsuccessfully.

The FTCE does not require you to know grammatical terms such as *gerund, subject complement,* or *dependent clause,* although general familiarity with such terms may be helpful to you in determining whether a sentence or part of a sentence is correct or incorrect. You should watch for errors in grammar, spelling, punctuation, capitalization, sentence structure, and word choice. Remember: this is a test of written language skills; therefore, your responses should be based on what you know to be correct for written work, not what you know to be appropriate for a casual conversation. For instance, in informal speech, you might say "Who are you going to choose?" But in formal academic writing, you would write "Whom are you going to choose?" Your choices, then, should be dictated by requirements for *written*, not *conversational* English.

Skill 8: Use a Variety of Sentence Patterns Effectively

Parallelism

Sentences should use the same kind of grammatical construction for all items in a series—those usually joined by a coordinating conjunction (*and, but, or,* and *nor*). "No smoking, eating, or drinking" is parallel; "No smoking, food, or drinking" is not, because *food* is not a verb form. Making elements parallel also requires knowledge of parallel correlative pairs, that is, the use of appropriate pairs together: *neither* and *nor, either* and *or, both* with *and, whether* with *or,* and *not only* with *but also.*

Parallel structure is used to express matching ideas. It refers to the grammatical balance of a series of any of the following:

Phrases. The squirrel ran *along the fence, up the tree,* and *into his hole* with a mouthful of acorns.

Adjectives. The job market is flooded with *very talented, highly motivated,* and *well-educated* young people.

Nouns. You will need a *notebook, pencil,* and *dictionary* for the test.

Clauses. The children were told to decide *which toy they would keep* and *which toy they would give away.*

Verbs. The farmer *plowed, planted,* and *harvested* his corn in record time.

Verbals. *Reading, writing,* and *calculating* are fundamental skills we should all possess.

Correlative Conjunctions. *Either* you will do your homework *or* you will fail. *Note:* Correlative conjunctions must be used as pairs and not mixed with other conjunctions, such as *neither* with *or* or *not only* with *also.*

Near-parallelisms. Sometimes a string of seemingly parallel thoughts are not in fact parallel. Consider this sentence: "I *have quit* my job, *enrolled* in school, and *am looking* for a reliable babysitter." In this sentence the writer has already *quit* and *enrolled* but is still looking for a babysitter; therefore she cannot include all three in a parallel structure. A good revision of this sentence is, "I have quit my job and enrolled in school, and I am looking for a babysitter."

Misplaced and Dangling Modifiers

Many people, probably including at least some parents of your students, consider misplaced and dangling modifiers to be a sure sign of ignorance about the English language. Although this belief on their part may be unfair, teachers need to be aware that it is firmly held. As the name suggests, a misplaced modifier is one that is in the wrong place in the sentence. Misplaced modifiers come in all forms—words, phrases, and clauses. Sentences containing misplaced modifiers are often very comical: *Mom made me eat the spinach instead of my brother.* Misplaced modifiers, like the one in this sentence, are usually too far away from the word or words they modify. This sentence should read *Mom made me, instead of my brother, eat the spinach.*

Such modifiers as *only, nearly,* and *almost* should be placed next to the word they modify and not in front of some other word, especially a verb, that they are not intended to modify. For example, *I only sang for one reason* is wrong if the writer means to say that there was *only one* reason for singing.

A modifier is misplaced if it appears to modify the wrong part of the sentence or if the reader cannot be certain what part of the sentence the writer intended it to modify. To correct a misplaced modifier, move the modifier next to the word it describes.

UNREVISED: She served hamburgers to the men on paper plates.

REVISED: She served hamburgers on paper plates to the men.

A *squinting modifier* is one that may refer to either a preceding or a following word, leaving the reader uncertain about what it is intended to modify. Correct a squinting modifier by moving it next to the word it is intended to modify.

UNREVISED: Snipers who fired on the soldiers often escaped capture.

REVISED: Snipers who often fired on the soldiers escaped capture. OR
Snipers who fired on the soldiers escaped capture often.

A *dangling modifier* is a modifier or verb in search of a subject: the modifying phrase (usually a participle phrase—an *-ing* word group or an *-ed* or an *-en* word group—or an infinitive phrase—a *to + verb* word group) has nothing to modify. It is figuratively *dangling* at the beginning or the end of a sentence. The sentences often look and sound correct at first glance: *To be a student government officer, your grades must be above average.* However, the verbal modifier has nothing to describe. *You* are supposed *to be a student government officer*; *your grades* cannot become an officer.

To correct a dangling modifier, reword the sentence by either (1) changing the modifying phrase to a clause with a subject, or (2) changing the subject of the sentence to the word that should be modified. Here are some other examples of correct revision of dangling modifiers:

UNREVISED: Shortly after leaving home, the accident occurred.

REVISED: Shortly after we left home, the accident occurred.

UNREVISED: To get up on time, a great effort was needed.

REVISED: To get up on time, I made a great effort.

Sentence Fragments

A fragment is an incomplete construction that either (1) lacks a subject or a verb or (2) is preceded by a subordinating conjunction (e.g., *because, which, when, although*). A complete construction, such as a sentence or an independent clause, expresses a complete thought.

UNREVISED: Traffic was stalled for ten miles on the freeway. Because repairs were being made on potholes. (The second "sentence" is a dependent, or subordinate, clause.)

REVISED: Traffic was stalled for ten miles on the freeway because repairs were being made on potholes.

UNREVISED:	It was a funny story. One that I had never heard before. (The second "sentence" has no verb for its subject, "One.")
REVISED:	It was a funny story, one that I had never heard.

Run-On/Fused Sentences

A run-on, or fused, sentence is not necessarily a long sentence or a sentence that the reader considers too long; in fact, a run-on might consist of two short sentences: *Dry ice does not melt it evaporates.* A run-on results when the writer fuses, or runs together, two separate sentences without any correct mark of punctuation separating them.

UNREVISED:	Knowing how to use a dictionary is no problem each dictionary has a section in the front of the book that tells you how.
REVISED:	Knowing how to use a dictionary is no problem. Each dictionary has a section in the front of the book that tells you how.

The most common type of run-on sentence is characterized by a comma splice—the incorrect use of only a comma to separate what are really two separate sentences. There are three quick ways to fix a comma splice: (1) replace the comma with a period and start a new sentence; (2) replace the comma with a semicolon; and (3) add a coordinating conjunction, such as *and* or *but,* after the comma.

UNREVISED:	Bob bought dress shoes, a suit, and a nice shirt, he needed them for his sister's wedding.
REVISED:	Bob bought dress shoes, a suit, and a nice shirt. He needed them for his sister's wedding.
UNREVISED:	One common error in writing is incorrect spelling, the other is the occasional use of faulty diction.
REVISED:	One common error in writing is incorrect spelling; the other is the occasional use of faulty diction.
UNREVISED:	We have never won the track championship, we have won the cross-country title.
REVISED:	We have never won the track championship, but we have won the cross-country title.

If one of the complete thoughts is subordinate to the other, you may also use a subordinate conjunction to connect the two:

UNREVISED:	Neal won the award, he had the highest score.
REVISED:	Neal won the award because he had the highest score.

Subordination, Coordination, and Predication

Suppose that you wanted to combine the information in these two sentences to create one statement: *I studied a foreign language. I found English quite easy.* How you decide to combine this information should be determined by the relationship you'd like to show between the two facts. *I studied a foreign language, and I found English quite easy* adds little or nothing to the original meaning. The **coordination** of the two ideas (connecting them with the coordinating conjunction *and*) is therefore ineffective. Using **subordination** instead (connecting the sentences with a subordinating conjunction) clearly shows the relationship between the expressed ideas:

> *After I studied a foreign language, I found English quite easy. OR*
>
> *Because I studied a foreign language, I found English quite easy.*

When using any conjunction—coordinating or subordinating—be sure that the sentence parts you are joining are in agreement:

> UNREVISED: She loved him dearly but not his dog.
>
> REVISED: She loved him dearly, but she did not love his dog. OR
> She loved him, but not his dog, dearly.

Another common mistake is to forget that each member of the pair must be followed by the same kind of construction.

> UNREVISED: She complimented her friends both for their bravery and thanked them for their kindness.
>
> REVISED: She both complimented her friends for their bravery and thanked them for their kindness.

While refers to time and should not be used as a substitute for *though, and,* or *but.*

> UNREVISED: While I'm usually interested in Fellini movies, I'd rather not go tonight.
>
> REVISED: Although I'm usually interested in Fellini movies, I'd rather not go tonight.

Where refers to a place and should not be used as a substitute for *that.*

> UNREVISED: We read in the paper where they are making strides in DNA research.
>
> REVISED: We read in the paper that they are making great strides in DNA research.

After words such as *reason* and *explanation,* use *that,* not *because.*

> UNREVISED: His explanation for his tardiness was because his alarm did not go off.
>
> REVISED: His explanation for his tardiness was that his alarm did not go off.

Skill 9: Maintain Consistent Point of View

Depending on the audience, essays may be written from one of three points of view:

1. *Subjective/Personal* Point of View:

   "I think . . ."

   "I believe cars are more trouble than they are worth."

   "I feel . . ."

2. *Second Person* Point of View (We . . . You; I . . . You):

   "If *you* own a car, *you* will soon find out that it is more trouble than it is worth."

3. *Third Person* Point of View (focuses on the idea, not what "I" think of it):

   "*Cars* are more trouble than *they* are worth."

It is very important to maintain a consistent point of view throughout your essay. If you begin writing in the first-person ("I"), do not shift to the second- or third-person in the middle of the essay. Such inconsistency is confusing to your reader and will be penalized by the graders of your essay.

Skill 10: Observe the Conventions of Standard American English

Make sure to leave yourself enough time at the end to read over your essay for errors such as misspellings, omitted words, or incorrect punctuation. You will not have enough time to make large-scale revisions, but take this chance to make any small changes that will make your essay stronger. Consider the following when proofreading your work:

- Are all your sentences really sentences? Have you written any fragments or run-on sentences?

- Are you using vocabulary correctly?

- Did you leave out any punctuation? Did you capitalize correctly?

- Are there any misspellings, especially of difficult words?

If you have time, read your essay backwards from end to beginning. By doing so, you may catch errors that you missed reading forward only.

Drill: Essay Writing

DIRECTIONS: You have 50 minutes to plan and write an essay on the topic below. You may write on one of the assigned topic choices only.

Make sure to give specific examples to support your thesis. Proofread your essay carefully and take care to express your ideas clearly and effectively.

> ### ESSAY TOPIC:
>
> In the last 20 years, the deterioration of the environment has become a growing concern among both scientists and ordinary citizens.
>
> ### ASSIGNMENT:
>
> Choose one pressing environmental problem, explain its negative impact and discuss possible solutions.

Drill: Essay Writing

This Answer Key provides three sample essays that represent possible responses to the essay topic. Compare your own response to those given on the next few pages. Allow the strengths and weaknesses of the sample essays help you to critique your own essay and improve your writing skills.

ESSAY I (Score: 5–6)

There are many pressing environmental problems facing both this country and the world today. Pollution, the misuse and squandering of resources, and the cavalier attitude many people express all contribute to the problem. But one of the most pressing problems this country faces is the apathetic attitude many Americans have towards recycling.

Why is recycling so imperative? There are two major reasons. First, recycling previously used materials conserves precious national resources. Many people never stop to think that reserves of metal ores are not unlimited. There is only so much gold, silver, tin, and other metals in the ground. Once it has all been mined, there will never be any more unless we recycle what has already been used.

Second, the United States daily generates more solid waste than any other country on earth. Our disposable consumer culture consumes fast food meals in paper or styrofoam containers, uses disposable diapers with plastic liners that do not biodegrade, receives pounds, if not tons, of unsolicited junk mail every year, and relies more and more on prepackaged rather than fresh food.

No matter how it is accomplished, increased recycling is essential. We have to stop covering our land with garbage, and the best ways to do this are to reduce our dependence on prepackaged goods and to minimize the amount of solid waste disposed of in landfills. The best way to reduce solid waste is to recycle it. Americans need to band together to recycle, to preserve our irreplaceable natural resources, reduce pollution, and preserve our precious environment.

Analysis

This essay presents a clearly defined thesis, and the writer elaborates on this thesis in a thoughtful and sophisticated manner. Various aspects of the problem under consideration are presented and explored, along with possible solutions. The support provided for the writer's argument is convincing and logical. There are few usage or mechanical errors to interfere with the writer's ability to communicate effectively. This writer demonstrates a comprehensive understanding of the rules of written English.

ESSAY II (Score: 3–4)

A pressing environmental problem today is the way we are cutting down too many trees and not planting any replacements for them. Trees are beneficial in many ways, and without them, many environmental problems would be much worse.

One of the ways trees are beneficial is that, like all plants, they take in carbon dioxide and produce oxygen. They can actually help clean the air this way. When too many trees are cut down in a small area, the air in that area is not as good and can be unhealthy to breath.

Another way trees are beneficial is that they provide homes for many types of birds, insects, and animals. When all the trees in an area are cut down, these animals lose their homes and sometimes they can die out and become extinct that way. Like the spotted owls in Oregon, that the loggers wanted to cut down the trees they lived in. If the loggers did cut down all the old timber stands that the spotted owls lived in, the owls would have become extinct.

But the loggers say that if they can't cut the trees down then they will be out of work, and that peoples' jobs are more important than birds. The loggers can do two things—they can either get training so they can do other jobs, or they can do what they should have done all along, and start replanting trees. For every mature tree they cut down, they should have to plant at least one tree seedling.

Cutting down the trees that we need for life, and that lots of other species depend on, is a big environmental problem that has a lot of long term consequences. Trees are too important for all of us to cut them down without thinking about the future.

Analysis

This essay has a clear thesis, which the author does support with good examples. But the writer shifts between the chosen topic, which is that indiscriminate tree-cutting is a pressing environmental problem, and a list of the ways in which trees are beneficial and a discussion about the logging profession. Also, while there are few mistakes in usage and mechanics, the writer does have some problems with sentence structure. The writing is pedestrian and the writer does not elaborate on the topic as much as he or she could have. The writer failed to provide the kind of critical analysis that the topic required.

ESSAY III (Score: 1–2)

The most pressing environmental problem today is that lots of people and companies don't care about the environment, and they do lots of things that hurt the environment.

People throw littur out car windows and don't use trash cans, even if their all over a park, soda cans and fast food wrappers are all over the place. Cigarette butts are the worst cause the filters never rot. Newspapers and junk mail get left to blow all over the neighborhood, and beer bottles too.

Companies pollute the air and the water. Sometimes the ground around a company has lots of toxins in it. Now companies can buy credits from other companies that let them pollute the air even more. They dump all kinds of chemicals into lakes and rivers that kills off the fish and causes acid rain and kills off more fish and some trees and small animals and insects and then no one can go swimming or fishing in the lake.

People need to respect the environment because we only have one planet, and if we keep polluting it pretty soon nothing will grow and then even the people will die.

Analysis

The writer of this essay does not define his or her thesis for this essay. Because of this lack of a clear thesis, the reader is left to infer the topic from the body of the essay. It is possible to perceive the writer's intended thesis; however, the support for this thesis is very superficial. The writer presents a list of common complaints about polluters, without any critical discussion of the problems and possible solutions. Many sentences are run-ons and the writer has made several spelling errors. While the author manages to communicate his or her position on the issue, he or she does so on such a superficial level and with so many errors in usage and mechanics that the writer fails to demonstrate an ability to effectively communicate.

FTCE

Florida Teacher Certification Examination
General Knowledge Test

Practice Test 1

Answer Sheet – Practice Test 1

Subtest I: Reading

1. Ⓐ Ⓑ Ⓒ Ⓓ
2. Ⓐ Ⓑ Ⓒ Ⓓ
3. Ⓐ Ⓑ Ⓒ Ⓓ
4. Ⓐ Ⓑ Ⓒ Ⓓ
5. Ⓐ Ⓑ Ⓒ Ⓓ
6. Ⓐ Ⓑ Ⓒ Ⓓ
7. Ⓐ Ⓑ Ⓒ Ⓓ
8. Ⓐ Ⓑ Ⓒ Ⓓ
9. Ⓐ Ⓑ Ⓒ Ⓓ
10. Ⓐ Ⓑ Ⓒ Ⓓ

11. Ⓐ Ⓑ Ⓒ Ⓓ
12. Ⓐ Ⓑ Ⓒ Ⓓ
13. Ⓐ Ⓑ Ⓒ Ⓓ
14. Ⓐ Ⓑ Ⓒ Ⓓ
15. Ⓐ Ⓑ Ⓒ Ⓓ
16. Ⓐ Ⓑ Ⓒ Ⓓ
17. Ⓐ Ⓑ Ⓒ Ⓓ
18. Ⓐ Ⓑ Ⓒ Ⓓ
19. Ⓐ Ⓑ Ⓒ Ⓓ
20. Ⓐ Ⓑ Ⓒ Ⓓ

21. Ⓐ Ⓑ Ⓒ Ⓓ
22. Ⓐ Ⓑ Ⓒ Ⓓ
23. Ⓐ Ⓑ Ⓒ Ⓓ
24. Ⓐ Ⓑ Ⓒ Ⓓ
25. Ⓐ Ⓑ Ⓒ Ⓓ
26. Ⓐ Ⓑ Ⓒ Ⓓ
27. Ⓐ Ⓑ Ⓒ Ⓓ
28. Ⓐ Ⓑ Ⓒ Ⓓ
29. Ⓐ Ⓑ Ⓒ Ⓓ
30. Ⓐ Ⓑ Ⓒ Ⓓ

31. Ⓐ Ⓑ Ⓒ Ⓓ
32. Ⓐ Ⓑ Ⓒ Ⓓ
33. Ⓐ Ⓑ Ⓒ Ⓓ
34. Ⓐ Ⓑ Ⓒ Ⓓ
35. Ⓐ Ⓑ Ⓒ Ⓓ
36. Ⓐ Ⓑ Ⓒ Ⓓ
37. Ⓐ Ⓑ Ⓒ Ⓓ
38. Ⓐ Ⓑ Ⓒ Ⓓ
39. Ⓐ Ⓑ Ⓒ Ⓓ
40. Ⓐ Ⓑ Ⓒ Ⓓ

Subtest II: Mathematics

1. Ⓐ Ⓑ Ⓒ Ⓓ
2. Ⓐ Ⓑ Ⓒ Ⓓ
3. Ⓐ Ⓑ Ⓒ Ⓓ
4. Ⓐ Ⓑ Ⓒ Ⓓ
5. Ⓐ Ⓑ Ⓒ Ⓓ
6. Ⓐ Ⓑ Ⓒ Ⓓ
7. Ⓐ Ⓑ Ⓒ Ⓓ
8. Ⓐ Ⓑ Ⓒ Ⓓ
9. Ⓐ Ⓑ Ⓒ Ⓓ
10. Ⓐ Ⓑ Ⓒ Ⓓ
11. Ⓐ Ⓑ Ⓒ Ⓓ

12. Ⓐ Ⓑ Ⓒ Ⓓ
13. Ⓐ Ⓑ Ⓒ Ⓓ
14. Ⓐ Ⓑ Ⓒ Ⓓ
15. Ⓐ Ⓑ Ⓒ Ⓓ
16. Ⓐ Ⓑ Ⓒ Ⓓ
17. Ⓐ Ⓑ Ⓒ Ⓓ
18. Ⓐ Ⓑ Ⓒ Ⓓ
19. Ⓐ Ⓑ Ⓒ Ⓓ
20. Ⓐ Ⓑ Ⓒ Ⓓ
21. Ⓐ Ⓑ Ⓒ Ⓓ
22. Ⓐ Ⓑ Ⓒ Ⓓ

23. Ⓐ Ⓑ Ⓒ Ⓓ
24. Ⓐ Ⓑ Ⓒ Ⓓ
25. Ⓐ Ⓑ Ⓒ Ⓓ
26. Ⓐ Ⓑ Ⓒ Ⓓ
27. Ⓐ Ⓑ Ⓒ Ⓓ
28. Ⓐ Ⓑ Ⓒ Ⓓ
29. Ⓐ Ⓑ Ⓒ Ⓓ
30. Ⓐ Ⓑ Ⓒ Ⓓ
31. Ⓐ Ⓑ Ⓒ Ⓓ
32. Ⓐ Ⓑ Ⓒ Ⓓ
33. Ⓐ Ⓑ Ⓒ Ⓓ

34. Ⓐ Ⓑ Ⓒ Ⓓ
35. Ⓐ Ⓑ Ⓒ Ⓓ
36. Ⓐ Ⓑ Ⓒ Ⓓ
37. Ⓐ Ⓑ Ⓒ Ⓓ
38. Ⓐ Ⓑ Ⓒ Ⓓ
39. Ⓐ Ⓑ Ⓒ Ⓓ
40. Ⓐ Ⓑ Ⓒ Ⓓ
41. Ⓐ Ⓑ Ⓒ Ⓓ
42. Ⓐ Ⓑ Ⓒ Ⓓ
43. Ⓐ Ⓑ Ⓒ Ⓓ
44. Ⓐ Ⓑ Ⓒ Ⓓ
45. Ⓐ Ⓑ Ⓒ Ⓓ

Subtest III: English Language Skills

1. Ⓐ Ⓑ Ⓒ Ⓓ
2. Ⓐ Ⓑ Ⓒ Ⓓ
3. Ⓐ Ⓑ Ⓒ Ⓓ
4. Ⓐ Ⓑ Ⓒ Ⓓ
5. Ⓐ Ⓑ Ⓒ Ⓓ
6. Ⓐ Ⓑ Ⓒ Ⓓ
7. Ⓐ Ⓑ Ⓒ Ⓓ
8. Ⓐ Ⓑ Ⓒ Ⓓ
9. Ⓐ Ⓑ Ⓒ Ⓓ
10. Ⓐ Ⓑ Ⓒ Ⓓ

11. Ⓐ Ⓑ Ⓒ Ⓓ
12. Ⓐ Ⓑ Ⓒ Ⓓ
13. Ⓐ Ⓑ Ⓒ Ⓓ
14. Ⓐ Ⓑ Ⓒ Ⓓ
15. Ⓐ Ⓑ Ⓒ Ⓓ
16. Ⓐ Ⓑ Ⓒ Ⓓ
17. Ⓐ Ⓑ Ⓒ Ⓓ
18. Ⓐ Ⓑ Ⓒ Ⓓ
19. Ⓐ Ⓑ Ⓒ Ⓓ
20. Ⓐ Ⓑ Ⓒ Ⓓ

21. Ⓐ Ⓑ Ⓒ Ⓓ
22. Ⓐ Ⓑ Ⓒ Ⓓ
23. Ⓐ Ⓑ Ⓒ Ⓓ
24. Ⓐ Ⓑ Ⓒ Ⓓ
25. Ⓐ Ⓑ Ⓒ Ⓓ
26. Ⓐ Ⓑ Ⓒ Ⓓ
27. Ⓐ Ⓑ Ⓒ Ⓓ
28. Ⓐ Ⓑ Ⓒ Ⓓ
29. Ⓐ Ⓑ Ⓒ Ⓓ
30. Ⓐ Ⓑ Ⓒ Ⓓ

31. Ⓐ Ⓑ Ⓒ Ⓓ
32. Ⓐ Ⓑ Ⓒ Ⓓ
33. Ⓐ Ⓑ Ⓒ Ⓓ
34. Ⓐ Ⓑ Ⓒ Ⓓ
35. Ⓐ Ⓑ Ⓒ Ⓓ
36. Ⓐ Ⓑ Ⓒ Ⓓ
37. Ⓐ Ⓑ Ⓒ Ⓓ
38. Ⓐ Ⓑ Ⓒ Ⓓ
39. Ⓐ Ⓑ Ⓒ Ⓓ
40. Ⓐ Ⓑ Ⓒ Ⓓ

Practice Test 1

Subtest I: Reading

TIME: 40 Minutes
40 Questions

> **DIRECTIONS:** A number of questions follow each of the passages in the reading section. Answer the questions by choosing the best answer from the four choices given.

Questions 1 and 2 refer to the following passage:

America's national bird, the mighty bald eagle, is being threatened by a new menace. Once decimated by hunters and loss of habitat, this newest danger is suspected to be from the intentional poisoning by livestock ranchers. Authorities have found animal carcasses injected with restricted pesticides. These carcasses are suspected to have been placed to attract and kill predators such as the bald eagle in an effort to preserve young grazing animals. It appears that the eagle is being threatened again by the consummate predator, humans.

1. One can conclude from this passage that

    (A) the pesticides used are detrimental to the environment.
    (B) the killing of eagles will protect the rancher's rangeland.
    (C) ranchers must obtain licenses to use the pesticides.
    (D) the poisoning could result in the extinction of the bald eagle.

2. The author's attitude is one of

    (A) detached observation.   (C) informed acceptance.
    (B) concerned interest.   (D) unbridled anger.

Questions 3 and 4 refer to the graph below.

Number of Boys and Girls in Scouting in 1989 (in millions)

Source: 1991 Census Bureau's Statistical Abstract of the U.S.

3. In what year was the involvement in scouting closest to being equal between girls and boys?

   (A) 1970
   (B) 1975

   (C) 1980
   (D) 1985

4. How much difference between the number of boys and the number of girls involved in scouting was there (in millions) in 1970?

   (A) 1.6 million
   (B) .9 million

   (C) 1.5 million
   (D) 2.4 million

5. The disparaging remarks about her performance on the job made Alice uncomfortable. The word "disparaging" is closest in meaning to

   (A) complimentary.
   (B) evil.

   (C) technical.
   (D) insulting.

Questions 6 to 8 refer to the following passage:

INSTRUCTIONS FOR ABSENTEE VOTING

   These instructions describe conditions under which voters may register for or request absentee ballots to vote in the November 2, 2004, election.

   (1) If you moved on or prior to October 5, 2004, and did not register to vote at your new address, you are not eligible to vote in this election.
   (2) If you move after this date, you may vote via absentee ballot or at your polling place, using your previous address as your address of registration for this election.
   (3) You must register at your new address to vote in future elections.
   (4) The last day to request an absentee ballot is October 28, 2004.
   (5) You must be a registered voter in the county.

(6) You must sign your request in your own handwriting.

(7) You must make a separate request for each election.

(8) The absentee ballot shall be issued to the requesting voter in person or by mail.

6. A voter will be able to participate in the November 2, 2004, election as an absentee if he or she

   (A) requested an absentee ballot on November 1, 2004.
   (B) voted absentee in the last election.
   (C) moved as a registered voter on October 13, 2004.
   (D) moved on October 5, 2004.

7. On October 15, 2004, Mr. Applebee requested an absentee ballot for his daughter, a registered voting college student, to enable her to participate in the election process. Mr. Applebee will most likely need clarification on which of the following instructions?

   (A) 2   (C) 5
   (B) 4   (D) 6

8. Which of the following best describes the most important piece of information for potential voters who want to participate in the election process, either in person or by absentee ballot?

   (A) Do not change precincts.
   (B) Do register to vote in the appropriate precinct.
   (C) You may vote at your nearest polling place.
   (D) The last day to register is always October 28.

Questions 9 and 10 refer to the following statement:

The atrophy and incapacity that occur when a broken bone is encased in plaster and immobilized clearly demonstrate what a sedentary lifestyle can do to the human body.

9. In the passage above, "atrophy and incapacity" refer to

   (A) a strengthened condition brought about by rest.
   (B) a decrease in size and strength.
   (C) a type of exercise.
   (D) rest and recuperation.

10. Which of the following statements does NOT reflect the author's view of sedentary living?

   (A) If you don't use it, you lose it.
   (B) Mobility is affected by lifestyle.
   (C) A sedentary lifestyle is a healthy lifestyle.
   (D) A body is as a body does.

Questions 11 to 15 refer to the following passage:

Frederick Douglass was born Frederick Augustus Washington Bailey in 1817 to a white father and a slave mother. Frederick was raised by his grandmother on a Maryland plantation until he was eight. It was then that he was sent to Baltimore by his owner to be a servant to the Auld family. Mrs. Auld recognized Frederick's intellectual acumen and defied the law of the state by teaching him to read and write. When Mr. Auld warned that education would make the boy unfit for slavery, Frederick sought to continue his education in the streets. When his master died, Frederick was returned to the plantation to work in the fields at age 16. Later, he was hired out to work in the shipyards in Baltimore as a ship caulker. He plotted an escape but was discovered before he could get away. It took five years before he made his way to New York City and then to New Bedford, Massachusetts, eluding slave hunters by changing his name to Douglass.

At an 1841 anti-slavery meeting in Massachusetts, Douglass was invited to give a talk about his experiences under slavery. His impromptu speech was so powerful and so eloquent that it thrust him into a career as an agent for the Massachusetts Anti-Slavery Society.

Douglass wrote his autobiography in 1845 primarily to counter those who doubted his authenticity as a former slave. This work became a classic in American literature and a primary source about slavery from the point of view of a slave. Douglass went on a two-year speaking tour abroad to avoid recapture by his former owner and to win new friends for the abolition movement. He returned with funds to purchase his freedom and to start his own anti-slavery newspaper. He became a consultant to Abraham Lincoln and throughout Reconstruction fought doggedly for full civil rights for freedmen; he also supported the women's rights movement.

11. According to the passage, Douglass's autobiography was motivated by

   (A) the desire to make money for his anti-slavery movement.
   (B) the desire to start a newspaper.
   (C) his interest in authenticating his life as a slave.
   (D) his desire to educate people about slavery.

12. The central idea of the passage is that Frederick Douglass

   (A) was influential in changing the laws regarding the education of slaves.
   (B) was one of the most eminent human rights leaders of the century.
   (C) was a personal friend and confidant to a president.
   (D) wrote a classic in American literature.

13. According to the author of this passage, Mrs. Auld taught Frederick to read because

   (A) Frederick wanted to learn like the other boys.
   (B) she recognized his natural ability.
   (C) he needed to read to work in the home.
   (D) she obeyed her husband's wishes in the matter.

14. The title that best expresses the ideas of this passage is

   (A) The History of the Anti-Slavery Movement.
   (B) The Dogged Determination of Frederick Douglass.
   (C) Frederick Douglass's Contributions to Freedom.
   (D) The Oratorical and Literary Brilliance of Frederick Douglass.

15. In the context of the passage, "impromptu" is closest in meaning to

   (A) unprepared.
   (B) in a quiet manner.
   (C) forceful.
   (D) elaborate.

Question 16 refers to the following passage:

   Acupuncture practitioners, those who use the placement of needles at strategic locations under the skin to block pain, have been tolerated by American physicians since the 1930s. This form of Chinese treatment has been used for about 3,000 years and until recently has been viewed suspiciously by the West. New research indicates that acupuncture might provide relief for sufferers of chronic back pain, arthritis, and, recently, pain experienced by alcoholics and drug users as they kick the habit.

16. According to the passage, acupuncture has been found to help people suffering from all of the following EXCEPT

   (A) recurring back pain.
   (B) alcoholics in withdrawal.
   (C) liver disease.
   (D) drug addicts in withdrawal.

Question 17 refers to the following passage:

   Each time a person opens his or her mouth to eat, he or she makes a nutritional decision. These selections make a definitive difference in how an individual looks, feels, and performs at work or play. When a good assortment of food in appropriate amounts is selected and eaten, the consequences are likely to be desirable levels of health and energy to allow one to be as active as needed. Conversely, when choices are less than desirable, the consequences can be poor health or limited energy or both. Studies of American diets, particularly the diets of the very young, reveal unsatisfactory dietary habits as evidenced by the numbers of overweight and out-of-shape young children.

17. The author's attitude toward Americans' dietary habits may be characterized as

   (A) concerned.
   (B) informational.
   (C) angry.
   (D) amused.

Question 18 refers to the following passage:

   Commercial enterprises frequently provide the backdrop for the birth of a new language. When members of different language communities need to communicate or wish to bargain with each other, they may develop a new language through a process called "pidginization." A pidgin language, or pidgin, never becomes a native language; rather, its use is limited to business transactions with members of other language communities. Pidgins consist of very simple grammatical structures and small vocabularies. They have tended to develop around coastal areas where seafarers first made contact with speakers of other languages.

18. The passage suggests which of the following about pidgins?

   (A) We could expect to hear pidgins along the west coast of Africa and in the Pacific islands.
   (B) Pidgins are located in inland mountain regions.
   (C) Pidgins become the main language after several generations of use.
   (D) Pidgins are the languages of seafarers.

Question 19 refers to the following passage:

There are two ways of measuring mass. One method to determine the mass of a body is to use a beam-balance. By this method, an unknown mass is placed on one pan at the end of a beam. The known masses are added to the pan at the other end of the beam until the pans are balanced. Since the force of gravity is the same on each pan, the masses must also be the same on each pan. When the mass of a body is measured by comparison with known masses on a beam-balance, it is called the gravitational mass of the body.

The second method to determine the mass of a body is distinctly different; this method uses the property of inertia. To determine mass in this way, a mass is placed on a frictionless horizontal surface. When a known force is applied to it, the magnitude of the mass is measured by the amount of acceleration produced upon it by the known force. Mass measured in this way is said to be the inertial mass of the body in question. This method is seldom used because it involves both a frictionless surface and a difficult measurement of acceleration.

19.   Which of the following statements can best be supported from the passage?

   (A)   The gravitational and inertia mass methods measure different properties of the object.
   (B)   The masses are equal when the weights are equal and cause the beam to be balanced.
   (C)   Gravitational and inertial measurements do not give the same numerical value for mass.
   (D)   The mass of a body depends on where it is located in the universe.

Question 20 refers to the following statement:

Her introductory remarks provided a segue into the body of the speech.

20.   In this context the word "segue" means

   (A)   delivery.   (C)   direction.
   (B)   a pause.   (D)   credential.

Questions 21 to 23 refer to the following passage:

One of the many tragedies of the Civil War was the housing and care of prisoners. The Andersonville prison, built by the Confederates in 1864 to accommodate 10,000 Union prisoners, was not completed when prisoners started arriving. Five months later the total number of men incarcerated there had risen to 31,678.

The sounds of death and dying were not diminished by surrender of weapons to a captor. Chances of survival for prisoners in Andersonville were not much better than in the throes of combat. Next to over-crowding, inadequate shelter caused unimaginable suffering. The Confederates were not equipped with the manpower, tools, or supplies necessary to house such a population of captives; prisoners themselves gathered lumber, logs, anything they could find to construct some sort of protection from the elements. Some prisoners dug holes in the ground, risking suffocation from cave-ins, but many hundreds were left exposed to the wind, rain, cold, and heat.

Daily food rations were exhausted by the sheer numbers they had to serve, resulting in severe dietary deficiencies. The overcrowding, meager rations, and deplorable unsanitary conditions resulted in rampant disease and a high mortality rate. The consequences of a small scratch or wound could result in death in Andersonville. During the prison's 13-month existence, more than 12,000 prisoners died and were buried in the Andersonville cemetery. Most of the deaths were caused by diarrhea, dysentery, gangrene, and scurvy that could not be treated due to inadequate staff and supplies.

21. What is the central idea of the passage?

    (A) The prison was never fully completed.
    (B) Prison doctors were ill-equipped to handle emergencies.
    (C) Andersonville prison was not adequate to care for three times as many prisoners as it could hold.
    (D) Many prisoners died as a result of shelter cave-ins.

22. From this passage the author's attitude toward the Confederates is one of

    (A) impartiality.   (C) indifference.
    (B) contempt.   (D) denial.

23. The first sentence of the second paragraph of this passage can best be described as

    (A) a digression.   (C) an exposé.
    (B) a hypothesis.   (D) an irony.

Question 24 refers to the following statement:

Maria commented to Joe, "Ted's nose is out of joint because he wasn't invited to the reception."

24. Someone hearing the conversation would most likely conclude that Ted

    (A) had a swollen nose.
    (B) was upset about not being asked to the reception.
    (C) was not invited to the reception because his nose was hurt.
    (D) had a bandage on his nose at the reception.

Questions 25 to 27 refer to the following passage:

To the Shakers, perfection was found in the creation of an object that was both useful and simple. Their Society was founded in 1774 by Ann Lee, an Englishwoman from the working classes who brought eight followers to New York with her. "Mother Ann" established her religious community on the belief that worldly interests were evil.

To gain entrance into the Society, believers had to remain celibate, have no private possessions, and avoid contact with outsiders. The order came to be called "Shakers" because of the feverish dance the group performed. Another characteristic of the group was the desire to seek perfection in their work.

Shaker furniture was created to exemplify specific characteristics: simplicity of design, quality of craftsmanship, harmony of proportion, and usefulness. While Shakers did not create any innovations in furniture designs, they were known for fine craftsmanship. The major emphasis was on function, and not on excessive or elaborate decorations that contributed nothing to the product's usefulness.

25. The passage indicates that members of the religious order were called the Shakers because

    (A) they shook hands at their meetings.
    (B) they did a shaking dance at their meetings.

(C) they took their name from the founder.

(D) they were named after the township where they originated.

26. Which of the following is the most appropriate substitute for the use of the term "innovations" in the third paragraph?

(A) Corrections

(B) Changes

(C) Functions

(D) Brocades

27. The passage suggests which of the following about the Shakers?

(A) Shakers believed in form over function in their designs.

(B) Shaker furniture has seen a surge in popularity.

(C) Shakers appeared to believe that form follows function.

(D) Shaker furniture is noted for the use of brass hardware.

Questions 28 and 29 refer to the following passage:

James Dean began his career as a stage actor, but in motion pictures he symbolized the confused, restless, and idealistic youth of the 1950s. He excelled at film parts that called for brooding, impulsive characterizations, the personification of frustrated youthful passion. Dean made three such movies: *East of Eden, Rebel Without a Cause,* and *Giant,* and established himself as a cult hero. Tragically, his career was cut short in an automobile crash before the release of *Giant.*

28. One conclusion that could be drawn from this passage is that

(A) James Dean was not well regarded because of the kind of characters he portrayed.

(B) James Dean had to be replaced by another actor in *Giant* due to his death.

(C) James Dean was adept at portraying sensitive, youthful characters.

(D) James Dean was a promising stage actor.

29. The author's attitude is one of

(A) regret.

(B) anger.

(C) pessimism.

(D) indifference.

Questions 30 to 32 refer to the following passage:

Benjamin Franklin began writing his autobiography in 1771, but he set it aside to assist the colonies in gaining independence from England. After a hiatus of 13 years, he returned to chronicle his life, addressing his message to the younger generation. In this significant literary work of early United States, Franklin portrays himself as benign, kindhearted, practical, and hardworking. He established a list of ethical conduct and recorded his transgressions when he was unsuccessful in overcoming temptation. Franklin wrote that he was unable to arrive at perfection, "yet I was, by the endeavor, a better and happier man than I otherwise should have been if I had not attempted it."

30. Which of the following is the LEAST appropriate substitute for the use of the term "ethical" near the end of the passage?

(A) Moral   (C) Virtuous

(B) Depraved   (D) Qualifiable

31. The passage suggests which of the following about Franklin's autobiography?

(A) It was representative of early American literature.
(B) It fell short of being a major work of literary quality.
(C) It personified Franklin as a major political figure.
(D) It was a notable work of early American literature.

32. Which of the following slogans best describes Franklin's assessment of the usefulness of attempting to achieve perfection?

(A) Cleanliness is next to Godliness.
(B) Nothing ventured, nothing gained.
(C) Ambition is its own reward.
(D) Humility is everything.

Questions 33 to 35 refer to the graph below:

How the Average Consumer Spent Money in 2002
Total: $25,893

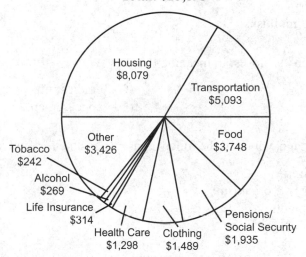

Source: Census Bureau's Statistical Abstract of the U.S.

33. According to the graph, the average consumer spent approximately 50 percent of her/his earnings on

(A) housing and health care costs.
(B) transportation and housing.
(C) food.
(D) transportation and pensions.

34. After transportation, the next greatest amount of money was spent on

(A) clothing.   (C) food.

(B) other.   (D) pensions/social security.

35. According to the graph, expenditure on health care was approximately equal to

(A) clothing.
(B) pensions.
(C) food.
(D) other.

Questions 36 to 38 refer to the following passage:

The scarlet flamingo is practically a symbol of Florida. Once the West Indian flamingo population wintered in Florida Bay and as far north as St. John's River and Tampa Bay, but the brilliantly colored birds abandoned these grounds around 1885 due to the decimation of their numbers by feather hunters. The flock at Hialeah Race Track is descended from a handful of birds imported from Cuba in the 1930s. It took seven years before the first flamingo was born in captivity, but several thousand have since been hatched.

Flamingo raisers found that the birds require a highly specialized diet of shrimps and mollusks to maintain their attractive coloring. It is speculated that hunters as well as the birds' selective breeding habits perhaps caused the disappearance of these beautiful birds from the wild in North America.

36. The central idea of the passage is that the flamingos of Florida

(A) are a symbol of Florida.
(B) are no longer found in the wild in North America.
(C) came from Cuba.
(D) eat shrimps and mollusks.

37. The word "decimation" is closest in meaning to

(A) desecration.
(B) restoration.
(C) eradication.
(D) appeasement.

38. According to the passage, which of the following is responsible for the flamingo's brilliant plumage?

(A) Selective breeding
(B) Their diet of marine organisms
(C) Shallow water plants
(D) Fish and water snakes

Questions 39 and 40 refer to the following passage:

Teachers should be cognizant of the responsibility they have for the development of children's competencies in basic concepts and principles of free speech. Freedom of speech is not merely the utterance of sounds into the air, rather, it is couched in a set of values and legislative processes that have developed over time. These values and processes are a part of our political conscience as Americans. Teachers must provide ample opportunities for children to express themselves effectively in an environment where their opinions are valued. Children should have ownership in the decision-making process in the classroom and should be engaged in activities where alternative resolutions to problems can be explored. Because teachers have such tremendous power to influence in the classroom, they must be careful to refrain from presenting their own values and biases that could "color" their students' belief systems. If we want children to develop their own voices in a free society, then teachers must support participatory democratic experiences in the daily workings of the classroom.

39. The title that best expresses the ideas in the passage is

   (A) The Nature of the Authoritarian Classroom.
   (B) Concepts and Principles of Free Speech.
   (C) Exploring Freedom in American Classrooms.
   (D) Developing Children's Citizenship Competencies.

40. It can be inferred from the passage that instructional strategies that assist children in the development of citizenship competencies include all of the following EXCEPT

   (A) children's participation in rule making.
   (B) fostering self-esteem.
   (C) indoctrination in principles of society.
   (D) consideration of cultural and gender differences.

Subtest II: Mathematics

TIME: 100 Minutes
45 Questions

> <u>DIRECTIONS:</u> **Each of the questions or incomplete statements below is followed by four suggested answers or completions. Select the one that is best in each case.**

1. Simplify the following expression: $6 + 2(x - 4)$.

   (A) $4x - 16$ (C) $2x - 2$
   (B) $2x - 14$ (D) $-24x$

2. Referring to the following figure, if the measure of $\angle C$ is 20° and the measure of $\angle CBD$ is 36°, then what is the measure of $\angle A$?

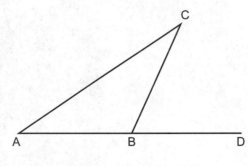

   (A) 16°   (C) 56°
   (B) 20°   (D) 144°

3. If six cans of beans cost $1.50, what is the price of eight cans of beans?

   (A) $.90   (C) $1.60
   (B) $1.00   (D) $2.00

4. Bonnie's average score on three tests is 71. Her first two test scores are 64 and 87. What is her score on test three?

   (A) 62   (C) 74
   (B) 71   (D) 151

5. In the figure below, what is the perimeter of square *ABCD* if diagonal *AC* = 8?

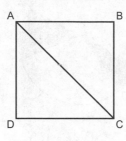

    (A) 32   (C) $4\sqrt{2}$
    (B) 64   (D) $16\sqrt{2}$

6. Three small circles, all the same size, lie inside a large circle as shown below. The diameter *AB* of the large circle passes through the centers of the three small circles. If each of the smaller circles has an area of 9π, what is the circumference of the large circle?

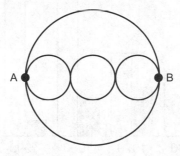

    (A) 9   (C) 18π
    (B) 18   (D) 27π

7. A jar contains 20 balls. These balls are labeled 1 through 20. What is the probability that a ball chosen from the jar has a number on it which is divisible by 4?

    (A) $\dfrac{1}{20}$ (C) $\dfrac{1}{4}$

    (B) $\dfrac{1}{5}$ (D) 5

8. If $2x^2 + 5x - 3 = 0$ and $x > 0$, then what is the value of *x*?

    (A) $-\dfrac{1}{2}$ (C) 1

    (B) $\dfrac{1}{2}$ (D) $\dfrac{3}{2}$

9. The center of the following circle is the point *O*. What percentage of the circle is shaded if the measure of arc *AB* is 65° and the measure of arc *CD* is 21.4°?

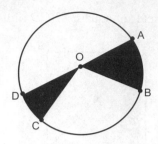

(A) 86.4%   (C) 27.4%

(B) 43.6%   (D) 24%

10. According to the following chart, in what year was the total sales of Brand X televisions the greatest?

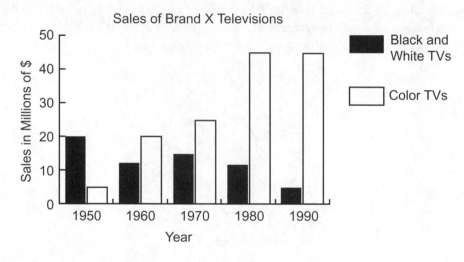

(A) 1960   (C) 1980

(B) 1970   (D) 1990

11. How many odd prime numbers are there between 1 and 20?

(A) 7   (C) 9

(B) 8   (D) 10

12. Two concentric circles are shown in the figure below. The smaller circle has radius $OA = 4$ and the larger circle has radius $OB = 6$. Find the area of the shaded region.

(A) 4π (C) 20π
(B) 16π (D) 36π

13. Solve the following inequality for x: $8 - 2x \leq 10$.

(A) $x \leq 1$ (C) $x \geq -1$

(B) $x \leq -1$ (D) $x \leq \dfrac{5}{3}$

14. Calculate the expression shown below and write the answer in scientific notation.
     0.003×1.25

(A) 0.375×10^{-2} (C) 3.75×10^{-3}
(B) 0.375×10^{2} (D) 3.75×10^{3}

15. In the figure below $l_1 \parallel l_2$, ΔRTS is an isosceles triangle, and the measure of $\angle T = 80°$. Find the measure of $\angle OPR$.

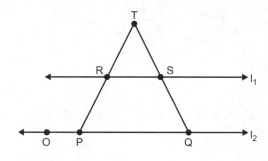

(A) $50°$ (C) $105°$
(B) $80°$ (D) $130°$

16. What is the midpoint of $\overline{MN}$ in the figure below?

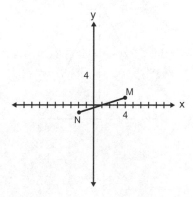

(A) $(-4, 2)$ (C) $(1, 0)$

(B) $\left(-\dfrac{3}{2}, 1\right)$ (D) $\left(-\dfrac{1}{2}, 1\right)$

17. The ratio of men to women at University X is 3:7. If there are 6,153 women at University X, how many men are at University X?

    (A) 879

    (B) 1,895

    (C) 2,051

    (D) 2,637

18. Find the slope of the line passing through the points W and Z in the following figure.

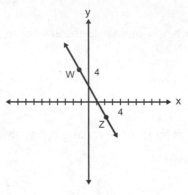

    (A) $-\dfrac{1}{2}$

    (B) $\dfrac{1}{4}$

    (C) -2

    (D) 2

19. Linda bought a jacket on sale at a 25 percent discount. If she paid $54 for the jacket, what was the original price of the jacket?

    (A) $72.00

    (B) $67.50

    (C) $40.50

    (D) $36.00

20. Assume that $\triangle ABC$ below is an equilateral triangle. If $CD \perp AB$ and $CD = 6$, what is the area of $\triangle ABC$?

    (A) $3\sqrt{3}$

    (B) 12

    (C) $12\sqrt{3}$

    (D) 36

21. The formula relating the Celsius (C) and the Fahrenheit (F) scales of temperature is shown below. Find the temperature in the Celsius scale when the temperature is 86° F.

$$F = \frac{9}{5}C + 32$$

(A) 25°   (C) 105°
(B) 30°   (D) 124.6°

22. In the number 72104.58, what is the place value of the 2?

(A) Thousands   (C) Tenths
(B) Ten thousands   (D) Thousandths

23. Mrs. Wall has $300,000. She wishes to give each of her six children an equal amount of her money. Which of the following methods will result in the amount that each child is to receive?

(A) 6 × 300,000   (C) 300,000 ÷ 6
(B) 6 ÷ 300,000   (D) 300,000 − 6

24. Referring to the figure below, what is the length of $\overline{PQ}$?

(A) $2\sqrt{5}$ (C) 5
(B) $5\sqrt{2}$ (D) 7

25. Bob wants to bake some cupcakes. His recipe uses 2²/₃ cups of flour to produce 36 cupcakes. How many cups of flour should Bob use to bake 12 cupcakes?

(A) $\dfrac{1}{3}$ (C) $1\dfrac{2}{9}$

(B) $\dfrac{8}{9}$ (D) $1\dfrac{2}{3}$

26. The area of rectangle *EFGH* below is 120 and $\overline{EF}$ is twice as long as $\overline{EH}$. Which of the following is the best approximation of the length of $\overline{EH}$?

(A) 7   (C) 10
(B) 8   (D) 12

27. Ricky drove from Town A to Town B in 3 hours. His return trip from Town B to Town A took 5 hours because he drove 15 miles per hour slower on the return trip. How fast did Ricky drive on the trip from Town A to Town B?

    (A) 25.5 mph
    (B) 32 mph
    (C) 37.5 mph
    (D) 45 mph

28. Which of the following inequalities represents the shaded region in the figure below?

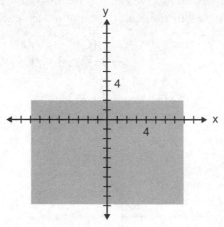

    (A) $x \geq 2$
    (B) $x \leq 2$
    (C) $y \geq 2$
    (D) $y \leq 2$

29. Given that $x, y,$ and z are any real numbers, which of the following statements are true?
    I.   If $x > y$, then $x^2 > y^2$.
    II.   If $x > y$, then $x + z > y + z$.
    III. If $x > y$, then $x - y > 0$.
    IV.   If $x > y$, then $xz > yz$.

    (A) II and III only
    (B) II and IV only
    (C) I, II, and III only
    (D) II, III, and IV only

30. Round the following number to the nearest hundredths place: 287.416.

    (A) 300
    (B) 290
    (C) 287.41
    (D) 287.42

31. Simplify the following expression.

    $$\frac{x^2 \times x^7}{x}$$

    (A) x^6
    (B) x^7
    (C) x^8
    (D) x^{10}

32. List the fractions shown below from least to greatest.

    $$\frac{1}{9}, \frac{2}{15}, \frac{3}{21}$$

(A) $\dfrac{1}{9}, \dfrac{2}{15}, \dfrac{3}{21}$ (C) $\dfrac{1}{9}, \dfrac{3}{21}, \dfrac{2}{15}$

(B) $\dfrac{3}{21}, \dfrac{1}{9}, \dfrac{2}{15}$ (D) $\dfrac{2}{15}, \dfrac{1}{9}, \dfrac{3}{21}$

33. A rectangular box with a square base is shown below. If the volume of the box is 256 cubic feet and the height of the box is one-half the length of a side of the base, find the height of the box.

(A) 4 feet   (C) 8 feet
(B) 6 feet   (D) 10 feet

34. If $x = -3$, then find the value of $-x^2 + 2x$.

(A) -15 (C) 3
(B) -3 (D) 15

35. If $a = b^3$ and $a = \dfrac{1}{8}$, what is the value of b?

(A) $\dfrac{1}{512}$ (C) $\dfrac{1}{2}$

(B) $\dfrac{3}{8}$ (D) $\dfrac{3}{2}$

36. In a barn there were cows and people. If we counted 30 heads and 104 legs in the barn, how many cows and how many people were in the barn?

(A) 16 cows and 14 people   (C) 22 cows and 8 people
(B) 18 cows and 16 people   (D) 24 cows and 4 people

37. Solve for x in the following proportion.

$$\dfrac{12}{x-1} = \dfrac{5}{6}$$

(A) 14.6   (C) 16.6
(B) 15.4   (D) 16.8

38. If two lines, l_1 and l_2, which lie in the same plane, are both perpendicular to a third line, l_3, in the same plane as the first two, what do you definitely know about l_1 and l_2?

    (A) l_1 and l_2 are perpendicular.   (C) l_1 and l_2 intersect.
    (B) l_1 and l_2 are parallel.   (D) l_1 and l_2 are skew.

39. What is $\frac{1}{2} + \frac{1}{3}$?

    (A) $\dfrac{1}{5}$ (C) $\dfrac{2}{6}$

    (B) $\dfrac{2}{5}$ (D) $\dfrac{5}{6}$

40. Given that $\overline{BC} \parallel \overline{DE}$ in the following figure, write down the pair of similar (~) triangles.

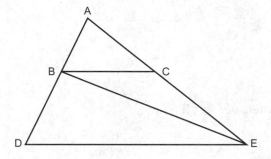

    (A) $\triangle ABC \sim \triangle ADE$ (C) $\triangle ABC \sim \triangle AED$
    (B) $\triangle ABC \sim \triangle ABE$ (D) $\triangle BCE \sim \triangle BAC$

41. The cost of gas heating a house in Riverview, Florida, is $1.83 per cubic foot. What is the monthly gas bill if the customer uses 145 cubic feet?

    (A) $265.35   (C) $183.00
    (B) $145.00   (D) $79.23

42. Which of the following figures below represent simple closed curves?

    a   b   c   d   e

    (A) a and b   (C) c and d
    (B) a, b, and c   (D) d and e

43. The wear-out mileage of a certain tire is normally distributed with a mean of 30,000 miles and a standard deviation of 2,500 miles, as shown below. What is the percentage of tires that will last at least 30,000 miles?

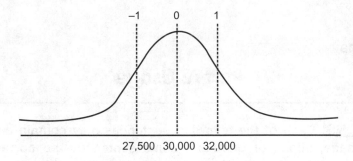

27,500 30,000 32,000

(A) 40%   (C) 50%
(B) 45%   (D) 55%

44. How many lines of symmetry, if any, does the following figure have?

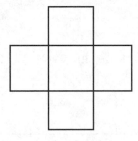

(A) 1   (C) 3
(B) 2   (D) 4

45. Suppose a person 2 m tall casts a shadow 1 m long when a tree has an 8 m shadow. How high is the tree?

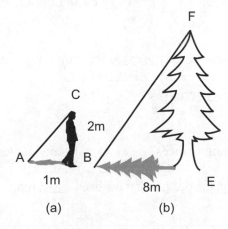

(A) 8 m   (C) 14 m
(B) 10 m   (D) 16 m

Subtest III: English Language Skills

TIME: 40 Minutes
40 Questions

Part A: Usage

<u>DIRECTIONS:</u> Each of the following sentences may contain an error in diction, usage, idiom, or grammar. Some sentences are correct. Some sentences contain one error. No sentence contains more than one error.

If there is an error, it will appear in one of the underlined portions labeled A, B, or C. If there is no error, choose the portion labeled D. If there is an error, select the letter of the portion that must be changed in order to correct the sentence.

<u>EXAMPLE:</u>

He drove <u>slowly</u> and <u>cautiously</u> in order to <u>hopefully</u> avoid having an
       A   **B**   **C**
accident. <u>No error</u>.
      D   Ⓐ Ⓑ ● Ⓓ

1. In 1877 Chief Joseph of the Nez Perces, <u>together with</u> 250 warriors and 500 women and children,
                                                    A
<u>were praised</u> by newspaper reporters for bravery during the 115-day fight <u>for</u> freedom. <u>No error</u>.
   B   **C**   **D**

2. The ideals <u>upon which</u> American society <u>is based</u> <u>are</u> primarily those of Europe and not ones derived
               A   **B** **C**
from the native Indian culture. <u>No error</u>.
                        D

3. <u>An astute and powerful</u> woman, Frances Nadel <u>was</u> a beauty contest winner before she became
        A   **B**
president of the company <u>upon the death</u> of her husband. <u>No error</u>.
                     C   **D**

4. Representative Wilson pointed out, however, that the legislature <u>had not finalized</u> the state budget
                                                  A
and salary increases <u>had depended</u> on decisions <u>to be made</u> in a special session. <u>No error</u>.
           B   **C**   **D**

5. Now the city librarian, doing more than checking out books, must help to plan puppet shows and
                                                                          A

   movies for children, garage sales for used books, and arranging for guest lecturers and exhibits for
                                                           B   **C**

   adults. No error.
           D

6. In order to completely understand the psychological effects of the bubonic plague, one must realize
              A   **B**

   that one-fourth to one-third of the population in an affected area died. No error.
                                                        C   D

7. Rural roads, known in the United States as farm to market roads, have always been a vital link in
                                                                                               A

   the economy of more advanced nations because transportation of goods to markets is essential.
                      B   **C**

   No error.
   D

8. Many a graduate wishes to return to college and abide in the protected environment of a university,
   A   **B**

   particularly if someone else pays the bills. No error.
                   C   **D**

9. Confronted with a choice of either cleaning up his room or cleaning out the garage, the teenager
   A   **B**

   became very aggravated with his parents. No error.
                C   **D**

10. My brother and I dressed as quickly as we could, but we missed the school bus, which made us late
                    A   **B**   **C**

    for class today. No error.
                     D

11. Among the activities offered at the local high school through the community education program are
    A   **B**   **C**

    singing in the couples' chorus, ballroom dancing, and Chinese cooking. No error.
                                                                           D

12. If you are disappointed by an inexpensive bicycle, then an option you might consider is to work this
                A

    summer and save your money for a more expensive model. No error.
              B   **C**   **D**

13. Also being presented to the city council this morning <u>is</u> the mayor's city budget for next year and
                      A
    plans to renovate the <u>existing</u> music theater, so the session <u>will focus</u> on financial matters. <u>No error</u>.
          B   **C**   **D**

14. Even a movement <u>so delicate</u> as a <u>fly's walking</u> triggers the Venus flytrap to grow extra cells on the
                    A   **B**
    outside of <u>its</u> hinge, immediately closing the petals of the trap. <u>No error</u>.
           C   **D**

15. Although outwardly Thomas Hardy seemed quite <u>the picture</u> of <u>respectability</u> and contentment, his
                                    A   **B**
    works, especially the prose, <u>deals with</u> the theme of man's inevitable suffering. <u>No error</u>.
                   C   **D**

16. Though unequal in social standing, the everyday lives of ancient Egyptian kings and commoners
    <u>alike</u> are visible in the pictures of <u>them</u> found <u>inside of</u> tombs and temples. <u>No error</u>.
    A   **B**   **C**   **D**

17. Sometimes considered <u>unsafe for</u> crops, land around river deltas <u>can be</u> excellent land for farming
                   A   **B**
    because periodic flooding deposits silt rich <u>in</u> nutrients. <u>No error</u>.
                            C   **D**

18. For years, people concerned with the environment <u>have compiled</u> information that <u>show</u> many
                               A   **B**
    species are extinct and others <u>are either</u> endangered or bordering on becoming endangered. <u>No error</u>.
                       C   **D**

19. Little is known about Shakespeare's boyhood or his early career as an actor and playwright, but he
    <u>appears to have been</u> a financial success because he bought many properties, including <u>one of the finest</u>
    A   **B**
    homes in Stratford, the town he <u>was born in</u>. <u>No error</u>.
                      C   **D**

20. *Scared Straight*, a program designed <u>to inhibit</u> criminal behavior in juvenile offenders <u>who</u> seemed
                               A   **B**
    bound for prison as adults, had a significant <u>affect</u> on the youngsters. <u>No error</u>.
                              C   **D**

21. The average American tourist feels <u>quite</u> at home in a Japanese stadium filled <u>at capacity</u> with sports
                               A   **B**
    fans watching Japan's <u>most</u> popular sport, baseball. <u>No error</u>.
                      C   **D**

22. My brother is engaged to a woman <u>who</u> my parents <u>have</u> not met because she has not yet
          A   B
<u>emigrated from</u> her native country of Ecuador. <u>No error</u>.
      C   D

23. Colonel Jones <u>denies that</u> he illegally delivered funds to a foreign government agent or that <u>he</u> was
              A   B
involved in <u>any other</u> covert activity. <u>No error</u>.
          C   D

24. In the United States, <u>testing for</u> toxicity, determining the proper dose and timing between doses, and
                    A
evaluating the vaccine for <u>effectiveness</u> <u>is</u> the method used in researching new drugs. <u>No error</u>.
                  B   C   D

25. George wants <u>to know if</u> <u>it is her</u> driving that expensive red sports car at a rate of speed
              A   B
<u>obviously exceeding</u> the posted speed limit. <u>No error</u>.
          C   D

Part B: Sentence Correction

<u>DIRECTIONS:</u> In each of the following sentences, some portion of the sentence is underlined. Under each sentence are four choices. The first choice has the same wording as the original. The other three choices are reworded. Sometimes the first choice containing the original wording is the best; sometimes one of the other choices is the best. Choose the letter of the best choice. Your choice should produce a sentence which is not ambiguous or awkward and which is correct, clear, and precise.

This is a test of correct and effective English expression. Keep in mind the standards of English usage, punctuation, grammar, word choice, and construction.

<u>EXAMPLE:</u>

When you listen to opera, <u>a person may not appreciate it</u>.

    (A) a person may not appreciate it.
    (B) it may not be appreciated by a person.
    (C) you may not appreciate it.
    (D) appreciating it may be a problem for you.

26. <u>Being that you bring home more money than I do</u>, it is only fitting you should pay proportionately more rent.

    (A) Being that you bring home more money than I do
    (B) When more money is made by you than by me
    (C) Because you bring home more money than I do
    (D) If your bringing home more money than me

27. So tenacious is their grip on life, that sponge cells will regroup and form a new sponge even <u>when they are</u> squeezed through silk.

    (A) when they are
    (B) as they will be
    (C) after they have been
    (D) because they should be

28. <u>Seeing as how the plane is late</u>, wouldn't you prefer to wait for a while on the observation deck?

    (A) Seeing as how the plane is late
    (B) When the plane comes in
    (C) Since the plane is late
    (D) Being as the plane is late

29. Only with careful environmental planning can we protect the <u>world we live in</u>.

    (A) world we live in
    (B) world in which we live in
    (C) living in this world
    (D) world in which we live

30. In the last three years we have added more varieties of vegetables to our garden <u>than those you suggested in the beginning</u>.

    (A) than those you suggested in the beginning
    (B) than the ones we began with
    (C) beginning with your suggestion
    (D) which you suggested in the beginning

31. As you know, I am not easily fooled by flattery, and while <u>nice words please you</u>, they don't get the job done.

    (A) nice words please you
    (B) nice words are pleasing
    (C) nice words please a person
    (D) flattering words please people

32. Some pieces of the puzzle, in spite of Jane's search, <u>are still missing and probably will never be found</u>.

    (A) are still missing and probably will never be found
    (B) is missing still but never found probably
    (C) probably will be missing and never found
    (D) are still probably missing and to never be found

33. *Gone With the Wind* <u>is the kind of a movie</u> producers would like to release because it would bring them fame.

    (A) is the kind of a movie   (C) is the kind of movie
    (B) is the sort of movie   (D) is the category of movie

34. Eighteenth-century architecture, with its columns and balanced lines, <u>was characteristic of those of previous times in Greece and Rome</u>.

    (A) was characteristic of those of previous times in Greece and Rome
    (B) is similar to characteristics of Greece and Rome
    (C) is similar to Greek and Roman building styles
    (D) was similar to architecture of Greece and Rome

35. Plato, one of the famous Greek philosophers, won many wrestling prizes when he was a young man, thus <u>exemplifying the Greek ideal of balance between the necessity for physical activity and using one's mind</u>.

(A) exemplifying the Greek ideal of balance between the necessity for physical activity and using one's mind

(B) serving as an example of the Greek ideal of balance between physical and mental activities

(C) an example of balancing Greek mental and athletic games

(D) this as an example of the Greek's balance between mental physical pursuits

36. Allied control of the Philippine Islands during World War II proved to be <u>another obstacle as the Japanese scattered resistance</u> until the end of the war.

(A) another obstacle as the Japanese scattered resistance

(B) difficult because of the Japanese giving resistance

(C) as another scattered obstacle due to Japanese resistance

(D) difficult because the Japanese gave scattered resistance

37. Flooding abated and the river waters receded as the <u>rainfall finally let up</u>.

(A) rainfall finally let up

(B) rain having let up

(C) rainfall, when it finally let up

(D) raining finally letting up

38. Unless China slows its population growth to zero, that country <u>would still have</u> a problem feeding its people.

(A) would still have

(B) might have had still

(C) will still have

(D) would have still

39. In *The Music Man*, Robert Preston portrays a fast-talking salesman who comes to a small town in Iowa <u>inadvertently falling in love with</u> the librarian.

(A) inadvertently falling in love with

(B) and inadvertently falls in love with

(C) afterwards he inadvertently falls in love with

(D) when he inadvertently falls in love with

40. Many naturalists have a reverence for the woods and wildlife, <u>which exhibits itself through their</u> writings or paintings.

(A) which exhibits itself through their

(B) and this exhibits itself through their

(C) and exhibiting itself in

(D) when they produce

Subtest IV: Essay

TIME: 50 Minutes

DIRECTIONS: Two topics are presented below. Select one of the topics as the basis for your essay. READ THE TOPICS VERY CAREFULLY TO MAKE SURE YOU KNOW WHAT YOU ARE BEING ASKED TO DO.

TOPIC 1:

In the twentieth century, the concept of heroism is dead. Do you agree or disagree with the statement? Support your opinion with specific examples from history, current events, literature, or personal experience.

OR

TOPIC 2:

Television often causes the viewer to lose touch with reality and become completely passive and unaware. Like other addictions, television provides a pleasurable escape route from action to inaction. Do you agree or disagree with these statements? Support your opinion with specific examples from history, current events, literature, or personal experience.

Practice Test 1

ANSWER KEY

Subtest I — Reading

1.	(D)	11.	(C)	21.	(C)	31.	(D)
2.	(B)	12.	(B)	22.	(A)	32.	(B)
3.	(C)	13.	(B)	23.	(D)	33.	(B)
4.	(C)	14.	(C)	24.	(B)	34.	(C)
5.	(D)	15.	(A)	25.	(B)	35.	(A)
6.	(C)	16.	(C)	26.	(B)	36.	(B)
7.	(D)	17.	(A)	27.	(C)	37.	(C)
8.	(B)	18.	(A)	28.	(C)	38.	(B)
9.	(B)	19.	(B)	29.	(A)	39.	(D)
10.	(C)	20.	(C)	30.	(B)	40.	(C)

Subtest II — Mathematics

1.	(C)	13.	(C)	25.	(B)	37.	(B)
2.	(A)	14.	(C)	26.	(B)	38.	(B)
3.	(D)	15.	(D)	27.	(C)	39.	(D)
4.	(A)	16.	(C)	28.	(D)	40.	(A)
5.	(D)	17.	(D)	29.	(A)	41.	(A)
6.	(C)	18.	(C)	30.	(D)	42.	(A)
7.	(C)	19.	(A)	31.	(C)	43.	(C)
8.	(B)	20.	(C)	32.	(A)	44.	(D)
9.	(D)	21.	(B)	33.	(A)	45.	(D)
10.	(C)	22.	(A)	34.	(A)		
11.	(A)	23.	(C)	35.	(C)		
12.	(C)	24.	(C)	36.	(C)		

Subtest III — English Language Skills

1.	(B)	11.	(D)	21.	(B)	31.	(B)
2.	(D)	12.	(A)	22.	(A)	32.	(A)
3.	(B)	13.	(A)	23.	(B)	33.	(C)
4.	(B)	14.	(A)	24.	(D)	34.	(D)
5.	(C)	15.	(C)	25.	(B)	35.	(B)
6.	(A)	16.	(C)	26.	(C)	36.	(D)
7.	(B)	17.	(D)	27.	(C)	37.	(A)
8.	(D)	18.	(B)	28.	(C)	38.	(C)
9.	(C)	19.	(C)	29.	(D)	39.	(B)
10.	(B)	20.	(C)	30.	(A)	40.	(B)

Detailed Explanations of Answers

Subtest I: Reading

1. **(D)**

   It is implied that the poisoning of animal carcasses in the habitat of bald eagles presents a new danger of extinction for America's symbol. Choices (A) and (C) are not mentioned in the passage. Choice (B) suggests a reason for the poisoning; however, the overall focus of the passage does not support this.

2. **(B)**

   The author's use of words such as "mighty bald eagle" and "threatened by a new menace" supports concern for the topic. Therefore, choices (A) and (C) are not applicable. The author appears for the most part to be objective. Choice (D) is too strong to be correct.

3. **(C)**

   In 1980, the difference between the numbers of boys and girls in scouting was .9 million. This represents the closest margin, the largest being 1.6 in 1985.

4. **(C)**

   In 1970, the difference between the numbers of boys and girls in scouting was 1.5 million.

5. **(D)**

   If Alice is uncomfortable with remarks about her performance on the job, it could mean either that the remarks were unkind or that compliments might lead to embarrassment. However, the prefix "dis" means to take away or not. In this instance then, we can assume that the remarks were not complimentary, choice (A). Nothing in the text indicates that the remarks were evil or technical, choices (B) and (C).

6. **(C)**

   Choice (C) fulfills requirements stated in rules 2 and 4 of the instructions for absentee voting. All other choices do not.

7. **(D)**

Mr. Applebee's daughter must sign her own request for an absentee ballot. Since the passage indicates that she is registered, the most important instruction for her is number 6, choice (D).

8. **(B)**

Choices (A) and (D) are not stated in the passage. Choice (C) is not true unless voters have registered, choice (B).

9. **(B)**

Atrophy and incapacity mean to experience a decrease in size and strength.

10. **(C)**

The passage associates loss of mobility with a sedentary lifestyle.

11. **(C)**

Douglass was interested in raising social consciousness about slavery. The passage stresses his interest in refuting those who doubted his claim to have been a slave.

12. **(B)**

Choice (A) is not supported by the text. All other choices, while true, are irrelevant to the question.

13. **(B)**

This choice is supported by the statement, "Mrs. Auld recognized Frederick's intellectual acumen . . ." Choice (D) contradicts information in the passage. The passage does not support choices (A) and (C).

14. **(C)**

Choices (A) and (B) are either too broad or too general. Choice (D) is too specific and limited to cover the information in the passage.

15. **(A)**

An "impromptu" speech is one given suddenly without preparation.

16. **(C)**

    All other choices are mentioned as providing relief from pain.

17. **(A)**

    Use of terms "good," "consequences," and "desirable" indicate a concern for a healthy diet. Choice (B) contradicts the author's attitude. Choices (C) and (D) are not supported by the text.

18. **(A)**

    Choices (B) and (C) are contradicted in the passage, and choice (D) is not relevant.

19. **(B)**

    All other choices are not supported in the text.

20. **(C)**

    A "segue" provides a direction or lead into the speech.

21. **(C)**

    The passage states that housing of prisoners was "one of the many tragedies of the Civil War," and that "overcrowding, meager rations . . . resulted in rampant disease and a high mortality rate," implying that the prison facility was inadequate for the number of prisoners. All other choices are discussed, but the main issue was overcrowded conditions.

22. **(A)**

    The author emphasizes a lack of supplies and manpower to care for the prisoners, not a lack of interest in doing so by the Confederates. Hence, choices (B), (C), and (D) are not appropriate.

23. **(D)**

    An irony is a result that is the opposite of what might be expected or appropriate. The passage implies that being captured was not a guarantee of survival in Andersonville. This choice is supported by the second sentence of the second paragraph.

24. **(B)**

    The figure of speech "his or her nose is out of joint" is an expression used to indicate that someone feels slighted. It has nothing to do with the condition of someone's nose.

25. **(B)**

   This choice is supported by the second paragraph of the passage. All other choices are irrelevant to information in the passage.

26. **(B)**

   "Innovations" means changes or new features that have been introduced.

27. **(C)**

   The passage discusses the importance of usefulness as well as simplicity to the Shakers; therefore, the function of the piece of furniture would be more important than the particular form. Choices (A) and (D) are contradictory to the information given, while choice (B) is beyond information given in the text.

28. **(C)**

   The passage states that Dean "symbolized the confused, restless, and idealistic youth," which implies that he was adept at portraying sensitive, youthful characters. Choices (A) and (B) are contradictory to information in the text. Choice (D) is a conclusion not supported by the text.

29. **(A)**

   The author's use of the word "tragically" in reference to Dean's death indicates a feeling of regret.

30. **(B)**

   Depraved means corrupted or perverted. All other choices have to do with accepted standards of conduct.

31. **(D)**

   The author states that Franklin's work was a "significant literary work of early United States." Each of the other choices is not supported by the text.

32. **(B)**

   The final sentence of the paragraph supports this choice. Choice (C) might apply, but choice (B) is closest to the overall mood of the passage. Choices (A) and (E) are not relevant to the question.

33. **(B)**

   Transportation and housing total about half of the $25,892.

34. **(C)**

According to the graph, food is next after transportation in amount of expense paid by the consumer.

35. **(A)**

According to the graph, health care was closest to clothing in total amount spent.

36. **(B)**

The author's use of the word "decimation" as well as the last sentence in the second paragraph supports this choice. All other choices are secondary to the central idea of the passage.

37. **(C)**

"Decimation" is the eradication or destruction of a large part of something.

38. **(B)**

This choice is supported by the first sentence of the second paragraph. All other choices are irrelevant to the discussion of the flamingo's plumage.

39. **(D)**

The first and last sentences of the passage support this choice. Choice (A) contradicts information in the passage, and choices (B) and (C) are too broad in nature and go beyond the scope of the passage.

40. **(C)**

Reviewing the author's discussion of developing children's citizenship competencies, we may conclude that indoctrination is contradictory to information given in the passage.

Subtest II: Mathematics

NOTATION: $m\angle PQR$ will represent "the measure of angle PQR."

1.   **(C)**

When simplifying algebraic expressions, always work from left to right. First perform all multiplications and divisions; then, once this is done, start again from the left and do all additions and subtractions.

SUGGESTION: It can be helpful to translate the algebraic statement to English. For example, $6 + 2\,(x - 4)$ is "six plus two *times* the quantity x minus 4." The word *times* indicates multiplication, so we must first perform $2(x - 4)$ by using the *distributive property* $a(b - c) = ab - ac$:

$$6 + 2(x - 4) = 6 + 2 \times x - 2 \times 4 = 6 + 2x - 8.$$

Then we perform the subtraction to combine the terms 6 and 8:

$$6 + 2x - 8 = 2x + (6 - 8) = 2x - 2.$$

Note that we did not combine the $2x$ term with the other terms. This is because they are not *like terms*. Like terms are terms that have the same variables (with the same exponents). Since the terms 6 and 8 have no variable x, they are not like terms with $2x$.

2.   **(A)**

The sum of the measures of the interior angles of a triangle is 180º, therefore;

$$\angle A + m\angle ABC + m\angle C = 180°.$$

We also know that $m\angle C = 20°$, so if we substitute this into the previous equation we have

$$m\angle A + m\angle ABC + 20° = 180°.$$

Subtracting 20° from both sides of this equation gives us

$$m\angle A + m\angle ABC = 160°$$

or $m\angle A = 160° - m\angle ABC.$

Therefore, if we know $m\angle ABC$, we are done! To find $m\angle ABC$, notice that $\angle ABD$ is a straight angle and, thus, $m\angle ABD = 180°$. But

$$m\angle ABC + m\angle CBD = m\angle ABD.$$

So, using the facts that

$$m\angle CBD = 36° \text{ and } m\angle ABD = 180°,$$

and substituting, we have

$$m\angle ABC + 36° = 180°$$

or $m\angle ABC = 180° - 36° = 144°.$

Hence, $m\angle A = 160° - m\angle ABC = 160° - 144° = 16°.$

3.   **(D)**

Let x be the cost of one can of beans. Then $6x$ is the cost of six cans of beans. So $6x = \$1.50$. Dividing both sides of the equation by 6, we get $x = \$.25$ and, hence, since $8x$ is the cost of eight cans of beans, we have

$$8x = 8 \times \$.25 = \$2.00.$$

4.   **(A)**

Let t_1, t_2, and t_3 represent Bonnie's scores on tests one, two, and three, respectively. Then the equation representing Bonnie's average score is

$$\frac{t_1 + t_2 + t_3}{3} = 71.$$

We know that $t_1 = 64$ and $t_2 = 87$. Substitute this information into the equation above:

$$\frac{64 + 87 + t_3}{3} = 71$$

Combining 64 and 87 and then multiplying both sides of the equation by 3 gives us

$$3 \times \frac{151 + t_3}{3} = 3 \times 71$$

or $151 + t_3 = 213.$

Now subtract 151 from both sides of the equation so that

$$t_3 = 213 - 151 = 62.$$

5.   **(D)**

Let s be the length of each side of square $ABCD$. Since triangle ADC is a right triangle, we can use the Pythagorean Theorem to solve for s. We have

$$AD^2 + DC^2 = AC^2$$

or $s^2 + s^2 = 8^2.$

Simplifying the equation, we get: $2s^2 = 64$. Now divide both sides of the equation by two:

$$s^2 = 32 \text{ so } s = \sqrt{32} = \sqrt{16} \times \sqrt{2} = 4\sqrt{2}.$$

Therefore, the perimeter of square $ABCD$ is

$$P = 4s = 4 \times 4\sqrt{2} = 16\sqrt{2}.$$

6.   **(C)**

Let r be the length of the radius of each of the small circles and let R be the length of the radius of the large circle. Then, $R = 3r$. The area of each of the small circles is $\pi r^2 = 9\pi$. Now divide both sides of the equation by π:

$$r^2 = 9 \rightarrow r = 3.$$

Then, $R = 3r = 3 \times 3 = 9$.

Therefore, the circumference of the large circle is

$$C = 2\pi R = 2\pi \times 9 = 18\pi.$$

7. **(C)**

Note that the numbers 4, 8, 12, 16, and 20 are the only numbers from 1 through 20 that are divisible by 4. The probability that a ball chosen from the jar has a number on it which is divisible by 4 is given by

$$\frac{\text{total number of balls with numbers that are divisible by 4}}{\text{total number of possible outcomes}} = \frac{5}{20} = \frac{1}{4}$$

8. **(B)**

To solve the equation

$$2x^2 + 5x - 3 = 0,$$

we can factor the left side of the equation to get

$$(2x - 1)(x + 3) = 0.$$

Then use the following rule (this rule is sometimes called the Zero Product Property): If $a \times b = 0$, then either $a = 0$ or $b = 0$. Applying this to our problem gives us

$$2x - 1 = 0 \text{ or } x + 3 = 0.$$

Solve these two equations:

$$2x - 1 = 0 \rightarrow 2x = 1 \rightarrow x = \frac{1}{2} \text{ or } x + 3 = 0 \rightarrow x = -3.$$

But $x > 0$, so $x = \frac{1}{2}$.

9. **(D)**

$\angle AOB$ and $\angle COD$ are central angles, meaning that their vertices are at the center of a circle. The measure of a central angle is equal to the measure of its intercepted arc. Hence, since arc AB and arc CD are the intercepted arcs of $\angle AOB$ and $\angle COD$, respectively, $m\angle AOB = 65°$ and $m\angle COD = 21.4°$. So,

$$m\angle AOB + m\angle COD = 86.4°.$$

Therefore, since one revolution of a circle is 360°, the shaded portion of the circle is represented by the following:

$$\frac{86.4}{360} = 0.24 = 24\%.$$

10. (C)

First find the total sales for each year by reading the graph for the sales of (i) black and white televisions and (ii) color televisions. Then combine these numbers:

1950	$20,000,000 + $5,000,000 = $25,000,000
1960	$10,000,000 + $20,000,000 = $30,000,000
1970	$15,000,000 + $25,000,000 = $40,000,000
1980	$10,000,000 + $45,000,000 = $55,000,000
1990	$5,000,000 + $45,000,000 = $50,000,000

The greatest total sales occurred in 1980.

11. (A)

A prime number is an integer which is greater than one and which has no integer divisors other than 1 and itself. So, the prime numbers between 1 and 20 (not including 1 and 20) are: 2, 3, 5, 7, 11, 13, 17, 19. But 2 is not an odd number, so the odd primes between 1 and 20 are: 3, 5, 7, 11, 13, 17, 19. Hence, there are seven odd primes between 1 and 20.

12. (C)

The area of the shaded region is equal to the area of the large circle (which has $\overline{OB}$ as a radius), minus the area of the smaller circle (which has $\overline{OA}$ as a radius). Since the area of a circle with radius r is $A = \pi r^2$, the area of the shaded region is:

$$\pi(OB)^2 - \pi(OA)^2 = 36\pi - 16\pi = 20\pi.$$

13. (C)

To solve this inequality, we shall use the following rules:

(i)   If $a \leq b$ and c is any number, then $a + c \leq b + c$.

(ii) If $a \leq b$ and $c < 0$, then $ca \geq cb$.

The goal in solving inequalities, as in solving equalities, is to change the inequality so that the variable is isolated (i.e., by itself on one side). So, in the equation $8 - 2x \leq 10$, we want the term $-2x$ by itself. To achieve this, use rule (i) above and add -8 to both sides obtaining

$$8 - 2x + (-8) \leq 10 + (-8)$$

or $-2x \leq 2$.

Now we use rule (ii) and multiply both sides of the inequality by $-\frac{1}{2}$ as follows:

$$-\frac{1}{2} \times 2x \geq -\frac{1}{2} \times 2$$

or $x \geq -1$.

14. **(C)**

Since 0.003 has three numbers to the right of the decimal point and 1.25 has two numbers to the right of the decimal point, our answer will have (three plus two) or five numbers to the right of the decimal point. Multiplying 0.003 and 1.25, we get 0.00375, since 3 times 125 is 375. Numbers of the form $A \times 10^n$, where A is a number between 0 and 1 inclusive, and n is an integer, are in scientific notation. Thus, 0.00375 in scientific notation is 3.75×10^{-3}. Notice that when the exponent $n < 0$, the original number is smaller than A.

15. **(D)**

Since $\angle OPQ$ is a straight angle, $m\angle OPQ = 180°$. But

$$m\angle OPQ = m\angle OPR + m\angle RPQ,$$

so $\qquad m\angle OPR + m\angle RPQ = 180°$

or $\qquad m\angle OPR = 180° - m\angle RPQ.$

Thus, we need to find $m\angle RPQ$. Now, $l_1 \parallel l_2$, therefore, $m\angle RPQ = m\angle TRS$ since $\angle RPQ$ and $\angle TRS$ are corresponding angles. Recall that corresponding angles are two angles which lie on the same side of the transversal (i.e., a line intersecting other lines, in this case line TP is a transversal since it intersects both line l_1 and l_2) are not adjacent, and one is interior ($\angle RPQ$ in this problem) while the other is exterior ($\angle TRS$). Also, we know that the sum of the measures of the interior angles of a triangle is 180° and

$$m\angle T = 80°, \text{ so } m\angle TRS + m\angle RST = 180° - m\angle T = 100°.$$

But $\qquad m\angle TRS = m\angle RST$

since $\triangle RTS$ is isosceles. Thus, $m\angle TRS = 50°$. Thus,

$$m\angle RPQ = 50°$$

and $m\angle OPR = 180° - m\angle RPQ = 180° - 50° = 130°$.

16. **(C)**

The midpoint of a segment with endpoints (x_1, y_1) and (x_2, y_2) is

$$\left(\frac{x_1 + x_2}{2}, \frac{y_1 + y_2}{2} \right).$$

Endpoints are $M = (4, 1)$ and $N = (-2, -1)$, so the midpoint of $\overline{MN}$ is

$$\left(\frac{4 + (-2)}{2}, \frac{1 + (-1)}{2} \right) = (1, 0).$$

17. **(D)**

Let m = the number of men at University X. Then we have the following proportion:

$$\frac{3}{7} = \frac{m}{6,153}$$

To solve this equation, we isolate the variable (i.e., get m by itself) by multiplying both sides of the equation by 6,153 to get

$$\left(\frac{3}{7}\right)6{,}153 = \left(\frac{m}{6{,}153}\right)6{,}153 \text{ or } m = 2{,}637.$$

18. **(C)**

Note that the line passing through W and Z slants downward as we look at it from left to right. This means our slope should be a negative number! To find the slope of the line passing through the points (x_1, y_1), and (x_2, y_2) we use the following formula:

$$\text{slope} = \frac{y_2 - y_1}{x_2 - x_1}.$$

Our points are $W = (-1, 4)$ and $Z = (2, -2)$ and so our slope is

$$\frac{(-2) - 4}{2 - (-1)} = \frac{-6}{3} = -2.$$

19. **(A)**

Let p be the original price of the jacket. Linda received a 25 percent discount so she paid 75 percent of the original price. Thus, 75 percent of p equals 54. Writing this in an equation, we get

$$0.75p = 54 \text{ or } \frac{3}{4}p = 54.$$

To solve this equation, multiply both sides of the equation by the reciprocal of ¾ which is ⁴⁄₃. This will isolate the variable p.

$$\frac{4}{3}\left(\frac{3}{4}p\right) = \left(\frac{4}{3}\right)54 \text{ or } p = \frac{216}{3} = 72$$

20. **(C)**

The area of

$$\triangle ABC = \frac{1}{2}\,(\text{base})(\text{height}) = \frac{1}{2}(AB)(CD) = \frac{1}{2}(AB)(6) = 3(AB).$$

So we need to find AB. Let $s = AB$. Then since $\triangle ABC$ is equilateral (i.e., all the sides have the same length), $BC = s$. Also, since $\triangle ABC$ is equilateral, D is the midpoint of AB, so $DB = \frac{s}{2}$. Now $CD \perp AB$ so $\triangle CDB$ is a right triangle and we can use the Pythagorean Theorem:

$$(CD)^2 + (DB)^2 = (BC)^2.$$

As $CD = 6$, this equation becomes

$$6^2 + \left(\frac{s}{2}\right)^2 = s^2,$$

or

$$36 + \frac{s^2}{4} = s^2.$$

To solve for s, subtract $\frac{s^2}{4}$ from both sides:

$$36 = s^2 - \frac{s^2}{4} = \frac{3}{4}s^2.$$

Now multiply both sides of the equation by the reciprocal of ¾ which is ⁴⁄₃:

$$\frac{4}{3}(36) = s^2$$

or $\quad s^2 = 48.$

Hence, $s = \sqrt{48} = \sqrt{16} = \sqrt{3} = 4\sqrt{3}$

The area of $\triangle ABC =$

$$3s = 3\left(4\sqrt{3}\right) = 12\sqrt{3}$$

21. **(B)**

Substituting $F = 86$ into the formula

$$F = \frac{9}{5}C + 32$$

we get

$$86 = \frac{9}{5}C + 32.$$

To solve for C, first subtract 32 from both sides:

$$86 - 32 = \frac{9}{5}C + 32 - 32$$

or

$$54 = \frac{9}{5}C.$$

Now multiply both sides of this equation by the reciprocal of ⁹⁄₅ which is ⁵⁄₉:

$$\left(\frac{5}{9}\right)54 = \left(\frac{5}{9}\right)\frac{9}{5}C \text{ or } \frac{270}{9} = C \text{ or } C = 30$$

22. **(A)**

72104.58 is read "seventy-two thousand, one hundred four and fifty-eight hundredths."

23. **(C)**

Another way to phrase the second sentence is: She wants to divide her money equally among her six children. Therefore, each child is to receive $300,000 \div 6$.

24. **(C)**

To find the distance between two points (x_1, y_1) and (x_2, y_2), we may use the following formula:

$$d = \sqrt{(x_2 - x_1)^2 + (y_2 - y_1)^2}$$

For our two points, $P = (1, 4)$ and $Q = (-2, 0)$, the above formula gives us the length of segment PQ:

$$d = \sqrt{(-2 - 1)^2 + (0 - 4)^2} = \sqrt{(-3)^2 + (4)^2} = \sqrt{9 + 16} = \sqrt{25} = 5.$$

25. **(B)**

Bob wants to bake 12 cupcakes. The recipe is for 36 cupcakes. Therefore, Bob wants to make $^{12}\!/_{36}$ or $\frac{1}{3}$ of the usual amount of cupcakes. Thus, Bob should use $\frac{1}{3}$ of the recipe's flour or

$$\left(\frac{1}{3}\right)\left(\frac{8}{3}\right) = \frac{8}{9}.$$

Note we used $^8\!/_3$ since $2\frac{2}{3} = {^8\!/_3}$.

26. **(B)**

Let x be the length of EH, then the length of EF is $2x$. The area of a rectangle is length (EF) times width (EH). So we have

$$(2x)(x) = 120 \text{ or } 2x^2 = 120.$$

To solve for x divide both sides of the equation by 2 to get $x^2 = 60$. Note that $49 < x^2 < 64$, so

$$\sqrt{49} < \sqrt{x^2} < \sqrt{64} \text{ or } 7 < x < 8.$$

But 60 is closer to 64 than it is to 49, so 8 is the best approximation of x which represents the length of EH.

27. **(C)**

Let s_1 and s_2 be Ricky's speed (rate) on the trip from A to B and the return trip from B to A, respectively. Then, since he drove 15 miles per hour slower on the return trip, $s_2 = s_1 - 15$. Recall that rate times time equals distance. So the distance from A to B is $(s_1)3 = 3s_1$ and the distance from B to A is

$$(s_2)5 = 5s_2 = 5(s_1 - 15) = 5s_1 - 75.$$

But the distance from Town A to Town B is the same as the distance from Town B to Town A, so we have the following equation:

$$3s_1 = 5s_1 - 75.$$

To solve this equation, first add 75 to both sides of the equation:

$$3s_1 + 75 = 5s_1 - 75 + 75 \text{ or } 3s_1 + 75 = 5s_1.$$

Now to isolate the variable, subtract $3s_1$ from both sides:

$$3s_1 + 75 - 3s_1 = 5s_1 - 3s_1 \text{ or } 75 = 2s_1.$$

To finish the problem, divide both sides of the equation by 2:

$$s1 = \frac{75}{2} = 37.5.$$

Thus, Ricky drove 37.5 miles per hour on his trip from Town A to Town B.

28. **(D)**

The shaded region consists of all the points on the horizontal line passing through the point (0, 2) and those below the line. All of these points have $y =$ coordinate less than or equal to 2. Thus, our answer is $y \le 2$.

29. **(A)**

Statement I is not always true. For example, let $x = 2$ and $y = -3$. Then $x > y$, but $x^2 = 4$ and $y^2 = 9$ so $x^2 < y^2$. Statement IV is not always true. For example, let $x = 5$, $y = 1$, and $z = -2$. Then $xz = -10$ and $yz = -2$ so that $xz < yz$. Statements II and III are true.

30. **(D)**

The 1 is in the hundredths place. If the number to the immediate right of the 1 (i.e., the number in the thousandths place) is greater than or equal to 5, increase 1 to 2; otherwise do not change the 1. Then leave off all numbers to the right of the 1. In this problem a 6 is in the thousandths place, so change the 1 to a 2 to get 287.42 as the answer.

31. **(C)**

Recall the following Laws of Exponents:

$$x^p \times x^q = x^{p+q} \text{ and } \frac{x^p}{x^q} = x^{p-q}.$$

So, $x^2 \times x^7 = x^{2+7} = x^9$. Hence,

$$\frac{x^2 \times x^7}{x} = \frac{x^9}{x^1} = x^{9-1} = x^8.$$

32. **(A)**

   We need to write the three fractions with the same denominator. So, find the least common multiple (LCM) of 9, 15, and 21.

$$9 = 3^2, 15 = 3 \times 5, \text{ and } 21 = 3 \times 7$$

Therefore, the LCM is

$$3^2 \times 5 \times 7 = 315.$$

Then

$$\frac{1}{9} = \frac{5 \times 7}{5 \times 7} \times \frac{1}{9} = \frac{35}{315},$$

$$\frac{2}{15} = \frac{3 \times 7}{3 \times 7} \times \frac{2}{15} = \frac{42}{315},$$

and

$$\frac{3}{21} = \frac{3 \times 5}{3 \times 5} \times \frac{3}{21} = \frac{45}{315}.$$

Clearly,

$$\frac{35}{315} < \frac{42}{315} < \frac{45}{315}$$

and hence, in order, from least to greatest, we have:

$$\frac{1}{9}, \frac{2}{15}, \frac{3}{21}.$$

33. **(A)**

   The volume of a rectangular box is the area of the base times the height. So if we let s be the length of each side of the base (it is a square), the area of the base is s^2. The height of the box is one-half the length of a side of the base. Thus, the height is $\frac{1}{2}$. The volume is then

$$V = s^2 \times \frac{1}{2}s = \frac{1}{2}s^3.$$

But the volume is given as 256. Substituting this into the equation

$$V = \frac{1}{2}s^3 V$$

gives us:

$$256 = \frac{1}{2}s^3.$$

Now multiply both sides of the equation by 2 to get

$$2 \times 256 = 2\frac{1}{2}s^3 \text{ or } 512 = s^3.$$

But, $512 = 8^3$ so that we have $8^3 = s^3$ or $s^3 = 8$. The height of the box is

$$\frac{1}{2}s = \frac{1}{2} \times 8 = 4 \text{ feet}.$$

34. **(A)**

If $x = -3$ then

$$-x^2 + 2x = -(-3)^2 + 2(-3) = -(9) + (-6) = -15.$$

35. **(C)**

If $a = b^3$ and $a = \frac{1}{8}$, then substituting into the first equation we have

$$\frac{1}{8} = b^3 \text{ or } \left(\frac{1}{2}\right)^3 = b^3 \text{ so } b = \frac{1}{2}.$$

36. **(C)**

Let x be the number of people in the barn. Then, since each person and cow has only one head, the number of cows must be $30 - x$. Since people have two legs, the number of human legs totals $2x$. Similarly, since the number of legs each cow has is 4, the total number of cow legs in the barn is $4(30 - x)$. Thus, we have this equation:

$$2x + 4(30 - x) = 104.$$

To solve this equation, use the distributive property:

$$a(b - c) = ab - ac.$$

We get

$$4(30 - x) = (4 \times 30) - (4 \times x) = 120 - 4x.$$

Our equation reduces to:

$$2x + 120 - 4x = 104 \text{ or } 120 - 2x = 104.$$

Now subtract 120 from both sides of the equation to get

$$-2x = 104 - 120 = -16.$$

Dividing both sides of the equation by -2: $x = 8$. Therefore, there were 8 people and $30 - 8 = 22$ cows in the barn.

37. **(B)**

To solve the proportion

$$\frac{12}{x-1} = \frac{5}{6}$$

multiply both sides of the equation by 6 and by $(x-1)$ so that we have

$$6(x-1) \times \frac{12}{x-1} = 6(x-1) \times \frac{5}{6} \text{ or } 72 = 5(x-1).$$

Now, use the distributive property:

$$a(b-c) = ab - ac$$

to get $72 = 5x - 5$. Add 5 to both sides of the equation:

$$77 = 5x$$

and then divide both sides by 5:

$$x = \frac{77}{5} = 15.4.$$

38. **(B)**

If two lines, l_1 and l_2, which lie in the same plane, are both perpendicular to a third line, l_3, then l_1 and l_2 are parallel.

39. **(D)**

First of all, the least common multiple (LCM) of 2 and 3 is $2 \times 3 = 6$, so let's rewrite the expression so that both fractions have 6 as a common denominator:

$$\frac{1}{2} + \frac{1}{3} = \frac{3}{3} \times \frac{1}{2} + \frac{2}{2} \times \frac{1}{3} = \frac{3}{6} + \frac{2}{6} = \frac{5}{6}.$$

40. **(A)**

Two triangles are similar if we can find two pairs of angles, one in each triangle, that are congruent. Given that $BC \parallel DE$ we know that $(\angle ABC, \angle BDE)$ and $(\angle ACB, \angle CED)$ are two pairs of corresponding and hence congruent angles. Thus, taking care in the order that we write the angles so that we match the correct angles, $\triangle ABC \sim \triangle ADE$.

41. **(A)**

Multiply $1.83 by 145 and the answer is $265.35.

42. **(A)**

By definition, a simple curve is a curve that can be traced in such a way that no point is traced more than once with the exception that the tracing may stop where it started. A closed curve is a curve that can be traced so that the starting and stopping points are the same. Therefore, a and b are simple closed curves. The rest are not.

43. **(C)**

In a normal distribution, half the data are always above the mean. Since 30,000 miles is the mean, half or 50 percent of the tires will last at least 30,000 miles.

44. **(D)**

A line of symmetry for a figure is a line in which you can stand a mirror so that the image you see in the mirror is just like the part of the figure that the mirror is hiding. In this case there are four lines.

45. **(D)**

This can be solved using ratio and proportion. Thus, 2 is to 1 as x is to 8.

$$\frac{2}{1} = \frac{x}{8}$$

so $x = 16$ m.

Subtest III: English Language Skills

1. **(B)**

    "Were praised" is a plural verb; since the subject is Chief Joseph, a singular proper noun, the verb should be "was praised." The intervening phrase of choice (A), "*together with* 250 warriors and 500 women and children," does not change the singular subject. Choice (C), "for," is idiomatically correct in that phrase.

2. **(D)**

    Choice (A), "upon which," is a correct prepositional phrase. Choice (B), "is based," agrees with its subject, "society." In choice (C), "are" agrees with its subject, "ideals."

3. **(B)**

    Two past actions are mentioned. The earlier of two past actions should be indicated by past perfect tense, so the answer is "had been." Choice (A) contains two adjectives as part of an appositive phrase modifying the subject, and choice (C), "upon the death," is idiomatically correct.

4. **(B)**

    Choice (B) should be "depend," not "had depended," because that use of past perfect would indicate prior past action. There is a series of events in this sentence: first, the legislature "had not finalized" the budget (A); then, Representative Wilson "pointed out" this failure. Choice (B) needs to be present tense as this situation still exists, and choice (C) is future action.

5. **(C)**

    In order to complete the parallelism, choice (C) should be "arrangements." "To plan" (A) is an infinitive phrase followed by noun objects: "puppet shows and movies" and "garage sales." Choice (B), "used," is a participate modifying books.

6. **(A)**

    An infinitive, "to understand," should never be split by any adverbial modifier, "completely." Choice (B), "effects," is the noun form, and choice (C), "affected," is the adjective form.

7. **(B)**

    "More" is used to compare two things. Since the number of nations is not specified, "more" cannot be used in this sentence. Choice (A) is idiomatically correct; choice (C), "is," agrees in number with its subject, "transportation."

8. **(D)**

Choice (B) is idiomatically correct. In "someone else," (C), "else" is needed to indicate a person other than the student would pay the bills.

9. **(C)**

Choice (C) should read, "became very irritated." "To aggravate" means "to make worse"; "to irritate" means "to excite to impatience or anger." A situation is "aggravated" and becomes worse, but one does not become "aggravated" with people. Choices (A), and (B) are correctly used idioms.

10. **(B)**

The reference in choice (B) is vague because it sounds as if the bus made the two students late. Choice (A) is a correct subject pronoun; choice (C) is a correct object pronoun.

11. **(D)**

Choice (A), "among," indicates choice involving more than two things. The preposition in (B) is correct. "Are," (C), is a plural verb, agreeing in number with the compound subject "singing . . . dancing . . . cooking."

12. **(A)**

One is "disappointed by" a person or action but "disappointed in" what is not satisfactory. Parallel with "to work," choice (B), "save," had the word "to" omitted. Choice (C) compares the two models, one "inexpensive" and one "more expensive."

13. **(A)**

The verb should be plural, "are," in order to agree with the compound subject, "budget . . . plans." Choice (C) is part of an infinitive phrase which includes a participle, "existing," (B). Choice (C) is idiomatically correct.

14. **(A)**

The expression should be phrased "as delicate as." Choice (B) uses a possessive before a gerund; and choice (C) is a possessive pronoun of neuter gender which is appropriate to use in referring to a plant.

15. **(C)**

The verb "deal" must agree with the subject, "works," and not a word in the intervening phrase. Choices (A) and (B), "the picture of respectability," describe the subject; (C) is idiomatically correct.

16. **(C)**

The word "of" in "inside of" is redundant and should not be used. Choice (A), "alike," is appropriate when comparing two classes of people. Choice (B), "them," is correct pronoun usage.

17. **(D)**

Choice (A), "unsafe for," is idiomatically correct. Choice (B), "can be," is grammatically correct. The preposition "in," choice (C), is correct.

18. **(B)**

The verb in this subordinate clause is incorrect; the clause begins with "that," and this word refers to "information." Therefore, the clause, in order to agree with the antecedent, must read "that shows." The verb "shows" should not be made to agree with "species" and "others." Choice (A), "have compiled," agrees in number with people. "Either" in choice (C) is correctly placed after the verb to show a choice of "endangered" or "becoming endangered."

19. **(C)**

Do not end a sentence with a preposition; the phrase should read, "in which he was born." The verb shows proper time sequence in choice (A); choice (B) is correct pronoun usage and correct superlative degree of adjective.

20. **(C)**

The noun form "effect" is the correct one to use. Choice (A), "to inhibit," is an infinitive; in choice (B), the nominative case "who" is the correct subject of "seemed."

21. **(B)**

The idiom should be "filled to capacity." The adverb in choice (A), "quite," is correct. Choice (C), "most," is appropriate for the superlative degree.

22. **(A)**

The subordinate clause, "who my parents have not met," has as its subject "parents," which agrees with choice (B), "have . . . met." Therefore, the pronoun is a direct object of the verb and should be in the objective case, "whom." Choice (C) is idiomatically correct.

23. **(B)**

The pronoun reference is unclear. The meaning of the sentence indicated that Colonel Jones denies involvement in any other covert activity. The agent from a foreign country may or may not have been involved in other covert activities, but that is not the issue here. The verb tense of choice (A) is correct. The word "other" in choice (C) is necessary to the meaning of the sentence.

24. **(D)**

Choice (A), "testing," is parallel to "determining" and "evaluating." In choice (B), "effectiveness" is correct. In choice (C), "is" must be singular because all three steps mentioned comprise the one process.

25. **(B)**

Choice (A) is correct. Choice (B) should read "it is she"; nominative case pronoun is required following a linking verb. The correct form of the modifiers appears in choice (C).

26. **(C)**

"Because" is the correct word to use in the cause-and-effect relationship in this sentence. Choice (A), "being that," and choice (D), "than me," are not grammatically correct. Choice (B), "is made by you," is in the passive voice and not as direct as choice (C).

27. **(C)**

"After they have been" completes the proper time sequence. Choice (A), "when," and choice (B), "will be," are the wrong time sequences. Choice (D), "should be," is an idea not contained in the original sentence.

28. **(C)**

"Since the plane is late" shows correct time sequence and good reasoning. Choice (A), "seeing as how," and choice (D), "being as," are poor wording. Choice (B), "when," is the wrong time, logically, to be on the observation deck.

29. **(D)**

Since a sentence should not end with a preposition, choices (A) and (B) are eliminated. Choice (C), "living in this world," introduces a new concept.

30. **(A)**

The construction, "than those," clarifies the fact that more vegetables have been added. Choice (C), "your suggestion," and choice (D), "which," do not contain the idea of adding more varieties of vegetables. Choice (B) ends with a redundant preposition.

31. **(B)**

The voice must be consistent with "I," so (B) is the only possible correct answer. All other choices have a noun or pronoun that is not consistent with "I": choice (A), "you," choice (C), "a person," and choice (D), "people."

32. **(A)**

The correct answer has two concepts—pieces are missing and pieces will probably never be found. Choice (B) has a singular verb, "is." Choice (C) indicates the pieces "probably will be" missing, which is not the problem. Choice (D) indicates the pieces are "probably" missing, which is illogical because the pieces either are or are not missing.

33. **(C)**

Choice (A), "the kind of a," is incorrect grammatical structure. Choice (D) introduces the new concept of "category." Choice (B), "sort of," is poor wording.

34. **(D)**

Choice (D) is clear and concise and shows the correct comparison of architecture. The antecedent of "those" in choice (A) is not clear. Choice (B) is comparing "characteristics," not just architecture. Choice (C) is awkward.

35. **(B)**

Choice (B) is clear and direct. Choice (A) is too wordy. Choice (C) has the wrong concept, "balancing games." Choice (D), "this as an example," is poorly worded.

36. **(D)**

An opposing force "gives" scattered resistance; therefore, choice (A) is incorrect. Choices (B) and (C) are poorly worded and do not have the correct meaning.

37. **(A)**

Choice (A) produces a complete sentence: "rainfall" is the subject and "let up" is the verb. None of the other choices produces a complete sentence.

38. **(C)**

This choice uses the correct tense, "will have," showing action in the future. All the other verbs listed do not show correct future verb construction.

39.   **(B)**

The correct choice has a compound verb: "comes" and "falls in love." The salesman comes to town first, then meets and falls in love with the librarian. Choice (A), with its misplaced participial phrase, sounds as if either the town or Iowa is in love with the librarian. Choice (C) would produce a run-on sentence. Choice (D) has an unclear tense.

40.   **(A)**

Choice (A) has clear reference. Choice (B) will produce a run-on sentence. Choice (C) does not indicate whose writings or paintings. Choice (D) sounds as if the only time naturalists feel reverence is when they write or paint.

Essay Scoring Guide

The FTCE-GKT essay sections are scored by two writing experts on the basis of the criteria outlined below. In addition to comparing your essay to those included in our practice tests, you may use these guidelines to estimate your score on this section. Remember that your score is the sum of the scores of two writing experts, so provided you respond to the assigned topic, your score will fall somewhere between two and twelve. Scores will be assigned based on the following guidelines:

SCORE of 6: The paper has a clearly established main idea that the writer fully develops with specific details and examples. Organization is notably logical and coherent. Point of view is consistently maintained. Vocabulary and sentence structure are varied and effective. Errors in sentence structure, usage, and mechanics are few and insignificant.

SCORE of 5: The paper has a clearly established main idea that is adequately developed and recognizable through specific details and/or examples. Organization follows a logical and coherent pattern. Point of view is mostly maintained. Vocabulary and sentence structure are mostly varied and effective. Occasional errors in sentence structure, usage, and mechanics do not interfere with the writer's ability to communicate.

SCORE of 4: The paper has an adequately sated main idea that is developed with some specific details and examples. Supporting ideas are presented in a mostly logical and coherent manner. Point of view is somewhat maintained. Vocabulary and sentence structure are somewhat varied and effective. Occasional errors in sentence structure, usage, and mechanics may interfere with writer's ability to communicate.

SCORE of 3: The paper states a main idea that is developed with generalizations or lists. The paper may contain occasional lapses in logic and coherence, and organization is mechanical. Point of view is ambiguous. Vocabulary and sentence structure are repetitious and often ineffective. A variety of errors in sentence structure, usage, and mechanics sometimes interferes with the writer's ability to communicate.

SCORE of 2: The paper presents an incomplete or ambiguous main idea. Support is developed with generalizations and lists. Organization is mechanical. The paper contains occasional lapses in logic and coherence. Point of view is confusing and distracting. Word choice is simplistic, and sentence structure is disjointed. Errors in sentence structure, usage, and mechanics frequently interfere with the writer's ability to communicate.

SCORE of 1: The paper has no evident main idea. Development is inadequate and/or irrelevant. Organization is illogical and/or incoherent. Point of view has not been established. Vocabulary and sentence structure are garbled and confusing. Significant and numerous errors in sentence structure, usage, and mechanics interfere with the writer's ability to communicate.

Subtest IV: Sample Essays with Commentary

Topic 1

Strong Response

A poll was recently conducted to determine American heroes. Sadly, most of the heroes listed in the top ten are cartoon characters or actors who portray heroic roles. What does this say about American ideals? Perhaps we do not know enough, or perhaps we know too much in order to have heroes. Having access to instant information about a variety of military, political, and religious figures, citizens of modern society have outgrown the innocence of previous centuries.

The ancient hero possessed many idealized virtues, such as physical strength, honesty, courage, and intelligence. Oedipus saved his people from pestilence by solving the riddle of the Sphinx. As leader, he was sworn to find the murderer of the previous king; Oedipus' brave pursuit of justice was conducted with honesty and integrity. Beowulf, another famous ancient hero, existed at a time when life was wild, dangerous, unpredictable.

Modern society is missing several of the ingredients necessary to produce a hero of this calibre. For one thing, there are no mythical monsters such as the Sphinx or Grendel. War is left as the stuff of heroic confrontation, but modern wars only add to our confusion. Men have been decorated for killing their brothers and friends in the Civil War; America fought the Germans in World War I and the Germans and Japanese in World War II, but our former enemies are our current allies. As for honesty, modern role models too often let us down. The media exposes politicians who are involved in scandal, sports figures who do drugs, and religious leaders who make multi-million dollar incomes.

No wonder Americans name Superman and actors John Wayne and Clint Eastwood to the list of modern heroes. These heroes are larger than life on the theatre screen, and their vices are at least predictable and reasonably innocuous. Wisely, we have chosen those who will not surprise us with ugly or mundane reality.

Analysis

This essay has a score range of 5-6. It is the strongest of the four essays. Although it is not perfect, it shows a good command of the English language and depth of thought. The writer employs a traditional essay structure: the first paragraph is the introduction and ends with the thesis statement; the second and third paragraphs discuss traditional and contemporary heroes, as stated in the last sentence of the thesis paragraph; the fourth paragraph concludes. Each of the two body paragraphs has a clear topic sentence. The writer gives several distinct examples to support his ideas. Vocabulary is effective, and sentence structure is varied.

Topic 2

Strong Response

In the past thirty years, television has become a very popular passtime for almost everyone. From the time the mother places the baby in his jumpseat in front of the television so that she can relax and have a second cup of coffee until the time the senior citizen in the retirement home watches Vanna White turn the letters on "Wheel of Fortune," Americans spend endless hours in front of the "boob tube." I believe that television can become an addiction that provides an escape from the problems of the world and from facing responsibility for your own life.

When my mother was a little girl, what did children do to entertain themselves? They played. Their games usually involved social interaction with other children as well as imaginatively creating entertainment for themselves. They also developed hobbies like woodworking and sewing. Today few children really know how to play with each other or entertain themselves. Instead, they sit in front of the television, glued to cartoons that are senseless and often violent. Even if they watch educational programs like "Sesame Street," they don't really have to do anything but watch and listen to what the answer to the question is.

Teenagers, also, use television as a way of avoiding doing things that will help them mature. How many kids do much homework anymore? Why not? Because they come home from school tired and relax in front of the television. Even if they watch a controversial program about some problem in the world like AIDS or the war in the Middle East, they don't usually do anything about it.

In addition, young mothers use television to escape their own problems. The terrible woes of the people on the soap operas make their problems seem less important. This means that they don't need to solve their own problems.

Although it may seem as if television is really great for older people, I think even my grandma would have more fun if she had more interests rather than just watching quiz shows. I know she has blotted out the "real world" when she expects us to act like perfect kids when she comes to visit.

In conclusion, I believe that television really can become an addiction that allows people of all ages to avoid facing their own problems and lose themselves in the problems of other people.

Analysis

This essay has a score range of 5-6. It has a traditional structure; the first paragraph introduces the topic, even suggesting the chronological organization of the essay. Each of the next four paragraphs has a clear topic sentence and details that develop it. The concluding paragraph, although only one sentence in length, restates the main idea. The essay is, therefore, clearly unified around the writer's opinion, which the writer tries to prove in a logical fashion. The writer effectively employs transitional words to relate the main ideas, varied sentence structure, and controlled vocabulary. Although the writer misspells *pastime*, uses the colloquial word *kids*, and has some problem with parallelism, repetition, and pronoun usage, the essay is well written considering the time limit.

FTCE

**Florida Teacher Certification Examination
General Knowledge Test**

Practice Test 2

Answer Sheet – Practice Test 2

Subtest I: Reading

1. Ⓐ Ⓑ Ⓒ Ⓓ
2. Ⓐ Ⓑ Ⓒ Ⓓ
3. Ⓐ Ⓑ Ⓒ Ⓓ
4. Ⓐ Ⓑ Ⓒ Ⓓ
5. Ⓐ Ⓑ Ⓒ Ⓓ
6. Ⓐ Ⓑ Ⓒ Ⓓ
7. Ⓐ Ⓑ Ⓒ Ⓓ
8. Ⓐ Ⓑ Ⓒ Ⓓ
9. Ⓐ Ⓑ Ⓒ Ⓓ
10. Ⓐ Ⓑ Ⓒ Ⓓ

11. Ⓐ Ⓑ Ⓒ Ⓓ
12. Ⓐ Ⓑ Ⓒ Ⓓ
13. Ⓐ Ⓑ Ⓒ Ⓓ
14. Ⓐ Ⓑ Ⓒ Ⓓ
15. Ⓐ Ⓑ Ⓒ Ⓓ
16. Ⓐ Ⓑ Ⓒ Ⓓ
17. Ⓐ Ⓑ Ⓒ Ⓓ
18. Ⓐ Ⓑ Ⓒ Ⓓ
19. Ⓐ Ⓑ Ⓒ Ⓓ
20. Ⓐ Ⓑ Ⓒ Ⓓ

21. Ⓐ Ⓑ Ⓒ Ⓓ
22. Ⓐ Ⓑ Ⓒ Ⓓ
23. Ⓐ Ⓑ Ⓒ Ⓓ
24. Ⓐ Ⓑ Ⓒ Ⓓ
25. Ⓐ Ⓑ Ⓒ Ⓓ
26. Ⓐ Ⓑ Ⓒ Ⓓ
27. Ⓐ Ⓑ Ⓒ Ⓓ
28. Ⓐ Ⓑ Ⓒ Ⓓ
29. Ⓐ Ⓑ Ⓒ Ⓓ
30. Ⓐ Ⓑ Ⓒ Ⓓ

31. Ⓐ Ⓑ Ⓒ Ⓓ
32. Ⓐ Ⓑ Ⓒ Ⓓ
33. Ⓐ Ⓑ Ⓒ Ⓓ
34. Ⓐ Ⓑ Ⓒ Ⓓ
35. Ⓐ Ⓑ Ⓒ Ⓓ
36. Ⓐ Ⓑ Ⓒ Ⓓ
37. Ⓐ Ⓑ Ⓒ Ⓓ
38. Ⓐ Ⓑ Ⓒ Ⓓ
39. Ⓐ Ⓑ Ⓒ Ⓓ
40. Ⓐ Ⓑ Ⓒ Ⓓ

Subtest II: Mathematics

1. Ⓐ Ⓑ Ⓒ Ⓓ
2. Ⓐ Ⓑ Ⓒ Ⓓ
3. Ⓐ Ⓑ Ⓒ Ⓓ
4. Ⓐ Ⓑ Ⓒ Ⓓ
5. Ⓐ Ⓑ Ⓒ Ⓓ
6. Ⓐ Ⓑ Ⓒ Ⓓ
7. Ⓐ Ⓑ Ⓒ Ⓓ
8. Ⓐ Ⓑ Ⓒ Ⓓ
9. Ⓐ Ⓑ Ⓒ Ⓓ
10. Ⓐ Ⓑ Ⓒ Ⓓ
11. Ⓐ Ⓑ Ⓒ Ⓓ

12. Ⓐ Ⓑ Ⓒ Ⓓ
13. Ⓐ Ⓑ Ⓒ Ⓓ
14. Ⓐ Ⓑ Ⓒ Ⓓ
15. Ⓐ Ⓑ Ⓒ Ⓓ
16. Ⓐ Ⓑ Ⓒ Ⓓ
17. Ⓐ Ⓑ Ⓒ Ⓓ
18. Ⓐ Ⓑ Ⓒ Ⓓ
19. Ⓐ Ⓑ Ⓒ Ⓓ
20. Ⓐ Ⓑ Ⓒ Ⓓ
21. Ⓐ Ⓑ Ⓒ Ⓓ
22. Ⓐ Ⓑ Ⓒ Ⓓ

23. Ⓐ Ⓑ Ⓒ Ⓓ
24. Ⓐ Ⓑ Ⓒ Ⓓ
25. Ⓐ Ⓑ Ⓒ Ⓓ
26. Ⓐ Ⓑ Ⓒ Ⓓ
27. Ⓐ Ⓑ Ⓒ Ⓓ
28. Ⓐ Ⓑ Ⓒ Ⓓ
29. Ⓐ Ⓑ Ⓒ Ⓓ
30. Ⓐ Ⓑ Ⓒ Ⓓ
31. Ⓐ Ⓑ Ⓒ Ⓓ
32. Ⓐ Ⓑ Ⓒ Ⓓ
33. Ⓐ Ⓑ Ⓒ Ⓓ

34. Ⓐ Ⓑ Ⓒ Ⓓ
35. Ⓐ Ⓑ Ⓒ Ⓓ
36. Ⓐ Ⓑ Ⓒ Ⓓ
37. Ⓐ Ⓑ Ⓒ Ⓓ
38. Ⓐ Ⓑ Ⓒ Ⓓ
39. Ⓐ Ⓑ Ⓒ Ⓓ
40. Ⓐ Ⓑ Ⓒ Ⓓ
41. Ⓐ Ⓑ Ⓒ Ⓓ
42. Ⓐ Ⓑ Ⓒ Ⓓ
43. Ⓐ Ⓑ Ⓒ Ⓓ
44. Ⓐ Ⓑ Ⓒ Ⓓ
45. Ⓐ Ⓑ Ⓒ Ⓓ

Subtest III: English Language Skills

1. Ⓐ Ⓑ Ⓒ Ⓓ
2. Ⓐ Ⓑ Ⓒ Ⓓ
3. Ⓐ Ⓑ Ⓒ Ⓓ
4. Ⓐ Ⓑ Ⓒ Ⓓ
5. Ⓐ Ⓑ Ⓒ Ⓓ
6. Ⓐ Ⓑ Ⓒ Ⓓ
7. Ⓐ Ⓑ Ⓒ Ⓓ
8. Ⓐ Ⓑ Ⓒ Ⓓ
9. Ⓐ Ⓑ Ⓒ Ⓓ
10. Ⓐ Ⓑ Ⓒ Ⓓ

11. Ⓐ Ⓑ Ⓒ Ⓓ
12. Ⓐ Ⓑ Ⓒ Ⓓ
13. Ⓐ Ⓑ Ⓒ Ⓓ
14. Ⓐ Ⓑ Ⓒ Ⓓ
15. Ⓐ Ⓑ Ⓒ Ⓓ
16. Ⓐ Ⓑ Ⓒ Ⓓ
17. Ⓐ Ⓑ Ⓒ Ⓓ
18. Ⓐ Ⓑ Ⓒ Ⓓ
19. Ⓐ Ⓑ Ⓒ Ⓓ
20. Ⓐ Ⓑ Ⓒ Ⓓ

21. Ⓐ Ⓑ Ⓒ Ⓓ
22. Ⓐ Ⓑ Ⓒ Ⓓ
23. Ⓐ Ⓑ Ⓒ Ⓓ
24. Ⓐ Ⓑ Ⓒ Ⓓ
25. Ⓐ Ⓑ Ⓒ Ⓓ
26. Ⓐ Ⓑ Ⓒ Ⓓ
27. Ⓐ Ⓑ Ⓒ Ⓓ
28. Ⓐ Ⓑ Ⓒ Ⓓ
29. Ⓐ Ⓑ Ⓒ Ⓓ
30. Ⓐ Ⓑ Ⓒ Ⓓ

31. Ⓐ Ⓑ Ⓒ Ⓓ
32. Ⓐ Ⓑ Ⓒ Ⓓ
33. Ⓐ Ⓑ Ⓒ Ⓓ
34. Ⓐ Ⓑ Ⓒ Ⓓ
35. Ⓐ Ⓑ Ⓒ Ⓓ
36. Ⓐ Ⓑ Ⓒ Ⓓ
37. Ⓐ Ⓑ Ⓒ Ⓓ
38. Ⓐ Ⓑ Ⓒ Ⓓ
39. Ⓐ Ⓑ Ⓒ Ⓓ
40. Ⓐ Ⓑ Ⓒ Ⓓ

Practice Test 2

Subtest I: Reading

TIME: 40 Minutes
40 Questions

> <u>**DIRECTIONS:**</u> **A number of questions follow each of the passages in the reading section. Answer the questions by choosing the best answer from the four choices given.**

Questions 1 to 5 refer to the following passage:

Spa water quality is maintained through a filter to ensure cleanliness and clarity. Wastes such as perspiration, hairspray, and lotions, which cannot be removed by the spa filter, can be controlled by shock treatment or super chlorination every other week. Although the filter traps most of the solid material to control bacteria and algae and to oxidize any organic material, the addition of disinfectants such as bromine or chlorine is necessary.

As all water solutions have a pH that controls corrosion, proper pH balance is also necessary. A pH measurement determines if the water is acid or alkaline. Based on a 14-point scale, a pH reading of 7.0 is considered neutral while a lower reading is considered acidic, and a higher reading indicates alkalinity or basic. High pH (above 7.6) reduces sanitizer efficiency, clouds water, promotes scale formation on surfaces and equipment, and interferes with filter operation. When pH is high, add a pH decrease such as sodium bisulphate (e.g., Spa Down). Because the spa water is hot, scale is deposited more rapidly. A weekly dose of a stain and scale fighter also will help to control this problem. Low pH (below 7.2) is equally damaging, causing equipment corrosion, water that is irritating, and rapid sanitizer dissipation. To increase pH, add sodium bicarbonate (e.g., Spa Up).

The recommended operating temperature of a spa (98°–104°) is a fertile environment for the growth of bacteria and viruses. This growth is prevented when appropriate sanitizer levels are continuously monitored. Bacteria can also be controlled by maintaining a proper bromine level of 3.0 to 5.0 parts per million (ppm) or a chlorine level of 1.0–2.0 ppm. As bromine tablets should not be added directly to the water, a bromine floater will properly dispense the tablets. Should chlorine be the chosen sanitizer, a granular form is recommended, as liquid chlorine or tablets are too harsh for the spa.

1. Although proper chemical and temperature maintenance of spa water is necessary, the most important condition to monitor is

    (A) preventing growth of bacteria and viruses.
    (B) preventing equipment corrosion.
    (C) preventing scale formation.
    (D) preventing cloudy water.

2. Of the chemical and temperature conditions in a spa, the condition most dangerous to one's health is

    (A) spa water temperature above 104°.
    (B) bromine level between 3.0 and 5.0.
    (C) pH level below 7.2.
    (D) spa water temperature between 90° and 104°.

3. The primary purpose of the passage is to

    (A) relate that maintenance of a spa can negate the full enjoyment of the spa experience.
    (B) convey that the maintenance of a spa is expensive and time consuming.
    (C) explain the importance of proper spa maintenance.
    (D) detail proper spa maintenance.

4. The spa filter can be relied upon to

    (A) control algae and bacteria.
    (B) trap most solid material.
    (C) assure an adequate level of sanitation.
    (D) maintain clear spa water.

5. Which chemical should one avoid when maintaining a spa?

    (A) Liquid chlorine   (C) Sodium bisulfate
    (B) Bromine   (D) Baking soda

Questions 6 to 10 refer to the following passage:

The relationship of story elements found in children's generated stories to reading achievement was analyzed. Correlations ranged from .61101 (p = .64) at the beginning of first grade to .83546 (p = .24) at the end of first grade, to .85126 (p = .21) at the end of second grade, and to .82588 (p = .26) for fifth/sixth grades. Overall, the correlation of the story elements to reading achievement appeared to indicate a high positive correlation trend even though it was not statistically significant.

Multiple regression equation analyses dealt with the relative contribution of the story elements to reading achievement. The contribution of certain story elements was substantial. At the beginning of first grade, story conventions added 40 percent to the total variance while the other increments were not significant. At the end of first grade, story plot contributed 44 percent to the total variance, story conventions contributed 20 percent, and story sources contributed 17 percent. At the end of second grade, the story elements contributed more equal percentages to the total partial correlation of .8513. Although none of the percentages were substantial, story plot (.2200), clausal connectors (.1858), and T-units (.1590) contributed the most to the total partial correlation. By the fifth and sixth grades three other story elements—T-units (.2241), story characters (.3214), and clausal connectors (.1212)—contributed most to the total partial correlation. None of these percentages was substantial.

6. Which of the following is the most complete and accurate definition of the term "statistically significant" as used in the passage?

   (A) Consists of important numerical data
   (B) Is educationally significant
   (C) Permits prediction of reading achievement by knowing the story elements
   (D) Indicates two measures (reading achievement and story elements) give the same information

7. The passage suggests which of the following conclusions about the correlation of story elements to reading achievement?

   (A) That there are other more important story elements that should also be included in the analyses
   (B) That children's inclusion of story elements in their stories causes them to achieve higher levels in reading
   (C) That these story elements are important variables to consider in reading achievement
   (D) That correlations of more than 1.0 are needed for this study to be statistically significant

8. The relative contribution of story conventions and story plot in first grade suggests that

   (A) children may have spontaneously picked up these story elements as a result of their exposure to stories.
   (B) children have been explicitly taught these story elements.
   (C) these story elements were not important because in fifth/sixth grades other story elements contributed more to the total partial correlation.
   (D) children's use of story conventions and plots were not taken from story models.

9. The content of the passage suggests that the passage would most likely appear in which of the following?

   (A) *Psychology Today*   (C) *Language Arts*
   (B) *The Creative Writer*   (D) *Reading Research Quarterly*

10. "None of these percentages were substantial" is the last statement in the passage. It refers to

    (A) the story elements for fifth/sixth grades.
    (B) the story elements for second grade.
    (C) the story elements at the end of first grade.
    (D) the story elements for all of the grades, i.e., first grade, second grade, and fifth/sixth grade.

Questions 11 to 13 refer to the following passage:

There is an importance of learning communication and meaning in language. Yet the use of notions such as communication and meaning as the basic criteria for instruction, experiences, and materials in classrooms may misguide a child in several respects. Communication in the classroom is vital. The teacher should use communication to help students develop the capacity to make their private responses become public responses. Otherwise, one's use of language would be in danger of being what the younger generation refers to as mere words, mere thoughts, and mere feelings.

Learning theorists emphasize specific components of learning: behaviorists stress behavior in learning; humanists stress the affective in learning; and cognitivists stress cognition in learning. All three of these components occur simultaneously and cannot be separated from each other in the learning process. In 1957, Festinger referred to dissonance as the lack of harmony between what one does (behavior) and what one believes (attitude). Attempts to separate the components of learning either knowingly or unknowingly create dissonances wherein language, thought, feeling, and behavior become diminished of authenticity. As a result, ideas and concepts lose their content and vitality, and the manipulation and politics of communication assume prominence.

11. Which of the following best describes the author's attitude toward the subject discussed?

   (A) A flippant disregard   (C) A passive resignation
   (B) A mild frustration   (D) An informed concern

12. The primary purpose of the passage is to

   (A) discuss the relationships between learning and communication.
   (B) assure teachers that communication and meaning are the basic criteria for learning in classrooms.
   (C) stress the importance of providing authentic communication in classroom learning.
   (D) address the role of communication and meaning in classrooms.

13. Which of the following is the most complete and accurate definition of the term "mere" as used in the passage?

   (A) Small   (C) Little
   (B) Minor   (D) Insignificant

Questions 14 to 16 refer to the following passage:

In 1975, Sinclair observed that it had often been supposed that the main factor in learning to talk is being able to imitate. Schlesinger (1975) noted that at certain stages of learning to speak, a child tends to imitate everything an adult says to him or her, and it therefore seems reasonable to accord to such imitation an important role in the acquisition of language.

Moreover, various investigators have attempted to explain the role of imitation in language. In his discussion of the development of imitation and cognition of adult speech sounds, Nakazema (1975) stated that although the parent's talking stimulates and accelerates the infant's articulatory activity, the parent's phoneme system does not influence the child's articulatory mechanisms. Slobin and Welsh (1973) suggested that imitation is the reconstruction of the adult's utterance and that the child does so by employing the grammatical rules that he has developed at a specific time. Schlesinger proposed that by imitating the adult the child practices new grammatical constructions. Brown and Bellugi (1964) noted that a child's imitations resemble spontaneous speech in that they drop inflections, most function words, and sometimes other words. However, the word order of imitated sentences usually was preserved. Brown and Bellugi assumed that imitation is a function of what the child attended to or remembered. Shipley et al. (1969) suggested that repeating an adult's utterance assists the child's comprehension. Ervin (1964) and Braine (1971) found that a child's imitations do not contain more advanced structures than his or her spontaneous utterances; thus, imitation can no longer be regarded as the simple behavioristic act that earlier scholars assumed it to be.

14. The author of the passage would tend to agree with which of the following statements?

   (A) Apparently, children require practice with more advanced structures before they are able to imitate.
   (B) Apparently, children only imitate what they already do, using whatever is in their repertoire.
   (C) Apparently, the main factor in learning to talk remains being able to imitate.
   (D) Apparently, children cannot respond meaningfully to a speech situation until they have reached a stage where they can make symbol-orientation responses.

15. The primary purpose of the passage is to

   (A) explain the role of imitation in language acquisition.
   (B) assure parents of their role in assisting imitation in language acquisition.
   (C) relate the history of imitation in language acquisition.
   (D) discuss relationships between psychological and physiological processes in language acquisition.

16. An inference that parents may make from the passage is that they should

   (A) be concerned when a child imitates their language.
   (B) focus on developing imitation in their child's language.
   (C) realize that their child's imitations may reflect several aspects of language acquisition.
   (D) realize that their talking may over-stimulate their child's articulatory activity.

Questions 17 and 18 refer to the following passage:

A major problem with reading/language arts instruction is that practice assignments from workbooks often provide short, segmented activities that do not really resemble the true act of reading. Perhaps more than any computer application, word processing is capable of addressing these issues.

17. The author would tend to agree that a major benefit of computers in reading/language arts instruction is

   (A) that the reading act may be more closely resembled.
   (B) that short segmented assignments will be eliminated.
   (C) that computer application will be limited to word processing.
   (D) that reading practice will be eliminated.

18. The appropriate use of a word processor to assist in making practice resemble a reading act is

   (A) detailed.
   (B) desirable.
   (C) unstated.
   (D) alluded.

Questions 19 to 21 refer to the following passage:

In view of the current emphasis on literature-based reading instruction, a greater understanding by teachers of variance in cultural, language, and story components should assist in narrowing the gap between reader and text and improve reading comprehension. Classroom teachers should begin with students' meaning and intentions about stories before moving students to the commonalities of story meaning based on common background and culture. With teacher guidance, students should develop a fuller understanding of how complex narratives are when they are generating stories as well as when they are reading stories.

19. Which of the following is the intended audience for the passage?

(A) Teachers using literature-based curriculum
(B) Professors teaching a literature course
(C) Parents concerned about their child's comprehension of books
(D) Teacher educators teaching reading methods courses

20. Which of the following is the most complete and accurate definition of the term "variance" as used in the passage?

(A) Change
(B) Fluctuations

(C) Diversity
(D) Deviation

21. The passage supports a concept of meaning primarily residing in

(A) culture, language, and story components.
(B) comprehension.
(C) students' stories only.
(D) students and narratives.

Questions 22 to 25 refer to the following passage:

As noted by Favat in 1977, the study of children's stories has been an ongoing concern of linguists, anthropologists, and psychologists. The past decade has witnessed a surge of interest in children's stories from researchers in these and other disciplines. The use of narratives for reading and reading instruction has been commonly accepted by the educational community. The notion that narrative is highly structured and that children's sense of narrative structure is more highly developed than expository structure has been proposed by some researchers.

Early studies of children's stories followed two approaches for story analysis: the analysis of story content or the analysis of story structure. Story content analysis has centered primarily on examining motivational and psychodynamic aspects of story characters as noted in the works of Erikson and Pitcher and Prelinger in 1963 and Ames in 1966. These studies have noted that themes or topics predominate and that themes change with age.

Early research on story structure focused on formal models of structure, such as story grammar and story schemata. These models specified basic story elements and formed sets of rules similar to sentence grammar for ordering the elements.

The importance or centrality of narrative in a child's development of communicative ability has been proposed by Halliday (1976) and Hymes (1975). Thus, the importance of narrative for language communicative ability and for reading and reading instruction has been well documented. However, the question still remains about how these literacy abilities interact and lead to conventional reading.

22. This passage is most probably directed at which of the following audience?

    (A) Reading educators   (C) Psychologists
    (B) Linguists   (D) Reading researchers

23. According to the passage, future research should address

    (A) how story structure and story schema interact with comprehension.
    (B) how children's use and understanding of narrative interacts and leads to conventional reading.
    (C) how story content interacts with story comprehension.
    (D) how narrative text structure differs from expository text structure.

24. The major distinction between story content and story structure is that

    (A) story content focuses on motivational aspects whereas story structure focuses on rules similar to sentence grammar.
    (B) story content focuses on psychodynamic aspects whereas story structure focuses on formal structural models.
    (C) story content and story structure essentially refer to the same concepts.
    (D) story content focuses primarily on characters whereas story structure focuses on story grammar and schemata.

25. Which of the following is the most complete and accurate definition of the term "surge" as used in the following sentence? The past decade has witnessed a surge of interest in children's stories from researchers in these and other disciplines.

    (A) A heavy swell   (C) A sudden increase
    (B) A sudden rise   (D) A sudden rush

Questions 26 to 29 refer to the following passage:

Seldom has the American school system not been the target of demands for change to meet the social priorities of the times. This theme has been traced through the following significant occurrences in education: Benjamin Franklin's advocacy in 1749 for a more useful type of education; Horace Mann's zealous proposals in the 1830s espousing the tax-supported public school; John Dewey's early twentieth century attack on traditional schools for not developing the child effectively for his or her role in society; the post-Sputnik pressure for academic rigor; the prolific criticism and accountability pressures of the 1970s; and the ensuing disillusionment and continued criticism of schools until this last decade of the twentieth century. Indeed, the waves of criticism about American education have reflected currents of social dissatisfaction for any given period of this country's history.

As dynamics for change in the social order result in demands for change in the American educational system, so in turn insistence has developed for revision of teacher education (witness the more recent Holmes report (1986)). Historically, the education of American teachers has reflected evolving attitudes about public education. With slight modifications, the teacher education pattern established following the demise of the normal school during the early 1900s has persisted in most teacher preparation programs. The pattern has been one requiring certain academic and professional (educational) courses often resulting in teachers prone to teach as they had been taught.

26. The author of this passage would probably agree with which of the following statements?

    (A) Social dissatisfaction should drive change in the American school systems.
    (B) Teacher education programs have changed greatly since normal schools were eliminated.
    (C) Critics of American education reflect vested interests.
    (D) Teachers' teaching methods tend to reflect what they have learned in their academic and professional courses.

27. The evolving attitudes about public education are

    (A) stated.   (C) alluded.
    (B) unstated.   (D) unwarranted.

28. One possible sequence of significant occurrences in education noted in the passage is

    (A) Mann's tax-supported public schools, post-Sputnik pressures for academic rigor, and the Holmes' report.
    (B) Franklin's more useful type of education, Dewey's educating children for their role in society, and Mann's tax-supported public schools.
    (C) Franklin's more useful type of education, the Holmes' report, and accountability pressures of the 1970s.
    (D) Mann's tax-supported public schools, accountability pressures of the 1970s, and the post-Sputnik pressures for academic rigor.

29. Which of the following statements most obviously implies dissatisfaction with preparation of teachers in the United States?

    (A) Demands for change in the American education system lead to insistence for revision of teacher education programs.
    (B) The pattern of teacher education requires certain academic and professional education courses.
    (C) The education of U.S. teachers has reflected evolving attitudes about public education.
    (D) Teacher education has changed very little since the decline of the normal school.

Questions 30 to 33 refer to the following passage:

HAWK ON A FRESHLY PLOWED FIELD

My Lord of the Field, proudly perched on the sod,
You eye with disdain
And mutter with wings
As steadily each furrow I tractor-plod.
"Intruder!" you glare, firmly standing your ground,
Proclaim this fief yours
By Nature so willed—
Yet bound to the air on my very next round.

You hover and soar, skimming close by the earth,

Distract me from work

To brood there with you

Of changes that Man wrought your land—for his worth.

In medieval days, lords were god over all:

Their word was the law.

Yet here is this hawk

A ruler displaced—Man and Season forestall.

My Lord of the Field, from sight you have flown.

For purpose untold,

When brave, you return

And perch once again, still liege-lord—but Alone.

Jacqueline K. Hultquist (1952)

30. Which of the following is the most complete and accurate definition of the term "liege-lord" as used in the passage?

   (A) Monarch
   (B) King
   (C) Sovereign
   (D) Master

31. Which of the following best describes the author's attitude toward the hawk?

   (A) Romantic
   (B) Pensive
   (C) Intimidating
   (D) Fearful

32. Which of the following groups of words about the hawk carry human qualities?

   (A) Mutter, brood, and ruler
   (B) Brave, disdain, and perch
   (C) Brave, brood, and distract
   (D) Mutter, disdain, and skimming

33. Which of the following is the most complete and accurate definition of the term "medieval" as used in the passage?

   (A) Antiquated
   (B) Feudal
   (C) Old
   (D) Antediluvian

Questions 34 to 37 refer to the following passage:

Reduced to its simplest form, a political system is really no more than a device enabling groups of people to live together in a more or less orderly society. As they have developed, political systems generally have fallen into the broad categories of those which do not offer direct subject participation in the decision-making process, and those which allow citizen participation—in form, if not in actual effectiveness.

Let us consider, however, the type of political system that is classified as the modern democracy in a complex society. Such a democracy is defined by Lipset (1963) as "a political system which supplies regular constitutional opportunities for changing the governing officials, and a social mechanism which permits the largest possible part of the population to influence major decisions by choosing among alternative contenders for political office."

Proceeding from another concept (that of Easton and Dennis), a political system is one of inputs, conversion, and outputs by which the wants of a society are transformed into binding decisions. Easton and Dennis (1967) observed: "To sustain a conversion process of this sort, a society must provide a relatively stable context for political interaction, set of general rules for participating in all parts of the political process." As a rule, this interaction evolves around the settling of differences (satisfying wants or demands) involving the elements of a "political regime," which consists of minimal general goal constraints, norms governing behavior, and structures of authority for the input-output function.

In order to persist, a political system would seem to need a minimal support for the political regime. To insure the maintenance of such a support is the function of political socialization, a process varying according to political systems but toward the end of indoctrinating the members to the respective political system. "To the extent that the maturing members absorb and become attached to the overarching goals of the system and its basic norms and come to approve its structure of authority as legitimate, we can say that they are learning to contribute support to the regime." The desired political norm (an expectation about the way people will behave) is that referred to as political efficacy—a feeling that one's action can have an impact on government.

Adapted from Easton, B. and J. Dennis, "The Child's Acquisition of Regime Norms: Political Efficacy" *American Political Science Review,* March 1967.

34. Political efficacy according to the passage is

 (A) most likely to be found where citizen participation is encouraged.
 (B) in an expanding concept of political efficiency.
 (C) in a diminishing concept of political efficiency.
 (D) in a figurehead political system.

35. Political socialization is a process which

 (A) occurs only in democracies.
 (B) occurs in any type of political system.
 (C) occurs less frequently in recent years.
 (D) occurs when members reject the goals of the system.

36. As used in the passage, which of the following is the most complete and accurate definition of the term "conversion"?

 (A) Transformation   (C) Resolution
 (B) Changeover   (D) Passing

37. The major distinction between the concepts of Easton and Dennis as opposed to the concepts of Lipset is

 (A) that the concepts of Easton and Dennis are based on the wants of a society, whereas Lipset's concepts are based on change of governing officials.
 (B) that Easton and Dennis' concepts are based on arbitrary decisions, whereas Lipset's concepts are based on influencing major decisions.
 (C) that Easton and Dennis' concepts must have a set of general rules, whereas Lipset's concepts provide for irregular constitutional opportunities.
 (D) that Easton and Dennis' concepts evolve around the settling of differences, whereas Lipset's concepts permit the largest conflict possible.

Questions 38 to 40 refer to the following passage:

Assignment: Research for a White Paper Proposing U.S. Foreign Policy

Imagine you are in charge (or assigned to) a foreign policy desk in the U.S. Department of State. Select one of the following regions (descriptors are merely suggestions):

Western Europe—A Changing Alliance

Eastern Europe—Out from Behind the Iron Curtain

The U.S.S.R.—Still an Enigma

The Middle East—History and Emotions

Africa—Rising Expectations in the Postwar Continent

South and Southeast Asia—Unrest in Far Away Places

The Far East—Alienation and Alliance

The Western Hemisphere—Neighbors; Pro and Con

Through research, prepare a White Paper for that area which will indicate:

1. a General Policy Statement toward the nations of that region;

2. a statement as to how World War II set the stage for that policy;

3. a summary of the major events since 1945 in that region which have affected U.S. foreign policy;

4. a list of suggested problems and/or possibilities for near-future interactions of that region and the U.S.

38. In order to complete this assignment, research into which of the following disciplines (areas of study) would be most appropriate?

(A) History, Economics, Political Science, and Language
(B) History, Political Science, Education, and Economics
(C) Political Science, Economics, Geography, and Religion
(D) History, Political Science, Economics, and Culture

39. Which of the following is the most complete and accurate definition of the term "Enigma" as used in the passage?

(A) Riddle   (C) Secret
(B) Puzzle   (D) Mystery

40. Which of the following is the most appropriate secondary school audience for the assignment?

(A) Students in a World Geography class
(B) Students in a World History class
(C) Students in an Economics class
(D) Students in an American Government class

Subtest II: Mathematics

TIME: 100 Minutes
45 Questions

> **DIRECTIONS:** Each of the questions or incomplete statements below is followed by four suggested answers or completions. Select the one that is best in each case.

1. If 406.725 is rounded off to the nearest tenth, the number is

   (A) 406.5.
   (B) 406.7.

   (C) 406.8.
   (D) 407.0.

2. The mean IQ score for 1,500 students is 100, with a standard deviation of 15. Assuming normal curve distribution, how many students have an IQ between 85 and 115? Refer to the figure shown below.

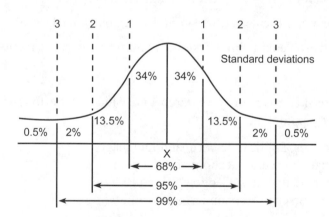

   (A) 750
   (B) 1,020

   (C) 1,275
   (D) 1,425

3. The sum of 12 and twice a number is 24. Find the number.

   (A) 6
   (B) 8

   (C) 10
   (D) 12

4. Twice the sum of 10 and a number is 28. Find the number.

   (A) 4
   (B) 8

   (C) 14
   (D) 24

5. Two college roommates spent $2,000 for their total monthly expenses. A pie graph below indicates a record of their expenses.

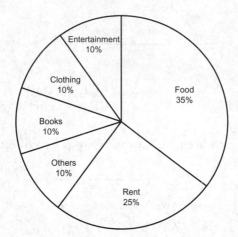

Based on the above information, which of the following statements is accurate?

(A) The roommates spent $700 on food alone.
(B) The roommates spent $300 on entertainment alone.
(C) The roommates spent $300 on clothing alone.
(D) The roommates spent $300 on books alone.

6. You can buy a telephone for $24. If you are charged $3 per month for renting a telephone from the telephone company, how long will it take you to recover the cost of the phone if you buy one?

(A) 6 months   (C) 8 months
(B) 7 months   (D) 9 months

7. What would be the measure of the third angle in the following triangle?

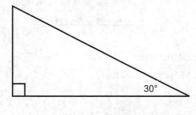

(A) 45°   (C) 60°
(B) 50°   (D) 70°

8. What is the perimeter of this figure?

(A) abc cm
(B) $(a + b + c)$ cm
(C) $(a + b + c)$ cm^2
(D) abc cm^3

9. What is the perimeter of the given triangle?

(A) 11 cm
(B) 12 cm

(C) 13 cm
(D) 15 cm

10. Assuming that the quadrilateral in the following figure is a parallelogram, what would be its area?

(A) 32 cm
(B) 40 cm^2

(C) 64 cm
(D) 64 cm^2

11. Refer to the figure below to determine which of the following statements is correct.

I. Figures A and B have the same area.
II. Figures A and B have the same perimeter.

(A) Only I
(B) Only II

(C) Neither I nor II
(D) Cannot be determined

12. Which of the following is NOT a proper subset of {1, 2, 3, 4}?

(A) {1, 2}
(B) {1, 2, 3}

(C) {1, 2, 4}
(D) {1, 2, 5}

13. Which of the following is an example of a rational number?

(A) $\sqrt{17}$
(B) $4\sqrt{11}$

(C) $7 + \sqrt{9}$
(D) $2 - \sqrt{15}$

14. Which of the following statements includes a cardinal number?

    (A) There are 15 volumes in the set of periodicals.
    (B) I received my 14th volume recently.
    (C) The students meet at Room 304.
    (D) James lives on 3448 Lucky Avenue.

15. In a group of 30 students, 12 are studying mathematics, 18 are studying English, 8 are studying science, 7 are studying both mathematics and English, 6 are studying English and science, 5 are studying mathematics and science, and 4 are studying all three subjects. How many of these students are taking only English? How many of these students are not taking any of these subjects?

    (A) 9 students take only English; 6 students take none of these subjects.
    (B) 10 students take only English; 5 students take none of these subjects.
    (C) 11 students take only English; 5 students take none of these subjects.
    (D) 12 students take only English; 6 students take none of these subjects.

16. For the given Venn diagram, find $n(A \cap B \cap C)$:

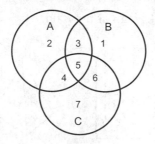

    (A) 3   (C) 5
    (B) 4   (D) 6

17. Find the next three terms in this sequence: 1, 4, 9, 16, . . .

    (A) 20, 25, 31   (C) 25, 36, 49
    (B) 21, 28, 36   (D) 25, 34, 43

18. Assume that one pig eats 4 pounds of food each week. There are 52 weeks in a year. How much food do 10 pigs eat in a week?

    (A) 40 lb.   (C) 208 lb.
    (B) 520 lb.   (D) 60 lb.

19. Suppose that a pair of pants and a shirt cost $65 and the pants cost $25 more than the shirt. What did they each cost?

    (A) The pants cost $40 and the shirt costs $25.
    (B) The pants cost $43 and the shirt costs $22.
    (C) The pants cost $45 and the shirt costs $20.
    (D) The pants cost $50 and the shirt costs $15.

20. There are five members on a basketball team. Supposing each member shakes hands with every other member of the team before the game starts, how many handshakes will there be in all?

    (A) 8   (C) 10
    (B) 9   (D) 12

21. Which figure can be obtained from figure Y by translation?

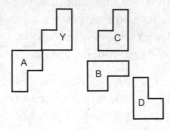

    (A) A   (C) D
    (B) C   (D) None of the above

22. Which of the polygons below is a triangular pyramid?

    (A) 1   (C) 3
    (B) 2   (D) 4

23. The figure below represents a portion of a square pyramid viewed from above. Which of the following statements is true?

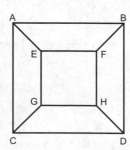

    (A) Edges $\overline{AE}$ and $\overline{BF}$ intersect.
    (B) Lines $\overline{AE}$ and $\overline{BF}$ intersect.
    (C) Face $\overline{CGEA}$ intersects plane $\overline{DHB}$.
    (D) Line $\overline{CG}$ intersects line $\overline{AB}$.

24. Below is a rectangular pyramid ABCDE.

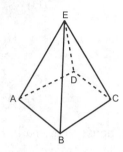

    How many vertices does it have?

    (A) 4   (C) 6
    (B) 5   (D) 7

25. Tom bought a piece of land selling for $20,000. If he had to pay 20 percent of the price as a down payment, how much was the down payment?

    (A) $2,500   (C) $4,500
    (B) $4,000   (D) $5,000

26. A personal computer sells for $3,200 to the general public. If you purchase one in the university, the price is reduced by 20 percent. What is the sale price of the computer?

    (A) $640   (C) $2,560
    (B) $2,410   (D) $3,180

27. In order for Sue to receive a final grade of C, she must have an average greater than or equal to 70% but less than 80% on five tests. Suppose her grades on the first four tests were 65%, 85%, 60%, and 90%. What range of grades on the fifth test would give her a C in the course?

    (A) 40 up to but excluding 95
    (B) 45 up to but excluding 95
    (C) 49 up to but excluding 98
    (D) 50 up to but excluding 100

28. A certain company produces two types of lawnmowers. Type A is self-propelled while type B is not. The company can produce a maximum of 18 mowers per week. It can make a profit of $15 on mower A and a profit of $20 on mower B. The company wants to make at least 2 mowers of type A but not more than 5. They also plan to make at least 2 mowers of type B. Let x be the number of type A produced, and let y be the number of type B produced.

    From the above, which of the following is NOT one of the listed constraints?

    (A) $x \le 5$ (C) $y < 5$
    (B) $x + y \le 18$ (D) $y \ge 2$

29. Mr. Smith died and left an estate to be divided among his wife, two children, and a foundation of his choosing in the ratio of 8:6:6:1. How much did his wife receive if the estate was valued at $300,000?

(A) $114,285.71   (C) $14,285.71
(B) $120,421.91   (D) $125,461.71

30. There were 19 hamburgers for nine people on a picnic. How many whole hamburgers were there for each person if they were divided equally?

   (A) 1   (C) 3
   (B) 2   (D) 4

31. George has four ways to get from his house to the park. He has seven ways to get from the park to the school. How many ways can George get from his house to school by way of the park?

   (A) 4   (C) 28
   (B) 7   (D) 11

32. If it takes one minute per cut, how long will it take to cut a 15-foot long timber into 15 equal pieces?

   (A) 10   (C) 20
   (B) 14   (D) 15

33. Ed has six new shirts and four new pairs of pants. How many combinations of new shirts and pants does he have?

   (A) 10   (C) 20
   (B) 18   (D) 24

34. The property tax rate of the town of Grandview is $32 per $1,000 of assessed value. What is the tax if the property is assessed at $50,000?

   (A) $32   (C) $1,562
   (B) $1,000   (D) $1,600

35. Ralph kept track of his work time in gardening. Refer to the broken-line graph below:

How many minutes did he average per day?

   (A) 20 min.   (C) 23.05 min.
   (B) 21.43 min.   (D) 25 min.

36. Mary had been selling printed shirts in her neighborhood. She made this pictograph to show how much money she made each week.

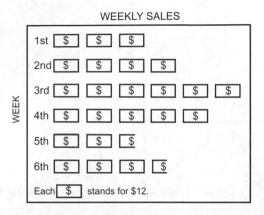

How many weeks were sales more than $55?

(A) 1 week
(B) 2 weeks

(C) 3 weeks
(D) 4 weeks

37. Find the volume of the following figure.

(A) 64 m²
(B) 128 m³

(C) 192 m³
(D) 384 m³

38. The results of Mary's spring semester grades follow. Find her grade point average for the term (A = 4, B = 3, C = 2, D = 1, F = 0).

Course	Credits	Grades
Biology	5	A
English	3	C
Math	3	A
French	3	D
P.E.	2	B

(A) 3.80
(B) 3.50

(C) 2.94
(D) 2.00

39. In a biology class at International University, the grades on the final examination were as follows:

91	81	65	81
50	70	81	93
36	90	43	87
96	81	75	81

Find the mode.

(A) 70　　　　　　　　　　　　　　　　(C) 87
(B) 81　　　　　　　　　　　　　　　　(D) 96

40. One commonly used standard score is a z-score. A z-score gives the number of standard deviations by which the score differs from the mean, as shown in the following example.

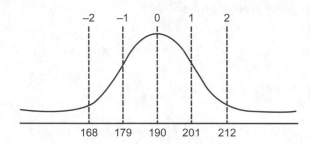

The mean (x) is 190 and the standard deviation(s) is 11. The score of 201 has a z-score of 1 and the score of 168 has a z-score of −2. Consider the mean height of a certain group of people as 190 cm with a standard deviation of 11 cm. Suppose Glenn's height has a z-score of 1.6. What is his height? (Note $z = x − x$.)

(A) 207.60 cm　　　　　　　　　　　(C) 179 cm
(B) 190 cm　　　　　　　　　　　　　(D) 212 cm

41. How many 12 oz. cans of orange juice would it take to give 75 people each an 8 oz. cup of orange juice?

(A) 112 cans　　　　　　　　　　　　(C) 600 cans
(B) 75 cans　　　　　　　　　　　　　(D) 50 cans

42. A car rental agency charges $139 per week plus $0.08 per mile for an average size car. How far can you travel to the nearest mile on a maximum budget of $350?

(A) 2,637 mi.　　　　　　　　　　　(C) 2,110 mi.
(B) 2,640 mi.　　　　　　　　　　　(D) 1,737 mi.

43. Suppose 4 people have to split 50 hours of overtime. Twice the number of hours must be assigned to one worker as to each of the other three. Find the number of hours of overtime that will be assigned to each worker.

(A) 10 hrs. for the first three workers; 20 hrs. for the 4th worker
(B) 8 hrs. for the first three workers; 16 hrs. for the 4th worker
(C) 9 hrs. for the first three workers; 18 hrs. for the 4th worker
(D) 11 hrs. for the first three workers; 22 hrs. for the 4th worker

44. Peter took a 1,500-mile trip in 5 days. Each day, he drove 30 miles more than the day before. How many miles did he cover on the first day?

(A) 375 mi.   (C) 230 mi.
(B) 294 mi.   (D) 240 mi.

45. Mr. Reagan needs 75 m to enclose his rectangular property. If the length of the property is 5 m more than the width, what are the dimensions of his property? Note the figure below.

$P = 2l + 2w$

$l = w + 5$

(A) $w = 16.25$ m; $l - 21.25$ m   (C) $w = 13.00$ m; $l = 24.50$ m
(B) $w = 18.25$ m; $l = 19.25$ m   (D) $w = 17.50$ m; $l = 20.00$ m

Subtest III: English Language Skills

TIME: 40 Minutes
40 Questions

Part A: Usage

<u>DIRECTIONS:</u> Each of the following sentences may contain an error in diction, usage, idiom, or grammar. Some sentences are correct. Some sentences contain one error. No sentence contains more than one error.

If there is an error, it will appear in one of the underlined portions labeled A, B, or C. If there is no error, choose the portion labeled D. If there is an error, select the letter of the portion that must be changed in order to correct the sentence.

<u>EXAMPLE:</u>

He drove <u>slowly</u> and <u>cautiously</u> in order to <u>hopefully</u> avoid having an accident.
       A   **B**   **C**

<u>No error</u>.
D

        Ⓐ Ⓑ ● Ⓓ

1. *Huckleberry Finn*, by <u>general consensus agreement</u> Mark Twain's greatest work, is <u>supremely</u> the
                    A   **B**
American <u>Classic</u>; it is also one of the great books of the world. <u>No error</u>.
       C   **D**

2. The U.S. Constitution <u>supposes</u> what the history of all governments <u>demonstrate</u>, that the executive
                    A   **B**
is the branch <u>most</u> interested in war and most prone to it. <u>No error</u>.
         C   **D**

3. Mama, the <u>narrator</u> of Alice Walker's short story "Everyday Use," speaks fondly of her daughter
         A
upon her return home after a long absence <u>like</u> Mama is <u>proud</u> of her. <u>No error</u>.
                              B   **C**   **D**

4. <u>Nearly</u> one hundred years after the impoverished Vincent Van Gogh died, his paintings <u>had sold</u> for
  A   **B**
more than a <u>million dollars</u>. <u>No error</u>.
          C   **D**

5. Many athletes recruited for football by college coaches <u>expect</u> that they will, <u>in fact</u>, receive an
                                                A   **B**

    education when they <u>accept</u> a scholarship. <u>No error</u>.
                       C   **D**

6. <u>Hopefully</u>, by the end of the <u>Twentieth Century</u>, computer scientists will invent machines with enough
        A   **B**

    intelligence to work without breaking down <u>continually</u>. <u>No error</u>.
                                   C   **D**

7. Studies <u>showing</u> that the earth includes a <u>vast series</u> of sedimentary rocks, some with embedded fossils
                  A   **B**

    <u>that</u> prove the existence of ancient organisms. <u>No error</u>.
    C   **D**

8. When Martin Luther King, Jr., wrote his famous letter from the Birmingham jail, he advocated neither

    evading <u>or</u> defying the law; <u>but</u> he accepted the idea that a penalty <u>results from</u> breaking a law, even an
               A   **B**   **C**

    unjust one. <u>No error</u>.
              D

9. <u>The Eighteenth Century</u> philosopher Adam Smith asserted that a nation <u>achieves</u> the best economic
              A   **B**

    results when individuals work both for their own interests and <u>to gain more goods</u>. <u>No error</u>.
                                          C   **D**

10. According to Niccolo Machiavelli, wise rulers <u>cannot</u> and <u>should not</u> keep their word when such
                                          A   **B**

    integrity would be to their disadvantage and when the reasons for the promise no longer <u>exist</u>. <u>No error</u>.
                                                         C   **D**

11. The Milky Way galaxy, which <u>comprises</u> millions of stars, has both thin and congested spots, but
                                A

    shines <u>their</u> <u>brightest</u> in the constellation Sagittarius. <u>No error</u>.
           B   **C**   **D**

12. <u>To learn</u> an ancient language <u>like</u> Latin or Greek is one way to discover the roots of Western Culture;
    A   **B**

    studying Judeo-Christian religious beliefs <u>is</u> another. <u>No error</u>.
                             C   **D**

13. Many political conservatives <u>contribute</u> the problems of modern American society to the twin evils of
                           A

    the New Deal and <u>secular humanism</u>, both <u>of which</u> are presumed to stem from Marxism. <u>No error</u>.
                  B   **C**   **D**

14. <u>Having minimal exposure</u> to poetry when they attended school, most Americans <u>chose</u> to watch
      A   **B**

television or <u>to read</u> popular magazines for entertainment. <u>No error</u>.
                   C   **D**

15. What makes <u>we</u> humans <u>different from</u> other animals <u>can be defined</u> at least partly by our powerful
                      A   **B**   **C**

and efficient intelligence. <u>No error</u>.
                                    D

16. When one contrasts the ideas of the Romantic William Wordsworth <u>with</u> those of Neoclassicist John
                                                                        A

Dryden, <u>one finds</u> that neither of the poets <u>differ</u> as much as one would expect. <u>No error</u>.
             B   **C**   **D**

17. Carl Jung's hypothesis of the collective unconscious suggests that we inherit <u>cultural-experimental</u>
                                                                                        A

memory in the form of mythological archetype, <u>which arise</u> from repeated <u>patterns</u> of human behavior.
                                                   B   **C**

<u>No error</u>.
   D

18. Bertrand Russell believed that a free person's liberation is <u>effected</u> by a contemplation of <u>Fate</u>; one
                                                                    A   **B**

achieves emancipation through passionate pursuit of eternal things, <u>not through</u> the pursuit of private
                                                                        C

happiness. <u>No error</u>.
               D

19. <u>Latin American</u> literature includes the works of Gabriel Garcia Marquez, Pablo Neruda, and Jorge
      A

Luis Borges; each of these <u>acclaimed</u> artists has won <u>their</u> share of prizes. <u>No error</u>.
                               B   **C**   **D**

20. The reason <u>a large percentage</u> of American college students <u>located</u> Moscow in California is <u>because</u>
                  A   **B**   **C**

they were not required to learn the facts of geography. <u>No error</u>.
                                                            D

21. Astronomers and physicists <u>tell</u> us that the universe is <u>constant</u> expanding and that it <u>comprises</u>
                                  A   **B**   **C**

numerous galaxies like ours. <u>No error</u>.
                                 D

22. <u>Less</u> students chose liberal arts and <u>sciences</u> majors in the 1980s than in the 1960s <u>because of</u> the
      A   **B**   **C**

contemporary view that a college education is a ticket to enter the job market. <u>No error</u>.
                                                                                    D

23. Span of control is the term <u>that</u> refers to the <u>limits</u> of a leader's <u>ability for managing</u> those employees
                                   A   **B**   **C**

    under his/her supervision. <u>No error</u>.
                               D

24. <u>Because some</u> people believe <u>strongly</u> that channelling, the <u>process by which</u> an individual goes into
        A   **B**   **C**

    a trance-like state and communicates the thoughts of an ancient warrior or guru to an audience, helps

    them cope with modern problems, but others condemn the whole idea as mere superstition. <u>No error</u>.
                                                                                                   D

25. The reed on a woodwind instrument is <u>essential</u> <u>being that</u> it controls the quality of <u>tone and sound</u>.
                                                 A   **B**   **C**

    <u>No error</u>.
      D

Part B: Sentence Correction

<u>**DIRECTIONS:**</u> In each of the following sentences some portion of the sentence is underlined. Under each sentence are four choices. The first choice has the same wording as the original. The other three choices are reworded. Sometimes the first choice containing the original wording is the best; sometimes one of the other choices is the best. Choose the letter of the best choice. Your choice should produce a sentence that is not ambiguous or awkward and that is correct, clear, and precise.

This is a test of correct and effective English expression. Keep in mind the standards of English usage, punctuation, grammar, word choice, and construction.

<u>**EXAMPLE:**</u>

When you listen to opera, <u>a person may not appreciate it</u>.

(A) a person may not appreciate it.
(B) it may not be appreciated by a person.
(C) you may not appreciate it.
(D) appreciating it may be a problem for you.

26. Two-thirds of American 17-year-olds do not know that the Civil War <u>takes place</u> between 1850–1900.

(A) takes place
(B) took place
(C) had taken place
(D) have taken place

27. Both professional and amateur ornithologists, <u>people that study birds</u>, recognize the Latin or scientific names of bird species.

(A) people that study birds
(B) people which study birds
(C) the study of birds
(D) people who study birds

28. Many of the oil-producing states spent their huge surplus tax revenues during the oil boom of the 1970s and early 1980s <u>in spite of the fact that</u> oil production from new wells began to flood the world market as early as 1985.

(A) in spite of the fact that
(B) even in view of the fact that
(C) even though
(D) when it was clear that

29. The president of the community college reported <u>as to the expectability of the tuition increase as well as the actual amount</u>.

    (A) as to the expectability of the tuition increase as well as the actual amount
    (B) that the tuition will likely increase by a specific amount
    (C) as to the expectability that tuition will increase by a specific amount
    (D) about the expected tuition increase of five percent

30. Although Carmen developed an interest in classical music, <u>she did not read notes and had never played an instrument</u>.

    (A) she did not read notes and had never played an instrument
    (B) she does not read notes and has never played an instrument
    (C) it is without being able to read notes or having played an instrument
    (D) it is without reading notes nor having played an instrument

31. Political candidates must campaign on issues and ideas that strike a chord within their constituency but <u>with their goal to sway</u> undecided voters to support their candidacy.

    (A) with their goal to sway
    (B) need also to sway
    (C) aiming at the same time to sway
    (D) also trying to sway

32. The major reasons students give for failing courses in college <u>is that they have demanding professors and work at</u> full- or part-time jobs.

    (A) is that they have demanding professors and work at
    (B) are demanding professors and they work at
    (C) are demanding professors, in addition to working at
    (D) are that they have demanding professors and that they have

33. <u>Having command of color, symbolism, as well as technique</u>, Georgia O'Keeffe is considered to be a great American painter.

    (A) Having command of color, symbolism, as well as technique
    (B) Having command of color, symbolism, and her technical ability
    (C) Because of her command of color, symbolism, and technique
    (D) With her command of color and symbolism and being technical

34. <u>Whether the ancient ancestors of American Indians actually migrated or did not</u> across a land bridge now covered by the Bering Strait remains uncertain, but that they could have has not been refuted by other theories.

    (A) Whether the ancient ancestors of American Indians actually migrated or did not
    (B) That the ancient ancestors of American Indians actually did migrate
    (C) Whether in actuality the ancient ancestors of American Indians migrated or not
    (D) That the ancient ancestors of American Indians may actually have migrated

35. Caution in scientific experimentation can <u>sometimes be related more to integrity than to lack of knowledge</u>.

    (A) sometimes be related more to integrity than to lack of knowledge
    (B) sometimes be related more to integrity as well as lack of knowledge
    (C) often be related to integrity as to lack of knowledge
    (D) be related more to integrity rather than lack of knowledge

36. Separated by their successful rebellion against England from any existing form of government, the citizens of the United States <u>have developed a unique constitutional political system</u>.

    (A) have developed a unique constitutional political system
    (B) had developed their constitutional political system uniquely
    (C) have developed their political system into a very unique constitutional one
    (D) have a unique political system, based on a constitution

37. <u>Returning to the ancestral home after 12 years, the house itself seemed much smaller to Joe</u> than it had been when he visited it as a child.

    (A) Returning to the ancestral home after 12 years, the house itself seemed much smaller to Joe
    (B) When Joe returned to the ancestral home after 12 years, he thought the house itself much smaller
    (C) Joe returned to the ancestral home after 12 years, and then he thought the house itself much smaller
    (D) After Joe returned to the ancestral home in 12 years, the house itself seemed much smaller

38. Historians say that the New River of North Carolina, Virginia, and West Virginia, <u>which is 2,700 feet above sea level and 2,000 feet above</u> the surrounding foothills, is the oldest river in the United States.

    (A) which is 2,700 feet above sea level and 2,000 feet above
    (B) with a height of 2,700 feet above sea level as well as 2,000 feet above that of
    (C) 2,700 feet higher than sea level and ascending 2,000 feet above
    (D) located 2,700 feet high above sea level while measuring 2,000 feet above

39. <u>The age of 36 having been reached</u>, the Ukrainian-born Polish sailor Teodor Josef Konrad Korzenio-wski changed his name to Joseph Conrad and began a new and successful career as a British novelist and short story writer.

    (A) The age of 36 having been reached
    (B) When having reached the age of 36
    (C) When he reached the age of 36
    (D) At 36, when he reached that age

40. During the strike, Black South African miners threw a cordon around the <u>gold mine, and they thereby blocked it to all white workers</u>.

    (A) gold mine, and they thereby blocked it to all white workers
    (B) gold mine, by which all white workers were therefore blocked
    (C) gold mine and therefore blocking it to all white workers
    (D) gold mine, thereby blocking it to all white workers

Subtest IV: Essay

TIME: 50 Minutes

DIRECTIONS: Two topics are presented below. Select one of the topics as the basis for your essay. READ THE TOPICS VERY CAREFULLY TO MAKE SURE YOU KNOW WHAT YOU ARE BEING ASKED TO DO.

TOPIC 1:

Many leaders have suggested over the last few years that instead of a military draft we should require all young people to serve the public in some way for a period of time. The service could be military or any other reasonable form of public service. Do you agree or disagree with the statement? Support your opinion with specific examples from history, current events, literature, or personal experience.

OR

TOPIC 2:

The old saying "Experience is the best teacher" suggests to some people that they would benefit more from learning on the job or in the world than from continuing their formal education in the school or college classroom.

ASSIGNMENT:

Write an essay in which you discuss the relative values of experiential and academic learning. Support your view with specific examples from literature, history, current events, or personal experience.

Practice Test 2

ANSWER KEY

Subtest I — Reading

1. (A)	11. (D)	21. (D)	31. (B)
2. (A)	12. (C)	22. (D)	32. (A)
3. (C)	13. (D)	23. (B)	33. (B)
4. (B)	14. (B)	24. (B)	34. (A)
5. (A)	15. (A)	25. (C)	35. (B)
6. (C)	16. (C)	26. (D)	36. (A)
7. (C)	17. (A)	27. (B)	37. (A)
8. (A)	18. (C)	28. (A)	38. (D)
9. (D)	19. (A)	29. (D)	39. (B)
10. (A)	20. (C)	30. (D)	40. (D)

Subtest II — Mathematics

1. (B)	13. (C)	25. (B)	37. (B)
2. (B)	14. (A)	26. (C)	38. (C)
3. (A)	15. (A)	27. (D)	39. (B)
4. (A)	16. (C)	28. (C)	40. (A)
5. (A)	17. (C)	29. (A)	41. (D)
6. (C)	18. (A)	30. (B)	42. (A)
7. (C)	19. (C)	31. (C)	43. (A)
8. (B)	20. (C)	32. (B)	44. (D)
9. (C)	21. (B)	33. (D)	45. (A)
10. (D)	22. (A)	34. (D)	
11. (B)	23. (B)	35. (B)	
12. (D)	24. (B)	36. (B)	

Subtest III — English Language Skills

1. (A)	11. (B)	21. (B)	31. (B)
2. (B)	12. (A)	22. (A)	32. (D)
3. (B)	13. (A)	23. (C)	33. (C)
4. (B)	14. (B)	24. (A)	34. (B)
5. (A)	15. (A)	25. (B)	35. (A)
6. (A)	16. (C)	26. (B)	36. (A)
7. (A)	17. (D)	27. (D)	37. (B)
8. (A)	18. (D)	28. (C)	38. (A)
9. (C)	19. (C)	29. (B)	39. (C)
10. (D)	20. (C)	30. (A)	40. (D)

Detailed Explanations of Answers

Subtest I: Reading

1. **(A)**

   Choices (B) and (D) present minor problems in spa maintenance. As bacteria and viruses are controlled by both temperature and chemicals, it becomes a possible source of health problems if ignored.

2. **(A)**

   Choices (B), (C), and (D) are correct levels or degrees.

3. **(C)**

   Choices (A) and (B) represent an inference that goes beyond the scope of the passage and would indicate biases of the reader. Although the passage explains spa maintenance, choice (D), the information is not adequate to serve as a detailed guide.

4. **(B)**

   The other choices, (A) and (C), refer to chemical or temperature maintenance. Although choice (D) helps to ensure clarity, choice (B) is explicitly stated in the passage.

5. **(A)**

   Choices (B), (C), and (D) are appropriate chemicals. Although chlorine is an alternative to bromine, this passage indicates it should be granular as indicated in choice (A).

6. **(C)**

   Choices (A) and (B) appear to be acceptable, whereas choice (D) indicates a perfect correlation. Choice (C) is correct as the passage is about correlational statistical significance, which permits prediction.

7. **(C)**

   Choice (A) goes beyond the information provided in the passage. Choice (B) is incorrect as correlation cannot indicate causality. Choice (D) is not statistically possible. The high positive correlation trend indicates that these variables are important to consider for future research. Thus, choice (C) is correct.

8.   **(A)**

Choices (B), (C), and (D) represent inferences that are based on inadequate information, which go beyond the scope of the passage. As these story elements are not taught explicitly in the first grade or prior to entering school, children apparently have picked up these elements from their exposures to stories as indicated by choice (A).

9.   **(D)**

Although the content might be appropriate for each of the journals, choices (A), (B), and (C), the style of writing suggests that it would be most appropriate for choice (D), *Reading Research Quarterly*, as this passage reports research results.

10.   **(A)**

The passage provides information for the grade level and mentions if it was significant or substantial. As this statement follows information provided for fifth/sixth grades, it refers to that level, thus choice (A).

11.   **(D)**

Choices (A), (B), and (C) all connote extreme or inappropriate attitudes not expressed in the passage. The author presents an informed concern—choice (D).

12.   **(C)**

For the other choices, (A), (B), and (D), the criteria, the role, the discussion, and the assurance for communication or learning are not provided in the passage. The passage stresses the importance of authenticity in communication—choice (C).

13.   **(D)**

Each of the choices is a possible definition, but the passage overall suggests that communication needs to be developed so that students' responses may become more significant and authentic—choice (D).

14.   **(B)**

Choices (A) and (D) are not supported by the passage. Choice (C) represents an incorrect conclusion. Choice (B) is supported by the various investigators' explanations.

15.   **(A)**

As stated explicitly in the passage, the various investigators have attempted to explain the role of imitation in language—choice (A). The other choices go beyond the scope of the passage.

16. **(C)**

As the investigators studied different aspects of language while attempting to explain the role of imitation in language, choice (C) is correct. The other choices go beyond the scope of the passage.

17. **(A)**

The passage explicitly states that computers are capable of addressing the issues of practice and the true act of reading, choice (A). The other choices represent inferences that are not supported by the passage.

18. **(C)**

Although the reader might make inferences to select choices (A), (B), and (D), ways to use a word processor to make practice resemble the true reading act are not stated in the passage. Thus, choice (C) is the correct answer.

19. **(A)**

Although audiences in choices (B), (C), and (D) may benefit from the information provided in the passage, the passage explicitly states that a greater understanding of the information in the passage should assist teachers—choice (A).

20. **(C)**

Each of the choices is a definition of variance. However, for this passage, choice (C) is the most appropriate.

21. **(D)**

Although meaning is found in the components of each choice, the passage states that we should begin with students' meaning before moving to the commonalities of story meaning—choice (D).

22. **(D)**

As the passage presents information by various researchers on children's stories, the passage ends with an unanswered question that still needs to be addressed by reading researchers as provided in choice (D).

23. **(B)**

Although more information may be needed about story content and story structure as indicated in choices (A), (C), and (D), the main question that remains to be answered is choice (B).

24. **(B)**

Each choice provides partially correct information about story content and story structure; choice (B) provides the most complete response.

25. **(C)**

    Each choice is a possible definition. However, choice (C) is most appropriate as there was an increased interest by researchers in these and other areas even though it has been an ongoing concern of some researchers.

26. **(D)**

    Choice (B) is not supported by the passage. Choices (A) and (C) go beyond the passage. The last sentence states "The pattern . . . resulting in teachers prone to teach as they had been taught"—thus choice (D).

27. **(B)**

    The other choices, (A), (C), and (D), are not supported by the passage. Although the passage mentions that teacher education has reflected evolving attitudes about education, the attitudes are not spelled out—choice (B).

28. **(A)**

    Only choice (A) has the correct sequence; the other sequences are incorrect.

29. **(D)**

    Choices (A), (B), and (C) are statements about education, teacher education, and teachers. Choice (D)'s statement that teacher education has changed very little implies that this lack of change could be a source of dissatisfaction.

30. **(D)**

    Choices (A), (B), and (C) suggest rights either by heredity or supreme authority. The hyphenated term "liege-lord" connotes both entitled rights and power to command respect. Thus choice (D), "master" (one who assumes authority and property rights through ability and power to control), best represents the hawk.

31. **(B)**

    Choices (C) and (D) are not supported by the passage. Choice (A) represents a possible conclusion, but choice (B) suggests real thought about the hawk.

32. **(A)**

    Each of the other choices contains a term that does not refer to human qualities. The other qualities may refer to the hawk, e.g., perch, or to the author of the passage, e.g., disdain.

33. **(B)**

Choice (D) is incorrect because of definition. Choices (A) and (C) are possible definitions, but *feudal* most clearly denotes an association to the Middle Ages.

34. **(A)**

The passage explicitly states that political efficacy is a feeling that one's actions can have an impact on government—choice (A). Choices (B), (C), and (D) are not supported by the passage.

35. **(B)**

Choices (A), (C), and (D) are not supported by the passage. The passage states ". . . political social- ization, a process varying according to political systems but toward the end of indoctrinating the members to the respective political system"—choice (B).

36. **(A)**

Although the other choices (B), (C), and (D) are possible definitions, the passage explicitly states that "a political system is one of inputs, conversions, and outputs by which the wants of a society are transformed into binding decisions"—thus choice (A).

37. **(A)**

Choices (B), (C), and (D) contain an incorrect concept of either Easton and Dennis or Lipset. Only choice (A) has the correct concepts for both Easton and Dennis and Lipset.

38. **(D)**

Choices (A), (B), and (C) each contain an area that is considered a component of culture, such as religion, education, and language. Thus, choice (D) is the most appropriate response.

39. **(B)**

Although each definition appears appropriate, choices (A), (C), and (D) assume that a solution is known, or has been known at one time, and could be solved. Choice (B) suggests a situation that is intri- cate enough to perplex the mind. Choice (B) is most appropriate for this passage as a definition of enigma is an inexplicable situation.

40. **(D)**

Although choices (A), (B), and (C) may touch on such a topic, the roles and functions of gov- ernmental offices and departments are generally addressed in an American Government class. Thus, choice (D) is correct.

Subtest II: Mathematics

1. **(B)**

   7 is in the tenth's place. Since the next digit (2) is below 5, drop this digit and retain the 7. The answer, therefore, is 406.7.

2. **(B)**

   The mean IQ score of 100 is given. One standard deviation above the mean is 34% of the cases, with an IQ score up to 115. One standard deviation below the mean is another 34% of the cases, with an IQ score till 85. So, a total of 68% of the students have an IQ between 85 and 115. Therefore, $1,500 \times .68 = 1,020$.

3. **(A)**

$$12 + 2x = 24$$
$$2x = 24 - 12$$
$$2x = 12$$
$$x = \frac{12}{2}$$
$$x = 6$$

4. **(A)**

$$(10 + x)2 = 28$$
$$20 + 2x = 28$$
$$2x = 28 - 20$$
$$2x = 8$$
$$x = \frac{8}{2}$$
$$x = 4$$

5. **(A)**

   $$\$2,000 \times .35 = \$700.$$

   The rest have wrong computations.

6. **(C)**

   Let x = length of time (# of mos) to recover cost.

$$3x = 24$$
$$x = \frac{24}{3}$$
$$x = 8 \text{ mos.}$$

7.   **(C)**

With one right angle (90°) and a given 30° angle, the missing angle, therefore, is a 60° angle.

$$90° + 30° = 120°; \ 180° - 120° = 60°$$

8.   **(B)**

The perimeter is the distance around the triangle, which is, therefore,

$$(a + b + c) \text{ cm}.$$

9.   **(C)**

The perimeter is the distance around the triangle. Therefore,

$$2 \text{ cm} + 6 \text{ cm} + 5 \text{ cm} = 13 \text{ cm}.$$

10.   **(D)**

The area of a parallelogram is base × height. Therefore,

$$A = bh = (16 \text{ cm}) \times (4 \text{ cm}) = 64 \text{ cm}^2.$$

11.   **(B)**

Figure A has an area of about 9 square units while Figure B has an area of about 7 square units. Both Figures A and B have the same perimeter of about 12 units.

12.   **(D)**

Only (D) has an element (which is 5) not present in the given set of {1, 2, 3, 4}.

13.   **(C)**

Nine is the square of an integer. 17, 11, and 15 are not squares of an integer. Therefore, they are irrational numbers. 7 is not the cube of an integer. Hence, it is an irrational number as well.

14.   **(A)**

15 is used as a cardinal number. The rest are either ordinal (B), or nominal (C), (D), numbers.

15.   **(A)**

Use the following Venn diagram (as shown below) with three circles to represent the set of students in each of the listed subject matter areas. Start with four students taking all three subjects. We write the number 4 in the region that is the intersection of all these circles. Then we work backward: Since seven are taking math and English, and four of these have already been identified as also taking English, math, and science, there must be exactly three taking only math and English. That is, there must be three in the region representing math and English, but not science. Continuing in this manner, we enter the given data in the diagram.

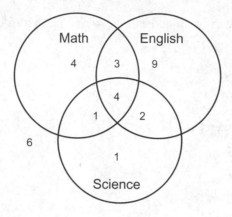

16. **(C)**

There is one element in the intersection of all three sets. Thus,

$n(A \cap B \cap C) = 5$.

17. **(C)**

The sequence 1, 4, 9, 16 is the sum of the odd numbers.

1. 1

2. $1 + 3 = 4$

3. $1 + 3 + 5 = 9$

4. $1 + 3 + 5 + 7 = 16$

18. **(A)**

Here, one must use only the needed information. Do not be distracted by superfluous data. Simple multiplication will do. If one pig eats four pounds of food per week, how much will 10 pigs eat in one week? $10 \times 4 = 40$ pounds. The problem intentionally contains superfluous data (52 weeks), which should not distract the reader from its easy solution. Ratio and proportion will also work here:

$\frac{1}{10} = \frac{4}{x}$, $x = 40$ pounds/week.

19. **(C)**

Let the variable S stand for the cost of the shirt. Then the cost of the pair of pants is $S + 25$ and

$$S + (S + 25) = 65$$
$$2S = 65 - 25$$
$$2S = 40$$
$$S = 20$$

$20 (cost of shirt)

$20 + $25 = $45 (cost of pants)

20. **(C)**

The possible handshakes are illustrated by listing all the possible pairs of letters. Thus,

AB	AC	AD	AE
BC	BD	BE	
CD	CE		
DE			

(a total of 10 handshakes)

21. **(B)**

Only (B) involves a change by only translation.

22. **(A)**

(B) is a rectangular prism. (C) is a square pyramid. (D) is neither a prism nor a pyramid.

23. **(B)**

If one continues lines $\overline{AE}$ and $\overline{BF}$, they intersect at a common vertex. The rest do not.

24. **(B)**

Points ABCDE are the vertices. Thus, 5 is correct.

25. **(B)**

Let

$D = $ down payment
$D = \$20,000 \times .20$
$D = \$4,000$

26. **(C)**

    20% of $3,200 = $640 (amount price reduced)

    $3,200 − $640 = $2,560 (sale price)

27. **(D)**

Let x = 5th grade

$$\text{Average} = \frac{65+85+60+90+x}{5}$$

For Sue to obtain a C, her average must be greater than or equal to 70 but less than 80.

$$70 \le \frac{65+85+60+90+x}{5}$$

$$70 \le \frac{300+x}{5} < 80$$

$$5(70) \le 5(300 + x \div 5) < 5(80)$$

$$350 \le 300 + x < 400$$

$$350 - 300 \le x < 400 - 300$$

$$50 \le x < 100$$

Thus, a grade of 50 up to but not including a grade of 100 will result in a C.

28. **(C)**

All but (C) are constraints. The constraint for y is to at least make two mowers.

29. **(A)**

    The ratio 8:6:6:1 implies that for each $8 the wife received, each child received $6 and the foundation $1. The estate is divided into $8 + 6 + 6 + 1$, or 21 equal shares. The wife received $\frac{8}{21}$ of $300,000 or $114,285.71, each child received $\frac{6}{21}$ of $300,000, or $85,714.29, and the foundation received $\frac{1}{21}$ of $300,000 or $14,285.71. As a check,

    $114,285.71 + $85,714.29 + $85,714.29 + $14,285.71 = $300,000.

30. **(B)**

Simple division: $\frac{19}{9} = 2$ whole hamburgers with one left over.

31. **(C)**

Simple multiplication: $7 \times 4 = 28$.

32. **(B)**

   For a 15 ft. log, it will take 14 cuts to make 15 equal pieces. Therefore, 14 minutes for 14 cuts.

33. **(D)**

   Simple multiplication.

   $6 \times 4 = 24$.

34. **(D)**

   First find out how many shares of $1,000 there are in $50,000.

   $$\$50,000 \div 1,000 = 50$$

   Then, multiply the shares by the cost ($50 \times \$32$) and the answer is $1,600.

35. **(B)**

   Find the sum of the seven days. Thus:

   $$M = 25;$$
   $$T = 30;$$
   $$W = 20;$$
   $$Th = 25;$$
   $$F = 10;$$
   $$Sat = 40;$$
   $$Sun = 0,$$

   or a total of 150 minutes. Find the average by dividing 150 by $7 = 21.43$ minutes.

36. **(B)**

   If each ☐$☐ stands for $12, only weeks 3 and 4 had a sale of $72 and $60, respectively. The rest are below $55.

37. **(B)**

   The volume of a pyramid is

   $$V = \frac{1}{3}Bh,$$

   where B is the area of the base and h is the height of the pyramid. Thus,

   $$V = \frac{1}{3}(64)(6)$$
   $$= \frac{1}{3}(384) = 128 \text{ m}^3.$$

38. **(C)**

Total the number of credits earned (in this case = 16 credits). Multiply the credit and the weight for the earned grade per subject (e.g., biology = $5 \times 4 = 20$). Then add the total of the products of the credits and corresponding weights (in this case = 47). Then divide 47 by 16 to get the grade point average of 2.94. See table below.

$$\text{Biology} = 5 \times 4 = 20$$

$$\text{English} = 3 \times 2 = 6$$

$$\text{Math} = 3 \times 4 = 12$$

$$\text{French} = 3 \times 1 = 3$$

$$\text{GPA} = \frac{\text{total cr} \times \text{wt}}{\text{total cr}} = \frac{47}{16} = 2.94$$

$$\text{P.E.} = \frac{2}{16 \text{ cr}} \times 3 = \frac{6}{47 \text{ cr} \times \text{ gr wt}}$$

39. **(B)**

Mode is the most frequent score. 81 appeared five times and is therefore the mode.

40. **(A)**

Following the formula

$$z = \frac{x - \bar{x}}{\text{s.d.}}$$

thus,

$$1.6 = x - \frac{190}{11}$$

$$17.60 = x - 190$$

$$x = 190 + 17.60$$

$$x = 207.60 \text{ cm (Glenn's height)}$$

41. **(D)**

First, find out how many ounces of orange juice are needed. So, multiply 75×8 oz. = 600 oz. needed. Then, divide 600 by 12 oz. = 50 12 oz. cans needed to serve 75 people with 8 oz. of juice each.

42. **(A)**

m = number of miles you can travel

$\$0.08m$ = amount spent for m miles travelled at 8 cents per mile,

(rental fee + mileage charge = total amount spent)

$\$139 + \$0.08m = \$350$

$139 - 139 + 0.08m = 350 - 139$

$$\frac{0.08m}{0.08} = \frac{211}{0.08}$$

$m = 2,637.5$

$m = 2,637$

Therefore, you can travel 2,637 miles (if you go 2,638 miles you have travelled too far).

43. **(A)**

Let x = number of hours of overtime for the 1st worker,

x = number of hours of overtime for the 2nd worker,

x = number of hours of overtime for the 3rd worker,

$2x$ = number of hours of overtime for the 4th worker.

$x + x + x + 2x = 50$

$\qquad 5x = 50$

$$\qquad x = \frac{50}{5}$$

$\qquad\qquad x = 10$ hrs of overtime for the 1st three workers

$\qquad\qquad 2x = 20$ hrs of overtime for the 4th worker

44. **(D)**

Let m = number of miles covered the 1st day.

$m + 30$ = number of miles covered the 2nd day,

$m + 30 + 30$ = number of miles covered the 3rd day,

$m + 30 + 30 + 30$ = number of miles covered the 4th day,

$m + 30 + 30 + 30 + 30$ = number of miles covered the 5th day.

$m + m + 30$ and so on . . . $= 1,500$

$5m + 30\,(10) = 1,500$

$\qquad 5m + 300 = 1,500$

$\qquad\qquad 5m = 1,500 - 300$

$\qquad\qquad 5m = 1,200$

$$\qquad\qquad m = \frac{1,200}{5}$$

$\qquad\qquad m = 240$ mi.

45. **(A)**

Using the formula

$$P = 2w + 2l$$

$$75 = 2w + 2(w + 5)$$

$$75 = 2w + 2w + 10$$

$$75 = 4w + 10$$

$$65 = 4w$$

$$16.25 = w$$

The width is therefore 16.25 m and the length is $w + 5$ or $16.25 + 5 = 21.25$ m.

Subtest III: English Language Skills

1. **(A)**

   Choice (A) is obviously wordy, "consensus" meaning the same as "general agreement," so it is the best choice. None of the others has a usage error. Choice (B) underscores the claim made in the whole sentence by establishing the book as the "best" American work. Finally, choice (C) is acceptable because of commas in other parts of the sentence. Choice (D) clearly does not apply.

2. **(B)**

   This question has several potential errors. Choice (A) calls to question the attribution of human rationality to an inanimate object, but since the Constitution actually does have logical premises, we can correctly say that the document can posit the premise stated. Choice (C) is acceptable because the superlative is referenced within the sentence; one should know that the U.S. government has three branches. That leaves choices (B) and (D). Choice (B) is the verb in the clause beginning with the word "what"; it is plural, and therefore, incorrect because it does not agree with its subject "history," a singular noun. Do not be fooled by the intervening plural word "governments." Since choice (B) is the error, choice (D) would no longer be considered.

3. **(B)**

   Even though people use "like" as a conjunction in conversation and public speaking, it is a preposition, and formal written English requires "as," "as if," or "as though" when what follows is a clause. No other choice is even suspect.

4. **(B)**

   One could question the use of "nearly" (A), but it is correct. One might argue also that "million dollars" (C) should be written "$1 million," but choice (B) is so clearly an incorrect use of the past perfect tense that the other possibilities, remote at best, pale by comparison. The simple past tense ("sold"), the present progressive tense ("are selling"), or the present perfect progressive tense ("have been selling") could each be used correctly depending on the meaning intended.

5. **(A)**

   This choice is not as obvious, but authorities agree that the use of "expect" to mean "suppose" or "believe" (the usage here) is either informal or colloquial, but again not formal written English. The next most likely choice, (D), would suggest that informal or colloquial usage is appropriate. The third most likely choice, (C), brings to mind the distinction between "accept" and "except," a word pair often confused. However, "accept" is correct here.

6. **(A)**

   Regardless of its popular usage "hopefully" is an adverb trying to be a clause ("it is hoped" or "I hope"). However, instances still exist that require a distinction between the two uses. To be clear, use, "hopefully" when you mean "in a hopeful manner." ["He wished hopefully that she would accept his proposal of marriage."] Choice (C) appears suspicious. "Continually" means recurrence at intervals over a period of time, so it is correctly used to imply that machines do break down often. (B) Capitalizing "Twentieth Century" is also appropriate as it is here used as the specific historical period (like the "Middle Ages"). We would not capitalize the phrase if it were used simply to count, as in "The twentieth century from now will surely find enormous changes in the world." It is incorrect to hyphenate a number-noun phrase like this one when it stands alone as a noun phrase.

7.   **(A)**

The two most suspicious choices are (A) and (C) because the item is a sentence fragment. No reasonable substitute for (C) would solve both the logic problem (incomplete thought) and the punctuation problem (comma splice if you omit "that"). Changing "showing" to "show" would, however, make the clause into a complete sentence with correct punctuation. Choice (B) does not provoke suspicion.

8.   **(A)**

Again, the two most questionable choices, (A) and (B), compete for our attention. The use of "but" makes sense because it shows contrast to the previous idea. ("Don't evade or defy the law, *but* if caught breaking a law, accept the penalty.") The use of "or," however, is clearly not parallel to the immediately preceding use of "neither." The proper phrase is "neither . . . nor" for negative alternate choices. Choice (C) does not demand a second look.

9.   **(C)**

This choice involves parallel construction, or the lack of it. The word "both" introduces a pair of phrases, one a prepositional phrase ("for their own interests"), the other an infinitive phrase ("to gain more goods"). Aside from being inelegant, "to gain more goods" is also not the same structure and should be changed to "their own gain" to make the two phrases perfectly parallel. Choice (C) is not problematic. Choice (A) is another candidate because of the capitalization and the lack of a hyphen between "Eighteenth" and "Century." The capitalization is correct and no hyphen is needed when the phrase becomes an adjective that has meaning as a single phrase, which the capitalization suggests, or if the first word forms a familiar pair with the following word and if there is no danger of confusion. [The sentence clearly does not mean that Smith is the eighteenth (small "e") philosopher, but *the* Eighteenth Century philosopher.]

10.   **(D)**

The other choices all fail to exhibit inappropriate usage. Choice (A), "cannot," is spelled as one word; choice (B), "should not," is parallel to "cannot" and adds meaning necessary to the thought. Finally, choice (C) is a third-person plural verb agreeing with its subject, "reasons."

11.   **(B)**

"Milky Way galaxy" is the singular antecedent, for which the pronoun referent should be "its" (inanimate object). Do not be confused by the intervening words ("stars" and "spots"); it is the galaxy which shines in this sentence, not the stars or the spots. Choice (A) is the correct usage of "comprises." Choice (C) is appropriate because the sentence has an internally supplied superlative sense; it does not need a "brightest of" phrase.

12. **(A)**

Again, non-parallel structure is the key of this and many other test items. Because of the overwhelming importance of understanding balance in sentence structure, tests like this one emphasize parallel sentence structures. "To learn" clashes with "studying" in the parallel clause. You cannot choose "studying." "Learning" substituted for "To learn" would make the clauses parallel. Choice (B) is a correct use of "like" as a preposition (objects: "Latin," "Greek"). Choice (C) is correctly singular as the verb of the noun phrase "studying . . . beliefs."

13. **(A)**

This is a colloquial, nonstandard substitution for the correct word, "attribute." Choice (B) is correctly lowercase, not capitalized. Choice (C) is a correct, if a bit stiff, phrase.

14. **(B)**

This is an incorrect simple past verb tense. You have to spot the context clue "most Americans" "attended" school in the past, which suggests they no longer do so now. They must then "choose" their entertainment. Choice (A) is questionable, but the present participial phrase suggests coincidence with the time "most Americans" "attended school." It is, therefore, correct. Choice (C) is correctly an infinitive that is parallel to "to watch."

15. **(A)**

The two most questionable choices are (A) and (B). Choice (A) is incorrectly a subjective case pronoun when it should be objective (object of verb "makes," subject "What"). If you know the difference between "different from" (correctly used in this sentence) and "difference than" (correctly used only to introduce a clause), then choice (B) is no longer viable. Besides being a passive construction, choice (C) has no objectionable qualities; it is grammatically correct.

16. **(C)**

This is a case of subject-verb disagreement related to the definition of the word "neither" (subject) as singular. Its verb must also be singular, and "differ" is plural. Choice (A) correctly uses English idiom ("compare to"—"contrast with"). Choice (B) is a singular verb agreeing with its subject, "one."

17. **(D)**

Everything in the sentence is acceptable or correct usage, even though some of it may be a bit stuffy and pedantic, i.e., choice (A). Choice (B) correctly agrees with its subject "which" (plural, antecedent "archetypes"). Choice (C) might be considered redundant ("repeated" and "patterns"), but that is not apparent from the context.

18. **(D)**

You are likely to have chosen either (A) or (B) here. The affect/effect word pair often confuses students, and this instance is one in which "effected" is correctly used as a verb meaning "brought about" or "caused to happen." The question in choice (B) is whether or not to capitalize the word "Fate." When it refers to the collective term for the Greek concept of destiny (actually gods, the Fates), as it does here, it is appropriately capitalized. Choice (C) does not seem questionable.

19. **(C)**

Again, the problem here is pronoun-antecedent agreement. "Their" does not refer to the three writers collectively; its antecedent is "each," which is always singular, not plural ("each one"). There is nothing wrong with choices (A) and (B).

20. **(C)**

The error here is known as faulty predication ("reason . . . is because"). The usage rule is that "because" is redundant for "reason." Choice (A) is appropriate, if a bit general (not 30 or 70 percent, for example). The verb in choice (B) is correct and in the past tense.

21. **(B)**

Choice (A) is a verb correctly in agreement with its compound subject. Choice (C) correctly uses the word "comprises" and makes it agree with its subject. Only (B) seems incorrect. The structure requires the adverb form "constantly," since it describes an adjective, "expanding."

22. **(A)**

This is the classic confusion of "less" for the correct "fewer." "Few(er)" refers to countable things or persons; "little (less)" refers to things that can be measured or estimated but not itemized.

23. **(C)**

Choice (A) is a correct use of the relative pronoun. Nothing is unusual about (B). (C) is the culprit here: it should be the infinitive form to adhere to the idiom, "ability to (verb)."

24. **(A)**

The sentence as it stands is illogical. Removing "Because" will make it sensible. (B) is an appropriate adverb modifying "believe"; (C) is a clear and effective subordination of an explanation of a term.

25. **(B)**

"Being that" is colloquial for "because," which is better for at least the reason that it is shorter, but also that it is more formal. No other choices seem out of bounds.

26. **(B)**

This question of appropriate verb tense requires the simple past tense verb "took" because the Civil War happened in a finite time period in the past. The other choices all fail that test. The original is present tense, and does not logically fit the facts. Choice (D) is the present perfect tense, which suggests a continuous action from the past to the present. Choice (C) is the past perfect tense, which suggests a continuing action from one time in the past to another in the more recent past.

27. **(D)**

We can eliminate fairly quickly choice (C) as either an inappropriate or awkward appositive to "ornithology," instead of "ornithologists." Neither is (A) the best choice even though some may consider it acceptable. Likewise, choice (B) tends to be limited to nonrestrictive clauses, unlike this one. Choice (D) then correctly uses a "personal" relative pronoun.

28. **(C)**

Choices (A), (C), and (D) are the best candidates because they are more concise than the other two choices. Each does express the same idea, but (D) does not as strongly indicate the contrast between the two clauses in the sentence as do choices (A) and (C). Choice (C) clearly makes its point in fewer words and is the better choice.

29. **(B)**

The phrase "as to" often is overblown and unclear, so it is best to eliminate it when there are other choices. Likewise, "expectability" does not exactly roll off your tongue. That leaves choices (B) and (D). Choice (D) adds a definite figure, unwarranted by the original sentence. It also is duller than (B), which does change the wording for the better and also indicates that the "actual amount" is to be announced, rather than that it is already known.

30. **(A)**

Choices (C) and (D) introduce unnecessary absolute phrases beginning with "it," which makes the sentences wordy. They can be eliminated immediately. Between (A) and (B) the difference boils down to the present tense vs. the past tense. Choice (A) uses past tenses, which seem better in sequence to follow the past tense verb "developed."

31. **(B)**

Choices (A), (C), and (D) can be disqualified quickly because they are not parallel to the structure of the main clause. Choice (B) reads well and has the virtue of brevity.

32. **(D)**

The choices are easy to discern in this sentence. The original verb does not agree with its subject, nor is the structure parallel. Choice (B) does not have parallel structure (phrase and clause). Choice (C) does not logically agree with the subject ("reasons") since it names one ("demanding professors") but relegates the other reason to an afterthought. Choice (D) has both parallel structure and subject-verb agreement; it also names two reasons.

33. **(C)**

The original suffers from inadequate causal relationship and non-parallel structure. Choice (D) is unnecessarily wordy; (D) is still not parallel. Choice (B) switches its structure at the end. Although it is technically parallel, it is still awkward because of the addition of the possessive pronoun "her." Choice (C) solves both problems by clearly showing cause and by being parallel (three nouns in series).

34. **(B)**

This sentence presents an incomplete comparison and a redundancy ("Whether"/"or did not"/ "remains uncertain"). Choice (B) eliminates both problems clearly. Choice (C) is worse in both respects. Choice (D) clears up the syntax but leaves some redundancy ("may actually have"/"remains uncertain"). Choice (B) eliminates both problems clearly.

35. **(A)**

The sentence as is reads well; it is perfectly balanced. Choice (B) introduces an incomplete comparison ("more" but no "than"). Choice (C) awkwardly uses "as to." Choice (D) makes a scrambled mess by introducing an illogical structure.

36. **(A)**

"Unique" means just that; it should not have qualifiers like "very" or "nearly." That eliminates choice (C). Choice (B) changes the meaning by making the development unique, instead of the system. Choice (D) uses an inappropriate verb tense because the first of the sentence suggests the Revolutionary War period, definitely in the past.

37. **(B)**

The original sentence, (A), has a dangling modifier (participial phrase). The house cannot return to itself, nor can "it" (pronoun for house). Choice (D) seems to leave something out: "returned to . . . home in 12 years." Choice (C) solves the original problem but is unnecessarily wordy. Choice (B) properly solves the dangling modifier problem by subordinating the return in an adverbial clause.

38. **(A)**

Choice (A) is the only response that makes sense. Each of the others introduces illogical comparisons or structures (non-parallel); (B) and (D) are also verbose. Choice (C) is concise but not parallel.

39. **(C)**

This sentence suggests causal relationships between the parts of the sentence that do not belong there. Choice (B) echoes the original (A) in that regard. Choice (D) has garbled syntax. (C) shows clearly that the cause-effect relationship is, rather, a time relationship.

40. **(D)**

This is essentially a problem of wordiness. (D) is the shortest and most clear of all the choices. The syntax of (B) complicates the idea unnecessarily. (C) does not use the appropriate conjunctive adverb; "thereby" is more precise than "therefore" when referring to an event.

Essay Scoring Guide

The FTCE-GKT essay sections are scored by two writing experts on the basis of the criteria outlined below. In addition to comparing your essay to those included in our practice tests, you may use these guidelines to estimate your score on this section. Remember that your score is the sum of the scores of two writing experts, so provided you respond to the assigned topic, your score will fall somewhere between two and twelve. Scores will be assigned based on the following guidelines:

SCORE of 6: The paper has a clearly established main idea that the writer fully develops with specific details and examples. Organization is notably logical and coherent. Point of view is consistently maintained. Vocabulary and sentence structure are varied and effective. Errors in sentence structure, usage, and mechanics are few and insignificant.

SCORE of 5: The paper has a clearly established main idea that is adequately developed and recognizable through specific details and/or examples. Organization follows a logical and coherent pattern. Point of view is mostly maintained. Vocabulary and sentence structure are mostly varied and effective. Occasional errors in sentence structure, usage, and mechanics do not interfere with the writer's ability to communicate.

SCORE of 4: The paper has an adequately stated main idea that is developed with some specific details and examples. Supporting ideas are presented in a mostly logical and coherent manner. Point of view is somewhat maintained. Vocabulary and sentence structure are somewhat varied and effective. Occasional errors in sentence structure, usage, and mechanics may interfere with writer's ability to communicate.

SCORE of 3: The paper states a main idea that is developed with generalizations or lists. The paper may contain occasional lapses in logic and coherence, and organization is mechanical. Point of view is ambiguous. Vocabulary and sentence structure are repetitious and often ineffective. A variety of errors in sentence structure, usage, and mechanics sometimes interferes with the writer's ability to communicate.

SCORE of 2: The paper presents an incomplete or ambiguous main idea. Support is developed with generalizations and lists. Organization is mechanical. The paper contains occasional lapses in logic and coherence. Point of view is confusing and distracting. Word choice is simplistic, and sentence structure is disjointed. Errors in sentence structure, usage, and mechanics frequently interfere with the writer's ability to communicate.

SCORE of 1: The paper has no evident main idea. Development is inadequate and/or irrelevant. Organization is illogical and/or incoherent. Point of view has not been established. Vocabulary and sentence structure are garbled and confusing. Significant and numerous errors in sentence structure, usage, and mechanics interfere with the writer's ability to communicate.

Subtest IV: Sample Essays with Commentary

Topic 1

Strong Response

The cynic in me wants to react to the idea of universal public service for the young with a reminder about previous complaints aimed at the military draft. These complaints suggest that wars might never be fought if the first people drafted were the adult leaders and lawmakers. Still the idea of universal public service sounds good to this concerned citizen who sees everywhere—not just in youth—the effects of a selfish and self-indulgent culture.

One reads and hears constantly about young people who do not care about the problems of our society. These youngsters seem interested in money and the luxuries money can buy. They do not want to work from the minimum wage up, but want instead to land a high paying job without "paying their dues." An informal television news survey of high school students a few years ago suggested that students had the well entrenched fantasy that with no skills or higher education they would not accept a job paying less than $20 an hour. Perhaps universal service helping out in an urban soup kitchen for six months would instill a sense of selflessness rather than selfishness.

The shiny gleam of a new expensive sports sedan bought on credit by a recent accounting student reflects self indulgence that might be toned down by universal service. That self indulgence may reflect merely a lack of discipline, but it also may reflect a lack of purpose in life. Philosophers, theologians and leaders of all types suggest throughout the ages that money and objects do not ultimately satisfy. Helping others—service to our fellow human beings—often does. Universal public service for that accounting student might require a year helping low income or senior citizens prepare income tax forms. This type of service would dim that self indulgence, give the person some experience in the real world, and also give satisfaction that one's life is not lived only to acquire things.

Universal service might also help young people restore faith in their nation and what it means to them. Yes, this is the land of opportunity, but it is also a land of forgotten people, and it is a land that faces outside threats. Part of the requisite public service should remind young people of their past and of their responsibility to the future.

Analysis

This essay has a score range of 5–6. It uses a traditional structure: the first paragraph states the topic, the second and third present development with specific examples from personal observation. The fourth ends the essay, but it is not as strong a conclusion as it could be. The writer probably ran out of time. The essay as a whole is unified and uses pertinent examples to support the opinion stated. The sentence structure varies, and the vocabulary is effective. Generally, it is well done within the time limit.

Topic 2

Strong Response

Years ago, before formal education was available, everybody learned what they needed to know by experience. The prehistoric hunter-gatherers had assigned roles in the tribe or community, and each person learned their role by following an expert around and by practicing skills like hurling a spear or keeping a fire going. In a way, they were "learning on the job." Today, however, learning on the job no longer works for many of the technologically oriented jobs in the marketplace. People need some academic learning before or at the same time as experiential learning.

In the distant past of low technology, people learned how to do their work by practicing it under the direction of a parent or another experienced adult. Even the so-called primitive people had to learn how to hunt and what plants are edible in the process of becoming hunters and gatherers. There was no manual and no school of hunting or gathering. They learned skills at the knee of their elders. As technology advanced, more knowledge became necessary. And when agricultural life began to dominate, skills such as knowing when and what to plant were learned by experience, often harsh experience at that. As technology advances farther into the use of complex machinery, more people will need more formal training. An IBM television commercial a few years ago showed how farmers can be more productive when they use an IBM personal computer to help manage their business. You don't have to go to college to learn how to use a computer, but you probably need some specialized formal training.

Today, job recruiters constantly say that they need workers who can learn by experience, who are prepared by academic training to learn work skills. If you want to work in accounting, for instance, you need to learn the rules and practices of accounting before you can start working. Then you learn even more in the practice of auditing other people's books. Some jobs also require a lot of formal education before you can work in that job. Real estate sales, for example, requires a state license that can only be acquired after a certain number of hours of formal training. Even relatively skilled jobs that do not require college degrees may require some prior academic training. If you have little or no knowledge of applied mathematics, you will have a hard time doing carpentry or machinery work.

On the other hand, classroom training is often out of touch with the "real world." Part of that is by design. Most people will not use directly a subject like algebra in their work. They won't write essays or interpret poetry. These academic skills often are used to do other academic work, but they can contribute to the ability to learn by experience. Algebra and poetry interpretation both train us in abstract thinking and creative problem solving, which should make us more valuable to an employer. Essay writing skills can be adapted fairly easily to business writing requirements. In other words, a large part of our academic learning prepares us to learn academically at a higher level or to apply the skills we learn in schools and college to real jobs.

Even college graduates are often assigned to a person on the job who is supposed to help the new employee learn by experience. Sometimes, though, there is no such help and the school of experience becomes the school of "hard knocks." Each time the new employee makes an error, they can either learn from that error and adapt or, ultimately, lose their job. By the same token, the new employee can learn through success as well. If they find out how to enter data into a microcomputer software program like a spreadsheet in accounting, they can build on that success and try to use or write a macro (a sort of mini-program) to help them become even more productive.

So, it seems that both academic learning and learning by experience are valuable in a technologically advanced culture. The best and most satisfying jobs aren't learned overnight or just in school or college. They require a mixture of academic or formal training and experience that helps them build on the academic learning.

Analysis

This essay has a score range of 5–6. The introduction is well thought-out and presents a strong thesis. The body paragraphs are detailed and support the thesis clearly and completely. Their sound structure steps through the author's argument clearly and there are few grammatical or punctuation errors. The conclusion could be stronger, but based on the length and considering the time constraints, it is adequate. The author uses language well except for a persistent pronoun-antecedent agreement problem and a few grammatical errors.

FTCE

Florida Teacher Certification Examinations
General Knowledge Test

Practice Test 3

Answer Sheet – Practice Test 3

Subtest I: Reading

1. Ⓐ Ⓑ Ⓒ Ⓓ
2. Ⓐ Ⓑ Ⓒ Ⓓ
3. Ⓐ Ⓑ Ⓒ Ⓓ
4. Ⓐ Ⓑ Ⓒ Ⓓ
5. Ⓐ Ⓑ Ⓒ Ⓓ
6. Ⓐ Ⓑ Ⓒ Ⓓ
7. Ⓐ Ⓑ Ⓒ Ⓓ
8. Ⓐ Ⓑ Ⓒ Ⓓ
9. Ⓐ Ⓑ Ⓒ Ⓓ
10. Ⓐ Ⓑ Ⓒ Ⓓ

11. Ⓐ Ⓑ Ⓒ Ⓓ
12. Ⓐ Ⓑ Ⓒ Ⓓ
13. Ⓐ Ⓑ Ⓒ Ⓓ
14. Ⓐ Ⓑ Ⓒ Ⓓ
15. Ⓐ Ⓑ Ⓒ Ⓓ
16. Ⓐ Ⓑ Ⓒ Ⓓ
17. Ⓐ Ⓑ Ⓒ Ⓓ
18. Ⓐ Ⓑ Ⓒ Ⓓ
19. Ⓐ Ⓑ Ⓒ Ⓓ
20. Ⓐ Ⓑ Ⓒ Ⓓ

21. Ⓐ Ⓑ Ⓒ Ⓓ
22. Ⓐ Ⓑ Ⓒ Ⓓ
23. Ⓐ Ⓑ Ⓒ Ⓓ
24. Ⓐ Ⓑ Ⓒ Ⓓ
25. Ⓐ Ⓑ Ⓒ Ⓓ
26. Ⓐ Ⓑ Ⓒ Ⓓ
27. Ⓐ Ⓑ Ⓒ Ⓓ
28. Ⓐ Ⓑ Ⓒ Ⓓ
29. Ⓐ Ⓑ Ⓒ Ⓓ
30. Ⓐ Ⓑ Ⓒ Ⓓ

31. Ⓐ Ⓑ Ⓒ Ⓓ
32. Ⓐ Ⓑ Ⓒ Ⓓ
33. Ⓐ Ⓑ Ⓒ Ⓓ
34. Ⓐ Ⓑ Ⓒ Ⓓ
35. Ⓐ Ⓑ Ⓒ Ⓓ
36. Ⓐ Ⓑ Ⓒ Ⓓ
37. Ⓐ Ⓑ Ⓒ Ⓓ
38. Ⓐ Ⓑ Ⓒ Ⓓ
39. Ⓐ Ⓑ Ⓒ Ⓓ
40. Ⓐ Ⓑ Ⓒ Ⓓ

Subtest II: Mathematics

1. Ⓐ Ⓑ Ⓒ Ⓓ
2. Ⓐ Ⓑ Ⓒ Ⓓ
3. Ⓐ Ⓑ Ⓒ Ⓓ
4. Ⓐ Ⓑ Ⓒ Ⓓ
5. Ⓐ Ⓑ Ⓒ Ⓓ
6. Ⓐ Ⓑ Ⓒ Ⓓ
7. Ⓐ Ⓑ Ⓒ Ⓓ
8. Ⓐ Ⓑ Ⓒ Ⓓ
9. Ⓐ Ⓑ Ⓒ Ⓓ
10. Ⓐ Ⓑ Ⓒ Ⓓ
11. Ⓐ Ⓑ Ⓒ Ⓓ

12. Ⓐ Ⓑ Ⓒ Ⓓ
13. Ⓐ Ⓑ Ⓒ Ⓓ
14. Ⓐ Ⓑ Ⓒ Ⓓ
15. Ⓐ Ⓑ Ⓒ Ⓓ
16. Ⓐ Ⓑ Ⓒ Ⓓ
17. Ⓐ Ⓑ Ⓒ Ⓓ
18. Ⓐ Ⓑ Ⓒ Ⓓ
19. Ⓐ Ⓑ Ⓒ Ⓓ
20. Ⓐ Ⓑ Ⓒ Ⓓ
21. Ⓐ Ⓑ Ⓒ Ⓓ
22. Ⓐ Ⓑ Ⓒ Ⓓ

23. Ⓐ Ⓑ Ⓒ Ⓓ
24. Ⓐ Ⓑ Ⓒ Ⓓ
25. Ⓐ Ⓑ Ⓒ Ⓓ
26. Ⓐ Ⓑ Ⓒ Ⓓ
27. Ⓐ Ⓑ Ⓒ Ⓓ
28. Ⓐ Ⓑ Ⓒ Ⓓ
29. Ⓐ Ⓑ Ⓒ Ⓓ
30. Ⓐ Ⓑ Ⓒ Ⓓ
31. Ⓐ Ⓑ Ⓒ Ⓓ
32. Ⓐ Ⓑ Ⓒ Ⓓ
33. Ⓐ Ⓑ Ⓒ Ⓓ

34. Ⓐ Ⓑ Ⓒ Ⓓ
35. Ⓐ Ⓑ Ⓒ Ⓓ
36. Ⓐ Ⓑ Ⓒ Ⓓ
37. Ⓐ Ⓑ Ⓒ Ⓓ
38. Ⓐ Ⓑ Ⓒ Ⓓ
39. Ⓐ Ⓑ Ⓒ Ⓓ
40. Ⓐ Ⓑ Ⓒ Ⓓ
41. Ⓐ Ⓑ Ⓒ Ⓓ
42. Ⓐ Ⓑ Ⓒ Ⓓ
43. Ⓐ Ⓑ Ⓒ Ⓓ
44. Ⓐ Ⓑ Ⓒ Ⓓ
45. Ⓐ Ⓑ Ⓒ Ⓓ

Subtest III: English Language Skills

1. Ⓐ Ⓑ Ⓒ Ⓓ
2. Ⓐ Ⓑ Ⓒ Ⓓ
3. Ⓐ Ⓑ Ⓒ Ⓓ
4. Ⓐ Ⓑ Ⓒ Ⓓ
5. Ⓐ Ⓑ Ⓒ Ⓓ
6. Ⓐ Ⓑ Ⓒ Ⓓ
7. Ⓐ Ⓑ Ⓒ Ⓓ
8. Ⓐ Ⓑ Ⓒ Ⓓ
9. Ⓐ Ⓑ Ⓒ Ⓓ
10. Ⓐ Ⓑ Ⓒ Ⓓ

11. Ⓐ Ⓑ Ⓒ Ⓓ
12. Ⓐ Ⓑ Ⓒ Ⓓ
13. Ⓐ Ⓑ Ⓒ Ⓓ
14. Ⓐ Ⓑ Ⓒ Ⓓ
15. Ⓐ Ⓑ Ⓒ Ⓓ
16. Ⓐ Ⓑ Ⓒ Ⓓ
17. Ⓐ Ⓑ Ⓒ Ⓓ
18. Ⓐ Ⓑ Ⓒ Ⓓ
19. Ⓐ Ⓑ Ⓒ Ⓓ
20. Ⓐ Ⓑ Ⓒ Ⓓ

21. Ⓐ Ⓑ Ⓒ Ⓓ
22. Ⓐ Ⓑ Ⓒ Ⓓ
23. Ⓐ Ⓑ Ⓒ Ⓓ
24. Ⓐ Ⓑ Ⓒ Ⓓ
25. Ⓐ Ⓑ Ⓒ Ⓓ
26. Ⓐ Ⓑ Ⓒ Ⓓ
27. Ⓐ Ⓑ Ⓒ Ⓓ
28. Ⓐ Ⓑ Ⓒ Ⓓ
29. Ⓐ Ⓑ Ⓒ Ⓓ
30. Ⓐ Ⓑ Ⓒ Ⓓ

31. Ⓐ Ⓑ Ⓒ Ⓓ
32. Ⓐ Ⓑ Ⓒ Ⓓ
33. Ⓐ Ⓑ Ⓒ Ⓓ
34. Ⓐ Ⓑ Ⓒ Ⓓ
35. Ⓐ Ⓑ Ⓒ Ⓓ
36. Ⓐ Ⓑ Ⓒ Ⓓ
37. Ⓐ Ⓑ Ⓒ Ⓓ
38. Ⓐ Ⓑ Ⓒ Ⓓ
39. Ⓐ Ⓑ Ⓒ Ⓓ
40. Ⓐ Ⓑ Ⓒ Ⓓ

Practice Test 3

Subtest I: Reading

TIME: 40 Minutes
40 Questions

> <u>DIRECTIONS:</u> A number of questions follow each of the passages in the reading section. Answer the questions by choosing the best answer from the four choices given.

Questions 1 to 3 refer to the following passage:

Representatives of the world's seven richest and most industrialized nations held a three-day economic summit in London on July 14–16, 1991. On the second day of the summit, Mikhail Gorbachev, who appealed for help, was offered support by the seven leaders for his economic reforms and his "new' thinking" regarding political reforms. However, because the allies were split on giving a big aid package to Gorbachev, the seven leaders decided to provide help in the form of technical assistance in fields such as banking and energy, rather than in hard cash.

1.   Which of the following statements best synthesizes what the passage is about?

   (A)   A seven-nation economic summit was held in London in July 1991.
   (B)   Mikhail Gorbachev appealed for help and the seven leaders agreed to support his economic reforms.
   (C)   At a three-day economic summit held in London in July 1991, leaders of the world's seven richest and most industrialized nations agrccd to provide technical assistance to Gorbachev.
   (D)   Representatives of the world's seven most industrialized nations, at a summit conference in London, were split on giving Gorbachev assistance in the form of hard cash.

2.   The passage implies that

   (A)   under the leadership of Gorbachev, the Soviet Union is faced with a financial crisis.
   (B)   Gorbachev's "new thinking" on democratic reforms needs support from the seven nations meeting in London.
   (C)   the seven leaders meeting in London were split on giving Gorbachev economic and political support.
   (D)   with the support of political and economic reforms along with provisions for technical assistance from the seven nations that met in London, the Soviet Union, under the leadership of Gorbachev, can achieve political and economic stability.

3.   The passage suggests that technical assistance will be provided to the Soviet Union
     (A)   only in the fields of banking and energy.
     (B)   in the fields of banking and energy and possibly other fields also.
     (C)   by the U.S. in the fields of banking and energy.
     (D)   by all seven nations—U.S., Great Britain, France, Germany, Italy, Canada, and Japan.

Questions 4 to 6 refer to the following passage:

A follow-up survey of the 1990 census showed an estimated undercount of 5.2 million people nationwide. This "undercount" was greatest in California where approximately 1.1 million people were not recorded. This estimated undercount was based on a post-census survey of 171,390 households nationwide. Failure to achieve an accurate count would affect federal funding and political representation. If the higher numbers were used, California would gain eight congressional seats instead of seven and about $1 billion in federal funds. Last July 14, 1991, however, Commerce Secretary Robert Mosbacher decided to stick to the original figures of the 1990 census.

4.   Which of the following statements gives the main idea of the passage you just read?

     (A)   California will gain an additional congressional seat and more federal money if the 1.1 million people undercounted in the census are included.
     (B)   An undercount in the census, if not considered, will be a disadvantage to any state.
     (C)   A post-census survey is necessary in getting to a more accurate population figure for the states.
     (D)   California will suffer the most because of the 1.1 million undercount in the 1990 census.

5.   If the 1.1 million undercount was considered for California

     (A)   it would settle any political dispute arising from the undercount.
     (B)   it would give California eight congressional seats and $1 billion in federal funds.
     (C)   it would discourage the practice of a post-census survey.
     (D)   it would reverse the decision made by Commerce Secretary Mosbacher.

6.   What would it mean for California if the original figures of the 1990 census were to remain the same?

     (A)   No additional federal funding will be given.
     (B)   There will be no additional political representation.
     (C)   The amount of federal funding and number of congressional seats will remain the same.
     (D)   The results of the follow-up survey of the 1990 census will be meaningless.

Questions 7 to 10 refer to the following passage:

A big toxic spill took place on the upper Sacramento River in California on July 13, 1991, about 10 p.m., when a slow moving Southern Pacific train derailed north of the town of Dansmuir. A tank car containing 19,500 gallons of pesticide broke open and spilled into the river. This pesticide is used to kill soil pests. Since the spill, thousands of trout and other fish were poisoned along a 45-mile stretch of river. In addition, 190 people were treated at a local hospital for respiratory and related illnesses. Residents along the river have been warned to stay away from the tainted water. Once this water reaches Lake Shasta, a source of water for millions of Californians, samples will be taken to assess the quality of the water.

7.   Which of the following statements conveys the message in the passage?

     (A)   Pesticides intended to kill soil pests can be dangerous to all living things.

(B) Water uncontaminated by pesticides is safe to drink.

(C) Take every precaution not to come in contact with the pesticide-infected water.

(D) Pesticides that killed thousands of trout and other fish will not necessarily kill human beings.

8. The Southern Pacific train that derailed was

(A) a passenger train.

(B) a cargo train.

(C) a cargo and passenger train.

(D) a special train.

9. The most serious problem that can come about as a result of the toxic spill is

(A) possible movement of residents in Dansmuir to another place of residence.

(B) the negative effects on those whose livelihood depends on the fishing industry.

(C) when the tainted water reaches Lake Shasta, which is a source of water supply for millions of Californians.

(D) the uncertain length of time it will take to make the tainted water safe and healthy again.

10. This unfortunate incident of toxic spill resulting from train derailment implies

(A) the need for more environmental protection.

(B) other means for transporting pesticides need to be considered.

(C) that there should be an investigation as to the cause of the train derailment and effective measures to prevent its occurrence again should be applied.

(D) that there should be research on how to expedite making infected water safe and healthy again.

Questions 11 to 13 refer to the following passage:

Labor Day, a national holiday observed in the United States, is really a day we should remember to give thanks to the labor unions. In the days before the unions became effective, a holiday meant a day off, but the loss of a day's pay to working people. It was not until World War II that unions succeeded, through negotiations with the federal government, in making paid holidays a common practice.

11. The main idea in the passage you just read is

(A) the role labor unions played in employer-employee relations.

(B) Labor Day as a national holiday in the U.S.

(C) the role labor unions played in effecting paid holidays.

(D) the dispute between paid and unpaid holidays.

12. The passage implies that before World War II

(A) a holiday gave working people a chance to rest from work.

(B) Labor Day meant losing a day's pay.

(C) a holiday was a day to make up for upon returning to work.

(D) labor unions were ineffective.

13. As a national holiday, Labor Day should really be a day to remember and be thankful for

(A) working people.

(B) paid holidays.

(C) labor unions.

(D) a free day.

Question 14 refers to the following passage:

President Bush's proposed educational "program of choice" will give parents more say in choosing schools for their children. This will encourage states and local districts to change their laws so that parents can apply their tax dollars toward the public or private school to which they choose to send their children, rather than be forced to send their child to the public school in their district or pay for private school tuition.

14. President Bush's proposed educational program implies

   (A) the freedom to choose.
   (B) competition among schools.
   (C) school standards need to be raised.
   (D) curricula should be improved.

Question 15 refers to the following passage:

Ash from Mt. Pinatubo in the Philippines has been found to contain gold and other precious metals. However, officials warned against any hopes of a new "gold rush." They found gold content of only 20 parts per billion, which is far below commercial levels. Other metals found were chromium, copper, and lithium.

15. The passage indicates

   (A) the possibility of existing gold mines beneath Mt. Pinatubo.
   (B) the need for further exploration of what else lies beneath the volcano.
   (C) other active volcanoes might be worth exploring as possible gold resources.
   (D) that the gold content of the ash from Mt. Pinatubo does not warrant a commercial level.

16. Which of the following makes a good title for the passage you just read?

   (A) A New Gold Rush
   (B) Ash Content from Mt. Pinatubo
   (C) A Philippine Discovery
   (D) Precious Metals

17. What might be a possible research project resulting from the ash content finding of Mt. Pinatubo?

   (A) Research on the ash content from the eruption of Mt. Fujiyama in Japan
   (B) Potential market value of the gold and other metals content in the volcanic ash from Mt. Pinatubo
   (C) Further excavation into possible gold underneath Mt. Pinatubo
   (D) Research on what lies underneath active volcanoes

Questions 18 to 20 refer to the following passage:

Gary Harris, a farmer from Conrad, Montana, has invented and patented a motorcycle helmet. It provides a brake light, which can signal traffic intentions to other drivers behind. In the U.S., all cars sold are now required to carry a third, high-mounted brake light. Harris' helmet will meet this requirement for motorcyclists.

18. The passage tells about

    (A) a new invention for motorcyclists.
    (B) a brake light for motorcyclists.
    (C) Harris' helmet.
    (D) Gary Harris, inventor.

19. An implication regarding the new invention is

    (A) the new brake light requirement for cars should likewise apply to motorcycles.
    (B) the new brake light requirement for cars cannot apply to motorcycles.
    (C) if you buy a car from outside of the U.S., you are exempted from the brake light requirement.
    (D) as an inventor, Gary Harris can make more money if he leaves farming.

20. Because of the new brake light requirement for cars

    (A) drivers can readily see the traffic signals of car drivers ahead of them.
    (B) less accidents can happen on the road.
    (C) car prices will go up and will be less affordable to buy.
    (D) more lights on the road can be hazardous.

Questions 21 to 24 refer to the following passage:

Lead poisoning is considered by health authorities to be the most common and devastating environmental disease of young children. According to studies made, it affects 15% to 20% of urban children and from 50% to 75% of inner-city, poor children. As a result of a legal settlement, all of California's medical-eligible children, ages one through five, will now be routinely screened annually for lead poisoning. Experts estimate that more than 50,000 cases will be detected in California because of the newly mandated tests. This will halt at an early stage a disease that leads to learning disabilities and life-threatening disorders.

21. Lead poisoning among young children, if not detected early, can lead to

    (A) physical disabilities.   (C) learning disabilities.
    (B) mental disabilities.   (D) death.

22. The new mandate to screen all young children for lead poisoning is required of

    (A) all young children in California.
    (B) all children with learning disabilities.
    (C) all medical-eligible children, ages one through five, in California.
    (D) all school-age children in California.

23. According to findings, more cases of lead poisoning are found among

    (A) urban children.   (C) immigrant children.
    (B) inner-city, poor children.   (D) children in rural areas.

24. The implication of this new mandate in California regarding lead poisoning is

    (A) non-eligible children will not be screened.

(B)   children older than five years will not be screened.

(C)   middle-class children will not be screened.

(D)   thousands of young children in California will remain at risk for lead poisoning.

Question 25 refers to the following passage:

As millions of children returned to school in the year 1991–1992, teachers in California had to face the reality of what many consider as the worst fiscal crisis to hit the schools in more than a decade. This crisis caused reductions in teaching positions, increases in class sizes, cuts in teacher paychecks in some school districts, reductions in special programs, reductions in school supplies, etc.

25.   Those who will be most affected by the effects of the financial crisis in California schools are

(A)   the teachers.   (C)   the paraprofessionals.

(B)   the school administrators.   (D)   the students.

Questions 26 to 28 refer to the following passage:

The U.S. Postal Service issued a 50-cent stamp in Anchorage, Alaska, on October 12, 1991, to commemorate the 500th anniversary of the arrival of the Italian explorer Christopher Columbus in the New World. The stamp depicts how Americans may have appeared to Asians crossing the Bering Strait. The stamp series showed the pre-Columbian voyages of discovery.

26.   Which of the following makes an appropriate title for the passage?

(A)   The Discovery of the Americas

(B)   500th Anniversary of the Discovery of America

(C)   The Significance of the Bering Strait

(D)   A Commemorative New U.S. Postal Stamp

27.   The passage implies that

(A)   historical facts need to be verified.

(B)   Christopher Columbus was not the first to arrive in the New World.

(C)   Native Americans came from Asia.

(D)   history books need to be rewritten.

28.   Which of the following would you consider as the most historically significant?

(A)   Asians crossed over the Bering Strait to the New World before Columbus came.

(B)   It has been 500 years since Christopher Columbus arrived in the New World.

(C)   A tribute to Christopher Columbus was held on October 12, 1991.

(D)   There were other voyages undertaken before Christopher Columbus'.

Questions 29 and 30 refer to the following passage:

A 150 million-year-old allosaurus skeleton, which appears to be intact, was found on September 9, 1991, by a Swiss team in north-central Wyoming. This Zurich-based company sells fossils to museums. They were digging on private property, but the fossil actually showed up on federal land.

Immediately, the federal government sealed off the site along the foot of Big Horn Mountains in Wyoming and deployed rangers from the Bureau of Land Management to prevent vandalism. Paleontologists believe that this discovery could lead them to a vast dinosaur graveyard.

29. The passage you just read can best be utilized by a classroom teacher in

(A) reading.
(B) biology.
(C) zoology.
(D) history.

30. A teaching strategy that the classroom teacher can use appropriately with the students regarding the allosaurus fossil discovery is

(A) the problem-solving approach.
(B) the survey approach.
(C) the deductive approach.
(D) the historical approach.

Questions 31 to 33 refer to the following passage:

Popular U.S. attractions such as Disneyland, the Golden Gate Bridge, Las Vegas, and the Statue of Liberty have attracted millions of foreign tourists whose spending helped the U.S. post a $31.7 billion service trade surplus in 1990 compared with a $101 billion merchandise trade deficit in the same year. The heavy-spending Japanese tourists accounted for the biggest portion of the tourism trade surplus, spending $5.5 billion more touring the U.S. than U.S. tourists spent visiting Japan. Canadians also outspent American tourists to Canada by $2.2 billion.

31. The main idea in the passage is

(A) foreign tourists in the U.S. spend more than American tourists spend abroad.
(B) Japanese tourists are the biggest spenders among tourists to the U.S.
(C) Canadians rank second to Japan in tourism spending in the U.S.
(D) tourism is very important to the economy of the U.S.

32. A significant implication of the passage is

(A) that the U.S. should increase its tourist spending in Japan.
(B) that tourist spending in the U.S. reduces its trade deficit.
(C) that Canada needs to improve its tourism attractions.
(D) that Japan has more money on which to spend on tourism than any other country.

33. Based on the passage, which of the following would be an appropriate topic of discussion with students?

(A) International relations
(B) Global relations
(C) Balance in global tourism industry
(D) Interdependency of nations

Questions 34 and 35 refer to the following passage:

San Francisco was named the world's favorite travel destination in the prestigious 1991 *Conde Nast Traveler* magazine poll. It was considered the best city in the world that year, beating out Florence, Italy (No. 2), and London and Vienna, which tied for No. 3. A red-carpet gala in the City Hall rotunda is planned in which Mayor Agnos will laud the city's 60,000 tourism industry workers including hotel maids, taxi drivers, bellhops, and others in the local hospitality industry.

34. An appropriate title for the passage is

    (A) San Francisco: World's Favorite Travel Destination.
    (B) A Gala for San Francisco's Tourism Workers.
    (C) San Francisco: Top in Ranking.
    (D) Top City in 1991.

35. The prestigious citation for the city of San Francisco could mean in practical terms

    (A) more openings for tourism industry workers.
    (B) higher pay demands from hotel maids, bellhops, and other workers.
    (C) more tourists will come to the city.
    (D) more money coming to the city from its tourism industry.

Questions 36 to 38 refer to the following passage:

Results of a study released by the College Board and the Western Interstate Commission for Higher Education projected that in 1994, the majority of California's high school graduates would be non-white and that by 1995, one-third of all the nation's students would be from minority groups. It is also predicted that, nationally, the total non-white and Hispanic student population for all grade levels would increase from 10.4 million in 1985–1986 to 13.7 million in 1994–1995. The figures suggest that, in the 1990s, equal educational opportunity for all students had taken hold as our nation's number one priority.

36. The passage suggests that, in the 1990s,

    (A) this nation was, educationally, at risk.
    (B) something needed to be done to reduce the growing numbers of minority students in the school system.
    (C) urgent educational reforms were needed to provide equal opportunity for all students.
    (D) immigration laws should have been strictly enforced to balance the numbers of white and non-white student populations.

37. Because of changes in demographics, what preparation would have been needed in California in the area of teacher preparation?

    (A) Recruit more minority teachers
    (B) Enforce school desegregation
    (C) Encourage non-Hispanic, white students to enroll in private schools
    (D) Revise teacher preparation programs to reflect appropriate preparation for multicultural class-rooms

38. What problem could have resulted from the increasing minority population in the nation?

    (A) Strong resentment from mainstream whites towards the school system

(B) Increase in enrollment in private and parochial schools

(C) "White flight" to the suburbs, where minorities had not yet become the majority

(D) Inappropriate and inadequate school curriculum and teacher preparation to meet the needs in multicultural classrooms

Questions 39 and 40 refer to the following passage:

The United States' final offer on a lease agreement for the Subic Bay Naval Base in the Philippines was rejected by the Philippine Senate. Hence, for the first time in nearly a century, U.S. military strategy for the Asia-Pacific region will no longer be centered on the Philippines, and the nation's economic survival and development will no longer rely on U.S. dependency. Somehow, this dependency on the U.S. has served as an impediment to the Philippines' ability to join East Asia's economic boom.

39. Which of the following best summarizes what the passage is about?

(A) The Philippines' economic dependency on the U.S. ended with its Senate's rejection of the U.S. lease offer.

(B) The U.S. lease offer for the Subic Bay Naval Base was rejected by the Philippine Senate. Hence, the U.S. will no longer have its military base in the Asia-Pacific region.

(C) The Philippines is now on its own in its economic survival and development.

(D) The U.S. military strategy for the Asia-Pacific region will no longer be on the Philippines following the Philippine Senate's rejection of the U.S. lease offer.

40. The U.S. military's pullout from Subic Bay would mean

(A) less Americans in the Philippines.

(B) a chance for the Philippines to survive on its own.

(C) weakening of U.S.-Philippine relations.

(D) less protection for the Philippines.

Subtest II: Mathematics

TIME: 100 Minutes
45 Questions

> **DIRECTIONS:** Each of the questions or incomplete statements below is followed by four suggested answers or completions. Select the one that is best in each case.

1. What is the least common denominator of $\dfrac{2}{15}, \dfrac{1}{21}$, and $\dfrac{4}{35}$?

    (A) 105
    (B) 415

    (C) 735
    (D) 175

2. On July 19, a Friday, Dick received a letter to have a class reunion exactly four years from that day. On what day of the week is his reunion?

    (A) Monday
    (B) Wednesday

    (C) Thursday
    (D) Friday

3. John and Mary are working on a job together. If John does it alone, it will take him seven days, while Mary can do it alone in five days. How long will it take them to do it together?

    (A) 2 days
    (B) 2 and $\dfrac{11}{12}$ days

    (C) 3 and $\dfrac{1}{2}$ days
    (D) 6 days

4. How much water is needed to add to a half-pint of syrup with 60 percent sugar to obtain a drink with 5 percent sugar?

    (A) 3 pints
    (B) 4 pints

    (C) 5.5 pints
    (D) 7 pints

5. Which of the following is true about triangle *ABC*?

(A) Angle *a* is the smallest angle.
(B) Side *a* is not the longest side.
(C) Angle *b* or *c* must be a right angle.
(D) Side *b* must be greater than side *a* in measurement.

6. If the diameter of circle *A* is twice that of circle *B*, what is the ratio of the area of circle *A* to the area of circle *B*?

   (A) 2 to 1   (C) π to 1
   (B) 4 to 1   (D) 8 to 1

7. A solid cube has a volume of 8. What is the volume of the cube whose sides are twice that of this cube?

   (A) 28   (C) 36
   (B) 32   (D) 64

8. Jack flies from New York to Los Angeles. His plane leaves New York at 2:15 p.m. The flying time is 5 hours and 45 minutes. Since New York is three hours ahead of Los Angeles, what time does he arrive in Los Angeles?

   (A) 11:00 p.m.   (C) 5:00 p.m.
   (B) 8:00 p.m.   (D) 4:45 p.m.

9. Bob has 50 coins, all nickels and dimes, worth a total of $4.85. How many nickels does he possess?

   (A) 15   (C) 37
   (B) 7   (D) 3

10. A steamboat goes 24 miles upstream and then returns to its original position. The round trip takes six hours. The water flows at three miles per hour. What is the speed of the boat in still water?

    (A) 9 miles/hour   (C) 7 miles/hour
    (B) 8 miles/hour   (D) 6 miles/hour

11. If ten babies drink a total of ten gallons of milk in ten days, how many gallons of milk will 20 babies drink in 20 days?

    (A) 20   (C) 30
    (B) 25   (D) 40

12. Jane has three kinds of coins, quarters, dimes, and nickels, totalling 24 in number and worth $3.00. How many coins of each kind does she have?

    (A) Jane has 12 nickels, 4 dimes, and 8 quarters.
    (B) Jane has 9 nickels, 8 dimes, and 7 quarters.
    (C) Jane has 6 nickels, 12 dimes, and 6 quarters.
    (D) There is no unique answer; further information is needed.

13. A parallelogram *ABCD* has all its sides measure 4, one of the diagonals $\overline{AC}$ also measures 4. What is its area?

    (A) Its area is 16.
    (B) Its area is $4\sqrt{3}$.
    (C) Its area is $8\sqrt{3}$.
    (D) Its area cannot be found; further information is needed.

14. Jack gave one-third of his money to his daughter and one-quarter of his money to his son. He then had $150,000 left. How much money did he have before he gave away some?

    (A) $225,000   (C) $360,000
    (B) $300,000   (D) $400,000

15. The fraction $\dfrac{1}{\left(\sqrt{3}-\sqrt{2}\right)}$ is equivalent to

    (A) $\sqrt{3}+\sqrt{2}$.   (C) 1.

    (B) $\sqrt{3}-\sqrt{2}$.   (D) None of the above.

16. If Don and Ron can paint a house in five days, and Ron can paint it alone in seven days, how long will it take Don to paint it alone?

    (A) 7 days   (C) 9.75 days
    (B) 17.5 days   (D) 11.25 days

17. If the volume of a cube is 8, how long is its main diagonal (the line segment joining the two farthest corners)?

    (A) $3\sqrt{2}$
    (B) $2\sqrt{3}$
    (C) $3\sqrt{3}$
    (D) The length of the main diagonal cannot be found for lack of information.

18. Norman lives six blocks north and six blocks east of Bob. The town is made up of all square blocks. How many ways can Bob walk to Norman's house walking only 12 blocks?

    (A) 2 ways   (C) 36 ways
    (B) 924 ways   (D) Infinitely many ways

19. If the area of a right isosceles triangle is 4, how long are its sides?

    (A) $2\sqrt{2}, 2\sqrt{2}, 4$
    (B) $2, 2, 2\sqrt{2}$
    (C) $3, 3, 3\sqrt{2}$
    (D) The lengths of the triangle cannot be found for lack of information.

20. Donald gave Louie a number of marbles to share with Dewey and Huey. Making sure that he got his share, Louie took one-third of the marbles and hid them. Dewey, after hearing from Donald that he

is entitled to one-third of the marbles as well, went and hid one-third of the remaining marbles. Not knowing what was going on, Daisy took two marbles from the pile. When Huey came, there were only 10 marbles left. How many marbles did Donald give to Louie in the beginning?

(A) 18
(B) 24
(C) 27
(D) That number cannot be found for lack of information.

21. A steamboat left Hong Kong on May 25, at 6 a.m., New York time. It sailed 400 hours and arrived in New York. When did it arrive?

(A) 10 p.m., June 10
(B) 10 p.m., June 11
(C) 4 p.m., June 10
(D) 4 p.m., June 11

22. Joan is eight years older than Georgette. Joan was twice as old as Georgette eight years ago. How old are they now?

(A) Joan is 28 and Georgette is 20.
(B) Joan is 26 and Georgette is 18.
(C) Joan is 24 and Georgette is 16.
(D) Further information is needed to figure their ages.

23. A river flows at a speed of five miles per hour. A steamboat went upstream for five hours and stopped at a point 20 miles from where it started. What is the speed of the steamboat in still waters?

(A) 9 miles per hour
(B) 12 miles per hour
(C) 14 miles per hour
(D) The speed of the boat cannot be found for lack of information.

24. Sarah bought 10 pounds of apples and nuts. Apples are 89 cents a pound, and nuts are $1.29 a pound. She spent a total of $10.10. How many pounds of nuts did she buy?

(A) 2
(B) 3
(C) 4
(D) 5

25. Jim and Joe were running together. Jim's average speed was 400 meters per minute. Jim started running four minutes before Joe. Ten minutes after Joe started, he caught up with Jim. What was Joe's average speed?

(A) 440 meters per minute
(B) 450 meters per minute
(C) 500 meters per minute
(D) 560 meters per minute

26. If 96 chickens and rabbits are put together, they have a total of 312 legs. How many chickens are there?

(A) 36
(B) 60
(C) 24
(D) 42

27. Harold decided to cut down his sugar consumption in coffee, tea, and other drinks. He had been consuming 120 grams of sugar a day. He was determined to cut down two grams per day until he no longer used sugar in his drinks. Starting from the first day that he began cutting down his sugar, how much sugar would he have consumed before he arrived at his goal?

    (A) 10,900 grams   (C) 8,200 grams
    (B) 72,000 grams   (D) 24,780 grams

28. John and Kevin have a total of $97. John has $9 more than Kevin. How much money does Kevin have?

    (A) $40   (C) $46
    (B) $44   (D) $48

29. Three circles of equal radii with centers A, B, and C are lying on a straight line and tangent to each other as in the figure shown below. A tangent line to circle C is drawn from A, meeting circle B at S and T, and tangent to circle C at D. What is the ratio of the line segment $\overline{ST}$ to the radii?

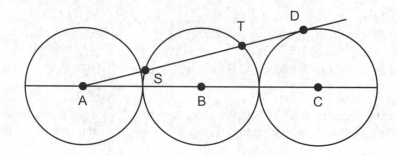

    (A) $\dfrac{\sqrt{3}}{2}$ (C) $\sqrt{3}$

    (B) $\dfrac{3}{2}$ (D) $\sqrt{2}$

30. If a number times itself is added to five times itself, the result is 24. What could this number possibly be?

    (A) 3 or 8   (C) 3 or −8
    (B) −3 or 8   (D) −3 or −8

31. Concerning the number π, which statement is the most accurate?

    (A) $\pi = 3.14$.   (C) $\pi = \dfrac{22}{7}$

    (B) $\pi = 3.1416$.   (D) π is an irrational number.

32. What is the measurement of an angle of a regular pentagon?

    (A) 72°   (C) 84°
    (B) 108°   (D) 104°

33. A boat travels 15 mph going downstream and 8 mph going upstream. How fast is the waterflow?

    (A) $\dfrac{7}{2}$ mph

    (C) $\dfrac{9}{2}$ mph

    (B) 3 mph

    (D) $\dfrac{5}{2}$ mph

34. The longest side of a triangle measures 2 and the shortest side measures 1. What cannot be the measurement of the angle between them?

    (A) 30°
    (B) 60°

    (C) 70°
    (D) 90°

35. Which of the following is closest to the graph of the equation $y = x^2$?

    (A)

    (C)

    (B)

    (D)

36. Roger took off at 8:00 a.m. driving 45 mph. Bill went after him two hours later and caught up with him at 4:00 p.m. How fast did Bill drive?

    (A) 70 mph
    (B) 65 mph

    (C) 60 mph
    (D) 50 mph

37. The expression $\dfrac{x+1}{x-1} - \dfrac{x-1}{x+1}$ simplifies to

    (A) -1.

    (C) $\dfrac{4x}{x^2-1}$.

    (B) $\dfrac{2x}{x^2-1}$.

    (D) $\dfrac{x}{x^2-1}$.

38. If an equilateral triangle has an area of $\sqrt{3}$, what are the lengths of its sides?

    (A) 1

    (C) 2

    (B) $\dfrac{3}{2}$

    (D) $\dfrac{5}{2}$

39. Jane went shopping. On her first trip, she bought six pairs of shoes, all at the same price, and three pairs of socks, also at the same price (shoes and socks are not necessarily of the same price), and she spent $96. On her second trip, she went to the same shop and bought four more pairs of the same socks and returned a pair of shoes; she spent $2. How much does a pair of her shoes cost?

    (A) $12
    (B) $14

    (C) $16
    (D) $18

40. Triangle *ABC* is inscribed in a circle with center *O* at the midpoint of the side *BC*. If angle *B* measures 47°, what is the measurement of angle *C*?

    (A) 43°
    (B) 47°

    (C) 53°
    (D) Insufficient information

41. The area of the circle below is 144π square feet. IF $\overline{OB}$ is increased by 2 feet, what is the area of the new circle (in square feet)?

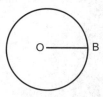

    (A) 4π
    (B) 121π

    (C) 146π
    (D) 196π

42. On what interval is the following function positive?

    (A) [0, 2]
    (B) (0, 2)

    (C) [1, 5]
    (D) (1, 5)

43. In the following figure, $\overline{AB} \perp \overline{BC}$, $\overline{AC} = 10$, and $\overline{AB} = 6$. What is the area of $\triangle ABC$?

(A) 24   (C) 121
(B) 48   (D) 240

44. According to the graph below, during how many months was supply greater than demand?

(A) 0   (C) 2
(B) 1   (D) 3

45. What is the greatest common divisor of 120 and 252?

(A) 2   (C) 6
(B) 3   (D) 12

Subtest III: English Language Skills

TIME: 40 Minutes
40 Questions

Part A: Usage

DIRECTIONS: Each of the following sentences may contain an error in diction, usage, idiom, or grammar. Some sentences are correct. Some sentences contain one error. No sentence contains more than one error.

If there is an error, it will appear in one of the underlined portions labeled A, B, or C. If there is no error, choose the portion labeled D. If there is an error, select the letter of the portion that must be changed in order to correct the sentence.

EXAMPLE: He drove <u>slowly</u> and <u>cautiously</u> in order to <u>hopefully</u> avoid having an
              A   **B**   **C**

accident. <u>No error</u>.
    D   Ⓐ Ⓑ ● Ⓓ

---

1. Which suspension bridge <u>is</u> the <u>longest</u>, the Verrazano-Narrows Bridge in New York City <u>or</u> the
                            A   **B**   **C**
Golden Gate Bridge in San Francisco? <u>No error</u>.
                                    D

2. A main function of proteins, whether <u>they come</u> from <u>plant or animal sources,</u> <u>is</u> the building of
                                    A   **B**   **C**
body tissue. <u>No error</u>.
             D

3. <u>Recognizing</u> that we <u>had worked</u> very hard to complete our project, the teacher told Janice and <u>I</u>
    A   **B**   **C**
that we could give it to her tomorrow. <u>No error</u>.
                                        D

4. <u>According to</u> the United States Constitution, the legislative branch of the government has powers
    A
<u>different than</u> <u>those</u> of the executive branch. <u>No error</u>.
    B   **C**   **D**

5. After <u>being studied</u> for the <u>preceding ten years</u> by the National Heart, Lung, and Blood Institute,
            A   **B**

    the relationship of high levels of cholesterol in the blood to the possibility of <u>having</u> heart attacks
                 C

    was reported in 1984. <u>No error</u>.
           D

6. The book *Cheaper By the Dozen* demonstrates that each of the children of Frank and Lillian Gilbreth
    <u>was expected</u> <u>to use</u> <u>his or her</u> time efficiently. <u>No error</u>.
     A   **B**   **C**   **D**

7. His aversion <u>with</u> snakes made camping an unpleasant activity <u>for him</u> and <u>one</u> that he tried dili-
           A   **B**   **C**

    gently to avoid. <u>No error</u>.
             D

8. The story of the American pioneers, <u>those</u> who willingly left the safety of <u>their</u> homes to move into
                               A   **B**

    unsettled territory, <u>show</u> us great courage in the face of danger. <u>No error</u>.
                   C   **D**

9. <u>Because of</u> the long, cold winters and short summers, farming in high latitudes is <u>more difficult</u>
    A   **B**

    <u>than low latitudes</u>. <u>No error</u>.
         C   **D**

10. When my sister and <u>I</u> were in Los Angeles, <u>we</u> hoped that both of us could be <u>a contestant</u> on a quiz
                A   **B**   **C**

    show. <u>No error</u>.
       D

11. After he <u>had broke</u> the vase that his mother <u>had purchased</u> in Europe, he tried to buy a new one for
           A   **B**

    his father and <u>her</u>. <u>No error</u>.
            C   **D**

12. Some of the people <u>with whom</u> the witness worked were engaged in covert activities <u>on behalf of</u> the
                 A   **B**   **C**

    United States government. <u>No error</u>.
                   D

13. Because of their cold personalities and hot tempers, <u>neither</u> John Adams <u>nor</u> his son John Quincy
                                          A   **B**

    Adams <u>were</u> especially successful in politics. <u>No error</u>.
          C   **D**

14. <u>Among</u> the reasons <u>for United States participation</u> in World War II <u>were</u> the Japanese attack on the
    A   **B**   **C**

    naval base at Pearl Harbor on December 7, 1941. <u>No error</u>.
                                                D

15. Some parents make a <u>greater</u> attempt to frighten <u>their</u> children about the dangers of driving than
                        A   **B**

    <u>teaching</u> them safe driving habits. <u>No error</u>.
    C   **D**

16. The high standard of living in Sweden <u>is shown</u> by <u>their</u> statistics <u>of life expectancy</u> and per capita
                                  A   **B**   **C**

    income. <u>No error</u>.
           D

17. The snow leopard <u>is</u> a wild mammal in Central Asia <u>that has</u> large eyes, a four-foot body, and
                 A   **B**

    <u>white and bluish gray in color</u>. <u>No error</u>.
             C   **D**

18. Selecting a lifetime vocation, a young person may have to choose either a vocation that he enjoys
    <u>and</u> a vocation that will make <u>him</u> rich; that choice is perhaps the <u>most important</u> one he will ever
    A   **B**   **C**

    make. <u>No error</u>.
         D

19. Failing a test because the student is nervous <u>is</u> understandable; <u>to fail</u> because <u>he or she</u> did not study
                                    A   **B**   **C**

    is quite another matter. <u>No error</u>.
                          D

20. Although she <u>had grown up</u> in the North and <u>had been</u> neither a slave <u>or</u> a slave owner, Harriet
                A   **B**   **C**

    Beecher Stowe vividly portrayed life on a slave-holding plantation in her famous book. <u>No error</u>.
                                                                      D

21. The reason Jason failed <u>his</u> speech was <u>because</u> he suffered <u>such stage fright</u> that he refused to give
                      A   **B**   **C**

    his final speech. <u>No error</u>.
                 D

22. After completing the typing course, he made <u>less</u> errors and typed <u>more rapidly</u> than <u>anyone else</u> in
                                     A   **B**   **C**

    his office. <u>No error</u>.
          D

23. Learning the basic components of good nutrition is <u>important for</u> the young adult <u>who want</u> <u>to gain</u>
                                                        A   **B**   **C**

    <u>independence</u> by living in his or her own apartment. <u>No error</u>.
                                                         D

24. Because condominiums offer the advantages of property ownership <u>along with</u> those of apartment
                                                                            A

    rental, <u>this</u> <u>has made</u> condominiums popular since the 1970s. <u>No error</u>.
            B   **C**   **D**

25. Students <u>who</u> eat every day in the college cafeteria generally tire of the <u>frequent</u> repetitious menu
             A   **B**

    <u>that is provided</u>. <u>No error</u>.
         C   **D**

Part B: Sentence Correction

> **DIRECTIONS:** in each of the following sentences some portion of the sentence is underlined. Under each sentence are four choices. The first choice has the same wording as the original. The other three choices are reworded. Sometimes the first choice containing the original wording is the best; sometimes one of the other choices is the best. Choose the letter of the best choice. Your choice should produce a sentence which is not ambiguous or awkward and which is correct, clear, and precise.
>
> This is a test of correct and effective English expression. Keep in mind the standards of English usage, punctuation, grammar, word choice, and construction.
>
> **EXAMPLE:**
>
> When you listen to opera, <u>a person may not appreciate it</u>.
>
> (A) a person may not appreciate it.
>
> (B) it may not be appreciated by a person.
>
> (C) which may not be appreciated by one.
>
> (D) you may not appreciate it.
>
>

26. Wealthy citizens often protest <u>about the building of</u> low-cost housing in the affluent communities where they reside.

    (A) about the building of
    (B) whether they should build
    (C) the building of
    (D) whether or not they should build

27. Siblings growing up in a family do not necessarily have equal opportunities to achieve, <u>the difference being their placement in the family, their innate abilities, and their personalities</u>.

    (A) the difference being their placement in the family, their innate abilities, and their personalities.
    (B) because of their placement in the family, their innate abilities, and their personalities.
    (C) and the difference is their placement in the family, their innate abilities, and their personalities.
    (D) they have different placements in the family, different innate abilities, and different personalities.

28. Two major provisions of the United States Bill of Rights <u>is freedom of speech and that citizens are guaranteed a trial by jury</u>.

    (A) is freedom of speech and that citizens are guaranteed a trial by jury.
    (B) is that citizens have freedom of speech and a guaranteed trial by jury.

(C)   are freedom of speech and that citizens are guaranteed a trial by jury.

(D)   are freedom of speech and the guarantee of a trial by jury.

29.   Poets of the nineteenth century tried <u>to entertain their readers but also with the attempt of teaching them</u> lessons about life.

(A)   to entertain their readers but also with the attempt of teaching them
(B)   to entertain their readers but also to attempt to teach them
(C)   to both entertain their readers and to teach them
(D)   both to entertain and to teach their readers

30.   The city council decided to remove parking meters <u>so as to encourage</u> people to shop in Centerville.

(A)   so as to encourage
(B)   to encourage
(C)   with the desire
(D)   thereby encouraging

31.   Visiting New York City for the first time, <u>the sites most interesting to Megan were</u> the Statue of Liberty, the Empire State Building, and the Brooklyn Bridge.

(A)   the sites most interesting to Megan were
(B)   Megan found that the sites most interesting to her were
(C)   Megan was most interested in
(D)   Megan was most interested in the sites of

32.   Although most college professors have expertise in their areas of specialty, <u>some are more interested in continuing their research than in teaching undergraduate students.</u>

(A)   some are more interested in continuing their research than in teaching undergraduate students.
(B)   some are most interested in continuing their research rather than in teaching undergraduate students.
(C)   some prefer continuing their research rather than to teach undergraduate students.
(D)   continuing their research, not teaching undergraduate students, is more interesting to some.

33.   <u>Whether adult adoptees should be allowed to see their original birth certificates or not</u> is controversial, but many adoptive parents feel strongly that records should remain closed.

(A)   Whether adult adoptees should be allowed to see their original birth certificates or not
(B)   Whether or not adult adoptees should be allowed to see their original birth certificates or not
(C)   Allowing the seeing of their original birth certificates by adult adoptees
(D)   That adult adoptees should be allowed to see their original birth certificates

34.   <u>Having studied theology, music, along with medicine</u>, Albert Schweitzer became a medical missionary in Africa.

(A)   Having studied theology, music, along with medicine
(B)   Having studied theology, music, as well as medicine

(C)   Having studied theology and music, and, also, medicine
(D)   After he had studied theology, music, and medicine

35. When the Mississippi River threatens to flood, sandbags are piled along its banks, <u>and they do this to keep its waters from overflowing</u>.

(A)   and they do this to keep its waters from overflowing.
(B)   to keep its waters from overflowing.
(C)   and then its waters won't overflow.
(D)   and they keep its waters from overflowing.

36. <u>Because of the popularity of his light verse</u>, Edward Lear is seldom recognized today for his travel books and detailed illustrations of birds.

(A)   Because of the popularity of his light verse
(B)   Owing to the fact that his light verse was popular
(C)   Having written light verse that was popular
(D)   Being the author of popular light verse

37. Lincoln's Gettysburg Address, <u>despite its having been very short and delivered after a two-hour oration by Edward Everett</u>, is one of the greatest speeches ever delivered.

(A)   despite its having been very short and delivered after a two-hour oration by Edward Everett
(B)   which was very short and delivered after a two-hour oration by Edward Everett
(C)   although it was very short and delivered after a two-hour oration by Edward Everett
(D)   despite the fact that it was very short and delivered after a two-hour oration by Edward Everett

38. China, <u>which ranks third in area and first in population among the world's countries</u>, also has one of the longest histories.

(A)   which ranks third in area and first in population among the world's countries
(B)   which is the third largest in area and ranks first in population among the world's countries
(C)   in area ranking third and in population ranking first among the world's countries
(D)   third in area and first in the number of people among the world's countries

39. <u>Leonardo Da Vinci was a man who</u> was a scientist, an architect, an engineer, and a sculptor.

(A)   Leonardo Da Vinci was a man who
(B)   The man Leonardo Da Vinci
(C)   Leonardo da Vinci
(D)   Leonardo Da Vinci, a man who

40. <u>The age of 35 having been reached</u>, a natural-born United States citizen is eligible to be elected President of the United States.

(A)   The age of 35 having been reached
(B)   The age of 35 being reached
(C)   When having reached the age of 35
(D)   When he or she is 35 years old

Subtest IV: Essay

TIME: 50 Minutes

> <u>DIRECTIONS:</u> Two topics are presented below. Select one of the topics as the basis for your essay. **READ TOPICS VERY CAREFULLY TO MAKE SURE YOU KNOW WHAT YOU ARE BEING ASKED TO DO.**

TOPIC 1:

"There is a wonderful, mystical law of nature that the three things we crave most in life—happiness, freedom, and peace of mind—are always attained by giving them to someone else." Do you agree or disagree with the statement? Support your opinion with specific examples from history, current events, literature, or personal experience.

OR

TOPIC 2:

The rising cost of health care has been a hotly debated political topic in recent years. What are your opinions on this subject?

Practice Test 3

ANSWER KEY

Subtest I — Reading

1. (C)	11. (C)	21. (D)	31. (A)
2. (D)	12. (B)	22. (C)	32. (B)
3. (B)	13. (C)	23. (B)	33. (C)
4. (A)	14. (B)	24. (D)	34. (A)
5. (B)	15. (D)	25. (D)	35. (D)
6. (C)	16. (B)	26. (D)	36. (C)
7. (C)	17. (B)	27. (B)	37. (D)
8. (B)	18. (A)	28. (A)	38. (D)
9. (C)	19. (A)	29. (C)	39. (D)
10. (C)	20. (A)	30. (D)	40. (B)

Subtest II — Mathematics

1. (A)	13. (C)	25. (D)	37. (C)
2. (B)	14. (C)	26. (A)	38. (C)
3. (B)	15. (A)	27. (D)	39. (B)
4. (C)	16. (B)	28. (B)	40. (A)
5. (B)	17. (B)	29. (C)	41. (D)
6. (B)	18. (B)	30. (C)	42. (D)
7. (D)	19. (A)	31. (D)	43. (A)
8. (C)	20. (C)	32. (B)	44. (C)
9. (D)	21. (A)	33. (A)	45. (D)
10. (A)	22. (C)	34. (D)	
11. (D)	23. (A)	35. (A)	
12. (D)	24. (B)	36. (C)	

Subtest III — English Language Skills

1. (B)	11. (A)	21. (B)	31. (C)
2. (D)	12. (D)	22. (A)	32. (A)
3. (C)	13. (C)	23. (B)	33. (D)
4. (B)	14. (C)	24. (B)	34. (D)
5. (A)	15. (C)	25. (B)	35. (B)
6. (D)	16. (B)	26. (C)	36. (A)
7. (A)	17. (C)	27. (B)	37. (C)
8. (C)	18. (A)	28. (D)	38. (A)
9. (C)	19. (B)	29. (D)	39. (C)
10. (C)	20. (C)	30. (B)	40. (D)

Detailed Explanations of Answers

Subtest I: Reading

1. **(C)**

    The question asks for the best synthesis of the passage and (C) is the best and most complete answer. Choices (A), (B), and (D) are not as complete. For example, (A) left out the duration of the conference, (B) left out both the duration of the conference and the number of the nations represented at the summit, and (D) left out the number of nations represented and support for Gorbachev's "new thinking."

2. **(D)**

    Of the choices provided, (D) gives the most logical and sound implication of the passage. (A) falls short of the capabilities of Gorbachev's leadership; in (B) the "new thinking" referred to already has the support of the seven leaders at the summit; (C) is a rather sweeping, unfair statement.

3. **(B)**

    The mention of banking and energy did not rule out technical assistance in other fields, hence, (B) is the correct answer. Choice (A) limited the assistance to only the fields of banking and energy; in (C) the statement is only partly true—the U.S. is not alone in providing support; and in (D) technical assistance can likewise come from other nations outside of the seven.

4. **(A)**

    The question asks for the main idea in the passage and (A) gives the best and complete main idea. Choices (B) and (C) are generalizations derived from the passage and (D), while it is true and specific to the passage, is stated in the negative.

5. **(B)**

    (B) gives the most specific consequence for California. The other choices, while all plausible or possible answers, do not get to the "root" of the issue specific to California.

6. **(C)**

    Based on the passage read, the answer to this question is (C)—two things are mentioned that could affect California and these are federal funding and the number of congressional seats. While (A) and (B) are correct, they are incomplete. Choice (D) is a consequential generalization which is correct but lacks the preciseness of (C).

7.   **(C)**

The question asks for the "message" conveyed in the passage. Choice (C) is the correct answer, as it gives a warning. In choice (A), pesticides cannot necessarily be dangerous to all living things—some are good for the protection of plants, for example; in (B), water can be contaminated by something other than pesticides; the statement in choice (D) may be true, but it is certainly not the best answer.

8.   **(B)**

The train is definitely a cargo train, hence, (B) is the correct answer. In (A), if it were a passenger train, hundreds would have been killed; in (C), according to the clues, the choices here don't apply; and in (D) the answer used "special train" but could have appropriately used "cargo train" instead.

9.   **(C)**

The question here asks for the most "serious problem" that can come about; so, of all the choices, (C) provides the most serious problem resulting from the pesticide spill for Californians. Choices (A), (B), and (D) are not life-threatening as is (C)

10.   **(C)**

(C) is the most logical and straightforward answer. (C) prioritizes which action should be first taken, and is therefore the correct answer. While the choices in (A), (B), and (D) are sound answers, they don't list the most urgent thing to do.

11.   **(C)**

The correct answer here is (C) because this choice synthesizes the key or main idea in the passage. The other choices, while partly true, don't give the main idea.

12.   **(B)**

Before World War II, which were the depression years, one can easily presume that people were more practical or money minded, hence, Labor Day as celebrated then could mean the loss of a day's pay for working people. Hence, (B) is the correct answer. While choices (A), (C), and (D) are also possible answers they don't get to the "root" of the issue.

13.   **(C)**

Explicitly given in the passage is (C), the correct answer. Choices (A), (B), and (D), while they may all be true and correct, are not what is precisely given in the passage.

14. **(B)**

The question asks for implication. The most straightforward implication of the choices provided has got to be (B). Choice (A) is too general and is actually given in the passage. Choice (C) is an eventual consequence of the proposed program and the same can be said of (D).

15. **(D)**

The gold content found in the volcanic ash from Mt. Pinatubo could easily stir or trigger a "gold rush." However, people are warned that the gold content found is not at a "commercial level." Hence, (D) is the correct answer. The other choices provided are all mere speculations.

16. **(B)**

Choice (B) is the most appropriate answer—it also synthesizes the content of the reading passage; hence, it is the correct answer. Choice (A) is incorrect. Choices (C) and (D) are somewhat applicable as titles but do not really synthesize the main idea of the passage as choice (B).

17. **(B)**

If priorities will have to be established to determine the most immediate research needed on the ash content from Mt. Pinatubo, choice (B) will have to be the most logical choice because there is already some data with which to work. Other research possibilities such as those in choices (A), (C), and (D) will have to come later.

18. **(A)**

The best and correct answer here is (A)—it's the main idea of the passage. Choice (B) is partially correct—if it has to be specific, it should refer to the brake lights on the helmet. Choice (C) is incomplete as a key or main idea of the passage and the same could be said of choice (D).

19. **(A)**

It would follow that the rationale behind the new brake light requirement for cars in California is the same for all other vehicles on the road. Hence, choice (A) is the correct answer. (B) is illogical; in (C) any car driven in California, wherever its been bought, cannot be exempted from the requirement; in (D) Harris can go on inventing while remaining a farmer—he'll make more money doing both.

20. **(A)**

Choice (A) is the most logical and appropriate answer. Hence, it is the correct answer. Choice (B) can be, but is not necessarily true; (C) is a logical possibility but will not drastically raise car prices beyond affordability; (D) may be true, but not as road hazards.

21. **(D)**

All the choices in this question are possible answers; however, since the question asks what lead poisoning, if not detected early, "can lead to," it calls for the ultimate consequence. Hence, (D) is the correct answer inasmuch as the passage states "life-threatening disorders" as among the possible consequences.

22. **(C)**

The correct answer to this question is choice (C)—it gives the complete and precise category. Other choices are incomplete—(A) left out the age group and the medical eligibility; (B) is narrowed down and all inclusive of "children with learning disabilities" and choice (D) is incorrect.

23. **(B)**

As indicated by figures in the passage, the correct answer is (B). Other choices (A), (C), and (D) are obviously incorrect. This is an example of a question in which the incorrect choices are not possible answers. The correct answer is derived from the figures provided in the passage.

24. **(D)**

The implications provided in choices (A) through (D) are correct. However, each of the implications for (A) through (C) is narrowed down to only one specific category of children—not any one is inclusive of all that needs to be addressed. Hence, (D) is the best and appropriate answer because it addresses the thousands who will not be screened, which include those in choices (A) through (C).

25. **(D)**

If schools exist to serve the best interest of students, then the correct answer for this question is (D). Choices (A) through (C) are also correct; however, the group that will be most affected by the financial crisis in California would have to be the "students." The fact remains that schools exist to serve the best interest of students.

26. **(D)**

A title is supposed to synthesize the main idea and (D) does. Choice (A) left out the main idea of a commemorative stamp; choice (B) is incorrect because it implies Columbus discovered the Americas; choice (C) is not the main idea of the passage.

27. **(B)**

The underlying fact behind the passage is explicitly implied; therefore, (B) is the correct answer. Choice (A), while true, is a generalized implication, not addressing the specific issue; choice (C) is debatable; choice (D), like (A), is also a generalized implication.

28. **(A)**

Of the choices given, (A) is the most historically significant, and, therefore, the correct answer. Choice (B) is significant but left out the fact that Columbus was not the first to arrive in the New World, the main point in the passage; choice (C) is a mere commemoration day; and choice (D) is not specific enough as an historically significant fact.

29. **(C)**

Since zoology is the study of animals (C) is the correct and appropriate answer. The other choices, which are other subject areas, as in (A), (B), and (D), are not quite the most appropriate subject areas.

30. **(D)**

A study of a 150 million-year-old fossil will require digging up into history; hence, (D) is the correct answer. Choice (A) could be used if there is a problem focus in the passage; choices (B) and (C) are poor and incorrect choices. Survey applies to a descriptive study; deductive is an approach that proceeds from a generalization or theory.

31. **(A)**

(A) clearly synthesizes the main idea in the passage; hence, it is the correct answer. Choice (D) is merely stating a fact, which does not speak of the main idea; the same can be said of choice (C); and choice (D), while it may be true, is not really the passage's main idea.

32. **(B)**

The most sound and significant implication of the passage is stated in (B); hence, this is the correct answer. Choice (B) is not sound, and reflects rather immature reasoning; choice (C) merely states some degree of competitiveness, which is not the issue's focus; and (D) is a "so what" kind of statement and not a sound implication.

33. **(C)**

The passage is really on global tourism providing comparisons and implying some inter-nation balance in tourism trade; hence, (C) is the appropriate and correct answer. Choices (A), (B), and (D) are stated in general terms, missing out on the specific focus or topic of the passage. Hence, they are not the logical and immediate topics to discuss.

34. **(A)**

The most appropriate and complete title is expressed in (A); hence, this is the correct answer. Choice (B) merely states a planned activity and does not address the main idea; choice (C) is incomplete—it does not specify basis for ranking; the same can be said for choice (D), likewise, an incomplete title.

35. **(D)**

The best answer in considering "practical terms" will have to be (D), which is the correct answer. Choice (B) is a possible consequence but an undesirable one; and choice (C) is a true implication but the "practicality" is merely implied. (D) says this explicitly.

36. **(C)**

The suggestion in (C) is the most sound and logical if equal opportunity for all students is to be our nation's priority; hence, this is the correct answer. Choice (A) is a mere statement of concern and does not provide a plan for action; choice (B) is illogical—you cannot cut down the number of minority students who are already in the system; and (D) is only secondary to the major issue.

37. **(D)**

Since the passage points out the growing number of minority students in the classroom, priority should be in providing the appropriate teacher preparation; hence, the correct answer is (D). Choice (A) is a need but secondary to those who are already in the system; choice (B) is something that has triggered legislations since the 1950s—the natural composition of the classroom today is already desegregated. While the other choices are a need, the one that needs immediate action is (D).

38. **(D)**

The answer to this question has to tie in with the foregoing answer; hence, the correct choice should be (D). Choices (A), (B), and (C), while also problems that arose from the changes in demographics, are secondary to (D).

39. **(D)**

The most complete summary of the passage is stated in (D); hence, this is the correct answer. Choice (A) is rather put in general terms—the U.S. pullout is not the only issue related to the Philippine economy. The interdependence of nations will remain no matter what, i.e., trade relations will continue; choice (B) is incorrect. The U.S. military strategy will have to be relocated elsewhere in the Asia-Pacific region. The same can be said for choice (C)—the Philippines will not be completely on its own as it continues to maintain its trade relations with the U.S. and other trading partners.

40. **(B)**

The passage is quite explicit in stating that the U.S. presence on the Philippines has been an impediment to the nation's capability in joining East Asia's "economic boom"; hence, the correct answer is (B). Choices (A), (C), and (D) are all possible consequences but are all quite debatable.

Subtest II: Mathematics

1. **(A)**

    The least common denominator of the fractions is the least common multiple of their denominators: 15, 21, and 35. Since

$$15 = 3 \times 5,$$

$$21 = 3 \times 7,$$

and
$$35 = 5 \times 7,$$

we see that their least common multiple is $3 \times 5 \times 7 = 105$.

2. **(B)**

    Since his reunion will be $365 \times 4 + 1 = 1{,}461$ days from a Friday, dividing 1,461 by 7 yields a remainder of 5. Therefore, his reunion is 5 days from a Friday, which makes it on a Wednesday.

3. **(B)**

    In one day, John can do $\frac{1}{7}$ of the work, and Mary can do $\frac{1}{5}$; together, they can do

$$\frac{1}{5} + \frac{1}{7} = \frac{12}{35}$$

of the job. To finish the whole job, it takes

$$\frac{35}{12} = 2 \text{ and } \frac{11}{12} \text{ days.}$$

4. **(C)**

    Since the sugar content is 60 percent of $\frac{1}{2}$ pint and will not be changed after the water is added, we obtain an equation by equating the sugar content before and after adding in x pints of water. The equation is then

$$\left(\frac{1}{2}\right) \times 60\% = \left(\frac{1}{2} + x\right) \times 5\%$$

$$30 = \frac{5}{2} + 5x$$

or

$$60 = 5 + 10x$$

$$55 = 10x$$

$$5.5 = x$$

5.   **(B)**

Since the only information we have concerning the triangle is that angle A measures 30°, we know that in a triangle, the largest angle faces the longest side, the sum of the three angles of a triangle is 180°, and a 30° angle is not the largest angle. Therefore, a is not the longest side.

6.   **(B)**

The diameter of circle A is twice that of circle B, so if the radius of B is r, then the radius of A is $2r$. Since the area of a circle with radius r is πr^2, the area of B is πr^2, while the area of A is

$$\pi(2r)^2 = 4\pi r,$$

therefore the ratio is 4:1.

7.   **(D)**

Since the cube has a volume of 8, its sides have length 2. The cube whose sides are twice that would be of length 4, so the volume of the other cube is

$$4 \times 4 \times 4 = 64.$$

8.   **(C)**

$2:15 + 5:45 = 8:00$ means he arrives in Los Angeles at 8 p.m. New York time. But New York is 3 hours ahead of Los Angeles, so the Los Angeles time of arrival is 5 p.m.

9.   **(D)**

We set up two equations. Let n be the number of nickels, and let d be the number of dimes. We have

$$n + d = 50.$$

Since each nickel is worth 5 cents and each dime is worth 10 cents, we have

$$5n + 10d = 485.$$

Multiplying the first equation by 10, we obtain

$$10n + 10d = 500.$$

Subtracting the second equation from it, we obtain $5n = 15$, or $n = 3$.

10.   **(A)**

Let s be the speed of the boat in still water. Then the speed of the boat upstream is $(s - 3)$ miles per hour, and the speed of the boat downstream is $(s + 3)$ miles per hour. Therefore, the time going upstream,

$$\frac{24}{s - 3}$$

hours plus the time going downstream,

$$\frac{24}{s+3}$$

hours, equals 6 hours. Solving for s gives $s = 9$ miles/hour.

$$\frac{24}{s-3}+\frac{24}{s+3}=6$$

$$\frac{(s+3)}{(s+3)(s-3)}+\frac{(s+3)}{(s-3)(s+3)}=\frac{6}{24}=\frac{1}{4}$$

$$\frac{2s}{(s+3)(s-3)}=\frac{1}{4}$$

$$8s=(s+3)(s-3)$$

$$=s^2-9$$

$$s^2-8s-9=0;$$

$$(s \quad 9)(s+1)=0;$$

$$s=9 \text{ or } -1,$$

but we require $s > 0$. Thus $s = 9$ miles/hour.

11. **(D)**

Since 10 babies drink 10 gallons of milk in 10 days, each baby drinks; $\frac{1}{10}$ gallon of milk per day. Each baby drinks 2 gallons of milk in 20 days, so 20 babies will drink $2 \times 20 = 40$ gallons of milk in 20 days.

12. **(D)**

Let x be the number of nickels, y be the number of dimes, and z be the number of quarters. We have two equations:

$$x + y + z = 24$$

and

$$5x + 10y + 25z = 300$$

and three unknowns. Therefore, no unique answer can be found without one more equation.

13. **(C)**

Draw both diagonals to divide the parallelogram into four equal parts. Each part is a right triangle with hypotenuse measuring 4 and one side measuring 2. Therefore, the other side must measure $2\sqrt{3}$ by the Pythagorean Theorem. The area of this triangle is

$$\left(\frac{1}{2}\right) \times (2 \times 2\sqrt{3}) = 2\sqrt{3},$$

and the area of the parallelogram is four times that, which is $8\sqrt{3}$.

14. **(C)**

Let the amount of money he had before be x. We have

$$x - \left(\frac{1}{3}\right)x - \left(\frac{1}{4}\right)x = 150,000.$$

Or,

$$\left(\frac{5}{12}\right)x = 150,000.$$

Therefore, $x = 360,000$.

15. **(A)**

If we multiply both the numerator and denominator by the conjugate of the expression $\sqrt{3} - \sqrt{2}$ namely, $\sqrt{3} + \sqrt{2}$, the numerator becomes $\sqrt{3} + \sqrt{2}$, and the denominator becomes $3 - 2 = 1$.

16. **(B)**

Since Don and Ron can paint the house in 7 days, they finish $\frac{1}{5}$ of the job in a day. Now, Ron's contribution in a day is $\frac{1}{7}$ of the job, so

$$\frac{1}{5} - \frac{1}{7}$$

is Don's contribution in a day, which amounts to $\frac{2}{35}$. Therefore, if Don is to do it alone, it will take him

$$\frac{35}{2} = 17.5 \text{ days}.$$

17. **(B)**

Since the volume of the cube is 8, each side has a measure of 2, and the main diagonal is found with the Pythagorean Theorem.

18. **(B)**

Each way for Bob to walk to Norman's consists of six blocks northward and six blocks eastward in different orders. The total number of ways of walking is then the same as the number of ways to choose 6 out of 12 things, and the number is

$$12 \times 11 \times 10 \times 9 \times 8 \times 7 \text{ divided by } 6 \times 5 \times 4 \times 3 \times 2, \text{ or } 924.$$

19. **(A)**

For a right isosceles triangle, the area is half of the product of the two equal sides. Therefore, each of the equal sides measure $\sqrt{8}$, or $2\sqrt{2}$, and the hypotenuse must be 4.

20. **(C)**

Let the number of marbles in the beginning be x. We have

$$x - \left(\frac{1}{3}\right)x - \left(\frac{1}{3}\right)\left(\frac{2}{3}\right)x - 2 = 10.$$

Solving the equation, $x = 27$.

21. **(A)**

We divide 400 by 24 (number of hours in a day); we obtain a partial quotient of 16 and a remainder of 16. This means that it takes 16 days and 16 hours for the trip. With 31 days in May, the boat must arrive on June 10. And 16 hours from 6 a.m. is 10 p.m.

22. **(C)**

If we let Joan's age be x, then Georgette's age is $(x - 8)$. Solving the equation

$$(x - 8) = 2[(x - 8) - 8] = 2x - 32,$$

we obtain $x = 24$.

23. **(A)**

Since the boat took five hours to go 20 miles, its speed upstream was four miles per hour. But the water effect was five miles per hour. If that effect had been taken away, the boat would have been five miles faster; therefore, the boat in still waters goes $4 + 5 = 9$ miles per hour.

24. **(B)**

Suppose Sarah bought x pounds of apples and y pounds of nuts. We have the following equations to solve:

$$x + y = 10$$

$$89x + 129y = 1,010$$

Solving these equations gives $x = 7$, $y = 3$.

25. **(D)**

When Joe caught Jim, Jim had been running for $(10 + 4) = 14$ minutes, at the rate of 400 meters per minute. So the total distance covered was $(14 \times 400) = 5,600$ meters. But Joe covered this distance in 10 minutes. Thus, his average speed was

$$\frac{5,600}{10} = 560 \text{ meters per minute.}$$

26. **(A)**

Since a chicken has two legs and a rabbit has four legs, letting x be the number of chickens and y be the number of rabbits, we have the following equations to solve:

$$x + y = 96$$
$$2x + 4y = 312$$
$$x = 96 - y$$
$$\frac{2x + 4y}{2} = 312$$
$$x + 2y = 156$$
$$96 - y + 2y = 156$$
$$96 + y = 156$$
$$y = 60$$
$$x + 60 = 96$$
$$x = 36$$

27. **(D)**

In the first week, he consumed 118 grams of sugar daily; in the second week, he consumed 116 grams of sugar daily, etc. We are then to add

$$118 + 116 + 114 + \ldots + 2$$

and since there are seven days in a week, the result must be multiplied by 7. Observing that

$$118 + 116 + 114 + \ldots + 2 = 2 \times (1 + 2 + 3 + \ldots + 59)$$
$$= 2 \times (1 + 59)\left(\frac{59}{2}\right) = 3,540$$

And
$$3,540 \times 7 = 24,780.$$

28. **(B)**

Let x be the amount of money Kevin has, and let y be the amount of money John has. Then $y + x = 97$ and $y - x = 9$. Subtracting the two equations, we have

$$2x = 88, \text{ or } x = 44.$$

29. **(C)**

If we draw a perpendicular line from B to the tangent line, say BE, then the right-angled triangles ABE and ACD are similar, so BE equals half of CD, the radius. BET is also a right-angled triangle, and BT is a radius. Using the Pythagorean Theorem, ET measures

$$\frac{\sqrt{3}}{2}$$

of the radius. Thus, ST measures $\sqrt{3}$ of the radius.

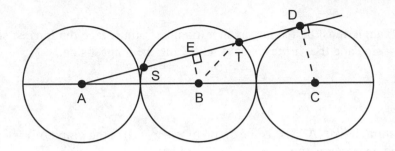

30. **(C)**

Letting this number be *x*, we have

$$x^2 + 5x = 24, \text{ or } x^2 + 5x - 24 = 0,$$

or

$$(x + 8)(x - 3) = 0,$$

so

$$x = 3 \text{ or } x = -8.$$

31. **(D)**

π is an irrational number, while (A), (B), and (C) are all approximate rational values of π, and the statement (D) is vague.

32. **(B)**

We do not need to memorize any formula. If we inscribe the regular pentagon in a circle, the angle with the vertex at the center facing each side is

$$\frac{360°}{5} = 72°,$$

and each of the other angles of that triangle must be

$$\frac{(180° - 72°)}{2} = 54°.$$

Thus, each of the angles is 108°.

33. **(A)**

Let *x* be the speed of the boat in still waters, and let *y* be the speed of the waterflow. Then $x + y = 15$ mph, and $x - y = 8$ mph. Subtracting the equations, we get $2y = 7$, or

$$y = \frac{7}{2}.$$

34. **(D)**

Since a 90° angle must be the largest in a triangle, it must face the longest side, and the angle between the longest side and the shortest side is not facing the longest side.

35. **(A)**

$y = x^2$ has a graph like (A). (B) is the graph of $x = y^2$; (C) is the graph of $x = -y^2$; (D) is not even the graph of a second degree equation.

36. **(C)**

Since Bill took six hours to catch up, and Roger has gone 90 miles, Bill was

$$\frac{90}{6} = 15$$

miles closer each hour. Thus, he was driving 60 miles per hour.

37. **(C)**

The common denominator is $x^2 - 1$, and the numerator is

$$(x + 1)^2 - (x - 1)^2 = 4x.$$

38. **(C)**

Using the Pythagorean Theorem and the formula for the area of a triangle,

$$b = a \text{ and } h = \sqrt{a^2 - \left(\frac{1}{2}a\right)^2}$$

where a is the length of the sides.

$$\frac{1}{2}bh = \text{area}$$

$$\frac{1}{2}a\sqrt{a^2 - \frac{1}{4}a^2} = \sqrt{3}$$

$$\frac{1}{2}a\sqrt{\frac{3}{4}a^2} = \sqrt{3}$$

$$\frac{1}{4}a^2\left(\frac{3}{4}a^2\right) = 3$$

$$a^2 = (3)\left(\frac{16}{3}\right)$$

$$a^2 = 2$$

39. **(B)**

Let the price for a pair of shoes be x, and let the price for a pair of socks be y. Then,

$$6x + 3y = 96,$$

and $$4y - x = 2.$$

Solving these equations, we have $x = 14$.

40. **(A)**

Since $\overline{BC}$ is the diameter of the circle, angle A is a right angle. Therefore, angle C is complementary to angle B, i.e.,

$$90° - 47° = 43°.$$

41. **(D)**

The area of a circle is πr^2 where r is the radius. In the given circle, $\overline{OB}$ is the radius and $A = 144\pi$. So, $144\pi = \pi r^2$ so that $r = 12$. If we increase the radius by 2 feet so that now $r = 14$, the area of the new circle is

$$A = \pi(14)^2 = 196\pi$$

42. **(D)**

A function is positive when the points on its graph lie above the x-axis. In our graph, this occurs when x is between 1 and 5 or $(1, 5)$.

43. **(A)**

Since $\overline{AB} \perp \overline{BC}$, we know that $\triangle ABC$ is a right triangle and, thus, we may use the Pythagorean Theorem to find the length of $\overline{BC}$ (let x be the length of $\overline{BC}$):

$$\overline{AC}^2 = \overline{AB}^2 + \overline{BC}^2$$

or $(10)^2 = 6^2 + x^2$

or $100 = 36 + x^2$.

To solve this, substract 36 from both sides of the euation to get: $64 = x^2$ so that $x = 8$. The area of $\triangle ABC =$

$$\frac{1}{2}(AB)(BC) = \frac{1}{2}(6)(8) = 24.$$

44. **(C)**

According to the graph, the supply was greater than the demand in March and May only.

45. **(A)**

The greatest common divisor (GCD) is the greatest integer that divides both 120 and 252. To find the GCD, factor both numbers and look for common factors.

$$120 = 2^3 \times 3 \times 5$$

and $\quad 252 = 2^2 \times 3^2 \times 7,$

so, the GCD $= 2^2 \times 3 = 12.$

Subtest III: English Language Skills

1. **(B)**

    As you read the sentence, you should recognize that choice (B) presents an error in comparison. The comparison of two bridges requires the comparative form "longer." All of the other choices are acceptable in standard written English. Choice (A), "is," agrees with its singular subject "bridge"; and choice (C), "or," is a coordinating conjunction joining the names of the two bridges.

2. **(D)**

    The correct response to this question is choice (D). All labeled elements are choices acceptable in standard written English. In choice (A), the pronoun "they" is plural to agree with its antecedent, "proteins," and the verb "come" is also plural to agree with its subject, "they"; choice (B), "plant or animal sources," is idiomatic; and choice (C), "is," is singular to agree with its singular subject, "function."

3. **(C)**

    The error is choice (C), "I," which is in the nominative case. Because the words "Janice" and "I" serve as indirect objects in the sentence, the correct pronoun is the first person objective form, "me." Choice (A), "Recognizing," is a participle introducing an introductory participial phrase modifying "teacher;" choice (B), "had worked," is a verb in the past perfect tense because the action in the phrase was completed before the action in the main clause occurred.

4. **(B)**

    The error occurs at choice (C), where the preposition "from" is idiomatic after the word "different." Although some experts insist upon the use of "from" after the adjective "different," others accept the use of "different than" in order to save words. An example would be "different than you thought;" the use of "from" would require the addition of the word "what." Choice (A), "According to," is a preposition correctly introducing a prepositional phrase; and choice (C), "those," is a plural pronoun to agree with its antecedent "powers."

5. **(A)**

    Choice (A) should be a gerund in the present perfect form (having "been studied") to indicate that the action expressed by the gerund occurred before the relationship was reported. Choice (B), "preceding ten years," is idiomatic. Choice (C), "having," is a gerund introducing the phrase "having heart attacks," which is the object of the preposition "of."

6. **(D)**

    Your answer should be choice (D), indicating that this sentence contains no error in standard written English. Choice (A), "was expected," uses the third person singular form of "to be" to agree with its subject "each;" choice (B), the infinitive "to use," is idiomatic after the passive verb "was expected;" and choice (C), "his or her," is singular to agree with its antecedent, the indefinite pronoun "each," and provides gender neutrality.

7.   **(A)**

You should recognize in choice (A) that the idiomatically acceptable preposition to follow "aversion" is "to." The other choices in the sentence are acceptable in standard written English. Choice (B), "for him," is a prepositional phrase modifying "activity;" choice (C), "one," is a pronoun appropriate to refer to its antecedent "activity."

8.   **(C)**

Choice (C) contains the error because the subject of the verb "show" is "story," a singular noun that calls for the third person singular verb, "shows." The rest of the sentence represents correct usage. Choices (A) and (B), "those" and "their," are plural pronouns that agree with the antecedent "pioneers."

9.   **(C)**

Choice (C) presents an error in comparison, appearing to compare "farming" with "low latitudes" when what is intended is a comparison of "farming in high latitudes" with "farming in low latitudes." The corrected sentence reads: "Because of the long, cold winters and short summers, farming in high latitudes is more difficult than farming in low latitudes." The other choices all represent appropriate usage in standard written English. Choice (A), "Because of," is idiomatically correct as a preposition. Choice (B), "more difficult," is the comparative form appropriate to compare two items.

10.   **(C)**

The error is in choice (C). The word "contestant" is a predicate nominative in the subordinate noun clause, and it must agree in number with the plural subject of the clause, the pronoun "both," to which it refers. The noun clause should, therefore, read: "that both of us could be contestants on a quiz show." Choice (A), "I," is part of the compound subject of the introductory adverb clause and is, correctly, in the nominative case. "We" is plural to agree with its compound antecedent, "sister and I," and is in the nominative case because it is the subject of the verb "hoped."

11.   **(A)**

The error is in choice (A). The auxiliary verb "had" calls for the past participle form of the verb "break," which is "broken." All of the other choices are acceptable in standard written English. Choice (B), "had purchased," is the past perfect form of the verb to indicate action completed in the past before the action of the verb in the main clause; and choice (C), "her," is the object of the preposition "for."

12.   **(D)**

This sentence contains no error in standard written English. Choice (A), the prepositional phrase "with whom," introduces an adjective clause modifying the word "people." The relative pronoun "whom" is in the objective case because it serves as the object of the preposition "with." The simple past tense "worked" is appropriate for choice (B); choice (C) is an idiomatic expression replacing the preposition "for."

13. **(C)**

Your reading of the sentence should indicate that choice (C), "were," presents an error in subject-verb agreement. A compound subject joined by "or" or "neither . . . nor" calls for a verb that agrees in number with the second part of the compound subject, which is, in this case, singular. The correct choice is the verb "was." The other choices represent correct usage. Choices (A) and (B) are correlative conjunctions.

14. **(C)**

Again the error is one of agreement of the subject and verb. Choice (C), "were," is plural; because its subject is "attack," not "reasons," which is the object of the preposition "among" and therefore cannot be the subject of the sentence, the verb should be the singular "was." Choice (A), "Among," introduces a prepositional phrase; choice (B) is an idiomatically acceptable prepositional phrase to modify the noun "reasons."

15. **(C)**

Your analysis of this sentence should disclose an error in parallelism in choice (C). "Teaching" should be replaced by "to teach," an infinitive parallel with "to frighten." Both infinitives modify the noun "attempt." The other choices all represent standard usage in written English. Choice (A), "greater," is the comparative form of the adjective, correctly used to compare two items; choice (B), "their," is a plural possessive pronoun agreeing in number with its plural antecedent, "parents."

16. **(B)**

You should recognize that the possessive pronoun in choice (B), "their," is not the appropriate pronoun to use in referring to a country. Choice (C), "of life expectancy," are both idiomatically acceptable prepositional phrases; choice (B), "is shown," is passive and agrees in number with its singular subject, "standard."

17. **(C)**

Choice (C), "white and bluish gray in color," is the third in a series of objects of the verb "has." The error lies in its lack of parallelism with the other two objects, "eyes" and "body." Corrected, the sentence reads: "The snow leopard is a wild mammal in Central Asia that has large eyes, a four-foot body, and a white and bluish gray color." The other choices are all acceptable in standard written English. Choice (A), "is," is singular to agree with its subject "leopard." Choice (B), "that has," is composed of the relative pronoun "that" referring to the noun "mammal," and the verb "has," that agrees with its subject in number.

18. **(A)**

You should recognize that choice (A), "and," is not the correct correlative conjunction to follow "either." The correct word is "or." The other choices all represent acceptable choices in standard written English. Choice (B), "him," is singular to agree with its antecedent "person" and objective because it is the object of the verb "make." Choice (C), "most important," is in the superlative form because the comparison involves more than two choices.

19. **(B)**

Choice (B), "to fail," is incorrect in standard written English. The sentence contains two parallel ideas that should be expressed with the same grammatical form. Because "Failing" is a gerund, the "infinitive" to "fail" should be replaced with "failing" to make the construction parallel. Choice (A), "is," agrees in number with its subject, "Failing"; and choice (C) is singular to agree with its antecedent, "student," and indicates no sexual preference.

20. **(C)**

You should recognize that choice (C), "or," is in error because the correlative conjunction that should follow "neither" is "nor." All other choices are correct. Choice (A), "had grown up," is idiomatically acceptable and it and choice (B), "had been," are in the past perfect tense to indicate that the actions occurred before the action mentioned in the main clause.

21. **(B)**

As you read the sentence, you should recognize that choice (B) is incorrect because "that" is the relative pronoun that should introduce a noun clause following "reason;" another option would be to revise the sentence by omitting the words "The reason," but that is not an option provided on this test. Choice (A), "his," is the correct possessive pronoun to refer to "Jason." Choice (C), "such stage fright," is idiomatic.

22. **(A)**

Your recognition that the word "less" is used with a singular noun and the word "fewer" is appropriate before a plural noun will lead you to locate the error in choice (A). Choice (B) is the comparative adverb, the correct choice to compare two people ("anyone else" is singular), and choice (C) is idiomatic as a singular indefinite pronoun.

23. **(B)**

You should recognize that the verb "want" in choice (B) does not agree with its subject "who," a pronoun that is singular to agree with its antecedent, "adult." The word ordering used in choices (A) and (C) are both idiomatic in standard written English.

24. **(B)**

As you read the sentence, you should recognize that the pronoun "this" in choice (B) does not have a clear antecedent in the sentence. The other choices are all correct in standard written English. Choice (A), "along with," is idiomatic and serves as one preposition. Choice (C), "has made," is in the present perfect tense because the action began in the past and continues into the present.

25. **(B)**

You should find the error at choice (B), where the adverb "frequently" is needed to modify the adjective "repetitious;" "frequent" is an adjective and does not correctly modify another adjective. Choice (A), the pronoun "who," correctly refers to its antecedent "Students;" and choice (C) is a relative pronoun "that" and its verb, "is provided," which comprise the adjective clause modifying "menu."

26. **(C)**

Because the verb "protest" can be transitive and have a direct object, choice (C) avoids awkward wordiness and use of the unnecessary preposition "about." Choices (B) and (D) include unnecessary words and use the pronoun "they" that has no clear antecedent.

27. **(B)**

Choice (B) best shows the causal relationship between sibling opportunities and their placement in the family, their abilities, and their personalities, and retains the subordination of the original sentence. Choice (A) provides a dangling phrase. Choice (C), with its use of the coordinating conjunction "and," treats the lack of opportunity and its cause as if they are equal ideas and does not show the causal relationship between them; choice (D) results in a run-on sentence.

28. **(D)**

Only choice (D) corrects the two major problems in the sentence, the lack of subject-verb agreement and the lack of parallelism. In choices (A) and (B), the verb "is" does not agree with its plural subject, "provisions." Choices (A) and (C) have unlike constructions serving as predicate nominatives, the noun "freedom" and the clause "that citizens are guaranteed a trial by jury." Choice (D) correctly uses the plural verb "are" to agree with the plural subject, and the predicate nominative is composed of two parallel nouns, "freedom" and "guarantee."

29. **(D)**

The errors found in the original sentence, choice (A), involve parallelism and redundancy. Choice (D) uses the parallel infinitives "to entertain" and "to teach" as direct objects and eliminates the repetition created in the use of both "tried" and "attempt" in the original sentence. Choices (B) and (C) provide parallel construction, but choice (B) retains the redundancy and choice (C) incorrectly splits the infinitive "to entertain."

30. **(B)**

Choice (B) adequately conveys the reason for removal of the parking meters with the least wordiness. Choices (A) and (C) contain unnecessary words; choice (D) has a dangling participial phrase.

31. **(C)**

Choice (C), in which "Megan" correctly follows the phrase, conveys the meaning with the least wordiness. The problem with choice (A) is the introductory participial phrase; it must be eliminated or followed immediately by the word modified. Choice (B) and (D) add words unnecessary to the meaning of the sentence.

32. **(A)**

The given sentence is acceptable in standard written English. Each of the alternate choices introduces a problem. Choice (B) uses the superlative form of the adjective, "most interested," when the comparative form "more interested" is correct for the comparison of two options; choice (C) introduces a lack of parallelism; and choice (D) is not idiomatic.

33. **(D)**

The noun clause in choice (D) is idiomatically acceptable. The use of "Whether" in choices (A) and (B) leads the writer to add "or not," words that contribute nothing to the meaning and result in awkwardness of construction. Choice (C) with its awkward gerund phrase is also not idiomatic.

34. **(D)**

This sentence presents two problems, namely use of a preposition instead of a coordinating conjunction to join the objects of the participle "having studied" and failure to show a time relationship. Choice (D) corrects both problems. Choice (B) simply replaces the preposition "along with" by "as well as"; choice (C) unnecessarily repeats the conjunction "and" rather than using the quite appropriate series construction. None of the choices (A), (B), or (C) correctly shows the time relationship.

35. **(B)**

This sentence contains the ambiguous pronoun "they," for which there is no antecedent and fails to show the relationship of the ideas expressed. Choice (B) eliminates the clause with the ambiguous pronoun and correctly expresses the reason for the sandbag placement. Choice (C) suggests that the two clauses joined by "and" are equal and does not show the subordinate relationship of the second to the first. Choice (D) retains both errors from the original sentence.

36. **(A)**

This sentence is correct in standard written English. Choice (B) introduces unnecessary words that add nothing to the meaning and make the sentence awkward and wordy; choices (C) and (D) do not correctly show relationship.

37. **(C)**

Choice (C) shows the relationship accurately and eliminates the awkward gerund construction as the object of the preposition "despite." The adjective clause in choice (B) fails to show the relationship of the original sentence; choice (D) introduces the superfluous words "the fact that."

38. **(A)**

This sentence is correct in standard written English. Choice (B) loses the strength of the parallelism in choice (A). Choice (C), although containing parallel construction, is idiomatically awkward with its participial phrases. Choices (B) and (D) all exhibit wordiness.

39. **(C)**

The original sentence, choice (A), contains the obvious and redundant words "was a man who." Choices (B) and (D) are also unnecessarily verbose. Choice (C) makes the statement in the most direct way possible and represents correct standard usage.

40. **(D)**

Choice (D) eliminates the awkward participial phrase with its passive verb, and, in direct fashion, clearly shows the desired relationship. Choices (A), (B), and (C) retain the awkward construction.

Essay Scoring Guide

The FTCE-GKT essay sections are scored by two writing experts on the basis of the criteria outlined below. In addition to comparing your essay to those included in our practice tests, you may use these guidelines to estimate your score on this section. Remember that your score is the sum of the scores of two writing experts, so provided you respond to the assigned topic, your score will fall somewhere between two and twelve. Scores will be assigned based on the following guidelines:

SCORE of 6: The paper has a clearly established main idea that the writer fully develops with specific details and examples. Organization is notably logical and coherent. Point of view is consistently maintained. Vocabulary and sentence structure are varied and effective. Errors in sentence structure, usage, and mechanics are few and insignificant.

SCORE of 5: The paper has a clearly established main idea that is adequately developed and recognizable through specific details and/or examples. Organization follows a logical and coherent pattern. Point of view is mostly maintained. Vocabulary and sentence structure are mostly varied and effective. Occasional errors in sentence structure, usage and mechanics do not interfere with the writer's ability to communicate.

SCORE of 4: The paper has an adequately stated main idea that is developed with some specific details and examples. Supporting ideas are presented in a mostly logical and coherent manner. Point of view is somewhat maintained. Vocabulary and sentence structure are somewhat varied and effective. Occasional errors in sentence structure, usage, and mechanics may interfere with writer's ability to communicate.

SCORE of 3: The paper states a main idea that is developed with generalizations or lists. The paper may contain occasional lapses in logic and coherence, and organization is mechanical. Point of view is ambiguous. Vocabulary and sentence structure are repetitious and often ineffective. A variety of errors in sentence structure, usage, and mechanics sometimes interferes with the writer's ability to communicate.

SCORE of 2: The paper presents an incomplete or ambiguous main idea. Support is developed with generalizations and lists. Organization is mechanical. The paper contains occasional lapses in logic and coherence. Point of view is confusing and distracting. Word choice is simplistic, and sentence structure is disjointed. Errors in sentence structure, usage, and mechanics frequently interfere with the writer's ability to communicate.

SCORE of 1: The paper has no evident main idea. Development is inadequate and/or irrelevant. Organization is illogical and/or incoherent. Point of view has not been established. Vocabulary and sentence structure are garbled and confusing. Significant and numerous errors in sentence structure, usage, and mechanics interfere with the writer's ability to communicate.

Subtest IV: Sample Essays with Commentary

Topic 1

Strong Response

Happiness, freedom, and peace of mind are goals that everyone wants in life. Yet they are very abstract and difficult to measure. Happiness is a frame of mind that means we enjoy what we do. Freedom is the ability to do what we want, although it is limited to not doing anything that takes away freedom from other people. Peace of mind is a feeling that we are all right and that the world is a good place. How does one achieve these important goals? They can best be acquired when we try to give them to other people rather than when we try to get them ourselves.

The people who feel happiest, experience freedom, and enjoy peace of mind are most often people who are concentrating on helping others. Mother Theresa of Calcutta is an example. Because she takes care of homeless people and is so busy, she probably doesn't have time to worry about whether she is happy, free, and peaceful. She always looks cheerful in her pictures.

There are other people in history who seem to have attained the goals we all want by helping others. Jane Addams established Hull House in the slums of Chicago to help other people, and her life must have brought her great joy and peace of mind. She gave to the mothers in the neighborhood freedom to work and know that their children were being taken care of; and Jane Addams apparently had the freedom to do what she wanted to help them.

On the other hand, there are people in literature who directly tried to find happiness, freedom, and peace of mind; and they were often miserable. The two people who come to mind are Scrooge and Silas Marner. Scrooge had been selfish in the past, and he wouldn't give anything for the poor. He wasn't a bit happy even at Christmas. Later, when he began helping others, he became happy. Silas Marner was very selfish, hoarding his money and thinking it would make him happy. Only when he tried to make little Eppie happy was he able to be happy, too, even without his stolen money.

If we want to achieve happiness, freedom, and peace of mind, we should get involved in helping others so much that we forget ourselves and find joy from the people we are helping. When we try to give away the qualities we want, we find them ourselves.

Analysis

This essay has a score range of 5–6. It is well organized, with the opening paragraph serving as the introduction and stating the thesis of the paper in its last sentence. Defining the terms serves as an effective way to introduce the paper. The last paragraph concludes the essay, restating the thesis. The three middle paragraphs support the thesis with specific examples that are adequately explained and have a single focus. Transitions effectively relate the ideas. The sentence structure varies, and the vocabulary is effective. There are no major errors in sentence construction, usage, or mechanics. Although the essay would benefit from some minor revisions, it is well done considering the time limit imposed upon the writer.

Topic 2

Strong Response

The rising cost of health care in the United States has become more than a national concern; it is now a national crisis. The situation has become so grave that the President made health care costs a major issue in his campaign and has appointed a task force to investigate ways of providing equitable health care for all Americans. One of the most pressing problems the task force is addressing is health insurance.

The cost of health insurance in this country has skyrocketed in the last two decades. Many middle class Americans cannot afford to insure themselves and their families, despite earning relatively large incomes, and for the working class, health insurance is completely out of reach. The result is that these people literally cannot afford to get sick. An illness means lost work wages, as well as exorbitant medical bills. Those who can afford to buy health insurance often find that their policy is inadequate for anything beyond rudimentary care. An unexpected surgery can involve thousands of dollars in out-of-pocket expenses, and a chronic disease like cancer or diabetes can eat up a policy's maximum allowable benefits in a matter of weeks or months.

The cost of providing group insurance has become so high that many employers, especially smaller companies, are trying to either cut benefits or find some cheaper way of providing coverage, while many prospective employees accept or reject job opportunities on the basis of benefits rather than salary.

Health-maintenance organizations (HMOs) and preferred-provider organizations (PPOs) are two common means that many employers have turned to in their attempts to regulate costs. HMOs and PPOs provide coverage for routine and preventive health care while keeping costs down by limiting benefits on certain types of care or by not covering certain expenses at all. However, these programs have serious limitations. Yearly out-of-pocket deductibles are generally high, and annual maximum benefits can be quite low. This means that for people who are in good overall health, these plans are beneficial, but if a family has an unexpected health emergency, whether it be a serious injury or a debilitating illness, these plans provide little assistance. It is also possible for a person with a rare illness not to be diagnosed because of the limitations on testing imposed by these plans.

One solution is to set national limits on how much certain procedures and tests can cost. By standardizing costs and then standardizing how much of the cost is covered by the government health care plan, costs can be managed. Many insurance companies already try to control costs by standardizing how much they will pay for various tests and procedures, but there are no regulations that restrict physicians or medical facilities from charging more than this standard rate. A national health care plan that did regulate fees would prevent some doctors and hospitals from overcharging for services. This type of fee schedule, combined with a sliding scale based on income for the amount of the fee that is covered by the government, could go far to easing this country's health care crisis. Other options are to base national health care on the plans already instituted in other countries. Canada and England are among the other countries that have instituted national health care and managed to control health care costs. A recent study showed that drug costs in Canada (for the same medications produced by the same companies) were less than half what they are in this country.

The health care problem in this country has reached crisis proportions. Many people who hold good jobs cannot afford to insure themselves or their families, and the working class and the poor cannot afford to get sick at all. Even those people who can afford health insurance find that the policies they buy do not cover catastrophic illnesses or injuries. Many employers have tried to provide health care coverage for their employees, but escalating costs have made it harder to provide comprehensive coverage. The only thing that can be said for certain is that health care reform is desperately needed, but the president's task force does not have an easy job ahead of it.

Analysis

This essay has a score rays of 5–6. If provides a clear thesis and develops that thesis in a clear and logical manner. The body of the essay expands on various aspects of the thesis, and provides concise and reasonable support. The few usage, structural, and mechanical errors do not interfere with the writer's ability to communicate effectively, and the writer demonstrates a solid understanding of the rules of written English. The essay is well-thought-out and the conclusion relates the various points raised in the essay to the general argument made throughout.

Index